BRUNO MADERNA

His Life and Music

Fig. 1: Bruno Maderna at the Holland Festival, 1972.
Photo Gisela Bauknecht.

BRUNO MADERNA
His Life and Music

Rossana Dalmonte and Mario Baroni

Translation by Michael Webb

ROWMAN & LITTLEFIELD
Lanham • Boulder • New York • London

Published by Rowman & Littlefield
An imprint of The Rowman & Littlefield Publishing Group, Inc.
4501 Forbes Boulevard, Suite 200, Lanham, Maryland 20706
www.rowman.com

86-90 Paul Street, London, EC2A 4NE

Distributed by NATIONAL BOOK NETWORK

Copyright © 2022 by The Rowman & Littlefield Publishing Group, Inc.
Copyright © 2021 Pendragon Press
Originally published as *Bruno Maderna: La Musica e la Vita* in Italian (Lucca: Libreria Musicale Italiana, 2020)

All rights reserved. No part of this book may be reproduced in any form or by any electronic or mechanical means, including information storage and retrieval systems, without written permission from the publisher, except by a reviewer who may quote passages in a review.

British Library Cataloguing in Publication Information Available

Library of Congress Cataloging-in-Publication Data

The previous edition of this book was catalogued by the Library of Congress as follows:

Library of Congress Control Number: 2021941719
ISBN 978-1-5381-7229-2 (cloth)
ISBN 978-1-5381-9640-3 (paperback)
ISBN 978-1-5381-7230-8 (e-book)

TABLE OF CONTENTS

List of Illustrations	vi
Introduction	vii
Chapter I: From Birth to the End of the War	1
Chapter II: From Venice to Darmstadt	29
Chapter III: Between Milan and Darmstadt	69
Chapter IV: Musica ex Machina	103
Photo Album	127
Chapter V: The Crisis of Total Serialism	139
Chapter VI: Changes in Life and Writing in the Sixties	165
Chapter VII: The Hyperion Cycle	217
Chapter VIII: The American Years	247
Bibliography	289
Bibliographic Abbreviations	301
Index of Cities, etc.	303
Index of Names	317
Index of Works	327

LIST OF ILLLUSTRATIONS

Fig. 1: Bruno Maderna at the Holland festival, 1972	ii
Fig. 2: Maderna in a typical conducting pose	128
Fig. 3: Brunetto Grossato in his father's band	129
Fig. 4: Brunetto Grossato conducting the orchestra at the Arena di Verona, 1933	129
Fig. 5: Young Maderna with Giacomo Manzoni (left) and Piero Santi (right)	130
Fig. 6: With Earle Brown in Darmstadt, 1959	130
Fig. 7: Maderna during a theory class, 1960	131
Fig. 8: At a rehearsal in Darmstadt, 1961	131
Fig. 9: Maderna and Nono in front of La Fenice in Venice, 1962	132
Fig. 10: Photo with dedication, 1968	132
Fig. 11: Maderna in Persepolis with the Empress Farah Diba (right) and Cathy Berberian (left), 1971	133
Fig. 12: Bruno Maderna and the tenor Paul Sperry	133
Fig. 13: Maderna at the WNCN in New York	134
Fig. 14: Bruno Maderna and Han de Vries during rehearsals for the Concerto per Oboe n. 3, 1973	135
Fig. 15: Bruno Maderna and Lucas Vis, Amsterdam, 1973	136
Fig. 16: Bruno Maderna and Maurice Béjart at La Scala in Milan (P. Boulez's ballet, *Le marteau sans maître*), January 1973	137
Fig. 17: Maderna in his home at Darmstadt	138

INTRODUCTION

Bruno Maderna (1920-73) is the first of the group of Italian composers born in the nineteen twenties who began their career in the period immediately before the Second World War and who made their mark in the post-war years, when they were given the opportunity to address the new world with fresh effort and hope. However, the figure of Maderna stands out not only because he was born some years before his fellow adventurers, but also because of the quite singular circumstances he was exposed to: his experience as a child prodigy may well have brought him early fame, but it also placed him in difficult and often unpleasant situations. And when, at the age of twenty, he graduated from the music conservatory after finally completing a regular course of studies in a situation of relative calm, his life was soon upset by the outbreak of the war.

His extraordinary musical talents immediately attracted the attention of Gian Francesco Malipiero, and it was largely thanks to the influence of this sullen and unpredictable figure that by the end of the war he could be said to have become a mature composer. At the Venice Conservatory, where he was given a small job, he came into contact with musicians of almost the same age whom he frequented as friends but also, quite unintentionally, as a sort of group leader or in any case a guide: not only in a technical sense but also spiritual, given his particular experience in terms of both art and life. To his great fortune, these friends and followers also included a young man called Luigi Nono. And so it was that a decade or so later Italian musicology began, perhaps rightly, to speak of the meetings between these young musicians as the birth of a New Venetian School.

The context in which they began to work was particularly dramatic. All of them had witnessed the destruction of many of the historic cities in which the central role of Europe in the field of culture had been born, and was now at risk of fading; and what is more, they had to endure the difficult task of living in a climate of underground civil war. They also found themselves facing a sudden change in economic models, and in the different social roles engendered within the new institutions that were emerging against a background of light and shadow, of struggles and tensions: the values that for centuries had been considered the unshakable pillars of human society were now being put into question. For those dedicating themselves to music or other forms of art, the very concept of communication and language was now being challenged, making it indispensable to search for new forms of expression. From this point of view Maderna's role was by no means secondary: he had already moved beyond his period of apprenticeship and had assimilated the ideas not only of the generation of Italian composers immediately preceding him, first and foremost Dallapiccola and of course Malipiero, but also those of the great international protagonists, from Bartók to Stravinsky; nor should we forget that he was among the first in Italy to read Hindemith's *Unterweisung im Tonsatz*, which he had purchased just two years after its publication. Indeed, it was this very book that brought him into contact with Nono, thanks to the mediation of Malipiero, an event that marked the beginning of an association destined to last throughout the most significant years of their achievements.

The role of Malipiero in the vocation of his two most promising pupils was also decisive in another sense: he was able to transmit to them his passion for ancient music, ranging from the great Flemish masters to Monteverdi and Vivaldi, an aspect that would always distinguish them from their European contemporaries. In particular Maderna, also in his work as a conductor, remained consistently attached to the history of music and had no qualms about staying faithful to the past, even at a time when much of the European avant-garde insisted that "new music" had the duty to start again from "year zero": the only composers worthy of consideration were, allegedly, those able to make a clean sweep of the past, which was implicitly held responsible for the crimes, both material and ideal, committed by the dominant classes of the twentieth century.

Some years later Maderna and Nono, the first of the Italians to frequent Darmstadt – the focal center of New Music – were joined by Luciano Berio, who had spent some time in the USA and, together with Maderna, founded the *Studio di Fonologia Musicale* in Milan, one of the most advanced centers in the field of so-called electronic music in Europe. These three "pioneers" shared many features in the way they responded to the revolution in musical language that had arisen in the post-war years, even though they each continued to pursue their own personal paths. For example, none of them assumed the extreme position adopted by some composers at Darmstadt regarding the audience they were writing for; Boulez and Stockhausen, in particular, made little pretense about their contempt for the concert-going public, whom they often defined as "bourgeois," using a term that was surely not intended in a sociological sense, but rather as a kind of insult. Instead, both Maderna and Nono, and Berio as well, chose a more problematic approach, which on the one hand defended the need to promote the transformations in musical language, but on the other raised the question of which type of public could appreciate the sense of their musical communication. Throughout the Sixties, Nono fearlessly explored and discussed the reactions of the public to whom he felt most politically linked, whereas Berio was more inclined towards the kind of mass-media experimentation proposed by the likes of Umberto Eco.

Maderna excluded neither of these directions, but his ear, finely tuned to the reactions of the public whom he routinely encountered during his work as a conductor, and to the feedback from the young people with whom his passion for teaching brought him into contact, led him to calibrate and systematically modify his choices. His approach therefore tended to be somewhat volatile, not prompted by any philosophical or ideological convictions, but rather by his relationship with different audiences. Moreover, another aspect that marked him out from his contemporaries was the fact that he made no attempt to support the contents of his music with any underlying theories, an attitude particularly rare among those involved in any branch or type of art. He undoubtedly relished his success as a composer, but without being particularly convinced of the "goodness" of his own point of view or message to the extent of feeling the need to promote or propagate it. This reticence to speak of himself may perhaps have increased the risk of his figure as a composer being overshadowed by his prestige as a conductor.

By the turn of the millennium, however, the appeal of the unpredictable and the unexpected – for several decades one of the mainstays of New Music – had begun to dwindle, and the contestation value that had previously rendered the function of the avant-garde so vital had gradually declined. We should nevertheless not confuse the general picture of the programs offered at theaters and concert halls with the perception of the cultural, educational and historical importance of this genre of music. This is confirmed by the fact that interest in avant-garde music has fortunately never waned; on the contrary, over the last few decades many important studies have heightened our knowledge of the sector.

Within this context, the figure of Maderna has been examined by numerous studies covering a wide range of perspectives. Without false modesty, we recall how the work carried out from the early 1980s by the study group formed at the University of Bologna bore numerous positive fruits, including the various books published in those years and the many articles dealing with particular aspects of the composer's work (conducting, concert recordings, music for radio), carried to fruition thanks to the tireless efforts of Maurizio Romito. We should also add the many works by Angela Ida de Benedictis, Veniero Rizzardi and Gianmario Borio, who with great clarity have elaborated on various aspects of Maderna's linguistic choices and aesthetics. The literature on Maderna is further enriched by the two significant volumes edited by Geneviève Mathon, Laurent Feneyrou and Giordano Ferrari, published by Basalte in 2007 and 2009; nor should we forget other important contributions such as those of Raymond Fearn and Markus Fein. Without all this, the present volume would not have been possible, and we offer our heartfelt thanks to these and to the many other scholars who are cited throughout the text.

Over and above what has already been written and said about the various aspects of Maderna's work, we thought it important to attempt, for the first time, a more global account, not limited to the single facets of his personality, but offering a reconstruction of his figure as a man, and therefore also of the biographical events that were often driven by unforeseen circumstances and by Maderna's evident thirst for ever new experiences and the most diverse of intellectual adventures. Our undertaking was certainly not made easy by the composer himself, who, despite his manifest cordiality and generosity towards all, was in reality never particularly open to confessions of a personal nature, not even with his adoptive mother, who often lamented this fact in the correspondence she held with him, but also with his closest friends.

Many of the biographical details are amply documented, especially with regards his constant movements and travels, but for certain other aspects we have had to content ourselves with following clues. This said, we have in any case limited ourselves to summarizing the most essential points, without pretending to offer an exhaustive account. We searched for the pieces of our puzzle in the correspondence, in the personal accounts of those that knew him, and in the reports of the journeys he made to take part in important artistic events. Many of the original letters referred to in the text are preserved at the Paul Sacher Foundation and our original intention was to travel to Basel to consult them. But unfortunately we were prevented from doing so by the sudden intervention of the Corona Virus pandemic. Some of the extracts quoted here are therefore based on the French versions found in *Extraits* 2007.

We are aware that the countless indications of the sources and bibliographic references may further burden the reading of a biography which is, per se, already complex. We apologize to our readers, but we believed it necessary to provide such copious documentation in order to allow each detail to be checked, thus circumventing the doubt that certain elements may have found their way into our book that are not based on fact, or derive from the unreliable accounts still in circulation today, which Maderna himself made no effort to deny.

The parts of the text giving details of Maderna's compositions run the risk, at times, of entering the domain of expert analysts, but here too we have tried to keep to the essentials. We have sought to describe as clearly as possible the salient moments that mark the changes in his style and language within the frame of international New Music. The "method" we used in our analyses cannot be strictly associated with any of the most widespread academic tools. Instead we have tried to provide the reader with an outline of each work that will act as an aid when listening to the piece in question. Basically, we have divided his stylistic tendencies into four main moments: a first phase in which he acquired the languages of the twentieth century, until approaching dodecaphony;

a second phase in which he applied serialism to different parameters (pitches, durations, dynamics, timbres), lasting until around the mid-Fifties; a third phase in which his interest in serialism began to take second place, gradually making way for experimentation with new sonorities and "open" forms, until the conclusion of the *Hyperion* cycle; and finally a fourth phase, characterized by his last substantial pieces for orchestra and a period spent largely in the USA, during which the composition of *Satyricon* led him to momentarily abandon the language of serialism. The typical reader we have in mind should be familiar to some extent with the music of the years in question, but not necessarily a composer or musicologist: we have tried to keep the use of technical terms to the bare minimum and have only adopted those that seemed indispensable. Furthermore, since we firmly believe that music should, above all, be listened to, we suggest that readers should supplement their reading with a tool such as "Youtube," where a very wide selection of Maderna's works and performances is available: the possibility to hear the music will prove fundamental in understanding and appreciating the facts and works described.

During the course of the years spent on the joint elaboration and writing of our book, we carefully deliberated, with changing fortunes, on the most suitable title for the volume and the precedence we should to give to the names of the two authors. In the end we decided not to be unduly concerned about the banality of the title, and to give the names of the authors in a different order in the Italian and in the English edition.

Bologna, June 1, 2020

CHAPTER I

FROM BIRTH TO THE END OF THE WAR

Bruno Maderna's life was very short, but so full of challenges and events that it reads like chapters from a novel. In particular, the accounts of his childhood and early youth have often come down to us in such conflicting versions that several different narratives could be written, as if we were speaking of a figure from far-off times and not of a contemporary of at least some of our readers. As far as his earliest years are concerned, since no new sources have emerged with respect to those referred to in a previous biography [*Documenti* 1985, 7-49], we will limit ourselves here to outlining only the main and most reliably documented details.[1]

Bruno Maderna was born in Venice on April 21, 1920, to Carolina Maderna and Umberto Grossato.[2] His father could not legally recognize him as his son as he was married to another woman, but he nevertheless took him under his protection and brought him up in the family's patriarchal home in Sant'Anna in Chioggia, where his grandfather Francesco, his uncles, aunts and numerous cousins welcomed him with great affection. So in the earliest part of his life he was known as Bruno (more often, Brunetto) Grossato, and nothing changed when his mother died when he was just over four years old. Carolina's family, who lived in the province of Pavia, made no attempt to remove the child from the environment in which had been nurtured since his birth.

In Sant'Anna, Bruno attended primary school, which at the time only lasted four years, and did well in all subjects. At the same time he was able to develop his precocious musical talent by learning to play the violin and drums from his grandfather, uncles and aunts, but he also learned the piano and accordion, instruments that various members of the family played in the dance

---

[1] The details are partly taken from local newspaper articles that underlined the unusual background of the "child prodigy," and partly from 32 more specific documents, collected by the present authors and published in *Documenti* 1985, 70-80. From 1933, many of the details are drawn from Maderna's correspondence.

[2] Curacy of S. Lazzaro of the Ospedale Civile di Venezia: "We hereby certify that the above-named Maderna Bruno Cesare son of Carolina daughter of Giuseppe (Dom. S. Maria del Giglio 2454) born in this pious place on April 21, 1920 at 4 o'clock was solemnly baptized in our Church on 25 April."

hall they managed in their *osteria*. In the 1940s the dance hall was still called "Bruno Grossato." Towards the end of his life, Maderna recalled his earliest musical experience with a curious remark:

> My grandfather thought that if you could play the violin you could then do anything, even become the biggest gangster. If you play the violin you are always sure of a place in heaven.[3]

Paradoxically, this was the most "normal" period of his eventful youth. Umberto Grossato, unlike the rest of his family, was little inclined to accept the quiet life of a small provincial village or the role as father of three children from three different women, all "adopted" by his relatives. When he noticed Brunetto's exceptional musical skills, he soon took advantage of the fact and gathered together a group of a dozen or so musicians to form a band – the Happy Grossato Company – which performed for some years on boats that took tourists to Venice, as well as in the most fashionable venues along the Adriatic Riviera, and even in well known restaurants in Rome and Milan. In Sesto San Giovanni Bruno was able to attend another year of school, albeit with many absences "due to sickness" and in the school year 1932-33 he obtained good marks at the Liceo Ginnasio Marco Foscarini in Venice. He did equally well at the Conservatorio B. Marcello, where on November 3, 1933 he passed the final exam of the "solfeggio" course with a respectable mark of 8.50.

The repertoire of the band of which Brunetto was the acclaimed star, consisted of fashionable dance tunes and popular songs, often orchestrated by Grossato himself. Even if in the photos Brunetto always has the air of a serious professional musician, one can easily imagine that he found this type of life by no means disagreeable; on the contrary, it suited his inclination to escape from the narrow ways of country life. Umberto may not have been a model father, but neither was he the "corrupt, pleasure-seeking man, fond of unrestrained revelry" that Brunetto describes some time later in his *Diario della mia vita*, a short piece written in a scandalistic-provincial style, with little (or no) correspondence to reality. On the other hand, Umberto contributed very little to the young man's human and artistic growth and apparently failed to put up much resistance when his son was taken away from him for various, not only philanthropic, reasons, leaving Brunetto to continue his life alone as an "adopted" child, without any legitimate family.

Sometime between the end of 1932 and the first months of 1933, certain influential figures from the Venetian musical world – including the Praetor

---

[3] From an interview given on WEFM Radio in Chicago in January 1970 [*Documenti* 1985, 90].

of Section II of the Magistrates court in Venice, justice Pietro Sielter, and the honorable lawyer Domenico Giuriati – who had admired Brunetto as the conductor of various orchestral groups (at the Chiosco di Piazza Dante in Diano Marina in August '32, at the Castello Sforzesco in Milan in September, and at La Fenice in Venice in October), decided to form a "Family council" or "Guardianship committee." The boy was duly taken away from the father (who was unable to prove his natural relationship to his son) and went to live in the home of Francesco Miotto, clarinetist of the orchestra of La Fenice in Venice. Through the intercession of the Guardianship committee, Mussolini granted Brunetto an annual scholarship of 12,000 Liras, and in exchange presented him to the Italian public in numerous concerts as a model of youth raised under Fascism[4]. This second series of concerts was held mainly in the Veneto area: at the Teatro Verdi in Trieste, at the Teatro Garibaldi and the Sala della Ragione in Padua, at the Malibran and La Fenice in Venice, on many occasions at the Filarmonico in Verona, and in front of a particularly large audience at the Arena in Verona (May 20, 1933). During the course of about a year in which he lived under the protection of the Guardianship committee, his religious education also began at the initiative of a young friar named Policarpo Crosara, who had heard about the young musician in April 1933 and was keen to meet him. In August of the same year Crosara was transferred to Fiume, but the friendship, trust and religious exchange that he had built up with Brunetto still continued on a regular basis for several years, as testified by their substantial correspondence.[5]

There is no way of knowing precisely how the transformation from a star of a light orchestra to the conductor of some of the most accredited groups and orchestras of Northern Italy took place, especially because his "entrepreneurs" – his father and the members of the Guardianship committee – even went as far as changing the boy's age: taking advantage of Brunetto's small stature and his childlike expression, they publicized him as a "nine-year-old child" when he was actually already 12 or 13. Also his father's interviews with the *Gazzettino di Venezia* after his first concerts [*Documenti* 1985, 13-14] are not entirely reliable, since they often contradict one another and are sometimes fanciful. Fortunately numerous concert bills or newspaper reviews (to date, nineteen can be consulted at the *Centro Studi Maderna*) document Brunetto's activity from August 1, 1932 (Chiosco di Piazza Dante in Diano Marina with the Overture from Verdi's *La forza del destino* and other "exquisitely Italian and melodic" pieces) to December 10, 1935 (at the

---

[4] Various letters and articles confirm the existence and composition of the Guardianship commission. Unfortunately, at least until now, it has not been possible to retrieve the legal document registering its formation.

[5] It could also be possible that the judgment of his father as corrupt and reckless was made under the influence of his friend Policarpo.

Radio di Torino headquarters, with pieces by Cherubini, Beethoven, Martucci, Pedrollo and Wagner). The list of concerts – now complete in *Romito* 2020 – provides a clear picture of how Maderna's early career as an orchestral conductor developed, first under the management of his father, and then overseen by the Guardianship committee, an emanation of the Fascist party.[6]

The day of July 1, 1934 was an important date for Brunetto. The competition that had grown up around his precocious artistic talents, involving varying interests, was eventually won by a well-to-do woman from Verona, named Irma Manfredi. She had been among the audience that had applauded him during the concert at the Arena and from that moment on did everything she could to reach her aim of giving the child a normal life and an education worthy of his abilities. Besides the resistance of the Guardianship committee, Manfredi also had to compete with the aspirations of a priest from Conselve, Don Bellucco, who struggled for years to obtain the custody of the boy. Having failed to prove his merits, Bellucco resorted to slandering the members of the Guardianship committee, who turned to the Court of Venice to defend themselves from such gratuitous violence.[7] But Manfredi too had no small difficulties to surmount in order to reach her aim. Some sources suggest that she paid a large sum of money to the Guardianship committee (under an unknown pretext),[8] and only with the support of the Curia of Padua, of the head of the carabinieri and the secretary of the Forensic Union of Verona, was she finally able to welcome the boy into her home. However, the custody of the child did not arrive through the Court but through the Vatican, and thus had no validity from a legal point of view. The official documents show that he was resident in Verona (first at Via Costa, 3, then at Via Anfiteatro, 6) from July 8, 1934, and his name appears in the registry of the same municipality from April 7, 1935 until March 15, 1963, when it was canceled due to his "definitive emigration abroad." Although the relation between Bruno and Irma Manfredi was always like that of mother and son, Irma never forgot their lack of legal recognition and tried again, many years later, to make things good.

---

[6] Particularly striking is the review of the concert held at the Arena in Verona on May 20, 1933, published in February of the following year in the Milanese journal *Pro Familia* and signed by Umberto Gelmetti. A photo shows the Arena with a packed audience on the steps of the Arena, the orchestra (described as made up of 120 members) and the young prodigy, who is said to be 12 years old, together with the composer Pino Donati, who was giving him music lessons at the time.

[7] The episode was taken up by the local press: see, for example, *Il Gazzettino di Venezia* of May 18, 1935.

[8] In 1942 a reform of the civil code officially revoked the institution of the Family Council, which had already lost much of its importance over the previous years.

Irma Manfredi had the spirit of an artist, both in her profession and in her private life.⁹ Thanks to her creative mind and manual skills she had set up a high quality tailoring business appreciated not only by the fashionable gentry of Verona, but also by those in Milan and Venice. At the time of her meeting with Bruno, she had sixty employees and lived with her mother in an elegant house decorated with antique furniture and paintings by reputable artists. His father, Umberto Grossato, carried on working as before and seems to have disappeared from the scene, and the only trace of his former life that Maderna took with him to Verona was his friendship with Policarpo Crosara. The correspondence between the two men and with Irma Manfredi is one of the richest sources for the reconstruction of Maderna's biography, at least until the end of the war.

While Manfredi began to see to his education, which she wanted to be excellent and equal to his musical and intellectual talents, Bruno prepared for his last two public appearances as an *enfant prodige*. On March 23, 1935, presenting himself for the first time as Maderna (his registered surname), he conducted part of the concert held at the Teatro Filarmonico in Verona in honor of the famous conductor from the same town, Franco Faccio.¹⁰ Once again, the concert – an exceptional occasion given his still youthful age – met with a clamorous success, so much so as to merit a letter of congratulations and thanks from the Podestà of Verona [*Centro Studi Maderna*, Section D 14.1]. While this event could be seen as an appendix to his memorable successes of the previous years, it is not clear how he subsequently came to conduct in a prestigious concert broadcast on the radio by the EIAR in Turin. The concert was widely covered by the press and, in a letter to Crosara, Maderna speaks of his impressions giving details in the manner of an expert conductor: the orchestra was excellent and responded readily to his remarks and gestures. [*Centro Studi Maderna*, Section L 1].¹¹

---

⁹ Irma Manfredi was born in Verona on July 4, 1896, and died in the same city on February 24, 1976.

¹⁰ L. Och, "Bruno Maderna a Verona: Istituzioni e protagonisti dell'ambiente musicale fra le due guerre," *Maderna e l'Italia musicale degli anni '40*, G. Bonomo, F. Zannoni, eds. (Milano: Suvini Zerboni, 2012), 35-36.

¹¹ The letter was written on December 22, 1935, about ten days after the concert. All letters referred to in the book with the shelf-mark *Centro Studi Maderna* Section L are copies of the originals that are mostly kept at the *Paul Sacher Stiftung* in Basel. The copies were made with the permission of Cristina Maderna, when the original letters were still in Darmstadt at the composer's home. In other instances the letters of Maderna are cited from extracts translated into French by A. I. De Benedictis and G. Ferrari and published in *Basalte* 1, 2007, 459-517. In some cases, then, the English version is based on the Italian translation from French. Unfortunately, as mentioned in the Introduction, our planned trip to Basel to consult the autographs was impeded by the Corona virus pandemic.

Irma Manfredi, with great foresight, did not think it necessary to enroll Bruno at the local lyceum, but, sparing no expense, organized private lessons for him with reputable teachers in the various subjects, bought him the entire *Enciclopedia Treccani* (as he himself enthusiastically tells his friend Policarpo in the previously cited letter) and sent him abroad to study languages, as he tells Policarpo in great detail, in a letter that is undated but, given the style of writing, probably dates from 1935-37: among other things he mentions that he was going to the Salzburg Festival and would then stay a while in Austria to learn German [*Centro Studi Maderna*, Section L 1]. He also appears to have been sent to England in 1939. A "specially-made" program, then, in which Bruno found himself in the privileged condition of being able to shape the direction of his educational path on his own personal interests. After attending a recent concert, the composer Pino Donati, who often met Maderna in those years, wrote a long article about him in the *Radiocorriere* (December 10, 1935) in which he points out, besides his musical studies, "his fondness of Letters, Latin and the language of Goethe."

As far as his musical education was concerned, Irma Manfredi's search was even more meticulous. Having rejected the Civico Liceo Musicale in Verona, as it was still being completed at the time,[12] she first thought of sending him to Milan, where he could study with Pizzetti, but then decided she preferred not to leave him alone in the big city and managed to persuade Arrigo Pedrollo, a concert pianist, composer and teacher at the Conservatory in Milan, to give Bruno private lessons at their home in Verona. Pedrollo has now almost disappeared from accounts of Italian music in the twentieth century, but a considerable amount of coeval literature depicts him as an excellent teacher and a generous, sensitive person, able to stimulate the imagination of his young pupils without dampening their unaffected enthusiasm.[13] Once again Manfredi proved to be an astute planner, since Pedrollo was able to teach Maderna the basic rudiments of harmony and composition, an area still totally unknown to him. But he may well have based his teaching more on his pupil's natural gifts and spontaneous curiosity rather than on the programs of the State Conservatory, for when Maderna took the final exam of the elementary composition course (summer session 1935), the commission of the Milan Conservatory passed him with a rather low average mark (6.50), while two years later he failed to pass the intermediate course at the same conservatory.

---

[12] M. Materassi, "Il Civico Liceo Musicale (1927-1967)," *Il Conservatorio di Musica "Evaristo Felice Dall'Abaco" di Verona. Gli edifici, la storia, il presente*, ed. L. Och (Conservatorio di Verona, 2008), 75-100.

[13] Pino Donati, in an article in *Il Brennero* (June 5, 1935), *Colloquio con Arrigo Pedrollo,* informs us that "the Maestro goes to Verona every week, on Mondays and Fridays." On Arrigo Pedrollo, see *Documenti* 1985, 41-43.

Irma Manfredi would not let herself be discouraged. She attributed the poor result to his young age, but also realized that she should now change direction. She understood that Bruno needed to attend a "regular" school that would offer him different perspectives and the chance to come into contact with other students of his own age. After a careful search, supported by the advice of various trustworthy counselors,[14] she decided that the best choice was the Conservatory of Santa Cecilia in Rome, where Alessandro Bustini, the professor of composition, was a renowned contrapuntalist and a strict teacher. Bustini tested Bruno in private and then accepted him among his pupils starting from the school year '37-38. Also the choice of lodgings was carefully thought out and she was even helped by a Secretary of State of the Vatican, Monsignor Giovanni Battista Montini, the future Pope Paul VI, who wrote as follows:

> From the Vatican, October 4, 1937 / Dear Madam, / Absolute lack of time has prevented me from answering you earlier and from dealing more thoroughly with the search you mention. I did, though, write again to my friend in Villa S. Francesco, to try again in the way you suggested. But he replied that the Director was adamant; that is, he would accept Bruno as a guest, on the condition that he practiced the piano elsewhere. I have asked various friends for other suggestions but with no result. / Finally I spoke with Mons. Giuseppe Trezzi, who has some dealings with the "Casa pensione S. Carlo." This is a guest house run by nuns, next to the Church of S. Carlo on the Corso (which is the main street of old Rome), in a fine house on the second or third floor, in rooms owned by the Lombard Brotherhood. I am told that there is good board and lodging, heating, and not many guests (there are about 18 places) many of whom are foreign. It is just a few steps from the school of Santa Cecilia. I asked specifically about the use of a piano. Mons. Trezzi tells me that, to avoid renting a piano (which is not so cheap in Rome today), the young man can make use of the one in the reading room, which appears to be quite separate from the other rooms. The rent, though, ranges from 28 Liras for the internal rooms and 30 Liras a day for those looking onto the Corso. The Pensione is only for men and clerics, just like Villa San Francesco. But there is no garden or open space nearby. However, it is very central. I have not made any commitment. / This is what was able to find out this evening, and I wanted to let you know immediately. / With devoted respect G.B. Montini. [*Documenti* 1985, 74-75]

---

[14] See the correspondence between Guido Bianchini – a Venetian musician, probably a member of the Guardianship committee – Irma Manfredi and Arrigo Pedrollo in various letters from July 1937; news of the first contact between Bustini and Maderna can be found in a letter to Irma Manfredi dated September 4, 1937, in which the Maestro invites Bruno to meet him at his home in Viale Carso 5 [*Centro Studi Maderna*, Section L 1].

The numerous attempts made by the high-ranking prelate to fulfill the mission that had been entrusted to him and the precision of his description, are clear indications of the high esteem in which Manfredi was held and of the fame that the young musician had already earned. At first Bruno seems pleased with his new lodgings, as he wrote to his friend Policarpo in a letter dated November 30, 1937 [*Centro Studi Maderna*, Section L 1]. But the charm of this sort of boarding school for adults soon faded. According to Guido Turchi, his fellow student at Santa Cecilia, he did not stay there long and preferred to move into privately rented rooms in the centre of Rome.[15]

His failure to pass the final exams of the intermediate composition course at the Milan Conservatory had, then, led to a further, profound change in the life of the young Maderna. After just three years of living a quiet and secluded existence in the home of Irma Manfredi, where his attempts to find an independent space of his own were seen as a worrying symptom of a personality disorder resulting from the turbulent years of his childhood, Bruno had now gained a certain amount of autonomy, for the first time without any "tutors." But he was nevertheless involved in organized structures that had the same rules for him and for all the others: the Casa San Carlo and the Conservatory of Santa Cecilia.

It is hard to give any precise details of the three years that Bruno spent in Rome, since the traces gleaned from his letters to "mamma Irma" describe the results of his studies, but not the more private aspects of his life. It is quite likely that this newfound freedom sometimes led him to behave in a way that his adoptive mother would not have approved of, especially his moments of escape in the company of women or in gambling, which Irma occasionally hints at when writing to Policarpo. And one can suppose that these were among the reasons why he left Casa S. Carlo, so as to feel totally free to follow his own rhythms of life. Nevertheless, in three years Bruno was able to bridge the gaps in the program of the intermediate composition course that had led to his failure at the Milan Conservatory and succeeded in completing the program of the advanced course, allowing him to graduate with full marks at the age of just twenty. His conduct may not have been impeccable in the eyes of his adoptive mother, but judging from the results of his musical studies, this side of his life does not seem to have taken up much of Bruno's time. In addition to the lessons at the conservatory, he often visited the home of Ildebrando Pizzetti, discussing technical problems about composing, as well as the question of musical poetics, a topic that began to increasingly trouble him. And he

---

[15] R. Pozzi, "Classicismo Romano. Maderna allievo di Bustini," in *Maderna e l'Italia*, cited in note 10, 48.

also completed his preparation as a pianist, just as Irma Manfredi had hoped, believing it to be a fundamental part of his musical education. But despite this intense activity, in one of his first letters to his mother, Bruno confesses that he missed being able to conduct.[16]

We should not of course underestimate the opportunities offered by the environment in Rome to a youngster free from the constraints of a "safe house": the chance to enjoy more frequent contact the musical life of the city and greater freedom in his relations with some of the notable figures among his fellow students like Carlo Maria Giulini and Guido Turchi, often joined by Giuseppe Rosati and Nazario Bellandi, who would later become teachers at the same music institution. With his colleagues – and sometimes alone – Maderna regularly went to hear the concerts and rehearsals at the Teatro Adriano, and he also organized meetings to listen to contemporary music while following the score. All the music Maderna had read as a child and had conducted with the somewhat blind confidence of his musical nature, together with the more recent repertoire he was discovering, began to take on a different aspect now that he could view it critically in the light of a richer musical environment and with the aid of more sophisticated tools of thought and analysis. A letter of December '39 [*Extraits* 2007, 470] is particularly revealing from this point of view. Bruno wrote to Irma to warn her that she would have to pay a quite substantial invoice from the shop of the publisher De Santis, where he had purchased several records and scores of music by Stravinsky[17], as well as a book, published by Schott just two years before, that he had wanted for some time: Hindemith's *Unterweisung im Tonsatzt*. One wonders how many Italian musicians of the time had studied this volume or even knew of its existence?

Other contacts were made by becoming a member of the *Gioventù Universitaria Fascista* (University Fascist Youth) in November '38, when nationalist tensions were beginning to grow stronger and the positions that would lead to the outbreak of the war were becoming more rigid – concerns that Bruno frequently expressed to his adoptive mother. This decision should not, however, be seen as evidence of his personal adherence to the Fascist party's plan for music. Many musicians – as well as critics, writers, performers – had, for some years, adhered to the directives of the party, though often taking a stand between the more traditionalist faction and the "modernists," the latter including especially Casella and Malipiero. Fiamma Nicolodi provides a clear and detailed picture of the situation with regards the protagonists of the so-called "Generazione

---

[16] Letter dated February 8, 1938.

[17] We have decided to adopt the form "Stravinsky" as opposed to the more correct transliteration from the Russian "Stravinskij" in order to conform with the usage of the literature in English.

dell'Ottanta" (Generation of the 1880s), but points out that, besides these, the same debate was also ongoing among younger composers, such as those of the intermediate generation including Dallapiccola and Petrassi, as well as those of the new generation like Guido Turchi and – we add – Bruno Maderna.[18]

Many of his letters talk about his relations with Maestro Bustini, who was not only an outstanding teacher, but from 1934 was also a member of the management board of the Teatro dell'Opera di Roma and had directed the Fascist union of musicians. The first meetings between the teacher and pupil seem to go well: "the professor is pleased with our first lesson" (letter of October '37, *Extraits* 2007, 464), and the good rapport persists throughout the period when Maderna is introduced to fugue writing, but tends to change when they start working on freer compositions, like accompanied melody, or pieces for small instrumental groups. Bustini apparently favored the models of the nineteenth century romantics and this made Maderna tremble and declare "I will not give up my personality!" (letter of January '39, *Basalte* 1, 2007, 467). The problem was, though, that Bruno still did not know what "his personality" was in terms of "free composition," to the extent that in various letters he describes his frustration at not being able to set D'Annunzio's poem *La sera fiesolana*, a text that he himself had chosen on February 6, 1938 [*Basalte* 1, 2007, 465]. One month later, on March 1, the poet died suddenly and Maderna dedicated a page in his diary to the fact, writing in a highly polished manner that reveals his clarity of judgment and his by no means superficial knowledge of recent Italian literature, even though he wrote it not to be published or to be read by others, but simply as a private record of his own thought:

> On March 3 [*recte*:1] Gabriele D'Annunzio suddenly died. / There is no doubt that with him Italy has lost a great poet. But in my opinion he had already died around fifteen years ago. One cannot, in fact, think of the work he produced over the last years without feeling a certain sense of pity. / He had become an old wreck. Aside from his senility, both eccentric and childlike, it must be said, and this has been true for some time, that he was one of those personalities of a world that in our sensations, in our evolution, which occurred so rapidly after the war, could be considered completely buried. / A "fish out of water." / His work nevertheless remains, which, one should rightfully acknowledge, bears witness to a great poet and, I believe, at least a third of this will survive, uncontaminated by the passing of time, intact for posterity to admire. He will always, I believe, have the right, and well earned, to be the third figure alongside Carducci and Pascoli, and to be recognized beside

---

[18] F. Nicolodi, *Musica e musicisti nel ventennio fascista* (Fiesole: Discanto, 1984), 140-165 *passim*.

them, and justly so, in the history of literature as the last marvelous gem and last substantial fruit of our glorious literature. [*Documenti* 1985, 76-77]

When he speaks of his compositions in this period his sense of uncertainty is great and often agonizing. The only thing he is certain of is his refusal of the romantic models: already three years earlier, while he was studying with Pedrollo, he had written to his friend Crosara that he could not stand the romanticism of Chopin, Schumann and their fellow composers. Declarations of this kind would seem to contradict his activity as a conductor. Over the previous years he had conducted works by Verdi, Wagner and Mendelssohn with extraordinary mastery and great engagement, but evidently what he objected to was not the romantic compositions themselves but the idea that he should compose romantically: the persistence of the nineteenth century works that circulated in the schools where he was studying simply made him irritable. This does not detract from the fact that, over and above his anti-romantic stance, he was also uncertain about his own direction. Although one or two of his pieces were considered worthy of appearing in the end-of-year concerts, he felt he had not managed to "resolve problems of color, of form and of expressive synthesis" (letter dated November 14, 1938, see *Extraits* 2007, 466).

However, such difficulties and uncertainties do not seem to have persisted much longer. At least, the letters he wrote after the conclusion of his scholastic period no longer contain such evident traces of these problems. Indeed, we must also consider that in May 1939 he managed to complete a challenging composition which, despite his doubts, still today reveals notable aspects of maturity and which he himself seems to have been satisfied with. The piece in question is *Alba*, for voice and strings, which, as he tells his mother, he defended vehemently against the initial sharp criticisms of his teacher Bustini who, whether or not convinced of what his talented pupil was proposing, in the end snapped: " 'Do whatever you like, I don't care'. And I left politely."[19] So this work deserves a more detailed examination.

First of all the selection of the text. After the difficulties he had met with *La sera fiesolana*, his choice to set Cardarelli's *Alba* seems to have been carefully meditated. The style adopted by the poet (following the inclination of *Ronda*, the "classically oriented" journal in which he actively participated in the early '20s) is far from the highly colored language of D'Annunzio. In choosing the piece Maderna may well have been influenced by the fact that Cardarelli was particularly well known in Rome, where he was in fact still working.[20] But it is possible that another aspect affected his choice: in Cardarelli's language one can also perceive

---

[19] Last part of the of the letter of May 7, 1939 to "mamma Irma" [*Extraits* 2007, 469].

[20] R. Pozzi, "Classicismo Romano," cited in note 16, 72.

the desire to contrast the search for "poetic nobility" underpinning D'Annunzio's artifices and Carducci's rhetoric, with a *sermo humilis*.[21] Maderna says nothing about Cardarelli, but his approach to setting the piece is not so far removed from these tendencies, if nothing else because the musical phrasing tends to "prosaicize" the poet's lines, to make them closer to the spoken word. Other features of the poem are mostly matched by more specifically musical choices. The language used by Maderna does not launch into any avant-garde flights, but presents certain novelties while keeping to a style in which harmony, melody and counterpoint maintain a reciprocal balance. While it cannot be ruled out that this apparent caution may have been due to his concerns about the judgment of his teacher, with whom he still had to complete his course of studies, the presence of some patently non-scholastic features leads us to conclusions of a different kind. We can, for example, observe that the piece is not like a true "accompanied monody" because the voice and instruments assume roles that are often quite distinct. The voice has long phrases divided asymmetrically by rests, while the strings follow a free, though rigorous internal logic of a contrapuntal nature, never taking up motives deriving from the voice part. In some cases the rests are longer, when Maderna prosaicizes the lines, based on the verbal syntax. As far as the relation between the verbal semantics and the music is concerned, the piece contains some examples of "neo-madrigalisms," as Pozzi calls them, referring to a well known theory of Massimo Mila. For instance, the dynamic peaks on adjectives like "rapinoso" ("turbulent") and "tenebrosa" ("dark"), or the imitative writing associated with the "fantasmi" ("phantoms") that are trying to flee. However, Maderna does not seem particularly interested in the dramatic relation that Cardarelli creates between the "morte affannosa" ("troubled death") of sleeplessness and the "alba dal freddo viso" ("the cold face of dawn"). Here the melody does not describe the sense of the words, it does not convey them through the expressive use of rhythms and intervals, a device typical of the romantic tradition. The melody is almost conceived as one of the lines of the counterpoint. It should also be added that dissonances are used, but not aggressively: the harmony remains within the framework of familiar scales and is not without the sporadic support of modes mentioned by Marina Giovannini in her study on the language of the early works of Maderna.[22] The overall result is one of a general sweetness, which does not overlook "il mare di luce incerta" ("the sea of uncertain light") with which Cardarelli ends the poem, or the restlessness and disquiet of the night, but avoids following either of these elements slavishly. Certainly, all this could

---

[21] R. Dalmonte, "Prima della serie. Orientamenti stilistici di Maderna negli Anni Quaranta: Le opere con testo poetico," in *Maderna e l'Italia*, cited in note 10, 132.

[22] M. Giovannini, "Il linguaggio armonico del giovane Maderna," *Bruno Maderna Studi e Testimonianze*, eds. R. Dalmonte, M. Russo (Lucca: LIM, 2004), 257-274.

be linked to the young composer's anti-romantic stance, but the work is inspired more directly by a modern aesthetics (constructive more than "expressive") most likely stimulated by his experiences of listening, study and thought during his stay in Rome.

It is not hard to deduce from these considerations that, despite its modest appearance, we are dealing with a composition that is not inspired by pre-existing models (it would in any case be difficult to pinpoint them) but one that is marked by a singular originality. The quantity of sketches that had led Giorgio Magnanensi, in the critical edition of the work [*Maderna* 1997], to presume a long period of gestation, has recently proved to be evidence of an intense bout of work lasting just a few weeks: from the middle of March to the beginning of May 1939.[23] And this aspect could be seen as further evidence that in writing *Alba* Maderna was moving away from his initial phase of uncertainty and felt within him a personal creative vein that was now starting to emerge.

In a brief telegram of June 15, 1940, Bruno informs Irma Manfredi that he obtained a mark of 9/10 in the composition exam he had taken the day before (June 14), and that he would soon be coming home [*Extraits* 2007, 474]. At last some good news for "mamma Irma!" Not only had he successfully completed his studies, but he had also decided not to prolong his stay in Rome. In reality, there was no real reason for him to return home immediately. He could well have chosen to continue his studies further after the diploma and set himself up in Rome as an "adult" orchestral conductor. And this was the idea strongly sustained by Pino Donati, who for some time had been zealously following Maderna's progress. Donati was a multifaceted figure with considerable influence in the world of Italian music. He too was a composer, but also a journalist, an organizer of musical events, and for many years the superintendent of the Arena di Verona. He had met Bruno when, at the age of thirteen, he had conducted his *Pastorale: Il presepio nella trincea* at the Filarmonico di Verona, alongside works by Beethoven, Verdi, Wagner, Mascagni and Wolf-Ferrari [*Documenti* 1985, 73]. From that moment on, they had grown increasingly closer to one another and their friendship also involved their respective families: for example, Donati's wife, the famous soprano Maria Caniglia, began to make use of Irma Manfredi's tailoring services. But other facts, documented by an ample correspondence, link Bruno's name to that of Pino Donati. His last youthful concert held in Turin with the orchestra of the EIAR (later the RAI) in December 1935 is reported in articles in the *Radiocorriere* and in various Veneto newspapers, all signed by Donati, and his first concert as an adult (February 17, 1941) was again

---

[23] From two letters from Maderna to his mother [*Extraits* 2007, 468-469].

at the EIAR in Turin, and was once more organized and sustained by Donati, who – not by chance – appears in the program with his own composition *Tre acquarelli paesani*. Nor was the radio the only opportunity that his mentor tried to find for Maderna: he busied himself trying to procure other engagements for him in both Milan and Florence. Numerous letters testify to Donati's plan to promote his young friend in the most important institutions across Italy rather than in just the Veneto region, where he risked being considered a sort of local phenomenon. This may also have been at the root of his plans to make him remain in Rome to attend the advanced composition course held by Ildebrando Pizzetti at the Accademia di S. Cecilia, and the orchestral conducting course held by Bernardino Molinari at the Augusteo. But Donati's aspirations did not coincide with those of Maderna, who probably intended to continue his preparation as a composer and conductor along different lines. He must have been quite aware that his studies with Bustini, his frequent contacts with Pizzetti and the academic program he had shared with his fellow students, had allowed him to develop a strong sense of self confidence in his ability to handle the technical devices of the classical German tradition from Bach to Beethoven. His ideological clashes with his inflexible teacher had, in fact, helped him to realize that his ability to exploit the tools of the trade could grow autonomously without losing any of his personal inventive capacity.

On leaving Rome he now felt the moment had arrived to change the direction in his choice of stimuli and ideas while furthering his studies after his diploma. His intuition led him towards a figure who was already well known and fully established on the national and international musical scene, a character who was variously judged, but unanimously acknowledged – albeit from different perspectives – as "exceptional" both as a composer and teacher, and perhaps also as a man: Gian Francesco Malipiero. He belonged to the group known as the "Generazione dell'80," whose general aims were to update the musical language they had inherited from the nineteenth century, but also to rediscover the musical patrimony of the Baroque era, especially that of Venice. The conviction that new Italian music should rebuild its identity based on both the study and teaching of the ancient masters and on the elaboration of new conditions and artistic expedients, united this recovery of the past with the exploration of new, original stylistic paths not without reference, but also not subservient, to the new ideas coming from France and the Germanic countries.

The encounter between ancient and modern formed the basis for much of the work of Malipiero, who lived in Venice, a place of memories, sentiments and wide cultural breadth. The Venice of the past was brought back to life in his modern transcriptions of vocal and instrumental music, in his studies of Vivaldi (who had only been recently rediscovered) and of Monteverdi (he edited the first modern edition of his complete works), who represented a model of civilization that he viewed with nostalgia but without conforming to the classicizing tendency of the early twentieth century. Already in the 1920s this fusion between ancient and modern was evident especially in his works for theater: Malipiero's theater is anti-realistic, allusive and fanciful, and above all anti-dramatic in that he frees his music from any subjection to the action and often condenses the different situations around lyrical themes in the form of songs. On the other hand, as Joachim Noller observes, his instrumental music is not without frequent "Impressions of the real" (*Impressioni dal vero*, the title of one of his works), while maintaining a distance from the poetics of program music. The relations between music and word, drama, history and reality are often defined as "fictional" in his numerous writings on aesthetics and by his commentators.[24]

Before the 1940s Maderna had never had any contact with Malipiero during his activity as a conductor; the concerts he conducted when he was young were organized on the basis of the well established repertoires favored by a large part of the public. But from 1941 the presence of Malipiero soon made itself felt. While the first two concerts conducted by the no longer youthful Maderna (in February and April '41) continued to show the influence of Donati,[25] his next appearance (May 22, Venice, Ca' Giustinian) was titled *Un'ora di classica musica veneta* (An hour of Venetian classical music) and included works by Dall'Abaco, Monteverdi, Bassani, Caldara, Galuppi, Lotti, Vivaldi and Marcello [*Documenti* 1985, 73]. Less than a year had passed since his return from Rome and this concert already bears witness to his surely not infrequent meetings with Malipiero. Their relationship was strengthened by Maderna's participation in the international advanced composition courses that Malipiero had held every year since 1932. The date of his first attendance can be inferred from a letter Malipiero sent him on June 1, 1941, in which he invites the young musician to join the other pupils in his class.[26] Maderna evidently accepted the invitation given that in a letter to his mother, undated but certainly from August '41, he mentions his friend Ettore Gracis as a colleague in Malipiero's class [*Extraits* 2007, 474]. He continued to frequent the class the following year, as testified by a document held at the Conservatorio B. Marcello dated December 16, 1942 in which Malipiero confirms that Maderna regularly attended his advanced composition course in the year 1942-43. Evidence of some contact

---

[24] J. Noller, "Malipiero: una poetica e un'estetica," *Rivista italiana di musicologia*, 26/1 (1991), 35-57.

[25] Donati's *Tre acquarelli paesani* was performed in both concerts. The second concert of April 5, 1941 held in Castelvecchio (Verona) was sponsored by the Unione Provinciale Fascista Professionisti e Artisti [L. Och, "Bruno Maderna a Verona," cited in note 10, 39].

[26] Letter cited by A. I. De Benedictis in her Introduction to the critical edition of the *Concerto per pianoforte e orchestra* [Maderna 2011, VI].

between Maderna and Malipiero before the concert at Ca' Giustinian can also be found in two letters of Pino Donati. The first (December 11, 1940) is written in reply to an "express letter" from Maderna, now lost, in which he cancelled his visit to Rome, an event that Donati had arranged with great care, as we gather from his unmistakable expressions of regret. Although Donati does not mention Malipiero, the cancellation of Maderna's appointments in Rome was probably linked to his interests in Venice but also to Malipiero. The second letter, written some weeks later (December 31), again in reply to a letter from Maderna, now lost, suggests a not infrequent contact between Maderna and Malipiero [*Centro Studi Maderna*, Section L 1].

It is hard to say what kind of impression Malipiero made on Maderna during their first meetings, but it was surely not a negative one, given that with the passing of time their friendship grew increasingly stronger. Certainly, Malipiero was very different from those who had previously influenced him in his choices, whether concerning his music or his life in general. His approach was a far cry from that of his first teacher Arrigo Pedrollo, always ready to highlight the positive sides of his pupil and to justify his failings; and quite different from that of the managerial "publicist" Pino Donati, and the strict and methodical Bustini. The figure of Malipiero could not be further away from the image of the "maestro" who becomes one's guide in art and in life. At the time he met Maderna he was living in perpetual conflict with himself and with the world, detached from the mainstream of music and in voluntary isolation, a position he had assumed even before the war. This attitude was by no means exempt from the criticism, more or less explicit, of the promoters of Fascist culture, who were nevertheless unable to undermine his choices or his independent and at times provocative stance. Reading his correspondence with Mussolini and with many influential figures of the regime, it would appear that Malipiero was very keen to gain official recognition of his works, which he dedicated (or asked to be dedicated) to the leader of the state.[27] On the other hand, it is hard to decipher his true political orientation from his copious correspondence with Guido M. Gatti, spanning over almost sixty years. Suffice it to read an extract from a letter written long after the facts to understand the irony and detachment with which Malipiero viewed those times:

> Now that the democracies have held out their hands across the borders, things are looking quite bad for me. Gone are the times when to spite the "hierarchs," notoriously hostile towards me, my music was played everywhere and often.[28]

---

[27] F. Nicolodi, *Musica e musicisti*, cited in note 19, 348-370.

[28] Asolo, October 15, 1952. See C. Palandri, ed., *Gian Francesco Malipiero. Il carteggio con Guido M. Gatti 1914-1972* (Firenze: Olschki, 1997), XIII.

While his concrete relations with Fascist culture and with the trends of post-war aesthetics offer us little insight into his physiognomy as a man, his modernity and originality as a musician can be measured in terms of his acute awareness of the alienation of contemporary culture from real life. Malipiero's cult of the antique, with its elusive re-evocations accompanied by bitter and angular music, is symptomatic of the incapacity of contemporary music to hide the impending crisis of values and to build a stable and unitary project with a positive outlook. It was not easy for those who encountered him for the first time to fathom the roots of his thought, even though in the course of his long and active career he often wrote about himself and his music, but in a style similar to that of his music: fleeting, ambiguous, ironic.

So what was it about this complex character that could have attracted the young Maderna, while he seems to have shown no particular interest in the work of other equally eminent figures of the time, like Pizzetti and Casella? Most studies on Maderna affirm that it was Malipiero who first oriented him towards the study of ancient music, but research into the sources raises questions about this hypothesis. The first records of Maderna's studies at the Biblioteca Marciana in Venice date, in fact, from 1948 and 1949,[29] while his interest in musical forms of the past – for example the Passacaglia – can be traced back to at least the early '40s and was probably stimulated by his experiences in Rome. In other words, rather than opening a new path, Malipiero's example was able to reinforce an interest already present in the young musician.

Whatever the case, during the early years of the decade his relations with Malipiero grew ever stronger, even though other circumstances took Maderna momentarily away from Venice. Some of these depended on his own free will, for example the period spent at the Accademia Chigiana in Siena to follow an advanced conducting course with Antonio Guarnieri (summer 1941), while others were beyond his control, for instance, the propaganda visit to Germany in June 1942, not to mention his duties associated with military service that began in August of the same year. In reality, even during his stay in Siena, which Maderna deemed important for his subsequent career, the figure of Malipiero did not disappear completely into the background. As he wrote to his mother shortly after his arrival at the Accademia Chigiana, out of sixteen applicants, he was one of the four admitted to Antonio Guarnieri's course; and along with him was another of Malipiero's pupils, Ettore Gracis. The description of his period in Siena continues in various letters to Irma Manfredi, in which Bruno tells her that the course is very demanding: six hours of rehearsals every

---

[29] R. Dalmonte, "Tracce di Malipiero e Maderna nei registri e negli schedari della Marciana," *Malipiero Maderna 1973-1993*, ed. P. Cattelan (Firenze: Olschki, 2000), 197-205.

day, which he followed diligently, as he found the Maestro's teaching useful even when not directed personally at him. But not everyone was able to keep up this pace and soon there were just two of them, Gracis and Maderna, who were nevertheless not particularly liked by Guarnieri precisely because they were pupils of Malipiero (letter of August 13). But after some days (letter of August 17) Bruno notes that the Maestro was showing greater kindness towards them, and the high consideration shown by Alfredo Casella finally made his stay in Siena a pleasant one (letter of August 23).[30] The change in Guarnieri's attitude towards Bruno was due – once again – to the intervention of Malipiero, who on August 8, 1941 sent two letters to Irma, one for Casella and one for Count Chigi Saracini, adding: "I hope these are able to counteract Guarnieri's bad mood," as in fact they were [*Centro Studi Madi Maderna*, Section L].

Another event, which this time took him outside of Italy, is widely documented. We learn from the *Allgemeine Thüringische Landeszeitung Deutschland* and the *Thüringer Gauzeitung*, newspapers both from the region of Weimar, one of the most important cultural centers in Germany, that from June 12 to 16 and from June 18 to 23, 1942, a large festival took place: "The days of European youth culture." Fourteen European countries actively participated in vocal and instrumental concerts, competitions, conferences, parades, art exhibitions and events focusing on poetry, film, theatre, science and radio. As many as 130,000 young people were present, involving 350 bands and 100 music schools. Numerous newspaper articles speak of the "Weimar-Florence bridge" intimating that young Europe would be born from these two cities. The festival would close, one month later, in Florence, but in June '42 the Florentine banner was already flying in Weimar and much space was devoted to the announcement and reports of the events that the *Hitlerjugend* and the *Gioventù Italiana del Littorio* were organizing together.[31]

Maderna's involvement in the festival had begun at the beginning of June, when he went to Rome, probably summoned there as a member of the Gioventù Universitaria Fascista and because of his growing fame as a young orchestral conductor. This invitation must have come as an unexpected and somewhat worrying turn of events for his mother Irma. Indeed, shortly afterwards Bruno wrote to reassure her: "nothing to worry about, here everything is fine […] we are leaving for Germany on the 16th […] a delegation of foreign journalists came to hear me conduct Verdi's *Vespri siciliani* and Paisiello's *Concerto* […] all this will help me greatly" [*Extraits* 2007, 475]. He was also introduced to Mussolini's eldest son and

---

[30] The three letters are pubished in *Extraits* 2007, 475.

[31] Copies of these newspapers are available at the *Centro Studi Maderna*, Section D 22.

to Aldo Vidussoni, secretary of the *Partito Nazionale Fascista*. And he was thus invited to Weimar for the second part of the festival. The head of the Italian delegation was General Bozzoni, who appears in many newspaper photos. Much space was also given to Natalino Sapegno's conference on Dante. There was a music prize for young people under 18 (males) or under 21 (females) and the award winners included many Italians, who were widely praised.[32] The above-mentioned German newspapers give wide coverage of the concerts at the Staatskapelle in Weimar, conducted by Paul Sixt, and those of the orchestra of the Nürnberg theater, conducted by Hubert Reicherts, which played famous works from the German and Italian repertory: Wagner, Verdi, Weber, Puccini, Strauss. But neither these newspapers, nor the Florentine newspaper *La Nazione* (consulted for the period from June 9 to July 2 1942) make any mention of the Italian music groups, let alone of Maderna. However, in some photos, now preserved in the library of the Accademia Filarmonica in Verona, he appears alongside other young people, probably during a parade.[33]

The other long absence from Verona, and from Malipiero's courses, occurred shortly after his return from Weimar, when Maderna was called to arms (August 10, 1942) and was assigned to the 62nd Alpine battalion, based at the school of non-commissioned officers in Merano. To his great fortune, the school was run by a certain Lieutenant Colonel Martinoja, a lover of music and theatre, and a special relationship soon developed between the officer and the composer and conductor Bruno Maderna. Suffice it to mention that just a few months after his conscription, Maderna obtained leave to conduct a concert in Castelvecchio di Verona on November 29, where he conducted *Intermezzi per l'Orfeo di Monteverdi* in Malipiero's transcription [*Documenti* 1985, 73]. And he was also able to continue composing, albeit in a quite particular context, since in place of military exercises he was asked to write music and instruct his fellow soldiers for the purposes of creating a new opera that would be staged at the end of the training course, a routine practice established by the music-loving Martinoja. The musical comedy in two acts and seven scenes *Via col tempo* has

---

[32] Mario Stasi was awarded a prize for his performance of Bruch's Violin Concerto, Giuseppe Bongera for playing Haydn's Oboe Concerto, Giuliana Bressan for Salzedo's Harp Concerto and Emilia Carlino for singing arias by Bellini.

[33] The journalist Gianni Villani published details of Maderna's trip to Weimar in the Verona newspaper *L'Arena* on August 12, 2012, based on information he obtained from Raffaele Capuozzo, a well known jeweller in Verona. Capuozzo, who was interviewed on separate occasions by Maurizio Romito and Mario Baroni, declared he had been a friend of Maderna's during their childhood and youth and had been given the photos of Weimar by Maderna himself when he returned from Germany. In the photos Capuozzo recognizes, standing next to Maderna, the singer Laura Cagol, who later became wife of the baritone Gian Giacomo Guelfi.

survived only as a libretto, written by Leo Chiosso, who after the war became a famous song lyric writer. Of the music – in the style of Gershwin and full of particular effects on the percussion – there remain only the memories of those who took part in the show, which was put on eight times in Merano and once in Arco di Trento [*Documenti*, 1985, 54-55]. In 1943 the battalion moved to the military base in Tarquinia, where Maderna was still stationed immediately after the fall of Mussolini on July 25, a fact that he tersely comments on in a letter to his mother of July 27. In his opinion Italy is at a decisive turning point in its history, and he is certain that this profound change will save and cleanse his country [*Extraits* 2007, 478].

Maderna's experience in the military camp in Tarquinia basically ended on September 10, 1943 when he obtained leave of absence from Martinoja to stay seventy days in Verona, with the order to present himself at the military barracks in Merano on December 20, 1943 [*Documenti*, 1985, 79-80]. But in the wake of the armistice proclaimed on September 8, Sergeant Bruno Maderna preferred to become one of the many "scattered" soldiers and to live in Verona in Manfredi's home rather than in the barracks. From this moment until the first months after the end of the war, life for those in their twenties became dangerous and the details we have are generally cloudy and often based on "heroic tales," in which Maderna too was marginally involved.

We know for sure that he met Raffaella Tartaglia, his future wife, in mid-September 1943, a fact that she herself confirmed to us in an interview. And Bruno often went to visit her brother Antonio at the home of his parents, a fellow soldier whom he had met some time before in Merano, where they had both been hospitalized. But his strongest interest at that moment was for Raffaella. She worked in the local prefectural office and shortly afterwards Bruno found a job at the police headquarters, and was thus able to conceal his "scattered" status and to live quite calmly, even finding time to compose and to conduct a concert at the Teatro Nuovo on January 11, 1945 [*Romito* 2020]. Another account comes from Ettore Manfredi, Irma's nephew, who was the same age as Maderna and his friend. He recalls that Bruno had some sort of contact with the activities of the partisans in Verona, until something was leaked, perhaps, to the German authorities. Manfredi states that Maderna was arrested by the SS in February 1945 and was released shortly afterwards thanks to Irma's important connections. There is, however, no written trace of this episode either in the official records or in private letters. Whatever the case, that winter Maderna decided to escape to the mountains. His position and some details of his activity are clearly described in Maderna's record card as a partisan:

p. 1 MINISTRY OF OCCUPIED ITALY/ N.. 056378 / Record card / of Maderna Bruno (Ras)/ son of N. N. / born 1920 /Partisan of the Brigade «V. AVESANI»; p. 2 Photo [not countersigned; personal details]; p. 3: Clandestine activity carried out by the holder / Place and division on September 8 [no data] / partisan group belonged to / BRIGATA AVESANI DISTACC. ROSSETTI [...] p. 5 [...] Paid the sum of L. 5000 (five thousand) as an award on demobilization as a partisan Verona August 1945 / Patriot Representative / (Magg. A.) Magri/ [signature]. [*Documenti* 1985, 80]

It is not clear whether Bruno actually took part in any operations, but the events surrounding his life in the last part of the war suggest that his conscience had taken a decisive anti-Fascist turn. He lived for some time in strict anonymity at Sant'Anna d'Alfaedo, in the Lessini mountains, where once a week Raffaella – as she herself recounts – reached him after a long bike ride. Their clandestine relationship came to an end when the couple were married, in secret, on November 10, 1945 in Mozzecane, a small town not far from Verona, with apparently no effect on their routine life, given that Bruno continued to live in his mother Irma's home [*Centro Studi Maderna*, Section Q 1]. His mother only learnt of the marriage some months later, on February 13, 1946, and Bruno subsequently "fled" to Venice. Irma Manfredi recounts these facts in a long letter to Policarpo Crosara, who had just returned after four years in prison, adding that the true reason for this sudden decision to marry appears to have been the parents' concern for the safety of their daughter.[34]

The five years that passed between the completion of his studies in Rome and the end of the war, although marked by experiences that doubtlessly disturbed his artistic growth and interrupted his career as a conductor, do not seem to have had any lasting effect on his character nor on the constancy of his passion for music. During his years of study with Malipiero, in which he also practiced his conducting skills with Guarnieri, and even when the events of the war began to involve him more directly, he worked on several compositions that were both important and mature in terms of their structure and language: a *Concerto per pianoforte ed orchestra*, the *Introduzione e Passacaglia "Lauda Sion Salvatorem"* for orchestra, a *Quartetto per archi* and finally the large-scale *Requiem*.

A. I. De Benedictis associates the *Concerto* with his advanced studies with

---

[34] Letter from Manfredi to Crosara in *Centro Studi Maderna* Section L 1. Manfredi's reference to the girl's safety can be explained by part of a letter Tartaglia wrote to Mario Baroni in May 1984: she recalls with bitterness (on p. 3) that shortly after the war she had been tried for alleged collaboration, but was exonerated "with the apologies of the Court." Letter from Tartaglia to Mario Baroni [*Centro Studi Maderna*, ibid., Section L 7].

Malipiero, since on the afternoon of its first performance at the Conservatory in Venice, in June 1942, all the composers appearing on the program were pupils from the course held by Malipiero in the previous year.[35] The composition of the *Concerto* and that of the *Introduzione e Passacaglia* took place in the same months, between 1941 and 1942, although the work for orchestra (concluded in 1942 according to the date given by Maderna on the score) was perhaps completed after the concerto. It should be added, though, that the order in which the two works were composed seems quite irrelevant seeing that there are no stylistic relations that would point to one being written before the other. Indeed, the only significant aspect is precisely their evident reciprocal independence: it is as if Maderna, in his early twenties, tended to experiment with different techniques of construction and expression, each coherent within itself, but none of them decisive for any future orientation. Over and above the difference in styles between the two compositions there is one feature, however, that they have in common: their anti-romanticism. Despite the fact that this element is manifest in both works (and that Maderna – as we saw – had admitted this position ever since he was under the schooling of Bustini), it never results in a provocative or, even less so, derisory approach. This kind of attitude of had, instead, been sometimes assumed in the previous decades, for instance by Stravinsky or Hindemith, not to mention the Italian futurists, but Maderna does not seem to have been attracted by this line of thought. It is almost tempting to suggest that his biographical background may have influenced his aesthetic choice. After leaving the primitive exhibitions of his father behind him, the gradual, exciting discovery of how rich the emotional and spiritual contents could be of an art that boasted centuries of refined development and that his teachers were skillfully and patiently helping him to appreciate, filled him with genuine enthusiasm.[36] His attitude towards music, whether ancient or modern, was therefore one of love and respect,

---

[35] The playbill for the performance (which was conducted by Ettore Gracis) can be found at the *Centro Studi Maderna*, Section D 3.5. In her introduction to the critical edition of the Concerto that she edited [*Maderna* 2011, V et seq] A. I. De Benedictis observes how the recent retrieval of three complete copies of the score made it finally possible to study and perform the work. Only four years before, Veniero Rizzardi ["Quasi perduto, quasi ritrovato Nota sulla riscoperta del giovanile *Concerto per pianoforte* di Bruno Maderna," *Atti dell'Istituto Veneto di Scienze, Lettere ed Arti*, no. 166 (2007-2008), 62] had stated that the score was "still lost," even though on that occasion he was able to publish a rediscovered version of it for two pianos that Maderna had compiled in 1946. In summary, in a short space of time, between 2007 and 2012, this concerto, which until around twenty years before we had known very little about, [*Documenti* 1985, 183] happily regained its historical presence.

[36] Hints of such enthusiasm, which at times are even moving, can be found in his diaries and in his school notes, some of which have been included in a study by Nicola Verzina, "Mutazioni storiche intorno a tre testi inediti di Bruno Maderna," *Studi musicali*, 28/2 (1999), 495-527.

and his unrelenting objective appears to have been to take full possession of its extraordinary secrets. This may explain the differences in style between the two works written contemporaneously, since he believed the secrets hidden within each one of them were equally worth exploring. This does not mean that he was dissatisfied with the outcome of such explorations or that he saw them simply as academic exercises: in 1946 he made a transcription of the *Concerto per due pianoforti* (see note 36) to allow it to be played in Great Britain and in 1947 he conducted the *Introduzione e Passacaglia* at the Teatro Comunale in Florence. One might also add that while the recent performances of the two works have allowed us to appreciate how in both compositions there are more or less evident references to some pre-existing model, what strikes the listener most is the originality with which these references have been re-elaborated, offering further confirmation of the trust he now had in his own creative abilities.[37]

The *Concerto per pianoforte* therefore shares the "modern" expression of the *Passacaglia*, but manages it in a different way. It is true that here and there we find various features common to both works: the rhythmic and contrapuntal play between the voices, dissonant encounters that are free and non violent, subtle melodic inventions with a certain modal leaning, and harmonies built on fourths. But, over and above these shared elements, the scheme of the two pieces diverges quite notably: the *Passacaglia* has a clear and ordered form, supported by rhetorically well organized tensions, whereas the *Concerto* plays on surprises, on sudden contrasts and irregular successions of episodes. With its polyphonic structure, the *Passacaglia* tends to allow the single parts to emerge and highlights the relations between them, whereas the *Concerto*, on the contrary, tends to hide the individual parts, not allowing them to be perceived singularly and at times presenting them as a magma of material as opposed to polyphony. The work often features outbursts of sound in which the instruments lack individual lines, but impose themselves collectively, often joined by the percussion. The *Concerto* nevertheless preserves some echoes of tradition, for example in the interplay between soloist and orchestra.

In *Introduzione e Passacaglia "Lauda Sion salvatorem"*, the choice of the archaic passacaglia form, and maybe also of some aspects of modalism and harmony in fourths, could well be put down to the influence of Malipiero, while the

---

[37] For details of the *Concerto per pianoforte* see the program notes and the bill for the concert in Verona on October 10, 2009, conductor Carlo Miotto, pianist Aldo Orvieto [*Centro Studi Maderna*, Section D 3.5]; the *Introduzione e Passacaglia* was conducted by Marco Angius at La Fenice in Venice on April 11 and 13, 2014. Recordings of the performances of both works can be found in the *Centro Studi Maderna*.

reference to *Lauda Sion* could be said to derive from Hindemith's symphony *Mathis der Maler*, where the German composer has quoted this ancient melody in the third movement. More detailed observations of this kind can be found in Mauro Mastropasqua's introduction to the critical edition of the work [*Maderna* 2005, X and XI], but we should add that Hindemith's symphony was played at S. Cecilia in Rome in December 1937 and that Maderna may have attended the performance or heard it being discussed. The *Passacaglia* appears to have gleaned some elements of the symphony's solid construction, but it is certainly not conceived on the turbulent models of the young Hindemith. We know, however, that Maderna had studied Hindemith's book of theory and this is perhaps reflected in what was his first symphonic composition, whose dramaturgical strategy is based on the alternation of tension and release, on a confident and free choice of consonant and dissonant intervals, and on an exemplarily sober approach to melody, besides the use of neo-Baroque counterpoint, vaguely inspired by Bach. This heritage is also borne out by a version he made for organ, dedicated to his organist friend Sandro Dalla Libera, which was donated to the *Centro Studi Maderna* [shelf-mark M 57 bis] by his son Francesco Dalla Libera.

The dramatic events that took place between July 1943 and April 1945, in which Maderna himself was directly involved, certainly allowed him little time to dedicate to composition. He was nevertheless able to work on a *Quartetto per archi* which has raised wide interest among Maderna scholars. The only clue as to the dating of the *Quartetto* comes from a letter he wrote to Irma in January 1943, while he was a soldier in Merano [*Extraits* 2007, 477-478]. He tells his mother that he is writing the Adagio of a quartet and that for the first time in his life he was forced to write from inside his head, because there was no piano where he was stationed. So he probably started the work sometime between 1942 and '43, but it is not clear when it was completed. The letter also offers some very interesting indications about his approach to composition in those years. The lack of a piano led him to reflect on the question of intervals, or rather on the "relations between the notes," as he puts it, and in particular the harmonic relations between the notes. Malipiero taught him to take these relations into account also between the different voices in counterpoint, and Hindemith similarly analyzed them in his *Unterweisung*, focusing above all on the relations between melodies. But despite these possible influences, Maderna underlines that he had always conceived his melody lines in terms of what he called their "harmonic atmosphere": basically he is experimenting with a more mature conception of the chord. He finds it hard to explain this to Irma and the only thing he finds to say is that in his new approach the material arrangement of the chord is almost "spiritualized."

Since the contemplation of intervals is a crucial issue in the music of the twentieth century, some scholars have wondered whether this playing with intervals, which began at the time of the *Quartetto*, might not be seen as a sort of premise to his later shift towards the Viennese school. Luigi Nono recalls how in those years Maderna was working particularly on major and minor seconds, on minor thirds and the tritone, intervals that are systematically used in some of Bartók's most famous works (the *Music for strings, percussion and celesta* and the *First String Quartet*).[38] Nono considers this aspect particularly significant, adding that from this point of view Bartók was just as innovative as the composers gathering around Schönberg in Vienna. Nicolò Palazzetti wrote a detailed article on Maderna's *Quartetto* starting from suppositions of this kind, but adding other considerations and insisting especially on a new aspect: the intervals mentioned by Nono are actually those typical of the so-called octatonic scale, which Maderna had thus began to use in this work.[39] Although Maderna and Nono never explicitly use this technical term, they may have felt its essence intuitively and tried to reproduce its "flavor" in their melodies and harmonies, or the "atmosphere" that Maderna mentions in his letter to Manfredi.

The last work conceived by Maderna during the war is a grandiose *Requiem*, which concludes his early period of composition that started with *Alba* in 1939. The date of the work is documented by a letter he wrote to Malipiero in August 1945, in which he announces that he has "recommenced" the work that had been "interrupted for many months."[40] From this we can deduce that he began to write the *Requiem* during the last years of the war; the date of its completion can be found at the bottom of the score: "Venice, September 1946." Once again the link between the style of this work and those that came before it lies, paradoxically, in its difference. It would appear that in his first years of activity as a composer his main aspiration was to explore and experiment with ideas that were always different from the previous ones. However, we should not underestimate one element that is shared by all five compositions and that

---

[38] A. I. De Benedictis, V. Rizzardi eds., *La nostalgia del futuro. Scritti scelti di Luigi Nono* (Milano: il Saggiatore, 2007), 212.

[39] N. Palazzetti, "Italian harmony during the Second World War: Analysis of Bruno Maderna's First String Quartet," *Rivista di Analisi e Teoria Musicale*, 21/1 (2015), 63-91. The octatonic scale, made famous over the last decades by Anglo-American musicology which suggests it forms the basis of much non dodecaphonic but non tonal music (e.g. that of Stravinsky, Bartók etc.), consists of a series of semitones and tones (a total of eight in an octave, and not seven as in a normal diatonic scale). The octatonic scale is characterized, in particular, by the presence of a minor second, major second, minor third and tritone: precisely the four intervals that Nono mentions in his article.

[40] Letter cited by V. Rizzardi in the Introduction to the critical edition of the *Requiem* [Maderna 2006, VI, IX].

we have already hinted at: a sort of "faith in his art." None of the previously mentioned compositions seem to have raised any doubt in his mind, and the same can be said of the *Requiem*.

Unfortunately the path undertaken by the composition was not entirely smooth. Malipiero (as testified by some of his letters) was enthusiastic and had promised he would try to arrange a performance, but nothing concrete came of this. And Maderna himself was unable to have it performed at the Biennale di Venezia in 1946. Another great admirer was the American composer and critic Virgil Thomson. During a visit to Venice in the same year he met Gian Francesco Malipiero, who introduced him to his young, brilliant pupil. On July 31 Maderna wrote to his mother that two days before, Thomson had come to his home and he had "let him listen" to his *Requiem*. Thomson was immediately struck by what he heard and was so impressed that a few days later (August 10) he published an article in the European edition of the *New York Herald Tribune* full of praise for the work. Not only this, he also promised to try to get it performed at various universities in America. The copy of the score that left for the USA some months later was destined to be the only one that survived, as the other copies disappeared with the passing of time and Maderna's interest in the work appears to have gradually diminished. More than half a century later, Veniero Rizzardi, thanks to a shrewd and fortunate piece of detective work, managed to uncover the score in a sector of the library of New York University, where it had ended after the last choral director approached by Thomson, Paul Boepple, had decided not to take on the work on account of its being too demanding.[41] The adventure of the creation and subsequent loss of the *Requiem* finally reached a happy conclusion: the composition was successfully performed on November 19, 2009 by the choir and orchestra of La Fenice in Venice, conducted by Andrea Molino.

To gain a general idea of the nature of the work it is perhaps worth considering two different accounts: that of Maderna, who spoke of it in 1970 in an interview on Radio Chicago, and that of Thomson in his previously mentioned article of 1946. In the interview [*Documenti* 1985, 90] Maderna comments that when it was written the piece was "a sort of visiting card; today it would seem rather naive." This minimizing attitude appears to be in stark contrast with the words of Thomson, who stated that the work reached an intensity of expression that rivals the requiems of Berlioz and Verdi. In the end, though, one might come to the conclusion that Thomson's affirmation (which perhaps in reality manages to capture the young composer's intentions)

---

[41] For details of the rediscovery of the work, see V. Rizzardi, *Esumazione di un Requiem* (Firenze: Olschki, 2007).

corresponds precisely with what Maderna would later consider pure and simple naivety. In the present context, though, we cannot share either of these points of view, even though they might prove helpful in trying to identify Maderna's poetics at the time, but also in understanding how these were transformed over the following decades. It seems more fruitful, instead, to take into account other important stylistic references: the grandeur of Verdi or of Berlioz recognized in this work also had other very different, but equally illustrious precedents. The double choir and its variable proportions (from 8 to 4 voices) is inextricably associated with the choral music of sixteenth century Venice, which may well have been Maderna's model, perhaps with a little encouragement from his teacher. And the kind of space that he had in mind for the performance of such a polychoral work may have been St. Mark's. Also the choice to include only brass groups, without the woodwind, could be seen as a tribute to the typical timbres of the Renaissance. As for the use of three pianos and a well stocked group of percussion instruments, the models (obviously not ancient) are quite easy to recognize in the examples set by Stravinsky and Bartók.

The musical language of the *Requiem* is varied and rich, which is also in keeping with the demands and tone of the text. The texture is mostly polyphonic, perhaps out of respect for the traditional use of polyphony in ancient sacred music: at times Maderna even pays homage to this tradition by inserting episodes in a fugato style. The contrapuntal interplay inevitably creates non-tonal harmonies with their resulting dissonances, while the formal structures are always very clear, each episode being internally coherent and well distinguished from those around it. Generally speaking the models that one perceives are not limited to those of the great European tradition, but also come from the more local Roman tradition of the twentieth century. It is not rare, for example, to hear distant echoes of the sacred works of Petrassi. Within each episode of the *Requiem* and also in the sequence of episodes, the rhetoric of the music is predominantly inspired by the ancient texts, with gradual intensifications and powerful peaks in dynamics and texture. In achieving these effects he exploits the wealth of timbres offered by the orchestral groups, as well as a wide variety of rhythmic invention. The "material" taste that the composer had experimented with in previous works now explodes in an often unprecedented fashion. Dramatic moments are alternated, in a carefully calculated manner, with more relaxed episodes featuring solo voices or instruments, or with ostinatos that may also be rhythmic and percussive, and at times there are even hints of dances with an ethnic flavor.

In conclusion, we might say this piece too belongs the "non-provocative" style of early Maderna. It is, however, only right to add that the choice to write a sacred work at such a time may also be interpreted as the desire to offer a prayer for the future. In his youth Maderna had passed through a phase in which, thanks above all to the influence of Policarpo and Irma, religion carried a significant weight. This work tells us that this weight was by no means secondary. The sheer faith that emanates from these notes leaves no doubt as to its authenticity. We know very little about this aspect of Maderna's character. We can only mention that almost thirty years later, when recalling those times during the interview in Chicago, he said half serious and half joking: "at that moment the only possibility was to write a requiem and then die" [*Documenti* 1985, 90-91].

CHAPTER II

FROM VENICE TO DARMSTADT

The end of the war also marked the end of Maderna's youthful years. He left Verona and Irma Manfredi's home, and chose to live in Venice with his wife, totally independent of his protectors and confidants. "Mamma Irma" was always ready to help him in any way he needed (especially financially), but would no longer be directly involved in his choices, and their correspondence became increasingly sporadic. There remains just a single trace of a request to his mother regarding the cost of sending copies of his *Requiem* to Brussels, which he would pay back later as soon as the work was published, perhaps by Suvini Zerboni, "and this will be the last time I'll ask you for money for music," as he writes in a letter, undated but probably sent in autumn 1946 [*Extraits* 2007, 481]. Given the complicated path that this work eventually took, it is not even certain that these expenses would be necessary. His relationship with his friend Policarpo Crosara also underwent a similar decline. Crosara had returned to Venice after the traumatic events he had suffered during the last years of the war (according to the oral account given to the present authors); some photos exist of a meeting between the two friends but little correspondence, and Bruno began to face the difficulties of life with the help of new friends and acquaintances.

Before moving on to the events characterizing Maderna's period in Venice, it is worth taking a closer look at his character as a person, as far as we can gather from the sparse details we have of his early life. In particular, certain apparently contradictory aspects of his behavior may seem rather surprising. Take, for example, the sincere and positive relation he had with his adoptive mother, who was nonetheless often concerned about the not always irreproachable conduct of her otherwise smart son. Similarly positive and genuinely sincere was his moral and religious relation with his friend Crosara, but this aspect too was often belied by the high spirited behavior that Bruno readily indulged in, according to the accounts of some of his companions in Venice during those years. Also his occasional comments about the "perverse" nature of his father did not prevent him from keeping in touch with his original family, as can be deduced from the musical material found in Sesto S. Giovanni at the home of his sister Italia Grossato, which he left there during his visits. The fact that the material includes music manuscripts, sketches and notes would seem to imply that these visits were not at all brief or even seldom, but are suggestive of a warm relationship and one of mutual trust. His very marriage to Raffaella

Tartaglia, although perhaps leaving much to be desired in terms of emotional stability, took place without the knowledge of his mother, who clearly saw it as yet another symptom of the undisciplined side of her son, who was by no means a rebel, though he sometimes behaved like one.

To understand the reasons behind these seemingly contradictory facets of his personality one does not have to be a psychologist or even a psychoanalyst: it is simply a matter of looking at the facts. The values transmitted by the easy-going life of his father and the libertarian environment of his family of origin, which he surely acquired and shared when he was a child, were suddenly overturned during his adolescence, and such an upheaval cannot fail to leave its traces on a person's character. From what we can gather it appears that two existential and moral models continued to coexist in his character, to the extent of leading him to yield alternatively to one side or the other. Fortunately they had no consequences on his musicality (which is the most important thing for us today), but we should not imagine that they had no influence on his way of thinking and behaving.

As he grew older he started to become more sure of his convictions, and his choices became more confident and solid. But one might wonder whether certain aspects of his adult personality were not the outcome of these earlier experiences. For example, the accounts passed on by his colleagues and by the performers he worked with unanimously stress his human cordiality and lack of any display of self-esteem that typically characterize great artists. This does not mean that he underestimated his intellectual and artistic qualities; on the contrary, he was perfectly aware of them. Suffice it to consider, for example, how in one of his interviews he spoke frankly of "the ignorant [...] stars of the podium" [*Documenti* 1985, 100]. But his greatest gift was the way he treated everybody with equal respect, regardless of their standing: he adopted the same simple manner whether he was speaking to one of his performers or to the superintendent of La Scala or even with the Shah of Persia.[1] Could it be that this type of behavior was in some way a reaction against how his gifts as a child prodigy had been exploited, and the discomfort that such a situation may have caused him? Finally, his apparently contradictory tendencies may, in the end, have become a sort of second nature. In an interview given in 1973, shortly before his death, he remarked:

> in life it is not necessary to be consistent [...] one should try to be so natural and alive that one can follow and express the different moments of our organism, both physical and psychological. I believe that the famous serial immutability has been one of the worst diseases [*Documenti* 1985, 117].

[1] See, for instance, photos 18 and 19 in *Documenti* 1985, 155 and the accounts given by many performers collected by Valerio Tura in *Pour Bruno* 2015, 171-234, *passim*.

Statements of this kind have led to further reflections about Maderna's apparent diffidence towards the ideologies that were circulating at Darmstadt.[2]

After 1945 the fact that he could no longer count on his exceptionally young age and peculiar private background to win over the public, made it less simple for him to enter the world of music as a conductor and composer. And he was weighed down even more by the tragic vestiges of the war and by the radical transformation in the outlook of a world that wished to rise from the ashes, but more especially to change direction, to distance itself as quickly as possible from the memories of the recent past. In the years immediately following the war Maderna too was in search of avenues that would bring him in touch with a more international dimension. And it was once again Malipiero who came to his aid by introducing him to important institutions and eminent figures both in Venice and in other cities.[3] It was, for instance, thanks to Malipiero that in the summer of 1946 he obtained a small job working in the library of the Venice Conservatory (contract drafted and signed on July 1, 1946). It is likely that he was given this job again, or something similar, over the following years, but it was not until the academic years 1949-50 and 50-51 that he finally obtained work as a substitute teacher on the entire course of "Teoria e Solfeggio" (12 hours of lessons a week). A later document dated March 6, 1962 reveals that Maderna had substituted for Nino Sanzogno in the orchestral conducting course from November 31, 1948 to May 28, 1949, while another document (January 10, 1953) shows that he stood in for the same teacher again in 1949-51. Basically, then, we can say that Maderna taught at the conservatory from 1946 to 1952, though without being classified in any precise ministerial role. The document in which Malipiero informs Maderna that he has had to terminate his contract because of the arrival of a new tenured teacher is dated February 21, 1952.[4]

His work at the conservatory gave Maderna the opportunity to meet a variety of young and promising musicians whose progress he followed carefully, in some cases also giving them private lessons. His students included Renzo Dall'Oglio, Gastone Fabris, Romolo Grano, Mario Messinis, and even Luigi Nono, who undertook the first part of his musical training with Maderna and would later share with him their first experience at Darmstadt. According to Renzo Dall'Oglio, Maderna and Nono had already met in 1946 thanks to their common interest in

---

[2] See G. Montecchi, "Il lavoro di precomposizione in Serenata n. 2," *Studi* 1989, 109.

[3] Besides introducing him to Virgil Thomson, he gave him a letter of introduction to Dimitri Mitropoulos (May 29, 1946) to help him obtain some possible engagements: "Bruno Maderna composer and orchestral conductor (excellent musician) [...] Listen to Bruno Maderna, he deserves it" [*Centro Studi Maderna*, Section L 1].

[4] All the documents cited in this paragraph can be found at the *Centro Studi Maderna* Section L 5.

the theories of Hindemith: Nono had asked Malipiero where he could find out more about the work of the German theorist and Malipiero had directed him to Maderna, who owned a copy of *Unterweisung im Tonsatz*.[5]

During his lessons – at the conservatory, and more especially at home – Bruno did not limit himself to critically examining his students' analyses of ancient music and their composition exercises, but broadened the discussion to include all that was happening in the world of music, and to accounts of his experiences with important figures like Casella, Pizzetti and Respighi, and with other composers from the "in-between" generation, such as Petrassi, Turchi and Dallapiccola, with whom he had come into contact during his studies in Rome and at the Accademia Chigiana in Siena. Since Maderna and his group of acquaintances were invariably present at concerts, in meetings with notable figures passing through Venice, at conferences at the conservatory and in the theaters, they became known as "The new Venetian school."[6] They were occasionally joined by other musicians, including the Brazilian composer Eunice Catunda, who exerted a strong influence on the group especially in terms of their political outlook: she had fled to Italy from Brazil along with other musicians, and was interested in the new dodecaphonic techniques. In his *Polifonica-Monodia-Ritmica* of 1951 Nono re-elaborated the rhythms and intervals of an Indo-Brazilian song that had probably been suggested to him by Catunda. Reliable sources inform us that during his lessons Maderna did not impart any prescriptions or details of methods, and above all he avoided insisting on his own personal thoughts or aesthetics; his main concern was to encourage his students to approach music through the analysis of different genres, outside of the usual repertoire. He placed particular emphasis on examples of ancient music indicated by Malipiero, a typical case being the enigmatic canons of the Flemish school.[7]

This attitude towards teaching in many ways reflects Maderna's own search for a personal path as a composer. In those years a wide variety of propositions, not always well formulated, circulated in the speeches and writings of musicians

---

[5] E. Schaller, "L'insegnamento di Bruno Maderna attraverso le fonti conservate presso l'Archivio Luigi Nono," *Bruno Maderna Studi eTestimonianze*, eds. R. Dalmonte, M. Russo (Lucca: LIM, 2004), 115.

[6] V. Rizzardi, "La nuova scuola veneziana. 1948-1951," *Le musiche degli anni Cinquanta*, eds. G. Borio, G. Morelli, V. Rizzardi (Firenze: Olschki 2004), 1-59.

[7] "Un'autobiografia dell'autore raccontata da Enzo Restagno," *Nono*, ed. E. Restagno (Torino: EDT, 1987). The references to Catunda can be found on pp. 22-23, those to the Flemish musicians on p. 12. Interesting reflections on the fundamental importance of the reciprical collaboration between Nono and Maderna in these years can be found in a book by J. Impett, where the author discusses what Nono called "musical thought," which (for the two musicians) included the way of organizing sound structures, their capacity to reveal an underlying element of imagination, and the network of relations linking individual imagination with the historical context in which it develops. See J. Impett, *Routledge Handbook to Luigi Nono and Musical Thought* (New York: Routledge, 2019).

and theorists, with the common aim of taking music away from the customary lines, towards new solutions: denotative or prescriptive statements, declarations proposing novel techniques or modes of performance open to countless possible interpretations. It was, in fact, quite hard for a young musician like Maderna to find his own direction in a world of music that wanted to be new, but was not sure of "new in what way." The language inherited from the developments that had taken place in the decades preceding the war, despite the clear and evident break away from the idioms of the late nineteenth century, was now in need of new forms of experimentation. This spurred the impulse to surpass any national barriers and to look towards what was happening in other countries, creating a kind of Europeanization whose borders were still uncertain, a way that had already been paved by the work of Alfredo Casella following his stay in Paris. Although his works written before the end of the war had shown a solid grounding and doubtless character, Maderna continued to search for solutions that would suit his way of conceiving music along new lines.

Maderna's first composition dating from the years immediately following the end of the war is the group of three *Liriche su Verlaine* for soprano and piano, which were written between 1946 and '47. "Aquarelles" (the first of the three songs) comes from the collection Romances sans paroles published by Verlaine in 1874, when the poet had first started experimenting with Parnassianism, a movement that aimed at a precise and rigid style, devoid of sentimental pathos. Maderna was most likely familiar with the settings already made by Debussy, Fauré and others, but his composition has little or nothing in common with these previous works. He seems instead to have been more inspired by the formal elegance of the original poem. The setting is made up of gently intertwining melodies with echoes and cross-references passing between the piano and vocal parts. The harmonies are non traditional and any associations with the semantics of the verbal text are only allusive. Basically he has chosen a form of expression that is somber but delicate, and without any evident passion. The second song is titled "Sérénade" and is taken from a collection of poems that the twenty-two year-old Verlaine had published in 1866 and called Poèmes saturniens. It is conceived in the vein of a genuine Italian popular song, "au son de la mandoline." Maderna's composition, in this case, is closely modeled on Verlaine's poem, as if the composer wanted to abandon himself freely to the simple pleasure of song. In reality, here too the situation is more complex: the twentieth century modernity of the setting, which is not lacking in occasional moments of harshness betrays an underlying intention that precludes any innocent abandon or presumed spontaneity. "Sagesse," the third and longest song, comes from the collection of the same name published later in the poet's life (in 1881) after his conversion to Roman Catholicism. The poem has the repetitive structure of a prayer and the affective relation with the contents is once again different: it has neither the impassibility of "Aquarelles," nor the feigned *naivety* of "Sérénade." Here Verlaine's poetry assumes the form of an authentic confession with no trace of pretence. And Maderna seems to identify with the poet's spirit: his setting is characterized by a gradual intensification, which reaches its powerful climax in the thirteenth of the fifteen strophes, with dissonances enclosed in a dense texture, until finding true peace in the final lines.

It is important to underline that Maderna had read Verlaine's poems with an extraordinary depth of attention, revealing the scrupulous nature of a man of culture. And we should not underestimate his choice of a poet like Verlaine, who, in his works, not only showed an unmatched skill in handling the language, but also his courage in testing the effects of a perilous social rejection, and in facing at his own risk, as a "damned" poet, what it meant to disobey the norms of behavior and moral values commonly upheld and respected in France at the time. In a period of transition such as that following the war, Maderna adopts the ethical model of Verlaine, which also holds significant aesthetic implications: discovering new social values and advocating "different" norms of behavior were part of a line of thought that was given new impetus by the collapse of Fascism, offering novel horizons that were still unpredictable. Unfortunately, though, his intentions were destined to remain unfulfilled. We know nothing of the performance of the work that was scheduled to take place in Rome in December 1947,[8] and the composition was left unpublished until its critical edition [*Maderna* 1997], while the first documented performance was given in Germany almost thirty years after the date of composition, in 1984 [*Documenti* 1985, 190], when the cultural climate was totally different and surely not such as to allow the Berlin audience to grasp Maderna's hypothetical aesthetic intentions. On the other hand, there is little doubt that this was a highly original work in a style that in no way resembled the five works written in the previous years,[9] and for this reason it represents, in a certain sense, the pinnacle of the composer's tendency to constantly look for new paths, which at one moment or another might offer some significant indication of his true deep-seated identity.

---

[8] In a letter of November 13, 1946 he tells his mother that he has finished the first of the three songs; in a letter written immediately afterwards he says: "On December 29 my songs on a text by Verlaine will be performed in Rome...." These letters were not known to the editor of the critical edition of the work, Benedetto Passannanti, who dates the composition to between the last months of 1946 and the first of '47. Unfortunately we still have no confirmation of the performance in Rome. The two letters are preserved in the *Paul Sacher Stiftung* in Basel [*Extraits* 2007, 484].

[9] As mentioned in the previous chapter, these were *Alba, Concerto per pianoforte e orchestra, Introduzione e Passacaglia, Quartetto* and the *Requiem*.

But in those years, no matter how successful it might be, his work as a composer was clearly not sufficient to resolve other more urgent problems concerning his material survival. He could no longer rely on the economic support of his adoptive mother as he had in the past, and his employment at the conservatory and the private lessons, though gratifying at an intellectual level, were barely enough to cover his financial needs. And to make matters worse, several of his pupils recall that as soon as they became friends with Bruno, he no longer wanted to be paid for his lessons. Moreover, despite his prodigious past, his merits as a composer and performer were still not fully acknowledged.

It was once again Malipiero who alleviated the situation by recommending him to the organizers of the first *Biennale Musica di Venezia* after the war as director of the "Gruppo Strumentale B. Marcello" and persuading them to include one of his pieces (the *Serenata per 11 strumenti*) in the program of the *Concerto della Giovane Scuola Italiana* (September 21, 1946). Besides this work by Maderna and one by Malipiero himself, the program also featured recent compositions by Valentino Bucchi, Guido Turchi and Camillo Togni. Some of these pieces offered examples of Italian dodecaphony, a technique Maderna was familiar with after associating with Luigi Dallapiccola, although he does not seem to have been particularly interested in using this approach for his own compositions. Knowing it would make her happy, on September 27 Bruno wrote to his mother about the concert, telling her how only the Venetian newspapers and Franco Abbiati in the *Corriere della Sera* of Milan had published negative reviews of his work (though not of his conducting), while on the contrary he had been widely covered and highly praised by Ferdinando Ballo on the radio and in the newspapers of Florence and Turin [*Extraits* 2007, 483].

The director of the Biennale, Giovanni Ponti, was not initially disposed towards the idea of giving the festival a clearly innovative slant, being more concerned about satisfying the expectations of the public in terms of a non challenging program and a particular emphasis on ballet. In the end the wider inclusion of composers and works from other countries helped to override the conservative tendencies and worries of an economic nature among the organizers of the festival.[10] But despite the far-sighted work of Ferdinando Ballo, technical-artistic director from 1947 to 1950, and the programming of works inspired by new musical currents, the Biennale in Venice did not immediately succeed in finding its own aesthetic identity compared to that of other festivals, such as the *Aprile Milanese* and the *Maggio Musicale Fiorentino*, particularly on account of the hostile attitude of the city's critics, which subsequently influenced the

---

[10] D. G. Leonardi, "Il Festival internazionale di musica contemporanea di Venezia (1946-54)," *Italia millenovecentocinquanta*, eds. G. Salvetti, B. M. Antolini (Milano: Guerini e Associati, 1999), 140.

decisions of the Ministry regarding financial support. However, by the end of the '40s the programs of the Biennale had begun to help the public become aware of the great European music of the twentieth century and to marvel at the pre-nineteenth century Italian repertoire. Suffice it to consider the theatrical works staged in the 1949 edition, which opened with Alban Berg's *Lulu*, followed by G. F. Ghedini's *Billy Budd* to a libretto by Quasimodo, and closed with Monteverdi's *Incoronazione di Poppea* (in Malipiero's revision), repeated on four consecutive evenings. Within this rich and varied setting, Maderna's name appears several times: besides his appearance as composer and conductor in the concert of 1946, he also features as the reviser of the concerto by Vivaldi played on September 30, 1947 and of Ziani's cantata *Il sepolcro* performed on September 12, 1950, while his *Concerto per due pianoforti e strumenti* is featured in the chamber concert of September 17, 1948, directed by Ettore Gracis.

Apart from the occasional work opportunities and teaching roles that presented themselves at the conservatory, another source of income (and of musical experience) came once more from Malipiero, who in March 1947 had been appointed artistic director of the *Istituto Italiano Antonio Vivaldi*, established by Antonio Fanna and Angelo Ephrikian, with support from the publishers, Casa Ricordi. The project to make modern transcriptions of the manuscripts that had recently arrived in the Foà Giordano Collection in Turin was monumental and was a further step in the direction already taken in various sectors of the world of music (musicologists, concert organizers, performers) ever since the start of the century and that had led, for example, to the founding of the *Società Antonio Vivaldi* (Venice 1938) and to the first Vivaldi festival in Siena. Malipiero's initiative, however, represented a truly historical milestone: it led to the publication of 530 easy-to-read editions of instrumental works, which increased the knowledge of Vivaldi's output at all levels and consolidated his artistic fame. The "Vivaldi revival" was a movement that also involved important foreign publishers such as Breitkopf, Eulenburg and Schott, although not matching the capacity for circulation and dissemination achieved by the editions of Ricordi.[11] In the celebrations marking the third centenary of Vivaldi's birth (1978), the world of Italian musicology was quite unanimous in recognizing the merits of the team in Venice, and here it suffices to quote just one example: "Malipiero took upon himself the burdensome task to personally revise, in the space of a quarter of a century, as many as 435 compositions, entrusting a further 46 to Ephrikian, while the remaining 48 volumes were revised by another six musicians, among whom the name of Bruno Maderna stands out."[12] It should be mentioned, though, that near the conclusion of the project, one of the most

---

[11] F. Nicolodi, "La riscoperta di Vivaldi nel Novecento," *Nuova Rivista Musicale Italiana*, 13/4 (1979), 820-844, *passim*.

[12] M. Abbado, "Antonio Vivaldi nel nostro secolo con particolare riferimento alle sue opere strumentali," *Nuova Rivista Musicale Italiana*, 13/1 (1979), 95 & 105.

accredited scholars of Vivaldi's works, Peter Ryom, who was preparing a *Grosse Ausgabe* of the composer's catalogue of works and a critical edition, often spoke negatively of the undertaking.

Various sources confirm that Malipiero asked Maderna to transcribe six of Vivaldi's concertos, published by Ricordi between 1947 and 1949. In doing so he not only helped Maderna financially but also found a significant outlet for his pupil's exceptional skills. The general norms for the series foresaw the transcription for string orchestra of manuscripts by Vivaldi, producing a score of the musical material that the composer had arranged only on a few staves. For example, for the *Concerto in do maggiore per violino archi e cembalo* (F I, no. 3), one of the pieces transcribed by Maderna, Vivaldi only wrote three parts: one with a treble clef, one with an alto clef and one with a bass clef. In such cases, both Malipiero and Ephrikian give the part with a treble clef to the violins, assigning to the soloist only the parts marked "Solo." The part in the alto clef is given to the violas, and the one written in the bass clef to the cello (and possibly the double bass an octave below) and to the bass line of the harpsichord. The rare additions of dynamic and agogic markings are given in brackets. The thorough bass is realized as a simple series of chords and is printed in smaller characters. Malipiero himself stated: "I have prepared over one hundred Concertos by Antonio Vivaldi for publication. I claim to have carried out only the work of a humble copyist, so correct, precise and indisputable are Vivaldi's manuscripts. I never gave in to the temptation to make speculative corrections."[13] Generally speaking, Maderna adheres carefully to the guidelines of the series, only occasionally taking greater liberty in the realization of the bass, which is often polyphonic and makes use of melodic fragments that are not included in the lines written by Vivaldi. In addition, he adds (without brackets) some accents and bowing marks, and gives some performing indications (in brackets). Although the series as a whole – and especially the six concertos revised by Maderna – could not be said to form a critical edition in the modern sense of the term, it is equally true that the musical essence of Vivaldi's original has not been modified, as instead happened, for example, in Casella's transcriptions.

The Malipiero-Ricordi editions of Vivaldi were not the only repertoire tackled by Maderna as a transcriber. He continued this line of work until the last years of his life, covering the most diverse of repertories for varying motives, but always in the knowledge – widely shared in Italy since the start of the century – that the study of ancient music would be an indispensable tool not only to save it from oblivion and enrich the repertory of music in general, but also to offer inspiration in the practice of modern music, in order to definitively set aside the

---

[13] G. F. Malipiero, Introduction to "*Vivaldiana* for orchestra" (Milano: Ricordi, 1953).

late-romantic models inherited from the previous generation. The first of these two aims most likely prevailed in the work of pioneers like Fausto Torrefranca, Luigi Torchi and Oscar Chilesotti, in their writings and transcriptions that appeared in the early decades of the twentieth century, but for those who looked towards the past after the war years – and especially for musicians of the "Venice school" who gathered around Malipiero and later Maderna – the two purposes often converged, obviously with differing emphasis, but always far from the lures of neo-classicism. To have an idea of Maderna's enormous contribution in this field it is sufficient to view the list compiled by Maurizio Romito in *Documenti* 1985, 320-326, which includes an incredible number of works, some still available and others lost, that together make up an entire repertory. And yet the list is not exhaustive, as it does not take into account the transcriptions of ancient music that Maderna used as a comment to works for radio, television and theater [*Romito* 2000/2 and 2002/1], often reducing them to single themes or fragments, assigned to voices or instruments, that were suited to the dramaturgical context, but were generally far removed from their original identity. In some cases, though, Maderna worked on "practical editions" for use in radio broadcasts, with the precise aim of extending the audience's knowledge of music history, as we learn from a letter of March 23, 1952 from Mario Labroca, co-director of the programs of the RAI:

> Dear Maestro, it is our intention to begin a new cycle of concerts whose theme will be the performance of a sort of "Anthology of opera." It will involve searching for operas from the past, those pieces for solo voice or *concertati*, even for chorus, that are worthy of being saved from the oblivion of time and that on account of their intrinsic artistic value do not merely represent a document of a philological kind, but can enrich our knowledge of the artistic values of opera in music [...].[14]

And we remain in the realm of transcription when the ancient text is not only prepared for modern instruments, but is also adapted to dramaturgic functions closer to those of the modern stage, as will be described in detail later when speaking of Belli's *Orfeo dolente* included in Maderna's *Hyperion* dating from the end of the '60s. The cultural importance of these transcriptions in the '50s (and in the wake of this initiative, also for many years to follow) can be deduced from the fact that Hermann Scherchen included Maderna's transcriptions in the catalogue of *Ars Viva* and similar reworkings by other composers were published by Ricordi, Schott and Bärenreiter.

---

[14] Cited in S. Pasticci, "Memorie di Petrucci a Venezia, quattro secoli dopo," in G. Cattin, P. Dalla Vecchia, *Venezia 1501: Petrucci e la stampa musicale*, Atti del Convegno (Venezia: Edizioni Fondazione Levi, 2005), 693.

Maderna and the "Venice school" were at the heart of this cultural phenomenon and worked with a wide range of repertory, also tackling music that was apparently far from the needs of the moment, such as Flemish polyphony. The transcription of Ottaviano Petrucci's *Odhecaton A* (1501) required an extremely delicate operation in order to translate as faithfully as possible the timbres and vocal nuances of the original using modern instruments. And both Nono and Maderna dedicated themselves to this task with great passion, as we learn from Susanna Pasticci's meticulous study of the sketches and preparatory drafts preserved at the *Paul Sacher Stiftung* in Basel (see note 14). The most interesting aspect of this particular transcription, besides the special care devoted to the timbre, lies in the way both composers assumed the transformational techniques that underpin the counterpoint starting from a *tenor*. When Maderna chose to use popular songs for the basis of one of his *Vier Briefe* and for his *Composizione in tre tempi* and Nono composed *Guernica* starting from the *Internationale* they both took the notes of the original songs to form units of pitches and durations that they applied throughout the composition, adopting the mechanisms of mathematical mutations, which they both used in a similar way. In doing so, they were both applying transformational techniques quite similar to those used by the Flemish composers to construct the melodies of their masses, drawing the structure from the single intervals and durations of the *tenores*, which were often taken from songs. The chosen *tenor* was broken up into its minimum structural units which were then dispersed throughout the whole composition. Of course Maderna and Nono were not solely interested in the musicological aspect, since the acquisition of such mechanisms was able to help them in their endeavor to reinterpret the dodecaphonic technique. Pasticci, however, suggests [709] that the procedures used by the Flemish composers also had a value that went well beyond any pure and simple technique: when the melody of a *tenor* was taken from liturgical fragments of Gregorian chant, the entire mass acquired the sacred tone of the original chant. Similarly, when Nono and Maderna used the melodies of political or popular songs as *tenores* and "disassembled" the structures in order to "reassemble" them in their works, they introduced a multitude of references not only relating to history, but also to the personal experience and beliefs that inspired their music.

Another by no means secondary sector that Maderna became involved in was that of the cinema. On September 27, 1946, he wrote to Irma Manfredi, clearly pleased with himself, to tell her that he was composing music for a film, which he had to deliver the following month; he also added that according to his wife Raffaella, receiving commissions as a composer was a great honor, which they were both happy about [*Extraits* 2007, 484]. At the start of December of the same year, in another letter to his mother, Maderna speaks of a trip to

Rome, where he met Gennaro Proto, co-screenwriter and general organizer of the films *Sangue a Ca' Foscari* and *Il fabbro del convento* for the Scalera company [*Extraits* 2007, 484]. Giorgio Mangini lists five films with music by Maderna between 1947 and 1951[15]; others came out between 1952 and '53 and another (*La morte ha fatto l'uovo*) in 1967. To these we might add his musical comment to Giuseppe Patroni Griffi's "ballata" for radio, *Il mio cuore è nel sud*, broadcast in 1950. Maderna sometimes recalled his collaborations with the mass-media principally as a means to earn money, but declarations of this kind are most likely apt to mask his real interest in the sector. This side of his work was neither episodic nor superficial, and continued (with varying results and involving considerable effort) for many years after this period. On the other hand, the participation in film or radio productions was not unusual for composers of the time. Pizzetti had written music for a silent movie as early as 1914 and was involved in other similar ventures up until 1949, when he wrote the score for Alberto Lattuada's *Mulino del Po*; Riccardo Zandonai wrote six movie scores in the space of just three years, between 1938 and 1941. And Malipiero himself was no stranger to the genre: Walter Ruttmann's *Acciaio* (1933) is a highly dramatic film in which the music, while retaining its own autonomy, takes into account the sounds produced by the action in the film; it is "authentic" music that derives from a concept where the score becomes part of the narration.[16]

It would nevertheless be reductive to consider film music as just a *particular* genre, in that it encompasses an extraordinarily rich and diversified range of styles, associated with different types of narration and with different moments in the actual narration, oscillating between the presentation (perhaps deliberate and referential) of stereotypes, and moments of original creation (a poetic function): in the words of Ennio Morricone, "Ten competent composers can write ten different scores, all good for the same film."[17] Over and above the extreme diversity of film music, the common difficulty shared by composers is how to adapt the language of art music and its need for meaningful autonomy, to a different language, with its own laws and objectives. In silent movies the narrative capacity of program music was at times able to characterize the atmosphere of certain scenes, especially in sequences without dialogue; but when the post-war avant-gardes began to conceive and promote music that tended towards the search for novel linguistic

---

[15] Three were directed by Max Calandri (*Sangue a Ca' Foscari, Il fabbro del Convento* and *Lohengrin*), one by Ignazio Ferronetti (*I misteri di Venezia*) and one by Antonio Leonviola (*Le due verità*) [G. Mangini, "Filmographie commentée," in *Basalte* 1, 2007, 229-240].

[16] S. Miceli, "La musica nel film e nel teatro di prosa. L'avvento dello specialismo," in *Italia milleno-vecentocoinquanta*, cited in note 10, 285-287.

[17] E. Morricone, "Un compositore dietro la macchina da presa," *Enciclopedia della Musica*, vol. I, *Il Novecento*, ed. J. J. Nattiez (Torino: Einaudi, 2001), 669.

paths and aimed at an absolute, self-contained expression, the merging of the two forms became more problematic, and led to the birth of different professional standpoints that were hard to reconcile.

Maderna's work for the mass-media, and in particular that of films, has been long forgotten or undervalued, due both to a lack of information and of interest. Only recently has there been an attempt to distinguish the commercial orientation of the earliest films from the experimental intentions of others, such as Giulio Questi's *La morte ha fatto l'uovo*, as well as Antonio Leonviola's *Le due verità* (1951), on which Leo Izzo has made a long and detailed study. Izzo shows that, despite some mismatching between the language of the film and that of the music, as well as a certain repetitiveness and lack of precision, in the final scenes "Maderna's contribution is determinant in rendering the anxious expectation, the gradual build-up of tension and the consequent inevitability of the tragic ending." But the most substantial and most interesting part of the article is the description of the numerous manuscript sheets that Maderna had prepared for the musical score of the film which was eventually, for reasons of production, reduced to around a third of the initial 150 pages. The complete set of manuscripts bears witness to the care he put into the work and his rich imagination in matching the plot.[18] Finally, particular mention should be made of Max Calandri's film version of Wagner's *Lohengrin*, since it represents an example of a genre that at the time (1946-47) was still in its experimental stages, and because the orchestra of La Fenice (with celebrated singers like Giacinto Prandelli and Renata Tebaldi) was actually conducted by Maderna himself.[19]

It is possible that the memories of his childhood experiences with his father's Happy Grossato Company and, even more so, his propensity to make music at all levels of complexity, engagement and social context, are reflected in his film scores, but also in his radio dramas and in a still unspecified number of jazz songs, transcriptions and arrangements, preserved in the archives of the SIAE, which still await adequate critical attention.[20] One of the few articles

---

[18] L. Izzo, "Il commento sonoro realizzato da Bruno Maderna per il film *Le due verità*," *Bruno Maderna Studi e Testimoniananze*, cited in note 5, 306-307.

[19] After many years of effort and searching Maurizio Romito recently managed to purchase a copy of this work. It is a very particular copy since it contains an off-camera commentary in English that describes the various moments of the opera. The original reel, without the voice-over, is preserved – in a single copy, not yet restored – at the Cineteca Nazionale del Centro Sperimentale di Cinematografia in Rome and has been purchased by the Videoteca Pasinetti in Venice.

[20] Giordano Montecchi recalls two disks of songs by Kurt Weill sung by Laura Betti and arranged by Maderna, and an album of 12 songs registered with the SIAE, which were originally written for Giulio Questi's film *La morte ha fatto l'uovo*. He also mentions some songs rearranged by Maderna, for example Modugno's "Volare" and fantasies on songs associated with Rome. See G. Montecchi, "Bruno Maderna e la musica leggera," *Musica/Realtà* no.10 (1983), 51-61.

focusing on this area of Maderna's work is that of Stefano Bellon, who examined some scores that the composer had written for a rhythm orchestra such as the one formed by the RAI in the '50s. Bellon notes Maderna's precise knowledge of the style then in fashion, but is surprised by the fact that no space is given to improvisation: the only parts not fully written out are those of the rhythm section, which are the only ones abbreviated in line with the usage of the time.[21]

Between the last months of 1946, when the *Liriche su Verlaine* were written, and the end of 1947 Maderna takes yet another of the unexpected steps we have become accustomed to while following his career as a composer. The *Concerto per due pianoforti e strumenti* has very little in common with the previous work, even though separated by a relatively short space of time. The first mention of the *Concerto* appears in a letter from Dallapiccola to Maderna on December 11, 1947.[22] Maderna had sent Dallapiccola the first part of the work, stating that he would add another two movements to complete it. Dallapiccola replied that in his opinion the piece was so well structured that it seemed practically complete as it stood. In the course of the following year Maderna nonetheless wrote the other two parts as he had intended and in September 1948, at its first performance in Venice, the work was presented in three movements; the same happened in Taormina when Maderna conducted the work on April 30, 1949.[23] And yet Dallapiccola's advice did not go unheeded, as Maderna made several subsequent changes to the composition, making additions and modifications until finally deciding to reduce it drastically, and in the same year he delivered a version in just one movement to the publishers Suvini Zerboni, who printed it in 1955.[24] Over and above these subsequent rethinkings, the *Concerto* can be considered a work that is not only different from his previous compositions, but one that can also be linked to the years to come, and it is this particular aspect that underlines its substantial novelty and importance. Many years after its composition Maderna recalls it as a sort of Opus 1: "here for the first time I found my personal expression after writing several works in the wake of Bartók and Stravinsky." [25] On that occasion he does not explain the reasons behind his

---

[21] See S. Bellon, "Maderna, entre improvisation et jazz," *Basalte* 2 (2009), 522-533.

[22] The letter can be found in M. Romito, "Lettere e scritti," *Studi* (1989) 56-57, and in the critical edition by P. Cattelan and R. Dalmonte [*Maderna* 2006, V].

[23] M. G. Sità, "I Festival," in *Italia millenovecentocoinquanta*, cited in note 10, 128.

[24] The critical edition of the *Concerto* [*Maderna* 2006] contains two slightly different drafts in three movements and the final version in a single movement.

[25] The quotation is taken from an autograph typescript, undated but probably written several years after the composition, in which Maderna describes the *Concerto* in German. The original is kept in the *Sammlung Bruno Maderna* of the *Paul Sacher Stiftung* in Basel, and is cited here by kind permission of the Foundation.

statement, but in the concert program for the Venice performance (not written by him but clearly based on his observations) we find the assertion that in this work "Maderna affirms his rigorous dodecaphonic orientation" [*Centro Studi Maderna*, Section D 3.4]. This singular remark has attracted the attention of various scholars. We can begin with Massimo Mila, who in his book [*Mila* 1976, 10], clearly states that the score of the *Concerto* contains no trace of dodecaphony. His refutation was based on the Suvini Zerboni edition of 1955, which in 1976 (when Mila's book was published) was the only one available; but even if he had seen the other two versions he would certainly have not changed his mind. And in fact the somewhat rash statement about his adherence to dodecaphony disappears from the program notes that Maderna wrote for the performance in Taormina.

Some years later, however, a careful analysis of the concerto was carried out by Stefano Bellon, which in some way could help find an explanation for the declaration that provoked the doubts and irony of Mila. The *Concerto* opens in a striking and original way: the two pianos play a single note in a decisive manner (a C reinforced by the other instruments), which is immediately followed by a series of numerous rapid notes. The alternation between the single note and the rapid notes is repeated eight times in a row, but each time the notes that follow the initial C are different. Bellon observes that, although they are different, the eight successions have some features in common. In the first four the rapid notes are governed by relations of reciprocal inversion (a rising interval becomes a falling interval of the same width, or vice versa), while in the fifth to eighth successions there is a retrograde relationship with the first four (that is, the sequence of the first four is read from the last note to the first).[26] It should not be forgotten that in the dodecaphonic system the series are governed by relations of inversion and retrogradation. So Maderna was not actually applying a "rigorous dodecaphonic" technique as stated in the first concert program, but was simply inspired by procedures deriving from the system. In any case the piece does not sound at all "Viennese" but rather Hungarian and, as happens in the music of Bartók, leaves no trace of any calculations on listening. The model that inspired Maderna's work is more likely to have been Bartók's *Sonata for two pianos and percussion* (1937).[27] But irrespective of its model, the three parts of the *Concerto*, including the second movement (Grave), which was initially conceived as a delightful "Tempo di siciliana," are indicative of an extraordinary inventive capacity.

---

[26] S. Bellon, "*Il Concerto per due pianoforti e strumenti* di Bruno Maderna verso Darmstadt: un'analisi della partitura," *Malipiero Maderna 1973-1993*, ed. P. Cattelan (Firenze: Olscki, 2000), 335-354.

[27] This similarity had already been noted in *Mila* 1976, 11.

A more direct reference to dodecaphony came in the same year, 1948, in which he had completed the *Concerto*.[28] At that time, perhaps on the suggestion of Malipiero, he was studying Dallapiccola's *Sex Carmina Alcaei* and in a letter of July he had asked for details of the techniques applied in these pieces. This led to the composition of *Tre Liriche Greche*, which bear distinct traces of Dallapiccola's model. The years from 1948 to 1950 were crucial for Maderna as a composer, since as many as six works inspired by dodecaphony were given their first performances in that period. Besides the *Concerto per due pianoforte e strumenti* and the *Liriche greche*, the same years also saw the composition of the *Fantasia e fuga* for two pianos, the *Composizione n. 1*, the *Composizione n. 2* (both for symphony orchestra) and finally the *Studi per "Il Processo" di F. Kafka*.

Joachim Noller points out, among other things, that many of Maderna's compositions, starting from 1948, "are based on the melodic and rhythmic constellations of a song, which [...] is elaborated using a serial technique." In other words, he organized a wide range of musical material in a serial fashion.[29] Nicola Verzina adds that Maderna often used "impure" series in which notes were missing or repeated.[30] Therefore, if we are to define dodecaphony as the method of composition proposed by Schönberg, adopted in personal ways by his pupils and systemized in treatises that were published immediately after the end of the war, we might conclude, paradoxically, that Maderna never actually applied the dodecaphonic technique as such. On the other hand, if instead of thinking of the method in its strictest sense, we consider its substance, then the situation changes. Noller, again [105], writes that Maderna

> takes a critical view of the traditions of the Viennese School [...]. For him, the strict prohibition of repetition seems to be a devitalized relict of a time now passed. He replaces it [...] with a compositional technique [...] characterized by changes, by transformations and by a use of the concept of the series that is broadened through that of permutation.

Speaking of permutation, it should be remembered that Maderna was particularly interested in the nature of intervals, an aspect that recurs throughout much of his work. This interest was likely the outcome of his reading Hindemith's treatise (*Unterweisung im Tonsatz*), which he had purchased in 1939. Early traces of this influence can already be found in his *Quartetto*

---

[28] G. M. Borio, "Influenza di Dallapiccola sui compositori italiani del secondo dopoguerra," *Dallapiccola, Letture e prospettive*, Atti del convegno, ed. M. De Santis (Milano: Ricordi & Lucca: LIM, 1997), 360.

[29] J. Noller, "Dimensioni musicali. Le composizioni di Bruno Maderna nel primo dopoguerra," *Studi* 1989, 95-96.

[30] *Verzina* 2003, 69.

of 1943. According to Rizzardi, Hindemith's theory of intervals, his typical schemes of calm and tension applied to both melody and harmony, can be found in the sketches of Maderna and Nono until at least 1953.[31] Similar notions are also mentioned in one of Maderna's rare theoretic writings.[32] But at that time, the two composers were more especially interested (with the doubtless encouragement of Malipiero) to discover whether there were links between the way intervals were treated in the polyphony of the Renaissance and even of Bach, and the way they were dealt with in dodecaphony. Their transcriptions of Renaissance canons and their description in Maderna's above-mentioned text moved precisely in this direction, as Susanna Pasticci points out in a highly detailed article.[33]

Maderna's approach to dodecaphony was underpinned by a clear and simple assumption, which he himself declared in handwritten notes probably prepared for a seminar to be held during the Darmstadt courses in 1954: "What I didn't like about the theory of dodecaphony was the principle that once a series had been presented, it had to [...] continuously reappear in its entirety." In other words, he proposed that a series need not always be presented in the same form but could be subject to some mutations.[34] Maderna's approach to dodecaphony (and that of his pupils) was always characterized by the numerical theory of mutations: a series could generate a practically infinite quantity of variants of itself.[35] It is beyond the scope of this book to go more deeply into the technical details of this matter. We will limit ourselves to pointing out some examples here and there, keeping in mind that instances of Maderna's use of serialism should be described work by work, given that his method of composition was never fixed or constant. On the contrary, one could say that he never established a definitive way of composing, but always preferred to search tirelessly for new and more effective solutions.

The *Tre Liriche greche* for small choir, soprano and instruments (1948) are the first example of Maderna's use of dodecaphony and his main source of inspiration appears to have been Dallapiccola's canonic writing. Various series are used throughout the work and are visible from the very first measures of "Canto mattutino" (the first song). The piece starts with a melody sung by the soprano consisting of twelve different notes, followed immediately by their

---

[31] V. Rizzardi, *La nuova scuola*, cited in note 6, 9.

[32] N. Verzina, "Mutazioni storiche intorno a tre testi inediti di Bruno Maderna," *Studi musicali*, 28/2 (1999), 517-518.

[33] S. Pasticci, *Memorie di Petrucci*, cited in note 14, 695.

[34] The notes are reproduced in the Appendix to N. Verzina, *Mutazioni storiche*, cited in note 32, 517.

[35] A technical analysis of many of the mutations applied by Maderna and Nono can be found in Verzina (see note 2) and in Rizzardi (see note 6).

inverted retrograde. But the serial organization in the rest of the piece is quite complex and is rarely as evident as in its incipit. An analysis of the dodecaphonic technique applied in the *Tre liriche greche* can be found in an in-depth study by Luca Conti.[36] But it is also worth adding that, irrespective of the use of series (or of fragments of series or their mutations), the listener will hear very little that recalls the style of three main Viennese exponents, nor anything that makes one think of expressionism. The reason for this probably derives from the fact that, as we have previously underlined, Maderna pays particular attention to the expressive functions of the intervals. In the melodies of the singers, for example, or in those of the flutes and clarinets, the intervals tend to maintain some form of "cantabilità." Furthermore, in many instances the intervals of the melodies proceed in thirds, creating vague affinities with traditional chords. And also in the intervals that make up the harmonies, Maderna takes great care (especially in the first and third song) to avoid an excess of harsh dissonances. Basically, he has adopted a free form of dodecaphony, one that is light and unaggressive, and this, together with the soft texture and ethereal register, creates a clear syntony with the words of the text. In fact, the first song ("Canto mattutino") describes the "dorati uccelli dall'acuta voce" ("the gilded birds with their shrill voice"), while the third ("Stellato") is made up of just one line that speaks of the "stelle lucentissime" ("sparkling stars"). The second song (about the savage "Danaidi") is denser and more violent: it is based on the ostinato figures of two contrasting percussion groups and on a menacing choir that at first speaks and then gradually starts to sing. In the space of just one or two measures their singing poignantly consumes all twelve notes of the chromatic scale. In short, one could say that once again this work, like those of the previous years, represents a new direction as far as Maderna's stylistic path is concerned.

Another of the three dodecaphonic works composed in the same months is the *Fantasia e fuga per due pianoforti*. And here too a different approach is taken compared to the techniques he was experimenting with in other works. In her introduction to the critical edition of the work [*Maderna* 2000, IX-X] Susanna Pasticci reconstructs the way in which Maderna has combined classical techniques of counterpoint with Viennese serialism. The main reference to the classical tradition is the fact that the composition is built on the set of four notes derived from the name BACH (Bb-A-C-B), which had already formed the basis for a long list of works by a wide range of composers, starting with Bach himself. Maderna not only creates his series on the basis of the name BACH, but also works on its transpositions. The application of these techniques leads

---

[36] L. Conti, "Le *Tre Liriche greche* di Maderna e la prima dodecafonia italiana," in *Bruno Maderna Studi e Testimoniananze*, cited in note 5, 275-286.

to the perception of two different aspects. Firstly, the inevitable abandonment of tonality; secondly, the use of certain parameters of musical discourse, defined by Meyer as "secondary" (the strength of the notes, the number of notes superimposed contemporaneously, the rapidity of their successions, their register – high or low) as significant elements of communication.[37] For example, the single, light and slow notes that open the piece give the idea of a mysterious suspension, and these are followed by denser and more violent episodes. Alternations of this kind, constantly varied and capable of producing surprises and novel forms of expectation, provide the basis for the whole piece. In its central part we find an imaginative fugue in which the name BACH is repeatedly presented in its different permutations. Unexpectedly, in the final measures there is a quotation of Bach's chorale *Vor deinen Thron tret' ich hiermit* ("herewith I come before thy throne"), his last composition purportedly dictated while on the point of death: a tonal melody set in a non tonal context, which gradually dissolves.

The third serial work composed in these months – certainly the most challenging and also the most problematic – is *Composizione n. 1* for orchestra. The date and place of the composition are given on the title page of the manuscript, but his correspondence with Nino Sanzogno (the conductor to whom the work is dedicated) offers us more precise details. In the first of two letters (December 17, 1948) Sanzogno asks how the work is progressing, while in the second (February 17, 1949) he is delighted to learn that the work is completed.[38] He conducted the Orchestra Sinfonica della RAI in the world premiere of the work in Turin in February 1950. This work too makes use of dodecaphony, albeit in the heterodox version that we are already familiar with. In describing the autograph score, De Benedictis states that in the bifolio that encloses the eighty-eight numbered pages there is an indication of the four series on which the work is built, while even more detailed information is given in a certain number of separate folios that contain more precise sketches of the series in question.

Over and above the absence of tonality, the listener can rarely perceive these technical mechanisms. However, rather than simply giving the traditional markings for the movements or the character of the episodes (Allegro, Adagio, etc.) he has added particular details of his intentions at the start of each episode in the score. For example, at m. 49 he announces "the theme is being built," and later indicates precisely the point where the

---

[37] L. B. Meyer, *Style and Music. Theory, History and Ideology* (Chicago: The University of Chicago Press, 1989), 14-15.

[38] See the Introduction to the critical edition of the work edited by A. I. De Benedictis: *Maderna* 2007, V.

theme and its subsequent "metamorphoses" are presented. A little further on he writes that "the theme has become a series" and shortly afterwards that "the four basic series are presented in strict canon." In deciding to communicate these details to his friend Sanzogno, who was to perform the work, and to other conductors that would follow, Maderna is clearly asking them to highlight these formal aspects during the performance, considering them important. But that is not all. Maderna also chooses to tell us that the *Composizione 1* is a piece based not only on series, but also on a theme, and on a theme "that should be heard." In the following episodes, though, the theme is "deconstructed" and modified by various "metamorphoses," then "integrated" by other material and finally "destroyed" and "dispersed." At the end of the work, in the last episode, "only the rhythm remains," gradually fading into silence. The narration that underpins the construction of the work seems almost like an apologue on the destiny of music: the new system (Maderna seems to remark, or to fear) is destined to unhinge not only the reassuring certainties of tonality, but also the trust in communication through "themes," which lies at the basis of over three centuries of European music. If we think of the discussions that started to emerge in those years on the concept of theme and the doubts about the legitimacy of avant-garde musical language, we can conclude that Maderna's conception of form in this work is by no means extravagant, but represents a precise aesthetic choice.[39] Even from such a brief description, it is easy to note that in the course of just a few months, between the writing of *Liriche Greche* and of *Composizione n. 1*, a very sudden change in direction has taken place. The ethereal Dallapiccolian climate has given way to a dense and controlled writing where the signs of structured thought become increasingly evident.

This transformation becomes even more evident in his next work, *Composizione n. 2*, which was premiered at Darmstadt under the baton of Hermann Scherchen on August 26, 1950. It is not known exactly when Maderna began to compose this work; he had certainly already started writing the piece in August 1949, when he includes it in a list of works available for performance,[40] but in a curriculum he writes "Venice 1950" [*Documenti* 1985, 198]. Given the amount of work testified by his sketches, it is plausible to imagine that its gestation was not particularly rapid. With these uncertainties in mind, the period of composition could be hypothesized as between 1949 and the first months of the following year, that is to say more or less in the same period that saw the birth of *Studi per "Il Processo" di F. Kafka*. The aspect of *Composizione n. 2* that immediately attracted the

---

[39] It is worth remembering that precisely in 1950, the German musician Hermann Heiss held a course in "athematic composition" at Darmstadt, see *Trudu* (1992), 60.

[40] See the Introduction to the critical edition of the work edited by S. Pasticci: *Maderna* 2006, VII.

attention and favor of listeners, and of the press, was the initial presentation of the *Seikilos Epitaph,* a melody already known in the first decades of the twentieth century as one of the few musical pieces surviving from the ancient Greek era. For example, in his review of the work Josef Rufer defined the music as "easy to listen to."[41] Nobody at the time appears to have asked themselves why the composer had made this peculiar choice. Maybe some people did, but were unable to find a convincing argument that was worth expressing openly; and Maderna himself typically offered no explanation. The first person to attempt an interpretation was Massimo Mila, who did so after the composer's death, when only a general overview of his life and work was available:

> There was in Bruno an instinctive desire to go back to the sources, to start from the origins: origins of sound, origins of music [...], to take into account the working material: material that was not just of a physical, acoustic kind, but that also comprises the historical situation in which we find ourselves working [*Mila* 1976, 15].

It should be added that this is the first of many later instances of references to ancient Greece: the myth of the aulos (here the cor anglais) would find its way into his music in a large number of guises over the next twenty years. But there is another equally important aspect that may help us find an interpretation, even if (again in the words of Mila) "it puts the stylistic coherence of the piece to hard test." In fact the numerical wizardry with which the melody is polyphonically elaborated immediately afterwards, and more especially the serial episodes of the waltzes and the rumba that make up the next two parts of the composition, appear to have nothing to do with the opening measures. In reality none of its critics has ever raised the issue of this singular contrast. Not even Nono, who considered the introduction too long, nor Scherchen, who with his notorious authoritarianism cut forty or so measures in his performance, measures that Maderna calmly put back in his performance a few years later.[42] But there may well be a reason for this apparent incoherence. Our theory is that the composer (who wrote *Composizione 2* shortly after *Composizione 1*) resumed the "narration" that he had begun in his previous work. In *Composizione 1* he had suggested that the atonal approach tended to destroy the conventions underpinning the idea of theme; in the new work he is saying how it destroys the primordial idea of melody. And he does so in a concrete fashion by demonstrating in the score, and to the listener, how the melody of the Epitaph can be deformed, that is to say

---

[41] Rufer's review in the Düsseldorf newspaper *Der Mittag* is cited in S. Pasticci, "'Una musica di facile ascolto': sulla *Composizione n. 2* di Bruno Maderna," in *Bruno Maderna Studi e Testimoniananze*, cited in note 5, 118.

[42] See the Introduction to the critical edition of the work edited by S. Pasticci: *Maderna* (2006), VII.

re-organized as a succession of intervals subjected to mutations, but destroyed as a perceptible living entity. We now need to take a step backwards and describe the form of the piece in a little more detail.

The work is divided into three parts: the first includes seven episodes narrating the adventures of the decomposition of the "Greek" theme. The second features two waltzes: an "English waltz" and a "Wiener Walzer." The third is a "Rumba." But this sequence of events will remain a puzzle (as it was for Mila) if it is not seen in the light of the narrative idea that almost certainly, we venture to say, lies at the roots of this work. Its deepest meaning is difficult to access simply by listening to the music, so some extra-musical references may be helpful. The whole of the first part of the work is shrouded in the mysterious musical mist of around twenty solo violins, in which Mila found an allusion to the "night of times": within this nebulous atmosphere the disintegration of the Greek theme takes on the aura of a rite that is being performed. The second part starts with the slow, and at times even pleasant, notes of a homely, not excessively rhythmic English waltz. A brief interruption is followed by the gradual introduction of a quite different Viennese waltz which, in the wake of other waltzes from the start of the century that celebrated the end of the spuriously joyful empire, becomes increasingly dense and compact in texture and rhythm until reaching a tragic, "Bergian" climate, of a clear expressionist stamp. A sudden silence is followed by the start of the "Rumba", which with its openly declared pointillism would appear to be alluding to the realms of Webern if it were not, as Mila suggests, more like a type of "wooden puppet ballet." At a certain point the voice of a timpano makes itself heard, heralding the entry of a dozen or so percussion instruments (perhaps explaining the title "Rumba"). And it is against this "woody" ensemble that the Greek melody makes its last dramatic appearance, now falling apart. A form of this type would remain beyond the limits of stylistic coherence if it were not viewed as having a narrative sense similar to that of *Composizione 1*: the description, in terms of a tragic rite, of what music was becoming.

These experiments with dodecaphonic techniques, and the subsequent afterthoughts, could perhaps stem from Maderna's meeting with two eminent figures from outside the Italian circle, Karl Amadeus Hartmann and Hermann Scherchen, although it would prove quite difficult to demonstrate exactly in what way they influenced the linguistic choices made in these works and in those that came immediately afterwards. And it is not easy, either, to establish when their first meeting took place. It is not unlikely, though, that Maderna had met Scherchen at the first Biennale in Venice after the war (1946), where the German musician conducted a concert on September 19, while Maderna himself conducted another on September 21 in which he performed music of the Young Italian School and his own *Serenata per 11 strumenti*.⁴³ At that time Scherchen had already become a legend: "der rote Kapellmeister" who at the young age of twenty had premiered Schönberg's *Pierrot lunaire* (1912) and then taken it across Europe. After a self-imposed exile lasting fifteen years he had finally returned to Germany to resume his role "as one of the most radical fighters for musical progress."₄₄ A curious and penetrating portrait of Scherchen in the '30s can be found in Elias Canetti's autobiography:

> The years in which music was being renewed, and in being renewed was becoming *ramified* as had never happened before, were for him like manna from heaven. [..] he did not allow any difficulty to stand in his way [...] the important point was to bring these new things to *victory*, that is to present them in the most perfect form to an unprepared audience for whom they were new and at first unrecognizable, unfamiliar and repellent, apparently horrible [...] in a city like Vienna, which had a very bad reputation for its inveterate conservatism with regards to music [...] He was taciturn, ruthlessly taciturn, when he had someone in front of him whom he intended to discover and encourage. For him, then, it was a question of life and death to not let loose a single word of praise.⁴⁵

Scherchen therefore arrived in Venice preceded by the fame of his performances of contemporary music that he had taken across the whole of Europe, both with the orchestra Ars Viva, which he himself had founded, and on behalf of the organization Musica Viva, founded by Karl Amadeus Hartmann in Munich in 1945. It was thanks to the efforts of Scherchen that Hartmann's reputation as a composer spread outside of Germany, something that had not yet occurred due to the composer's voluntary isolation, his "inner migration," the expression of his dissent towards Nazi politics. Born in 1905, Hartmann had lived through both world wars, and since he was born in Germany and openly professed his opposition to Nazi ideology, he was forced to withdraw from public musical life until the end of the Second World War, though still remaining in contact with his teachers and mentors Anton Webern and Hermann Scherchen. The common source of inspiration behind the works he wrote during this period of voluntary confinement can be gleaned already from their titles: *Des Simplicius Simplicissimus Jugend* (an opera against war written in the '30s), *Symphonic Fragment: Attempt at a Requiem*, *Musik der Trauer* for violin and orchestra (commemorating

---

[43] D. G. Leonardi, "Cronologia del Festival internazionale di musica contemporanea di Venezia (1946-54)," in *Italia millenovecentocoinquanta*, cited in note 10, 159-160.

[44] From an article in the Hamburg newspaper *Der Spiegel* of August 2, 1947, *Trudu* (1992), 41.

[45] Elias Canetti, *Il gioco degli occhi. Storia di una vita (1931-1937)* (Milano: Adelphi, 1985; our translation), 56-60, *passim*, italics in the original.

the occupation of Prague), and *Sinfonia tragica*, to mention just a few examples of his so-called degenerate music, which could only be performed in Germany after 1945. But in the changed political climate that followed the war, such criticism of the former regime was no longer enough to meet the expectations of the new generations, who were now in search of a fresh outlook for the future. Maderna, on the other hand, was quick to recognize certain interesting features in Hartmann's music, to the extent that in several letters (dating from between February and October 1950) addressed to the director of the Accademia di S. Cecilia [copies of the letters preserved in Section L 8 of the Centro Studi Maderna] he insistently proposed a performance of his *Symphonic Fragment*. However, it was not possible to perform the work in Rome and it was only played in Turin one year later. Hartmann nevertheless played an important role both as organizer of the Bavarian State Opera, and as the originator of the concert season Musica Viva (whose name not by chance is inspired by that of Scherchen's music publishing company) already inaugurated in November 1945, which helped to bring the music of emerging composers like Carl Orff, Iannis Xenakis, Olivier Messiaen, Bruno Maderna and Luciano Berio to the attention of a wider public.[46]

Scherchen had similarly distanced himself from the ideological hegemony by emigrating abroad in 1933, where he had continued his activity as a conductor in various important institutions. In 1946 both Scherchen and Maderna were present at the Biennale and again at the *Autunno Musicale Veneziano* of 1948, where Scherchen conducted the orchestral concert on September 14, and the concert of September 17 included Maderna's *Concerto per due pianoforti*, under the direction of Ettore Gracis. In the same year, Maderna, together with Nono, enrolled in the International Conducting Course held by Scherchen at the Venice Conservatory from September 16 to October 1.[47] According to some biographies Maderna was once again advised to do so by Malipiero, but perhaps in this case such encouragement was not really necessary, since his previous experiences with Scherchen had already fostered an ongoing relationship of mutual respect. In reality, Scherchen could be considered Maderna's last teacher, even though the course was not so much about teaching techniques of orchestral conducting, but focused more on music analysis and hermeneutics. Scherchen was, in fact, particularly concerned with the role of the conductor when faced with music that constantly demanded new approaches in order for it to be appreciated by a non specialist audience. "He [the conductor] must no longer merely give technically perfect form to the sonic body of musical works, but should also endeavor to endow them with a new and more intense sonic fascination. It is possible that the

---

[46] W. Heister, "La musica contro le ombre della politica fascista. L'opera e la vita di Karl Amadeus Hartmann," *Musica/Realtà*, 7 (1982), 25-44.

[47] D. G. Leonardi, *Cronologia*, cited in note 43, 147.

coming generations at the end of the twentieth century will find all music, from pre-classical to expressionist, increasingly lacking in artistic interest."[48]

Another opportunity to exchange views and opinions with other colleagues engaged in the exploration of New Music came in May 1949, during the First International Congress of Dodecaphony organized by Riccardo Malipiero and Wladimir Vogel in Milan, but already anticipated in a conference held in Orselina, a small town on the Swiss side of Lake Maggiore, not far from Locarno, on December 12 and 13, 1948, which was also attended, among others, by Maderna and Nono. The congress in Milan was felt to be a very important moment for all the Italian musicians and critics who took part; for the first time they were able to become familiar with the technical issues and compositional procedures that until then had been practiced seldom or not at all. Until the post-war period, apart from some important exceptions, musical criticism was the only means of learning about the music of the Viennese school of composers in Italy. Performances of their works were extremely rare and the scores practically unfindable. News and opinions about Schönberg and his followers were therefore obtained above all through the discussions printed in specialist journals.[49] The articles and essays published in Italy before 1945 were mostly about Schönberg, while mentions of Berg and Webern were scarce, inevitably resorting to stereotypes, with only isolated attempts at any critical analysis or commentary. The reception of the Viennese composers, limited in many cases to their founder, were heavily conditioned by ideological factors of a nationalist and/or Fascist frame. Schönberg was considered an innovator, and was maybe defined interesting, but "different" from the Italian tradition and therefore to be rejected from the outset, with the manifest purpose of blocking any attempt at emulation by the new generations of Italian musicians.

During the conference in Milan, Riccardo Malipiero added to the agenda the following question: is dodecaphony an aesthetic choice or a technique? The majority voted in favor of the second option.[50] There had clearly been a misrepresentation of Schönberg's fundamental idea that dodecaphony was to be seen in the wider and deeper sense of a method of composition, a position that shortly afterwards was destined to prevail. However, despite the presence of emerging figures on the international scene like John Cage, Karl Hartmann, Hermann Scherchen, René Leibowitz, and Luigi Dallapiccola, the younger participants – Camillo Togni, Bruno Maderna, Luigi Nono and the organizers themselves – saw the meeting above all

---

[48] H. Scherchen, "Die Kunst des Dirigierens," *Werke und Briefe*, vol. I (Bern: Peter Lang, 1991), 226.

[49] For a general overview of Italian journals, see *La Rassegna musicale. Antologia*, ed. L. Pestalozza (Milano: Feltrinelli, 1966), and in particular the editor's highly informative Introduction.

[50] R. Malipiero, "La dodecafonia come tecnica," *Rivista Musicale Italiana*, 55/3 (1953), 277-300.

as a starting point that needed to be built upon as soon as possible. Maderna took part in the preparations for a second conference that was scheduled to be held in Locarno in the late summer of 1950, but the meeting came up against a whole series of setbacks and had to be postponed until the following year, eventually taking place in Darmstadt from June 30 to July 2, 1951.

Maderna's first direct contact with Hartmann appears to date from the twenty-third Festival of the ISCM that was held in Palermo -Taormina from April 22 to 30, 1949. The International Society for Contemporary Music, which before the war had convened three times in Italy – in Venice in 1925, in Siena in 1928 and in Florence in 1934 – had chosen Palermo as the fourth venue for its post-war editions, after London, Copenhagen and Amsterdam. Maderna's invitation to the event was probably supported by Malipiero, a member of the international jury for the choice of compositions; the other members of the committee – including Hartmann – would certainly have had the opportunity to examine his work at close quarters. And his reputation as a conductor must not have been entirely unknown to them, given that his *Concerto per due pianoforti e strumenti* was not only chosen to close the meeting but was also entrusted to his baton.[51] On this occasion Maderna also met with great success as an organizer, managing to fill in the gaps in the Festival thanks to his association with the orchestra of Radio Roma. These details can be gleaned from a letter that Maderna sent to Nono, mistakenly dated April 2 but probably written on May 2, 1949 [*Extraits* 2007, 487-488]. The secretary of the international jury for the choice of compositions was Luigi Dallapiccola, who had already worked with Hartmann and most probably acted as an intermediary between the two musicians.

On April 9, Wolfgang Steinecke, director of the summer courses in Darmstadt, wrote to Maderna informing him that he had been given his address by Karl Amadeus Hartmann, who in addition to passing on Maderna's postal details, would almost certainly have spoken of the impression he had gained on reading the score of the *Concerto per due pianoforti e strumenti*, which Maderna had sent to him for admission to the Festival in Palermo-Taormina.[52] This, one can assume, was instrumental in fostering Steinecke's "very great interest" in performing a work by Maderna, of his own choice, at the end of the International Courses of Modern Music. This first letter was followed by an ample exchange of information about the state of Maderna's works that could be performed at Darmstadt, about the fee that Maderna would receive if he went to conduct them and how he would be pleased if he could come in the company of his wife Raffaella Tartaglia. The choice finally

---

[51] M. G. Sità, "I festival," in *Italia millenovecentocoinquanta*, cited in note 10, 126.

[52] The sources for this information, with more details of the relations between Maderna, Hartmann and Steinecke, can be found in the Introduction by the editors – P. Cattelan and R. Dalmonte – of the critical edition of the *Concerto* [*Maderna* 2006].

fell upon the *Concerto per due pianoforti e strumenti*, which was to be performed during the cycle "Music of the young generation" at the end of the courses held between June 19 and July 10, and more precisely on the penultimate day, July 9, 1949. As it turned out, Maderna announced at the last moment that it would be impossible for him to reach Darmstadt in time to conduct his piece, and so the work was replaced with the world premiere of the *Fantasia (B.A.C.H. Variationen)* for two pianos, played by Carl Zeeman and Peter Stadlen [*Carteggio* 2001, 23-37]. In the present state of research we do not know why Maderna was not able to be in Darmstadt on 9 July; we do know, however, that in the second half of 1949 and in the first months of the following year his activity as a composer – as we have said – showed no signs of any slackening, given that the *Composizione n. 2*, the *Studi per "Il Processo" di F. Kafka* and the radio comedy *Il mio cuore è nel sud* all date from that period. So the possibility of poor health can be essentially ruled out. It is true that in a letter to Wladimir Vogel on June 28, 1950 Maderna admits that in the previous few months he has gone through a particularly complicated moment in his life, but not everyone seems prepared to place too much weight on the contents of this letter:

> […] a bout of mental exhaustion has lately forced me to take complete rest. I can't tell you how difficult it is for me in this condition to attend to my commitments: writing a composition on a text by Kafka for the Venice festival, conducting a concert at the Basilica di Massenzio in Rome on August 24,[53] preparing my speech for the 2nd Congress in Locarno. […] I really don't feel like speaking about my personal approach to the harmonic and rational possibilities of the series, mainly because I still haven't devised any system, but also because the exhaustion I mentioned really limits my possibility to work.[54]

To anyone who has had (or will have) the occasion to study the "composition on a text by Kafka," later titled *Studi per "Il Processo" di F. Kafka*, this description of the composer's state of health in the first months of 1950 will appear somewhat curious, given the huge amount of work testified by the notes, sketches and all sorts of drafts that accompanied the writing of this work.[55]

---

[53] The concert actually took place on August 23 during the summer season of the Accademia di Santa Cecilia, when Maderna conducted works by Malipiero, Schumann, Mozart and Prokofiev [*Romito* 2020].

[54] The letter is reproduced in C. Piccardi, "Tra ragioni umane e ragioni estetiche: i dodecafonici a congresso," *Norme con ironie. Scritti per i settant'anni di Ennio Morricone*, ed. S. Miceli (Milano: Suvini Zerboni, 1998), 267-268.

[55] In her Introduction to the critical edition of the work [*Maderna* 2010, IX-XXIV] Rossana Dalmonte describes 180 sheets containing musical drafts, including portions already composed in an almost definitive form, and an even greater number of sheets and slips of paper containing the text of Kafka's work in Italian and in German.

Indeed, it would be more correct to say "of these works" because, whether before, after or at the same time as he wrote *Kafka* as we now know it, that is in a form similar to that of a cantata or an oratorio, Maderna was working seriously on a version of the same piece in the form of an opera in three acts, of which numerous drafts and sketches have survived, often written on sheets already half-used for previous academic counterpoint exercises. Probably Angela Ida De Benedictis is right when she suggests that Maderna complains about his health in his letter to Vogel because he has little will to put any effort into the organization of the second congress on dodecaphony.[56]

Maderna's notes give no indication of when he started work on the text by Kafka for one or the other of the realizations he had in mind. Besides the starting date, another point still shrouded in mystery is the date when it was completed. Indeed, despite the fact that Maderna himself wrote at the bottom of the score "Venice, August 16, 1950," that is to say about a month before the performance at the Biennale on September 13, two letters from Scherchen would appear to indicate that the score was ready more than four months before.[57] Already at the start of April Scherchen is enthusiastic about the work and asks Maderna if it would be better to publish it even before *Composizione n. 2*. And one month later he writes to Bruno telling him that he will take "Maderna-Kafka" with him to Prague. Another clue exists with regards the conclusion of the work, one that is worth mentioning since it is autograph. In the list of works that Maderna compiled in the documentation required for his participation in the Darmstadt summer courses in 1951, he includes the *Studi per "Il Processo" di F. Kafka* as his opus 6 and the radio drama *Il mio cuore è nel sud* as op. 7, but the latter work had already been broadcast on the radio on March 11, 1950 and so it is strange that he lists it after the work inspired by Kafka. This may, of course, have been an oversight on the part of Maderna, or perhaps the piece based on Kafka had really been completed long before the date that appears on the score, and was later revised only in one or two minor details.

In the definitive work, Kafka's text, taken from chapters six and seven of *The Trial*, is partly recited by a narrator and partly sung by a soprano, who assumes the role of Leni, while the protagonist never appears directly. The narration is not linear – as Maderna had intended for the opera version – but alternates between the main story and flashbacks. From the point of view of the musical language of the work, it can be considered a sort of transition

---

[56] A. I. De Benedictis, "Oltre il Primo Congresso di Dodecafonia. Da Locarno a Darmstadt," *Acta Musicologica*, 85/2 (2013), 234.

[57] The two letters of April 5 and June 5, 1950 are preserved at the *Paul Sacher Stiftung* and have been transcribed in R. Dalmonte, "Letture maderniane del *Processo* di Franz Kafka," in *Bruno Maderna Studi e Testimoniananze*, cited in note 5, 22-24.

between the extended dodecaphony of the *Liriche greche* of 1948 and the more overtly post-dodecaphonic thought of *Composizione n. 2*. There is again an evident refusal of any form of thematism, while there are clear signs of the durations being treated in a similar way to the pitches, that is using procedures of inversion and retrograde.[58] As far as the general form of the piece is concerned, Maderna experiments with a structure divided into two parts, quite different one from the other, though still following the sequence of the narration. The work begins with a sort of introduction featuring the narrator and a group of percussion instruments, which recounts the protagonist's decision to face the trial, since he is quite certain that "There was no guilt. The trial was nothing other than a large business deal." This is followed by the first part of the piece, which consists of a sequence of five episodes distinguishable through their pace and type of narration. It opens with an *Andante – Tempo di Wiegenlied* in 6/8, 9/8, in which Leni alternates between singing in a full voice, singing with closed mouth and speaking. The last portion of the singer's part is doubled by violin I. In the second episode (in 4/4), Leni's voice is always doubled by violin I and at times is joined by the voice of the narrator in a surreal dialogue, made up of short unrelated phrases. In the third episode the gently swaying rhythm of the *Wiegenlied* (lullaby) returns, and Leni sings alone against an increasingly lighter orchestral texture. After a passage for orchestra alone the instruments fall silent and the narrator describes the wretched room where the lawyers are located. The fifth episode again starts in 6/8 with the orchestra preparing the final return of the *Tempo di Wiegenlied*. Leni sings, *dolcissimo, espressivo*: "I like the accused, the accused are attractive....and they love me." The orchestra becomes increasingly sparser and the narrator takes up the theme of the attractiveness of the accused. At this point (m. 181) a long canon begins that runs through the whole of the second part. It begins with two instrumental voices and eventually involves as many as ten, with the music growing more and more violent. Leni has disappeared and the narrator dwells on the particular features of the legal procedures, introducing ever more alarming phrases against the thick texture of the orchestra: "The proceedings before the court are generally kept secret [...] the records and act of accusation were inaccessible to the accused and to his defense [...] The defense was not even granted by the law, but only tolerated [....] against this court one cannot defend oneself, only confess [...] confess... confess one's guilt! Beware! They are hunting you down!" until the final cry "Jooooosef KAPPA." The markings given for the orchestra stress the increase in tension and horror: *Andante implacabile.....Allegro violento...**fff** Allegro tumultuoso*.

---

[58] For a detailed description of the language of this work, see G. Borio, "La tecnica seriale in *Studi per "Il Processo" di Franz Kafka* di Bruno Maderna," *Musica/Realtà*, 32 (1990), 27-40.

Despite his complaining of excessive exhaustion, it could be said that by the end of the '40s Maderna had already laid a solid basis for the consolidation of his image as a composer and conductor at an international level. He had written several important works, he had taken part in various international festivals and conferences, he had been engaged to conduct in France and in Germany, and he had been invited by Steinecke to attend the International Courses in Darmstadt, an event that would soon have an important impact on his career as well as on his private life.

In the years that Maderna had his first dealings with the *Kranichsteiner Musikinstitut* in Darmstadt and subsequently decided to move there, the town was wearily recovering from the deep wounds caused by the war. During the massive bombing raid carried out on September 11-12, 1944 – the so-called *Brandnacht* ("Night of fire") – Darmstadt was reduced to a desert of rubble. Since the attack was focused on the central, densely populated part of the town, around 11,500 people were killed and 66,000 were left homeless. Overall, 99% of the old, central part of the town was destroyed, and 78% of the entire housing network fell victim to the bombs. The destruction was followed by a further blow for Darmstadt: in October 1945 the Americans took away its status as capital of the state of Hesse, which it had held for 400 years, and moved it to Wiesbaden. It was feared that the town would also be deprived of its main regional institutions, namely its theater, library and State Archives. Due to the limited economic means available, the reconstruction of Darmstadt focused essentially on the most pressing needs such as housing, but the plans to revive the town also foresaw the construction of new buildings for schools and the university, with the result that before the close of the century it had been awarded the title "City of science" by the Ministry of Hesse. As far as the more historic buildings were concerned, only the castle, the town hall, the cathedral and national museum were repaired; even the ruins of the ancient theater were abandoned and it was not until 1972 that a new theater was built in a new location. The old town, instead, was rebuilt on the basis of an urban planning scheme that took into account the needs of a new, more modern lifestyle.

Wolfgang Steinecke was one of the main actors in this rebirth. As town councilor responsible for culture he believed that "the needs dictate what is necessary. Culture is part of what is necessary; it must, and can, set the pace for the reconstruction. Without its inspirational power channeled into the objectives, chaos cannot be overcome."[59] With these principles in mind, he immediately, in 1946, organized summer courses of music in the castle of Kranichstein, an

---

[59] Steinecke's words were later repeated in a key text on the subject in question: *1946-1996, Von Kranichstein zur Gegenwart. 50 Jahre Darmstädter Ferienkurse* (Stuttgart: DACO, 1996), 30.

ancient hunting lodge about five kilometers away from the town, which had fallen into disuse in the nineteenth century. The courses remained there until 1948, but already then they involved only the teaching part of the activities, while the conferences were held at the *Technische Hochschule* and the concerts at the *Orangerie*. Although the *Internationales Musikinstitut* was officially founded in that year, it was only in the following year (1949) that it found a stable location in Marienhöhe, the seminary of the Seventh-day Adventists, which was free in the summer. It was here that important relations were established between the Frankfurt Radio Orchestra and that of Baden Baden for the concerts of the "Week of New Music" [*Trudu* 1992, 49-51], and it was in this year that the first contacts between Steinecke and Bruno Maderna took place.

Against the backdrop of this difficult situation in the post-war years, the plans for a renewed development of the arts in Darmstadt were implemented on various fronts. The music conservatory of Hesse started its activity in January 1946 with 600 registrants; the public library opened as early as December 1945, with a lending service for the small number of books that had been spared from the bombing (no more than 2000) and organized a collection of books from private sources to increase its stocks; already on December 15, 1945 a first series of theater plays began, which continued for several seasons, offering a mainly classical repertoire.[60] But the scenario changed quite significantly when the stage director Harro Dicks, previously active in Hanover, decided to move first to Frankfurt (1948) and then to Darmstadt in 1951, where he remained until 1976. He too chose to establish his place of work, his theater, outside the town, in the *Orangerie*, a small eigtheenth century castle surrounded by a park of orange and lemon groves (Darmstadt, as we have seen, did not have its own, true theater until 1972). Although he also worked in other German and western-European theaters, it was in Darmstadt that Dicks chose to set up a school and to promote his own personal way of combining dramaturgy and music. He referred to this as the "Darmstadt style," a style born out of the practical difficulties of the post-war years, but one that proposed new principles of composition and attained results of a high artistic level using very limited means. His style was widely emulated and also spread outside of Germany. Between 1952 and 1992 he held a school of opera at the *Akademie für Tonkunst*, as well as teaching at the Hochschule für Musik, Theater und Medien in Hanover. Maderna worked with him from 1952, and a warm friendship was soon established between the two men, to the extent that the German director was already a guest of Maderna in Venice that same year [*Carteggio* 2001, 56-57]. The numerous occasions in which

---

[60] E. Gerberding, "Darmstädter Kulturpolitik der Nachkriegzeit," in *1946-1996, Von Kranichstein*, cited in the previous note, 31-33.

they worked together in his theater included productions of Orff's *Carmina Burana*, Kurt Weill/Bertolt Brecht's *Rise and Fall of the City of Mahagonny*, Richard Strauss's *Salome*, Hindemith's *Neues vom Tage* and Berg's *Lulu*.

The material difficulties faced by any sort of cultural activity in Darmstadt are also reflected in the first letters from Steinecke to Maderna in which he speaks of the (very modest) fee for conducting the orchestra and even indicates which means of transport he should use from the station to reach Marienhöhe, where the participants were accommodated and the courses were held:

> The guest quarters of Marienhöhe can be reached from the central station with the tram no.1 or numbers 2 and 6 changing to no. 7 or 8 in the direction of Eberstadt. From the stop "Ludwigshöhe" a path will take you to the guest house in ten minutes […]. We are enclosing a declaration to obtain a discount on the travel ticket. [Letter of June 10, 1949 in *Carteggio* 2001, 30]

Even before visiting the town, Maderna doubtlessly knew what was going on in Darmstadt in the various fields of cultural reorganization. Both Hartmann and Steinecke would certainly have told him about the spirit of revival that the town was enjoying. In the first exchange of letters between Steinecke and Maderna, from April to June 1949, one can appreciate Steinecke's great interest in Maderna's works and in their being conducted by the composer himself, who seems quite flattered by the invitation. He even planned to travel there with his wife, sent the details of both of their passports, enrolled in the class and sent the scores of the *Concerto per due pianoforti e strumenti* and the *Fantasia e Fuga per due pianoforti*. He nevertheless stressed that he would only be able to be there to conduct his *Concerto* and perhaps meet Arnold Schönberg, if he kept his promise to visit the classes that year. The performance of the work was fixed for July 9. Unfortunately, though, the instrumental parts did not arrive in time and, as we have seen, Maderna himself was unable to go to Germany, and so on the evening in question his *Fantasia e Fuga* was performed, since no orchestral parts were required. The following year, Steinecke once again insisted that he should come to Darmstadt and perform one of his works:

> The most suitable one seems to be *Composizione n. 2* for chamber orchestra, dedicated to Scherchen, which he would conduct very willingly on this occasion. Naturally, if you want to conduct your own work personally, you are warmly invited to do so.[61]

---

[61] The quotation comes from the letter of May 24, 1950, reproduced in *Carteggio* (2001), 39-40. The details of the previous and subsequent relations between Steinecke and Maderna come from

In the end it was Scherchen who conducted *Composizione n. 2*, on the evening of August 26, 1950, and the work was well received by the critics, as we learn from the newspaper cuttings sent to Maderna by the secretary of the courses.[62] The following year (1951) no work by Maderna was performed at Darmstadt. He had hoped to take *Kafka* to Germany, which had been successfully premiered in Venice in September 1950, but for some reason the score arrived "after the jury had already established the program," as Steinecke states in a letter of May 12. Nonetheless, Maderna went to Darmstadt in any case, and his first encounter with the town's musical environment would prove determinant for rest of his life. On this occasion he was able to attend the main events, in particular the Second International Dodecaphonic Congress (July 2 to 4), during which Schönberg's *Dance around the Golden Calf* from *Moses and Aaron* was given its world premiere. During the congress Maderna had the opportunity to meet various eminent figures from the international music scene and witness (and perhaps take part in) the lively discussions that took place in the two sessions held behind closed doors. But on this occasion too – as had happened in Milan two years before – the meetings did not reach the goals that had been hoped for, and perhaps prompted more delusions than theoretic clarifications. Even Wladimir Vogel, who had put so much effort into organizing the two meetings, did not attend the congress. Instead, Schönberg's eminent example of the application of the dodecaphonic technique

> was an unforgettable experience for many young composers, among whom, apart from Luigi Nono, there were Bruno Maderna, Karel Goeyvaerts, Karlheinz Stockhausen and Camillo Togni. For Maderna, Nono and especially Togni it must have been a true revelation, the discovery of a totally new kind of music that pointed out the path to follow. [*Trudu* 1992, 66]

But in his exchange of letters with Steinecke between 1949 and '51, Maderna never explains why he was not able to take part in the courses personally in those years. The letters simply contain news about how his works were progressing, the delivery of orchestral material or practical details about their performance; all of them are sent from and to the same address, Castello 4002, where we know Maderna had settled after his marriage to Raffaella Tartaglia. We do not know exactly how long he remained in Darmstadt during his first stay. One can imagine that he took advantage of the occasion to visit the new cultural institutions of the town and maybe the theater school/workshop of Harro Dicks, with whom he

the same source.

[62] Documentation in *Centro Studi Maderna*, Section D 2.3.

quickly established a long and solid working relationship. And he would certainly have had the chance to meet Beate Christine Köpnik. Their mutual attraction seems to have been immediate and Maderna invited her to visit him in Venice soon afterwards. Proof of her visit comes from a picture postcard sent to Steinecke from Venice, on September 8, 1951, bearing the signatures and greetings, written very untidily, of a merry group that included the sisters Beate and Giselheid Köpnik, Bruno, his mother Irma, his friends Luigi Nono and Romolo Grano, and another couple of German acquaintances.[63]

This fortuitous encounter took place during a moment of crisis between Maderna and his first wife, and in fact on November 16, 1951 he began an appeal in the Law Courts of Verona against the request for separation made by Raffaella Tartaglia, who accused him of having deserted the marital home on June 17 of that same year. Their relations had clearly been deteriorating already for some time, apparently due to Bruno's frequent trips away from Venice and Raffaella's insistence that she should follow him during his professional engagements.[64] However, these domestic issues do not seem to have had any great effect on his artistic plans, since in a letter to Steinecke written on November 18 – that is, just two days after the legal appeal – Maderna informs him that he is composing a new work for the Darmstadt festival of the following year, and that he is preparing to conduct concerts in Hamburg, Munich and on Radio Zurich. His correspondence with Steinecke also gives some indications about the changes that were taking place in his life. On February 23, 1952, from Bologna, where he was conducting a concert at the Teatro Comunale, he urges Steinecke to send his letters to an address different from his usual one – Castello 5025 – an indication that the composer had changed his home. The two addresses cannot have been very far from one another, seeing that they are in the same district, but a few days later, on March 16, Maderna wrote to Steinecke again, giving him yet another address: c/o Pagan, Cannaregio 4633, Calle della Posta [*Carteggio* 2001, 45-48]. This fact is particularly significant, as it tells us that Maderna had no home of his own, but was living with another person/family, in a different district, where he nevertheless stayed for just a month. He then decided to leave Venice, as clearly emerges from this letter to Nono dated April 1952:

> Now I am going away [...] it is up to you to keep things going during these months [...] You are my best friend, you can take my place in everything

---

[63] We wish to thank Wilhelm Schlüter for sending us a copy of both sides of the postcard, preserved at the *Musikinstitut* in Darmstadt, and for his precious help in deciphering it.

[64] An example could be her request to follow him in his first invitation to Darmstadt in 1949 [*Carteggio*, 33]. For some unknown reason this trip did not take place.

and for everything. You must be the animator; help the lazy, be patient with those who don't understand [...] fill them with the love of music, of true life. [...] You have all the talents to do this [...] You must do it.[65]

Knowing how the story ends, one can easily guess that during this period, between 1951 and '52, he consolidated his relationship with Beate Christine Köpnik, his future second wife and mother of his three children. It would appear that Maderna had no qualms about making the situation public, as he dedicated his *Improvvisazione n. 1* to "meine Beata Christina [sic]," a work that was first performed in Hamburg on February 18, 1952. The legal action for his separation from Tartaglia went on until December 1971, when they were finally granted a divorce and he was at last free to marry Christine Köpnik, on April 28, 1972 [*Documenti* 1985, 63].

In the early '50s, the letters to and from Maderna mostly bear the address of Irma Manfredi, who had welcomed her adoptive son into her home after his separation from his wife, although it is unlikely that Maderna spent much time in Verona since his engagements as a conductor both at home and abroad were becoming increasingly more frequent. Alongside that of his mother we therefore find numerous temporary addresses. Broadly speaking, throughout 1952 he was often in Darmstadt, while in 1953 he was more frequently based in Verona. It was not until the following year that we find evidence of a more permanent residence in Darmstadt. When Maderna wrote to Varèse on December 4, 1954 to tell him about his performance of *Déserts* in Stockholm, he gave his address as "c/o Köpnik /Teichausserstr., 20."[66] The end of this letter also offers an interesting detail: "If you want to write to me, I'll be staying at the address I mentioned until January 5. Then I'll be in Verona, at Anfiteatro 6. Write to me when you come to Italy. We can go to Rome together. /Kind regards / Yours / Bruno Maderna/ (Doge of Venice)."[67] But despite all these shifts of address, his bond with Christine grew stronger and the most concrete sign of their union is the birth of their first child, Caterina, in February 1955.

---

[65] E. Schaller, "L'insegnamento di Bruno Maderna," in *Bruno Maderna Studi e Testimoniananze*, cited in note 5, 115.

[66] This was the address of the pharmacist Dr. Paul Köpnik, Beate's father, where Maderna usually stayed in this period, like a member of the family [W. Schlüter, "Anmerkungen zum Kapitel "Darmstadt 1949 bis 1973," *Bruno Madernas Biographie*, 2]. This typewritten document, until now unpublished, was kindly made available to us by the author.

[67] Typewritten letter with the signature and "self-definition" in brackets written by hand. Another phrase "(Emperor of China)" is also autograph, written above the opening "Dearest friend." See L. Cossettini, A. Orcalli, *L'invenzione della fonologia musicale. Saggi sulla musica elettronica sperimentale di Luciano Berio e Bruno Maderna*, (Lucca: LIM 2015), 86-87.

So who exactly was Beate Christine Köpnik? She was born on December 14, 1934 in Darmstadt and so when the thirty-one year-old Maderna met her in 1951 she was 17 and had just finished attending the *Viktoriaschule*, a high school for girls where she was known among her school companions for her passion for the theater and cinema, but evidently also for music, given that she was part of the team that organized the summer courses that year.[68] Her encounter with Maderna appears to have been a classic *coup de foudre* that then grew into a lifelong love, since she always remained faithful to him despite the difficulties and long periods of solitude she was forced to suffer on account of her partner's busy professional life. At the time of their meeting, although still very young, she was already working in the cinema. She had just appeared in a film by Rolf Thiele, *Die Primarinnen*, in a secondary role, but with a picture of her featured in the promotional poster. The following year she worked in *Der Tag der Hochzeit* by the same director, and in 1953 in Paul Verhoeven's *Vergiss die Liebe nicht*. In 1955 she appeared in Laszlo Benedek's film *Kinder, Mütter und ein General* that was also shown in the United States with the title *Sons, Mothers and a General*. Her last documented role is in a TV film by I. Moskowitz, *Napoleon in New Orleans* (1959), where she is listed among the principal parts.[69]

Throughout this period Bruno was still torn between a future that would push him towards becoming a citizen of the nascent Europe and the vocation to help alleviate the dire situation that Italian culture was undergoing in the years immediately after the war. The need to rise again from the ruins of the bombings was, in fact, not only a reality faced by the sorely battered Germany. Italy too was in urgent need of reconstruction and not only of houses and monuments. It was imperative to find a way out of the ideological-political confusion that had resulted not only from the twenty-year period of Fascism but also from the mistakes made while trying to escape from it. The chaotic reaction to the failure of one set of ideologies was inevitably followed by an attempt to find firm ground in others.

An exemplary case of the quest for cultural renewal is that of Vittorini's journal *Il Politecnico* first published in Milan on September 29, 1945. Despite making little impact and closing down after just two years, it left in its wake

---

[68] In the document by Wilhelm Schlüter cited in note 66, we read on p. 2: "Thanks to her interest in cultural life, already as a teenager she helped, together with her elder sister, in the organization of the sixth edition of the International Courses for New Music held at *Marienhöhe* in Darmstadt in the summer of 1951. Here she met Bruno Maderna, who was attending the courses for the first time, and fell in love with him."

[69] Details of Beate Köpnik's activity as an actress are taken from the following site, consulted on December 2, 2019: https://www.imdb.com/name/nm0462893/?ref_=nv_sr_1

an awareness of the close link between politics and culture and the exigency to make up for lost time, using as point of reference the thoughts of great authors and artistic movements that had been given little or no space during the Fascist era: Kafka, Freud, Brecht, Éluard, Surrealism, Pasternak, Mayakowsky and many others. The particular situation of Milan is aptly summarized in the words of Roberto Leydi, who recalls the city at a distance of fifty years:

> To understand the Milan of 1945, it should be remembered that already in the years before the war it had been a city with a very lively cultural scene; also in the years of Fascism, and despite Fascism. I certainly do not wish to take a revisionist line, but I believe that we need to reconsider the ideological *cliché* which sees '45, the end of the war, the fall of the last of vestiges of Fascism, the Liberation, as the moment that witnessed a sudden explosion of cultural vitality – obviously the question of political freedom is another thing – which magically (and unexplainably) appeared from nowhere. There is no doubt that the decisive events of April 25 opened the way for often unexpected initiatives, but we should not overlook the ferment that had already pervaded Milan during the gray years of Fascism. […] I am thinking of the lively European outlook of the architects grouped around Edoardo Persico and of the journal *Casabella*. I am thinking of the opening to international perspectives that allowed the development of modern Italian design and graphics, around the Studio Boggeri. [..] of the work […] of a poet like Alfonso Gatto. And I am thinking of the young artists of Brera [..]. Only by taking into account this background can we explain why in '45, in the space of just a few weeks, an extraordinary creative – but also organizational – vitality was established in this city, a vitality that would then continue to manifest itself until the end of the '60s, when also the national political climate changed so deeply, upsetting many hopes and, one should add, many illusions.[…] It was in this climate, in this atmosphere – which I venture to call magical – that the *Studio di Fonologia musicale della RAI* was born.[70]

The "ferment" that pervaded the city before the end of the war is also reflected in the choice of concert programs. Guido Salvetti reminds us that in the autumn season of 1942 various operas were staged that were wholly innovative compared to the Italian opera tradition: for example Berg's *Wozzeck*, Busoni's *Arlecchino*, Bartók's *Miraculous Mandarin*, Honegger's *Amphion*.[71] On this

---

[70] Roberto Leydi during the meeting "Lo Studio di Fonologia musicale della RAI di Milano a 40 anni dalla fondazione," organized by the University and Teatro Comunale of Bologna, on June 8, 1995, in *Esperienze allo Studio di Fonologia musicale della RAI di Milano 1954-1959*, eds. V. Rizzardi, A. I. De Benedictis (CIDIM-RAI, 2000), 217-221.

[71] G. Salvetti, "Ideologie politiche e poetiche musicali nel Novecento italiano," *Rivista Italiana di*

matter we should not forget the conflict between the secretary of the Italian Communist Party Palmiro Togliatti and the critic Massimo Mila on the subject of new music (1948). Basically, the event that sparked the debate was *Andrei Zhdanov's* condemnation of Soviet composers accused of allowing themselves to be influenced by the avant-garde tendencies circulating in the West. But since this condemnation attacked some of the fundamental principles of the poetics shared by the main promoters of musical renewal in Italy, and by important Soviet composers already well known and justly appreciated in the West, like Prokofiev and Shostakovich, the Italian composers and critics who were members of the Communist Party, or who in any case shared the position of the innovators, took sides against the theoretic principles of Zdanovism.[72] Underlying this situation was the conviction, which had already been sustained in *Il Politecnico*, that there was a firm link between political "progressiveness" and that of aesthetics. Being of the left also implied supporting the arts of the avant-garde, of renewal, of non conformism. Such principles constituted a line of thought that was fairly widespread throughout Italy. The discussion on the specific theme of Zdanovism spilled over into more general issues that involved the two opposing political forces: on the one hand the parties of the left – socialists and communists – and on the other the politically predominant parties of the right, among other things favored by the church, with the *Democrazia Cristiana* at the forefront. But while at a political level the control of the D.C. was always almost absolute, at a cultural level the principles of renewal tended to prevail. The debate was carried out above all in the newspapers but also within cultural institutions (for example, regarding the appointment of the directors of theaters, of festivals etc.). From this point of view Milan was one of the most typical and active centers. The most important music institutions (La Scala, *Società del Quartetto*, Casa Ricordi, RAI) represented the hard line in support of tradition, even though also on this front there were some tentative signs in the direction of renewal. For example, articles appearing the *Rassegna Musicale* in 1950 and 1951 provide evidence of the lively debate that was taking place in the city: there were those who appreciated the premiere of Ferrari Trecate's opera *L'orso re* and the staging of Wagner's complete *Tetralogy*

Musicologia, 35/1, (2000), 120. See also the articles by C. Fertonani, E. Sala and A. Alberti in *Milano laboratorio musicale del Novecento. Scritti per Luciana Pestalozza*, ed. O. Bossini (Milano: Archinto, 2009).

[72] Roderigo di Castiglia [P. Togliatti], "Orientamenti dell'arte," *Rinascita* (November 6, 1948), 453-454; M. Mila, "Disorientamento dell'arte", ibid. (December 6, 1948), 500-501. On this matter, see also L. Pestalozza, "Mila, Togliatti, la verità," *Musica/Realtà*, no. 64 (2001), 21-22.

in the original language, with the Bayreuth orchestra conducted by Wilhelm Furtwängler. But there were others who condemned the verbose rhetoric of Debussy's music for D'Annunzio's *Martyre de Saint Sebastien*.

It was therefore Milan that, along with Darmstadt, became Maderna's main focus of interest after separating from his wife, a choice that was further enhanced by the fact that his teaching engagement at the conservatory in Venice had now fallen through. In fact, in February 1952, the director Gian Francesco Malipiero informed him that on order of the ministry, and in compliance with the official list of candidates, he was obliged to appoint a new substitute teacher of "Teoria and Solfeggio" [*Documenti* 1985, 79].

The 1950s saw a steady rise in Maderna's commitments as a conductor, both at home and abroad. The Italian cities where he was most frequently engaged were Rome, Turin, Venice and Florence. Both Rome and Turin boasted permanent orchestras of the RAI which regularly broadcast orchestral concerts either live or recorded. Also in Florence and Venice he was invited by the RAI to record performances that would then be broadcast on the radio. From 1952, the year in which his association with Darmstadt became more stable, his engagements took him increasingly outside of Italy, and in particular to Germany, where the radio networks were particularly active in promoting contemporary music and where a large number of festivals had been set up. In 1952, '53 and '54 he took part in the festival of contemporary music *Das Neue Werk* in Hamburg, in which he featured not only as a conductor but also as a composer. The link with this important event and with the orchestra of the local radio (NWDR) was most likely Hermann Scherchen, who was a friend and former fellow-student of Rolf Liebermann, one of the main supporters of the festival. Another major festival was *Musica Viva*, founded in Munich by Karl Amadeus Hartmann, a friend and admirer of Maderna, which later spread to Heidelberg. Maderna was present at *Musica Viva* regularly from 1950 to '54. Cologne too hosted an important festival of contemporary music, *Musik der Zeit*, in which Maderna participated from 1952. And alongside his constant work in Darmstadt, he was also a regular visitor to nearby Frankfurt, where the radio of the federal state of Hesse had its headquarters [*Romito* 2020].

CHAPTER III

BETWEEN MILAN AND DARMSTADT

From the early 1950s, and in particular from 1952, Maderna began to spend an increasing amount of time in Darmstadt and he soon began think of the German city as one of the main bases for his work. This point in time seems to mark the start of new era in his daily experience, in his way of thinking about life and art, and in his work as a composer. Such changes would, however, take time to develop and this chapter will now try to outline how they gradually took effect.

As we have seen, 1948 was a decisive year for Maderna in terms of his contact with dodecaphony and with the world of music in Italy and in Europe. This date marks an important moment of transition for Maderna, but it is interesting to note that in the very same year musical trends started to change also in France, Germany and even in the United States, in directions that were not so different from those that Maderna was experiencing in Italy. News now traveled faster, through journalism and the radio, and through publishing and recording companies. The three or four years spanning the mid point of the century witnessed an increasingly more evident and concrete formation of new ideas and trends that began to stir the collective conscience across the western world. Old habits were being challenged and resistance to change was starting to give way.

We have already described certain changes that had taken place after the war in Darmstadt and Milan, a situation that was quite generalized in both Germany and Italy. It now seems important to outline, albeit briefly, the developments that progressively took shape in the field of culture, once the existential crisis of the post-war years had been largely overcome. The phenomenon was obviously not limited to music, but if we focus our attention on this particular sector, we can note that the main point of reference for all the new trends was the New Viennese School.

In the first decades of the century Schönberg, Berg and Webern had proposed far-reaching modifications to how the language of music was structured. But we also know that already from the late '20s the initial impetus was starting to decline, and the three progenitors of serialism no longer had sufficient consent and encouragement at a cultural level to have their music played or to allow their ideas to be spread; moreover, the age of expressionism was waning, and not only in music. But despite this they continued along the same path, now cultivating their beliefs in isolation. Schönberg then emigrated to the United States, where, at the time, he was still hardly known, and his two great pupils died prematurely. Subsequently, in the new climate that characterized the post-war years, a deep curiosity about the work of these pioneers began to surface, coupled with a sense of unfulfilled expectations and a feeling of sincere compassion for the personal suffering that the three musicians had experienced in those darker years.

All this created a renewed interest in dodecaphony, but did not prevent it from leading to highly divergent interpretations, often giving rise to intense and also contrasting debates. No musical grammar is absolute and must inevitably be applied in different ways by all those who work with it, even more so in this case, as we are dealing with a new generation of composers. It should be remembered that most of those who engaged in such lively discussions in the mid-century were born in the '20s; they did, of course, have "older brothers" born in the first decade of the century, like Dallapiccola, Schaeffer and Messiaen, whom they respected and at times assumed as models for their choices, but they may also have felt some sort of Freudian intolerance towards their forefathers. This was further fuelled by the desire for recognition typical of impetuous twenty-year-olds, who now had to face the resistance of a wizened audience in the concert halls and the banality of official music criticism. It is not hard to see, then, why the debates we are speaking of could easily reach extremes. And if finally we add that such a quest for a new common ground affected all the arts, and not only the arts but also the fields of science, philosophy, sociology and politics, one can fully appreciate the depth and wealth of such arguments.

The extensive organization of festivals witnessed in the late 1940s was not something new, but rather represented a revival of a practice that had been interrupted by the war and which now saw a veritable boom following the end of the conflict. First and foremost there was the Festival of International Music in Venice, which, as we have seen, was the training ground for Maderna's early career. But at the start of the '50s similar events grew up in many other parts of Europe: the Festival of Contemporary Music in Donaueschingen (linked to the Südwestfunk radio in Baden-Baden, which worked in close collaboration with the international music courses in Darmstadt), the concert season of the Ensemble Intercontemporain in Paris, the cycle *Das Neue Werk* in Hamburg (promoted by the Nordwestdeutscher Rundfunk), the Festival of the International Society for Contemporary Music (ISCM), which was held in different European cities each year and in the period following the end of the war took place in London, Copenhagen, Amsterdam and Palermo. Although the aim of these festivals was often to raise awareness about contemporary music, their programs also included works from the previous centuries so as not to risk the alienation of an audience unaccustomed to listening to the experimental work of the avant-garde.

The summer courses first held in Darmstadt in 1946 soon became a focus of attention for many musicians. The event was not merely a concert season but rather a cultural center where, in the space of a few vibrant weeks each summer, conferences and cycles of lessons on new techniques, new technology and new musical aesthetics were organized. Little by little the courses became a regular arena for the exchange of ideas between the protagonists of New Music. The meetings between young musicians, the chance to express their opinions directly, their furious discussions, their enthusiastic collaborations, the chance to deepen their knowledge of theory and to hear their music performed live, all constituted a particular case that had no precedent in the previous decades and could only rarely be matched in other arts or disciplines. This explains the symbolic (and sometimes rather over-simplified) significance that the name Darmstadt assumes in histories of twentieth century music. In reality Darmstadt did not represent a "style" and not even a "school" of composition: it was above all a unique place for the exchange of experiences and ideas.

From 1952 onwards, Maderna played a leading role in the *Ferienkurse*, not only on account of his experience as an organizer and conductor, but also because he spent long periods in the town and was very familiar with its inner workings and the various aspects of its cultural life. It should, however, be added that for various reasons his contribution and his personal identity always remained a little aloof from the mainstream of the courses. The important role assigned to him was likely due to his age (born in 1920, he was the oldest of the young enthusiasts that animated the courses), and also to the exceptionally precocious circumstances of his previous career as a musician; but he was also appreciated on account of the certain diffidence he showed towards any drastic theories and towards the convictions about the truth held by his fellow musicians. In effect, he wrote little and prudently about his thoughts, and perhaps his good sense made him prefer "doing" composition rather than "theorizing" about it in words. He certainly had theories, and ones that were solid and deep, but he preferred to keep them to himself or to reveal them in conversations or in interviews that were apparently less binding than a written article. There is no doubt, though, about his engagement in the courses, which was intense and wholly genuine. But in the absence of any detailed or first hand information about his thoughts, we believe it best first to give a general picture of the ideas that were emerging at the time, and which were subsequently taken up with great vigor in Darmstadt, and then try to understand to what extent Maderna assimilated such notions and elaborated them in his own work.

We will begin our overview of the European musical scenario in France, which from the '20s to the '40s had been less oppressed by the prohibition of "degenerate art" that was prevalent in Germany and to some extent also in

Italy. Again taking 1948 as our year of reference, we see that the young Boulez, who was then twenty-three, was concluding his studies with Leibowitz and Messiaen in Paris, and had already written various works for piano, as well as a cantata for soloists, choir and orchestra titled *Le Soleil des eaux*, on a text by the surrealist poet René Char, all of which, despite his later tendencies, became an acknowledged part of his output. In two articles published in the journal *Polyphonie* in 1948 he violently attacked his teacher Leibowitz, who had taught him classical dodecaphony, and had no qualms about expressing his scathing views about Alban Berg, whom he described as an old post-romantic "contrivance," even though, in the end, he was worth more than the various "little fools" who called themselves dodecaphonists in the "putrid" world of music in Paris. On the other hand, he was quite appreciative of his teacher Messiaen (and of Stravinsky), who had taught him to build asymmetric rhythms and to abandon the systems characterized by an orderly metrical framework that had dominated Europe for centuries. The question of rhythm was a burning and widely discussed issue, and that of the possible application of serial schemes also to durations and not only to pitches soon became a topic of heated debate in Darmstadt. The idea was to unhinge the conventional relations between durations, just as the system of series proposed by Schönberg had unhinged the pitch relations between the notes of a scale. In this way each note could have its own specific pitch and duration, and should be seen as a "point" with no relations to other notes or "points" (the term "pointillism" was soon taken up in the discussions in Darmstadt). Already in 1948 Boulez had understood that the music he had in mind would move beyond "classic" dodecaphony and that the other parameters of sound, besides the pitches, would need to be taken into account. In those years he also discussed these ideas in an assiduous correspondence with John Cage, who shared these perspectives even though coming from a very different experience such as that of the United States.[1]

When Boulez came to Darmstadt for the first time in 1952, the theme of "poly-parametric" serialism, which he had written articles about and had tried to apply in some of his works, was already known and was an object of contention and discussion.[2] Messiaen too, as the "Darmstadtians" were well aware, had worked a great deal on rhythm. In the introduction to his *Quatuor pour la fin du temps* (1942)

---

[1] J.-J. Nattiez, ed., *Pierre Boulez - John Cage. Correspondance et Documents* (Mainz: Schott, 2002).

[2] Boulez's articles, published in various journals, not only in French, and above all between 1948 and 1952, were collected in a book edited by Paule Thévenin in 1966. They were translated into English by Stephen Walsh and published by Clarendon press under the title *Stocktakings from an apprenticeship* (1991). Two articles in particular have justly retained a place in the bibliographic repertory: one on the rhythms of Stravinsky's *Sacre du Printemps* titled *Stravinsky remains*, 55-110, and the still more famous *Schoenberg is dead*, 209-14.

he had listed some of the techniques used in the work, such as duration values irrationally added to a note, or schemes for the diminution and augmentation of rhythmic values, and in his *Technique de mon langage musical* published two years later, he devoted six chapters to the subject of rhythm. Fundamentally, his treatise deals with the need to separate the parameters of pitch and duration at a theoretic and operative level. In 1949 he then wrote a composition (*Mode de valeurs e d'intensité*) in which also the parameter of dynamics assumes a separate role from that of the rhythms and pitches. The work caused a sensation at Darmstadt, but in the following years the composer considered it no more than a sort of exercise. In 1952 Messiaen was invited to teach in the summer courses; his lessons, however, were more a question of challenging and stimulating the participants rather than pointing out a particular path, since his practice and theory of composition never actually involved the systematic organization of series as such.[3]

The question of forsaking the relations between pitches, durations and dynamics had begun to take on importance also outside of France: in the United States composers like Milton Babbitt, Elliott Carter and George Perle (a pupil of Ernst Krenek) were curious about the trends that were starting to develop from dodecaphony in Europe, and in New York a small but active group of composers (including, among others, Earle Brown, John Cage, Christian Wolff and Morton Feldman) showed an interest in the theories of Joseph Schillinger regarding the *Mathematical basis of the arts*, published in 1948. In the same year Babbitt had written a *Composition for four instruments* in which he experimented with the extension of Schönberg's serial techniques to the durations.[4]

In Venice, Maderna had considered extending Schönberg's serialism to wider relations of mathematical organization between the twelve notes of the scale; others in Paris and New York had thought of applying the system to the duration of the notes, which was possible on the basis of their numerical divisions (in fractions: from the whole-note, to the half-, quarter- and eighth-notes, etc.). A similar calculation could also be applied to the sequence of dynamics (from pppp to ffff), which could even be assigned to single notes or 'points'. In 1949 John Cage maintained that sound as a physical phenomenon had four dimensions (which from then on were called 'parameters'): frequency, duration, loudness, and timbre.[5] While serial experiments with the first three of these parameters had already been carried out with some success, the parameter of timbre did not lend itself so readily to the numerical system. Among other

---

[3] A. Shenton, *Olivier Messiaen's System of Signs: Notes Towards Understanding His Music* (Aldershot: Ashgate, 2008).

[4] L. Cossettini, A. Orcalli, *L'invenzione della fonologia musicale. Saggi sulla musica elettronica sperimentale di Luciano Berio e Bruno Maderna* (Lucca: LIM, 2015), 7-9.

[5] *Pierre Boulez - John Cage* (2002), cited in note 1, 85.

things, timbre was traditionally associated with the use or combination of particular instruments, making it hard to separate one timbre from the other, while the idea of organizing timbres into twelve categories, just because there were twelve notes in a scale, appeared absurd. Some compositions attempted to move in this direction but the task was certainly not easy.

At this point the question of organizing the different timbres began to follow a separate path. The year 1948 could take on a symbolic significance in this respect: in March of that year Pierre Schaeffer made the following note in his journal: "Back in Paris I have started to collect objects. I have in mind a 'symphony of noises'; after all there has been a symphony of Psalms. I go to the sound effects department of the French radio service. I find clappers, coconut shells, klaxons, bicycle horns [...]. After some wrangles with the Administration [...] I take them away."[6] Basically, this was the beginning of what would be called *musique concrète*. In the same period Werner Meyer-Eppler, who worked at the Institute of Research for Phonetics and Communication of the University of Bonn, had started to study aspects of sound that would later be referred to as 'electronic music'. Meyer-Eppler spoke of his research in a conference (*Musik und Technik*) held during the Darmstadt courses in 1951, in which also Adorno, Schaeffer and Eimert took part, and on that occasion he presented some examples of the work that had been realized at his institute.[7] The new generation of composers, deprived of their traditional tools, now had to master new elements of sound, which involved the use of sine waves that could be generated through oscillators able to emit a single pre-determined frequency vibration. With the aid of a Magnetophon it was possible to superimpose other frequencies to produce artificial harmonic sounds that could create simulations of timbre. The data was measurable, distributed over time, modulable in amplitude and able to provide important information about the nature of the timbre.[8] Herbert Eimert, who worked for the radio in Cologne (Nordwestdeutscher Rundfunk) began, in his turn, to apply similar procedures. Although the Electronic Music Studio in Cologne was officially inaugurated in 1953, the first experiments had already been carried out in 1951.[9]

---

[6] F. Bayle, ed., *Pierre Schaeffer, l'oeuvre musicale. Textes et documents* (Paris: INA-GRM, 1990), 23. Cited in Pierre Schaeffer, *In Search of a Concrete Music*, trans. John Dack and Christine North (Berkeley: University of California Press, 2012), 4.

[7] A. I. De Benedictis, "Gli esordi dello Studio di Fonologia Musicale: Il risultato di un incontro fra la musica e le possibilità dei nuovi mezzi," in M. M. Novati, ed., *Lo Studio di fonologia. Un diario musicale 1954-1983* (Milano: Ricordi, 2009), 12.

[8] *L'invenzione della fonologia musicale* (2015), cited in note 4, 10.

[9] K. H. Wörner, *Stockhausen, life and work* (London: Faber and Faber, 1973), 129.

The discussions about multiparametric serialism and the experiments with timbre both focused on "sound materials" that had to be organized within a composition. In other words, the abandonment of the grammatical rules of tonal music created the need for new structural units that composers could use to build their work. Both of these new approaches, parametric and electronic, stemmed from scientific and mathematical thought, and thus required the application of logical principles quite different from those of the previous musical tradition. A more prudent aesthetically-oriented attitude saw these new procedures as providing pre-compositional material that could be adapted to form the basis of their compositions. On the contrary, a more extreme approach demanded a grammar that not only provided material but also scientific models that could be used to organize the macro-formal structure of their works.

During the composition seminar held by Theodor Adorno at the *Ferienkurse* of 1951, this issue gave rise to a heated debate between Karlheinz Stockhausen and Adorno himself. At the time Stockhausen was twenty-three and was apparently not yet familiar with the scores of Webern. He had, however, befriended a young Belgian composer, Karel Goeyvaerts, a pupil of Messiaen who had written a sonata for two pianos in which he systematically applied series of pitches and series of durations. During the seminar the two musicians performed a movement of the work, which prompted negative comments from Adorno but was defended vehemently, and in an irreverent tone, by Stockhausen [*Trudu* 1992, 71]. The core of the argument was the aesthetic sense of the sonata, which Adorno held to be meaningless as it had no communicative intentions. The two young pianists, on the other hand, defended the work saying it was based on a clear and precise musical logic, even if different from that of tradition. Shortly afterwards Adorno took up the issue again in his essay *The Aging of the New Music*, in which he contested the idea of replacing the process of composing with an "objective" mathematical arrangement of sonic parameters and attributed the phenomenon to the subservience of art to the nascent ideologies of technocratic capitalism.[10]

The fundamental question that was now leading to bitter disputes was that of communication in music and Maderna was clearly quite sensitive to the issue. In 1951 he was in Darmstadt and probably heard about this clash between Adorno and the two young musicians. Curiously, this was the same year in which, on July 2, Scherchen – as we mentioned before – performed, to great acclaim, Schönberg's *Dance around the Golden Calf* from *Moses und Aron*, one of the most noted examples of classical dodecaphony and of "expressive"

---

[10] "Das Altern der neuen Musik," *Der Monat* (May 7, 1955), translated by Susan Gillespie in *Essays on Music* (Berkeley: University of California Press, 2002), 181-202.

music. Stockhausen and Goeyvaerts respectfully attended the performance, but soon afterwards in a private letter Goeyvaerts defined it as a kind of "serial Verdi" [*Trudu* 1992, 66]. Boulez too was more inclined towards the notion of "objectivity" and in a letter to Cage, written two years before, he spoke of the numeric relations Cage had used in some rhythmic sequences, stating that he greatly appreciated them because they were "impersonal."[11] The theme of communication in music was closely linked to the need to reject any kind of subjectivity, fantasy or creative imagination. The composer's task was to listen to the "truth" of a piece of musical material, uncontaminated by the subject. In 1969 Mario Bortolotto, summing up two decades of experimentation with this kind of approach, wrote: "New Music means an epiphany of the material, that is to say illumination […] Just as in the musical philosophy of the primitives, music returns to being a song of the spheres, Pythagorean harmony."[12] Moreover, Adorno himself had helped to bring this theme to the forefront when, in line with the view of the Frankfurt school, he analyzed the pervasive aspects of the "reification" of thought. In his introduction to the Italian translation of Adorno's *Philosophy of Modern Music*, Luigi Rognoni underlined how "capitalist society [had] alienated subjectivity to the anonymous objectivity of the mass culture demanded by industrial civilization."[13] Adorno had by no means ruled out that a non-reified thought (whether philosophical or musical) could exist – he himself was clear proof of this. But the young generation of composers seemed wary of any form of subjectivity and dreamed of a musical world of astral and uncontaminated purity.

This, then, was the situation that characterized the international scenario of the mid-twentieth century. As for Maderna, over and above his participation in the activities at Darmstadt, we will now try to establish what his thoughts were regarding New Music, that is to say his theoretic position, a theme that was rarely touched upon in his articles, but was clearly present in the concrete choices he made in his works. Some clues can be drawn from a text he prepared for a conference-lecture to be held in Darmstadt.[14] After an introduction in which he speaks about Schönberg, he immediately points out that every composer always creates "a synthesis between means and application, this being the expression of his times." The document is

---

[11] J-J. Nattiez (ed. 2002), cited in note 1, p.74.

[12] M. Bortolotto, *Fase Seconda. Studi sulla Nuova Musica* (Torino: Einaudi, 1969), 52-53.

[13] L. Rognoni, "La musicologia filosofica di Adorno," in T. W. Adorno, *Filosofia della musica moderna* (Torino: Einaudi, 1960), XI; original title *Philosophie der neuen Musik* (Tübingen: Mohr-Siebeck, 1949).

[14] The conference took place in the context of a study group for young composers in 1954 [*Trudu* 1992, 357], but Maderna never published the text. It can now be read in N.Verzina, "Mutazioni storiche. Intorno a tre testi inediti di Bruno Maderna," *Studi Musicali* (1999), 517-525.

written in the form of brief notes that Maderna evidently intended to elaborate while he was speaking. However, from the context one can deduce that by "means" he was referring to the sonic materials and the general rules, including mathematical procedures, adopted to organize them, and by "application" he meant the way the materials are effectively used in a given work. He also adds (or implies) that the application of these materials has the function of "expressing" something, of manifesting the contents, which are inevitably subjective. He then concludes that the contents are the "expression of one's times," meaning that the musical thought of the composer reveals a cultural and conceptual trend to which he adheres. Throughout the rest of his varied and often complex lecture this opening premise is never contradicted, and is sometimes explicitly confirmed. His speech consisted mainly in listening to and analyzing in detail some works by Schönberg and Webern, with some final remarks about the "means" that he used in his compositions, namely mutations and magic squares.

Markus Fein, who wrote a book entirely devoted to Maderna's works from the early '50s, adds some thoughts of his own about the aspects we are considering.[15] In particular he suggests (on p. 282) that the reciprocal influences of Maderna's double activity as performer and composer often mentioned in the literature should – in his opinion – be viewed with some caution. On the contrary, we believe that it is not possible to underestimate the fact that his long experience as a conductor, starting from when he was a child, helped Maderna to become very sensitive to those that were listening to his performances. Furthermore, we cannot overlook his extraordinary ability, acknowledged by many who knew him, to immediately hear what he saw written on a score. Therefore, we sustain that his approach to composition and his experience as a conductor were surely closely linked.

Other important clues emerge from the discussions that Maderna had with Nono in that period, traces of which can be found in the letters the two composers wrote to one another. As we already mentioned in the previous chapter, in April 1952 Maderna moved away from Venice and left the fate of their "Venetian school" in the capable hands of Nono. In the same period he told Nono that he had become a member of the Italian Communist Party, spurred by an inner conviction he had felt ever since his involvement in the struggle for liberation during the final phases of the war [*Extraits* 2007, 491]. From the tone of the letter we can gather that they had already spoken about and discussed this decision at great length: it seems likely that joining the Communist party had different meanings for the two musicians.

---

[15] Markus Fein, *Die musikalische Poetik Bruno Madernas. Zum "seriellen" Komponieren zwischen 1951 und 1955* (Frankfurt am Main: Lang, 2001).

In November of the same year [ibid., 493-495], in another letter to his friend, Maderna returns to the question of politics. He wrote the letter from Barcelona, where he conducted two concerts, and speaks about the Spanish resistance to Franco. It is hard not to associate letters of this type with the music he would later call, during a lecture in Darmstadt, the "expression of one's times," clearly a reference to music that was politically engaged (more or less in the same period, he wrote the cantata *Vier Briefe*, whose texts include a letter from an Italian partisan who had been sentenced to death). In a letter from the start of 1953 [ibid., 496] he confides to his friend that he was still unsure about their position within the prevailing international trends. He confesses to Nono that he is afraid of becoming too submissive to the curious aesthetic views of Stockhausen and Boulez, or to those of Scherchen's entourage. Their way of seeing their own (true) music – and of composing it – should involve moving beyond these trends, so as to turn composition into a human question, one of communication.

Maderna, then, appears not to have shared the idea of impersonality or objectivity in music, even though he was convinced that pieces written from an objective point of view, like Stockhausen's *Kreuzspiel*, in whose performance he participated, or like Boulez's *Polyphonie X*, which he conducted in 1953, were doubtlessly to be appreciated, even though they lacked the intent to communicate and the notion of music as a human question that he himself truly believed in.

It should also be remembered that the Darmstadt courses, which Maderna attended with great enthusiasm, were born as a multifaceted event and would always continue to be so. It would be wrong to identify the environment at Darmstadt only with the extreme tendencies that were expressed there; certainly, those trends existed, but there was also room for other tendencies of a different kind that were equally appreciated. If an artist expressed aesthetic principles and built them into a personal philosophy, he was free to do so, but beneath Maderna's seemingly complacent *façade* and apparently contradictory behavior one can sense the belief that, for him, the value of a work of art did not depend on the theories on which it was based, but rather on the way the sonic materials were "applied" in a given piece of music, in other words on its underlying principles of imagination and not of philosophy.

Over and above his adhesion to or distancing from the poetics that were then in circulation, already in his works written between 1948 and 1950, Maderna shows he has his own clear idea of how to manage the technical procedures of dodecaphony. However, as we well know, he always tended to see his plans for a new work as a chance to look for and try out new approaches, and this continued to be the case also after 1950. Among the works composed in that period there is one that coincides exactly with the period in which he was moving between

Venice and Darmstadt. Given that it was premiered in Hamburg on February 18, 1952, *Improvvisazione 1* was probably written in Venice, or perhaps in Verona, in autumn 1951. Although the work contains structural techniques and sonic elements that could link it to *Composizione n. 2* or to other previous pieces, there are also certain aspects that are more sophisticated in comparison with his works dating from and immediately after 1948, to the extent that Fein considers it to be his first truly "Darmstadtian" work of the 1950s.

Without wishing to go too deeply into the details of the serial techniques adopted by Maderna, also because it is impossible to identify any precise organization that was applied to all his works, we have nevertheless attempted to give an approximate idea of how they worked in Table 1, a model that is totally invented and simplified in its mechanism.

Table 1.

C	1	7	9	6	8	12	5	4	10	11	2	3
F#	7	6	12	4	11	3	1	9	8	5	10	2
G#	9	5	2	7	12	11	1	8	10	6	4	3
F	6	3	9	2	12	1	10	4	5	7	11	8
G	8	6	9	12	10	5	11	3	2	1	4	7
B	12	5	3	1	7	8	9	10	11	2	4	6
E	5	1	8	10	2	6	12	3	7	9	11	4
Eb	4	5	8	2	12	7	11	1	10	6	3	9
A	10	3	5	2	7	1	6	9	4	8	12	11
Bb	11	10	5	7	6	4	12	3	2	1	9	8
C#	2	9	10	7	4	3	1	8	11	5	6	12
D	3	8	5	12	2	10	4	1	11	6	9	7

Our imaginary example uses a real series that was used by Schönberg in his Op. 31. The aim is to show how twelve variants could be derived from this initial series by means of well-defined numerical procedures. In our theoretic case the note *C* is indicated as 1, and so on:

(C C♯ D D♯ E F F♯ G G♯ A A♯ B
 1 2 3 4 5 6 7 8 9 10 11 12)

The first horizontal sequence and the first vertical sequence indicate (in numbers) the notes of Schönberg's series. From the second line onwards we see (horizontally) the numerical variants of the initial series. In this example the first variant (that begins with F♯, number 7) is obtained by taking every other note of the original series; the numerical series of the third line starts from note 9 (G♯) and again skips one note at a time of the previous series, and so on. In each of the twelve horizontal lines there must obviously be a different series of 12 notes.

Table 1 clearly illustrates how Maderna (along with Nono and the other Venetians) firmly rejected the principle proposed by Schönberg whereby an entire composition should derive from a single serial model. Such a constraint would drastically limit the composer's possibility to make choices, and risked making the resulting melodies and harmonies seem forced and unspontaneous. On the other hand, Schönberg's technique was born from the need to offer composers a secure and logically thought-out method that would allow them to avoid the tonal attractions that traditionally linked the notes of a scale: for centuries the western ear had been educated to these attractions, and to disregard this heritage was certainly no easy task. Numerous composers throughout the twentieth century tried to resolve the issue and Schönberg's solution was the most radical and systematic. But the use of a single series was not the only way to avoid the established tonal attractions: any sort of dodecaphonic series would provide the same result. The idea of using multiple series attained the objective of avoiding tonal links, but also broadened the possible range of choice, as the intervals that linked one note to the next were not only those present in a single basic series. In 1991 Borio and Rizzardi suggested calling these calculations the "technique of shifts"– shifts of numbers that corresponded to entities of sound – and asserted that this approach had been constantly applied from the time of *Improvvisazione n. 1* at least until the period of Nono's *Canto sospeso* (1956).[16]

The techniques used in the composition of *Improvvisazione n. 1*, documented by countless sketches, opened the way to later developments. In the works that followed, the possibilities of choice offered in this first work systematically evolved in different directions: for example, in some cases the numbers of the series were not applied to the pitches, but to the successions of durations, when it was deemed necessary to organize them in particular parts of a work. Maderna and Nono, however, never became totally subservient to the fascination of numerical calculations, even though they made abundant use of them. They used them in a free and flexible fashion, depending on the needs of each individual composition. The problem that some of the more ardent composers faced was that of working "in a sonic world beyond counterpoint and motivic-thematic thought."[17] But in Maderna's case these traditional elements do not seem to have been avoided out of principle: when they suited his communicative purposes he had no qualms about adopting them to characterize certain aspects of his works. On listening to *Improvvisazione 1* some examples of these complex decisions come to light.

---

[16] G. Borio, "Sull'interazione fra lo studio degli schizzi e l'analisi dell'opera," in *La nuova ricerca sull'opera diLuigi Nono*, eds. G. Borio, G. Morelli, V. Rizzardi (Firenze: Olschki, 1999), 15.

[17] ibid., 21.

The overall style of the work is well defined and derives from recourse to the numerical logic we have just described. From a perceptive point of view the arbitrariness of the numbers produces a sense of disorder and uncertainty, not only on account of the lack of any tonal reference but also due to the inconsistency of the durations, the constantly changing timbres, the sudden shifts between high and low zones of the sonic range, and the way that the notes have been reduced to single units (the so called pointillism). And yet this does not necessarily produce the sensation that everything has been flattened out and that all is equal to everything else. In *Improvvisazione 1* Maderna organizes small fragments of irregularly overlapping timbres, minimum pseudo-melodies of two to three notes, contemporary but uneven pulsations, and brief contiguous sonorities set in different registers. The overall effect is a kind of homogeneous carpet of sound, a mosaic of shifting elements in constant rotation. However, Maderna did not stop there. Even though he built textures that were similar to those of other young composers, he did not share their principle of "removing the subject": neither he nor Nono were willing to renounce the ethics of subjectivity, understood as the defense of ideal values. And in order to speak of ideal values it was necessary to find paths of sharing and tools of persuasion. In fact, *Improvvisazione 1* contains rhetorical constructions, allusions to existential situations and emotional contrasts, in other words the means that music had for centuries learned to adopt in order to dialogue with its listeners. And so the music of *Improvvisazione 1* slowly reveals an overall plan, a general "macro form": after some moments of expectation, hints of tension begin to appear and these gradually intensify until reaching a peak.

Another aspect (already tried out in *Composizione n. 2*) is the provocative reference to popular dances, in this case a Polka and a Can-can, which are broken up into various episodes that in the Can-can lead to arousing moments of disorderly and violent pulsations. Equally singular is the sudden and unexpected appearance, at the height of tension, of an actual melody in a recitative style. Finally, another "license" that Maderna allows himself is the conspicuous presence of repetitions of various kinds. These are not, of course, reiterations of themes, because there are no themes as such, but rather of sonic images that for varying reasons become recognizable: for example, the listener can perceive the fairly constant presence of the harps in some of the opening and closing episodes; elsewhere one can hear the repetition of short staccato notes, especially when they are repeated by the same instrument; and here and there pedal-notes stand out from the context, simply because they are perceived as different. All in all, one could say that in *Improvvisazione 1* Maderna was passionately attracted to the mathematical and geometrical regularities of his calculations, but he was also particularly careful to hold the attention of whoever might be listening to the result. He was enthusiastic about the unprecedented materials made available by the latest advances in musical research, but was unwilling to let them become absolute. He felt irresistibly attracted towards the new, but maintained a strong love for the historical configuration of musical language and was aware that every style had always been connected to the ideas and hopes of its time. He knew perfectly well that his way of embodying the new in music raised doubts among some of his colleagues, but was too wise to use arrogance as an instrument of discussion.

Once again it is difficult to reconstruct the more practical side of his life, particularly in the delicate moment of his separation from Venice before becoming definitively rooted in Darmstadt. Due to a lack of any explicit information from the protagonist of our story, we must base our narration on the dates of his appearances in public events, on the dates and addresses that are given in his letters and in those sent to him, and on any details appearing in letters of friends that shared some moments of their life and reflections with him. The picture of his life in this period is, then, inevitably sketchy, as we have few written traces of his private affairs – his work, his thoughts, his new personal relations.

The year 1952 was not only decisive in Maderna's private life, but was also particularly significant in terms of his professional involvement in the city of Darmstadt, over and above his participation in the *Ferienkurse*. From March onwards an intense exchange of letters took place between Maderna and Wolfgang Steinecke, to plan various events in the calendar of an especially important year. The courses that year were seen as a "new beginning," the "serial phase" of the institution seven years after its establishment, years that Steinecke himself had referred to as a phase of "orientation for young German musicians."[18] Alongside the presence of Nono, Boulez, Stockhausen and Goeyvaerts, one of the main features of the 1952 season was a closer relation with the Landestheater and especially with the classes on opera direction held by Harro Dicks. The previous year had already seen important changes within the hierarchy of the theater: Rudolf Sellner had been appointed superintendent and Hermann Scherchen principal conductor of the orchestra.[19] From the content of their letters we understand that Maderna already knew of this situation and was eager to take part in one of their projects. To achieve this aim, he first tells Steinecke, in great detail, about his idea to orchestrate Orazio Vecchi's *Amphiparnaso*, even specifying the exact group of players he would need and his intention to have the Prologue performed in German. He also speaks at length of

---

[18] G. Borio, H. Danuser, *Im Zenit der Moderne. Die Internationalen Ferienkurse für Neue Musik Darmstadt 1946-1966*, 4 vols. (Freiburg im Breisgau: Rombach, 1997), vol. I, 90.

[19] W. Schlüter, *Anmerkungen zum Kapitel "Darmstadt 1949 bis 1973" in Bruno Madernas Biographie*, an unpublished typescript kindly made available to us, page 5.

another two Italian works: Petrassi's *Coro di morti* (1940-41), and Dallapiccola's *Job*, which had been premiered at the Teatro dell'Opera in Rome two years before. This first exchange of ideas led the two correspondents to consider organizing an "Italian evening" that year. Maderna warns Steinecke that there could be some difficulties, as Dallapiccola had some very precise ideas about his work, but assures him: "I'll work for more than a month on the rehearsals" [*Carteggio* 2001, letters of March 16 and 30]. The discussion continues in their letters and after a couple of weeks Steinecke gives his approval: "I hope you can manage to stay in Darmstadt for a month; so we'll have time to talk about the concerts while we're making the preparations for the theatrical works" [ibid., letter of April 16 addressed to Calle della Posta, Venice]. It is not hard to imagine how, on receiving this letter, Maderna readily made his decision to leave for a lengthy stay in Darmstadt and wrote his farewell letter to Nono, assigning him the task of carrying on what he had begun with the "Venice school," the letter that closed the events described in Chapter Two. He then sent a telegram to Steinecke: "Due to engagements with the RAI, I will be in Darmstadt on 26 [April]" [ibid., 51-65]. After months of provisional planning, the "Italian evening" was finally held on July 15 the *Italienischer Opernabend*, which included Dallapiccola's sacred representation *Job*, a staged version of Petrassi's *Coro di morti*, and Orazio Vecchi's Comedia Harmonica *Amphiparnaso*, with staging by Harro Dicks and conducted by Maderna.[20] Part of the program was also repeated at the Landestheater, where *Amphiparnaso* was now paired with Orff's *Carmina Burana*, again directed by Dicks and conducted by Maderna. The project seems to have been widely appreciated as it was repeated seven times in the months of October, November and December.[21]

The *Ferienkurse* of 1952 were particularly intense for Maderna: he appears as a performer (percussionist) in the first performance of Stockhausen's *Kreuzspiel*, the work that created the greatest stir among participants of the course that year, and as conductor of the second concert in the cycle "Music of the New Generation" (in which he conducted, among other things, the *5 Espressioni* by his former pupil in Venice, Renzo Dall'Oglio) and of the third concert in the same cycle (in which he conducted Nono's *Epitaffio per Federico Garcia Lorca 1. España en el corazon*). This last concert also included the first performance of his new work with electronics, *Musica su due dimensioni*. The advent of electronic music was, in fact, another topic that was beginning to be discussed at Darmstadt in this period. In 1950 and 1951 two meetings had been organized that saw the participation of Schaeffer, Meyer Eppler, Eimert, Adorno and others.[22] Maderna

---

[20] *Chronik* 1997, 553.
[21] See documents in *Centro Studi Maderna*, Section D 12.
[22] The first was titled *Die Klangwelt der elektronischen Musik* and consisted of three seminars with musical examples. That of the following year included two seminars. The subject was then taken up again in 1953 [*Chronik* 1997, *passim*].

does not appear to have attended these meetings, but news of their contents had undoubtedly circulated and given rise to much discussion.

And so it was that on July 21, 1952 in Darmstadt he presented his new work for electronics and live instruments, whose novel combination of flute and magnetic tape proved a source of great interest. In his introduction to the critical edition of the work [*Maderna* 2002] Nicola Scaldaferri also gives details of the different phases entailed in the composition. The electronics part was recorded in Bonn using certain "timbres" and "noises" prepared by Meyer-Eppler, [23] and an instrument called the Melochord. According to Scaldaferri this was "a keyboard instrument with tones and semitones built in 1949 by Harald Bode," which had 5 octaves, various timbres and polyphonic possibilities. The instrument was therefore quite different from the one designed by Schaeffer at Radio France, and from the one that would be created shortly afterwards in Cologne. In Paris timbres recorded from external noises were filtered and manipulated, while in Cologne sine sounds were used ("pure" sounds of only one frequency, without harmonics), which were certainly not organized in the form of a scale, but on the basis of a continuum of frequencies: by summing various frequencies simultaneously, new timbres could be built, and a few years later Stockhausen worked enthusiastically on this mechanism. The Melochord, instead, involved working on the notes, not the timbres. And in fact the score originally prepared by Maderna indicated notes on a staff for the electronics part. And the instruments specified in the main surviving manuscript are the flute, electronics and piano.

The genesis of the work is quite complex and the diverse accounts in the literature make it difficult to reconstruct the various phases of its writing. The best path is perhaps to examine the existing documents one by one, starting with the letter in which Meyer-Eppler replies to Maderna, who had told him of his plans to write a work for real instruments – flute, piano, celesta and percussion – and electronic sounds. Meyer-Eppler, professor of Physics at the University of Bonn, pointed out that a piece for traditional instruments and electronically generated sounds might create "an impression of contrast." As an alternative, he suggested recording the instruments on a tape and then combining them with the electronic sounds.[24] But Maderna had another solution in mind and immersed himself in the task, filling as many as eighty-nine sheets of paper with drafts of series and sketches. However, he soon realized that something was not working and on May 30 he wrote to Nono explaining his problems: he tells him he had just started writing his new work (he had written eighty measures), but he had come to realize that the serial calculations they had been working on together

---

[23] *Im Zenit der Moderne*, cited in note 18, vol. II, 86-87.
[24] Letter of May 14, 1952, in *Studi* 1989, 62.

since 1948 were not compatible with the use of electronics. Evidently, the idea of combining two different types of sound sources had led to some practical problems in the writing [*Extraits* 2007, 492-493]. This can be gleaned not only from the doubts expressed in his letter to Nono, but also from some otherwise inexplicable developments. The work was originally conceived for at least three traditional instruments: besides the flute, also the piano, celesta and percussion, and in fact the concert bill included the name of the pianist Pietro Scarpini. However, in the end the only live instrument to appear on the score was the flute. This fact is generally put down to a lack of time, but there may also have been a more fundamental reason linked to the composition itself: in reality it would likely have taken him just a few hours to write a part for the piano once the problems he mentions had been overcome, maybe with the aid of the numerous sheets of calculations and notes he had already written and that had likely taken up much of the limited time available. Also the percussion part was reduced to a single stroke on the cymbal. The piece that was heard in Darmstadt on July 21 [copy at the *Centro Studi Maderna*, Section B 52] is clearly divided into three parts: the first is a montage on tape of three melodic lines indicated in the manuscript as flute, electronics and piano, all three played on the Melochord over a base of light electronic sounds (some of which were probably prepared by Meyer-Eppler); part B is a very "discursive" and agreeable solo for live flute; part C is almost entirely made up of electronic sounds of varying timbres, but mainly in the form of regular beats alternated with disjointed noises. In the coda, after the stroke on the suspended cymbal, the only remnant of the originally planned percussion part, the flute reappears, with a particular timbre on the Melochord – all this in the space of around nine minutes.

The performance made a considerable impact, especially on account of its combination of traditional instruments and artificially built sounds, and the singularity of the experiment continued to be a topic of interest for many months afterwards. The following year, on October 28, Maderna wrote an urgent letter to Steinecke asking him to send a copy of his tape of *Musica su due dimensioni* to Dr. Wohlgensinger of Zurich Radio, and to do so as soon as possible. We understand, then, that Maderna was by no means disappointed with the outcome of the work – on the contrary, he wanted to circulate the work, in other words promote it. But this was not to happen, because Steinecke tells him he had sent his tape to Radio France in Paris, who intended to include it in their *Centre de Documentation de Musique Internationale* (letter of October 31, 1953). However, shortly afterwards (November 2), Steinecke wrote to him again to say that he had found a copy of the tape (or the original) at Radio Frankfurt [the three letters cited can be read in *Carteggio* 2001, 81-85]. The extent to which this tape was initially appreciated is surely of no small significance, despite the fact that six years later Maderna composed another work that used the same title, but was totally different.

In his essay titled "Maderna e il mezzo elettronico," in *Studi* 1989, Alvise Vidolin writes that *Musica su due dimensioni* is "one of the very first works of mixed music." And this is undoubtedly the most remarkable aspect of the composition, but not the only one. Nicola Scaldaferri's painstaking reconstruction for the critical edition of 2002 clearly reveals moments of "free choice," both in the flute part and in the intersection with the tape, thus allowing us to assign another "first" to the piece, that of being the first "open work" in Maderna's output. But several years later, when his very different and highly successful work of the same name appeared, much water had passed under the bridges of Paris, Darmstadt, Cologne and especially Milan, where the *Studio di Fonologia* had been set up. In other words, when Maderna decided to return to the idea of contraposing the two "dimensions," only the title remained of the former piece, whereas the compositional idea changed radically. The practice of combining electronic and live sounds was no longer a novelty – other composers had followed the same route, with even greater ambitions, as we will see later.

After the end of the Darmstadt courses (July 24, 1952) Bruno went back to Venice, for what reason we do not know, but it was there, in August, that he was visited by Harro Dicks, maybe to discuss the staging of a new work, probably the ballet they both had in mind. In fact, some of the literary and musical material of the ballet *Das eiserne Zeitalter* ("The Age of Iron") on a text by Egon Vietta, to which Harro Dicks also contributed, dates from that very period.[25] Egon Vietta had settled in Darmstadt precisely in 1952, working as a consultant to Dicks at the Landestheater Rudolf Sellner and collaborating with him until 1955. This new figure in the literary scene of the town did not go unnoticed, since he brought with him his fame as an authoritative critic (he had recently published the philosophical work *The question of being in Martin Heidegger* in Stuttgart) and as director of the journal *Das Neue Forum*, in which he helped to sustain the idea of experimental and avant-garde tendencies in the sphere of theater, dance and the plastic arts, perfectly in line with the cultural plan of the *Ferienkurse*. Maderna probably met him through Dicks, and the three artists soon established a close working relationship, as can be gathered, for example, from a note written by Vietta at the bottom of one of the three manuscripts that have transmitted the text of the ballet: "This ballet, born in collaboration with my friend Bruno Maderna, was nurtured by an idea of Harro Dicks – the metamorphosis of Theseus."[26] The idea of working

---

[25] See *Documenti* 1985, 206. Vietta is the *nom de plume* of the writer, journalist and critic Karl Egon Fritz (1903-1959). In 1952, Harro Dicks had started teaching a course on musical theater direction at the *Ferienkurse* [*Chronik* 1997, 552].

[26] Maurizio Romito wrote a detailed article on *Das eiserne Zeitalter* in *Musica/Realtà*, 10 (April 1983), 63-69.

on a subject linked to an ancient myth must surely have attracted Maderna, as he too had recently fallen under the spell of antiquity: think, for example, of his *Liriche greche* of 1949, and the *Seikilos Epitaph* that opens *Composizione n. 2*. In this case the setting of the original tale of Ariadne, Theseus and the Minotaur was transported into an unlikely visionary future, involving robots, automatons and machines, which multiplied the number of characters and made them quite extraneous to the original context. And on reading this libretto one cannot help thinking of certain scenes from Maderna's future *Hyperion*.[27] Besides the three manuscripts mentioned above (one of which is by Maderna himself), a score has survived that is practically complete, divided into three parts and with a large number of sketches and other materials in preparation for a new phase of the project – which, however, never actually materialized.

After his meeting with Dicks, Maderna does not appear to have stayed much longer in Venice, also because no performances of his music were scheduled for the Biennale of that year and neither was he involved as a conductor. So it is likely that he soon went back to Darmstadt, where he would be reunited with Christine, and could also work on various projects for new works. However, over and above his understandable wish to be close to his young friend, it should also be remembered that Maderna no longer had his own home in Venice and was staying with another family as a lodger; and, as we have mentioned, his work as a teacher at the conservatory had come to an end. From this moment on, then, Maderna is a "man with a suitcase," a "freelancer," with neither a fixed job nor a permanent home.

The assumption that he returned to Darmstadt that autumn is further supported by the increasing number of engagements he took on as a conductor, many of which were in German territory. In between the seven performances at the Landestheater, featuring *Amphiparnaso* and *Carmina Burana*,[28] Maderna conducted various different orchestras: on September 17 he worked with the Münchener Philharmoniker to make a recording for the Bayerischer Rundfunk, and on October 7 he made another recording in Zurich for Radio Beromünster. On October 11 we find him in Rome for a concert at S. Cecilia, where his interpretation of Brahms was met with great enthusiasm by Nono, who speaks about it in his previously mentioned letter to Scherchen (see note 21). From November 7 to 10 he was in Barcelona and on November 14 in Heidelberg [*Romito* 2020]. But despite his constant travels, Darmstadt must still have been his main base of work. It was from here that Maderna wrote several letters to Nono, which

---

[27] Romito's study mentioned in the previous note also points out some basic aspects of the musical writing, such as the manipulation of the rhythms and the use of particular melodic materials.

[28] The concerts were held on September 19, 21 and 22, November 21 and December 13, 18 and 29 [*Romito* 2020].

provide valuable details about his private and professional life in this period. On October 23, still in 1952, he tells him with great self-satisfaction that he is working on the ballet – using its Italian title *L'età del ferro* – and that he has come up with an "interesting, simple and new" rhythmic idea, which could perhaps be taught to his pupil-friends in Venice.[29] From this letter, and also from the next, we learn of his nostalgia for what he liked to refer to as the "Venice school." The state of mind of a person that has decided to "change his life," but has not forgotten his recent close associations, also emerges from a letter he had written to Steinecke some months before (February 23) concerning the preparations for the concert programs of that year's *Ferienkurse*, in which he proposes replacing the works by Zafred with an important piece by Renzo Dall'Oglio [*Carteggio* 2001, 46-47].

On November 25 Maderna wrote two more letters to Nono (and this assiduous correspondence surely testifies to the deep bond of friendship that had developed between the two musicians). In the first letter he gives more news about his work on the ballet, which he appears to have taken much to heart, and in the second he gives an ample description of the concert he conducted on November 8 in Barcelona. He speaks of Chavez's *Toccata* and the astonishment of the audience who were unaccustomed to hearing contemporary music. But above all he describes his impressions on meeting the young people determined to struggle against Franco's regime. He appears to have stayed in Spain until November 11, and then towards the end of the month, as he tells Nono in another letter, he went to Bielefeld with Christine to visit a friend of hers, a competent pianist with whom he played some unfamiliar duets by Schubert and Mozart, on a brand new Steinway. He was so struck by this experience that he suggested to Nono that they should orchestrate these pieces together. After taking his leave of Christine (whom he always refers to in his letters as "Chris," implying that Nono too had become a close friend) Bruno continued northwards, where in Oldenburg he gave a concert of early romantic music: Beethoven and various works by Mendelssohn. The orchestra, Maderna recounts, was highly responsive, just like that of Darmstadt, and the two towns were even similar to one another in some respects. Maderna appears to have been overwhelmed by the beauty of this music, as if he were hearing it for the first time – maybe his frame of mind at that particular moment allowed him to appreciate this well known music in a different, more radiant way. This is yet another sign of how his frequent visits to Darmstadt, as documented by numerous public performances, and more especially the fact of having Christine at his side, had a significant effect on his life. It is no coincidence that in the above-mentioned

---

[29] On page 68 of the essay cited in note 26, Romito reproduces two examples of the rhythmic pattern for the ballet, prepared by Maderna but taken from the *Polonaise et Double* of J. S. Bach's *Suite in B minor* BWV 1067.

letter to Nono he defines 1952 as "the year of *Erlebnisse*," of deep experiences [the four letters cited are reproduced in *Extraits* 2007, 493-495].

In 1953, though maintaining a close association with Darmstadt, Maderna appears to have spent most of his time in Italy, not in Venice, but now in Verona at the home of his adopted mother Irma Manfredi. In the first letter he writes to Steinecke (January 21, 1953), he describes how hard it is to promote "true" music in Italy, both in theaters and at the RAI. He tells his friend (this is the first letter where he addresses Steinecke using the familiar "tu" form) that with the help of Barbara Giuranna, who for the past year had been recommending him to various music institutions, he had managed to obtain engagements for two concerts in Naples, this time in programs that included Petrucci's *Odhecaton* and Boulez's *Poliphonie X*. Maderna was probably confident that his choice of pieces would be well received, seeing that, despite all difficulties, some sort of change seemed to be taking place in the cultural institutions situated in Naples. Indeed, browsing through the issues of *Rassegna Musicale* of that year, one can note that a certain sector of the Neapolitan public was trying to shake off the old conservative listening habits and was starting to appreciate the rare efforts of the organizers to rejuvenate the repertory, well exemplified by the recent success of Schönberg's opera *Von heute auf morgen*.[30] Later in the same letter to Steinecke, Maderna recounts that thanks to Ferdinando Ballo – who had been director of the Biennale Musica in Venice until the previous year – and the support of Petrassi and Turchi, he was working on plans for a concert in Rome. But although he had various prospects for concerts elsewhere, as well as proposals for the premiere of the ballet, his main priority still appears to have been the Darmstadt courses. However, his relations with Darmstadt were still unclear, and so he asked his friend Steinecke to intercede through Sellner:[31]

> I've written to Sellner and asked him for an official invitation for the next Kranichstein festival. No reply. Here I have much to do and have many proposals for spring-summer, in Switzerland and in France too. [...] I don't wish to be arrogant, but Sellner must understand that I am not the permanent conductor of Darmstadt. I cannot turn down all the invitations just for a hypothetical engagement from Sellner. It really is impossible and I must tell you that if, within 10 days, I don't receive an official reply, I will unfortunately be forced to cancel our plans for Darmstadt this year [*Carteggio* 2001, 68-71].

---

[30] See *La Rassegna Musicale*, 23 (1953), 59.

[31] Gustav Rudolf Sellner, as Wilhelm Schlüter points out (see note 19), was not just superintendent of the Landestheater in Darmstadt, but also of the Deutsche Oper in Berlin.

In the meantime he continued to stay in touch with the world of cinema, in particular with the director Antonio Leonviola, with whom he had already worked in 1951 for the film *Le due verità*, in which he had successfully managed – and with decidedly interesting results – to underline the director's narrative intentions through his music.[32] Despite the critical (and also commercial) failure of Max Calandri's films *I misteri di Venezia* and *Il moschettiere fantasma* in 1952, one year later Maderna accepted Leonviola's invitation to write music for his film *Noi cannibali*, which turned out to be fairly well received. Other interesting ventures into this field include his music for the film *Opinione pubblica* directed by Maurizio Corgnati and for Charles Vildrac's television play *Padri nemici*.[33] Although Maderna dedicated himself assiduously to this type of work, which would continue in the years that followed with countless, and often noteworthy, productions for the radio, television, theater and cinema, in a letter to Nono he referred to this side of his work with a note of colorful sarcasm: "il faut que je gagne ma vie et je ne peux faire pour le moment qu'en composant de la merde pour de films" [undated letter, but probably from January-February 1953, translated in *Extraits* 2007, 496].

In the same period he continued to strengthen and consolidate his relations with the intellectual world of Milan. He learned from Nono that Piero Santi was interested in writing articles on the "dodecaphonists" for the journal *Il Diapason* [ibid., 498]; and Maderna may well have also been attracted by the political leaning of the magazine *Il Ponte* directed by Piero Calamandrei from 1945 to 1955. Maderna's political views had long been oriented toward the left: as we have seen, in 1952 he became a member of the Italian Partito Comunista, but he was nevertheless not insensitive to the liberal-socialist ideals promoted in this magazine. As far as music is concerned – as can also be gathered from the articles appearing in *Rassegna Musicale* – the world of music institutions (and of certain official critics like Guglielmo Barblan) remained firmly rooted in the more traditional repertory. However, tentative signs of an opening to new ideas were not lacking: for example, the staging of Richard Strauss's *Die Liebe der Danae* at La Scala, and performances of Ettore Desderi's *Architetture di Cattedrali* and Bruno Bettinelli's *Concerto da Camera* at the concerts of the Pomeriggi Musicali. Encouraged by these albeit timid signs, Maderna proposed to Antonio Ghiringhelli, superintendent of La Scala, the idea of staging the premiere of his ballet *L'età del ferro* and a one-act opera based on García Lorca's *Don Perlimplin*, insinuating that the theater in Darmstadt had already shown an interest in these

---

[32] L. Izzo, "Il commento sonoro realizzato da Bruno Maderna per il film *Le due verità*," in *Bruno Maderna. Studi e testimonianze*, eds. R. Dalmonte, M. Russo (Lucca: LIM, 2004), 299-341.

[33] Details of the films are taken from: G. Mangini, "Filmographie commentée," *Basalte* 1 2007, 229-237. For the television play, see *Romito* 2000/2, 249.

works [letter of June 6, 1953, ibid., 497]. Given that the ballet was still not finished (and unfortunately never would be) and the opera had not yet been started, one cannot help but admire the young composer's entrepreneurial spirit.

Whether or not the official invitation ever arrived is hard to say, but we do know that after conducting the concert he had long been planning with Ballo in Rome on July 8, he shortly afterwards arrived in Darmstadt, on July 16 (the first day of the courses), and on the last day of the series, July 30, he conducted "half" a concert. In fact, on the same evening, and despite Maderna's protests, Wolfgang Fortner, one of the founders of the *Ferienkurse* who had assumed various roles over the past years, conducted Bartók's *Divertimento* and his own cantata *Mitten des Lebens*, while Maderna concluded the evening by conducting his own cantata *Vier Briefe* and Milhaud's *La mort d'un tyran*.[34] Just how important Darmstadt was to him can be gleaned from the fact that, in order to take part in this concert (despite having to share it with Fortner!) he had not hesitated to cancel an engagement in Florence and had taken it upon himself to personally procure the score of Milhaud's work (premiered in Venice the year before). Presumably one of the reasons why he felt so strongly about going to Darmstadt was because he wanted to perform a new work that he had put much effort into and had dedicated to the Kranichstein institute: the original title of *Vier Briefe* had in fact been *Kranichsteiner Kammerkantate*. Although from 1949 the famous summer courses had been moved to Marienhöhe, concerts continued to be held in the hall of Kranichstein castle and the various venues were known collectively as the Kranichsteiner Musikinstitut. So he often referred to the piece in his correspondence as the *Krakaka* or the *Kranichsteiner Kammerkantate*.

The texts set to music in the *Vier Briefe* not only reflect the ideological stance inherited from his experience in Venice in the company of Nono, but were also highly topical. The first letter (for bass) had appeared in 1952 in a book published by Einaudi and edited by Piero Malvezzi and Giovanni Pirelli: *Lettere di condannati a morte della Resistenza italiana*. Maderna was immediately aware of the particular significance of this work and was the first to focus on a theme that was subsequently taken up by Fellegara in 1954 and by Nono in 1955-56.[35] The second piece is made up of a first episode (for bass) in which a German industrialist affirms to a colleague that the practice of sacking workers, no matter how painful at a human level, is necessary for the "higher cause" of economic progress; in the second, shorter episode (for soprano) a well-to-do woman invites a friend to join her on a vacation in the Riviera. The text of the third piece was similarly published in 1952, in a German book containing

---

[34] *Chronik*, 565.
[35] Vittorio Fellegara, *Lettere di condannati a morte della resistenza italiana* for narrators, choir and orchestra; Luigi Nono *Il canto sospeso*.

Franz Kafka's *Letters to Milena* (published two years later by Mondadori in an Italian translation) and Maderna had been struck by an imaginary love letter, which he now set for soprano. The fourth and final letter is taken from Antonio Gramsci's *Lettere dal carcere* published by Einaudi in 1947 and contains two intense personal accounts about his life in prison.[36] Maderna's choice of texts not only reflect his close attention to the political and literary issues of his time, but also follow a carefully planned dramaturgical sequence in the alternation of the letters and their diverse musical setting.

The instrumentation is for chamber ensemble: 4 woodwinds, 1 horn, 9 strings and a large battery of percussion and keyboard instruments; all the instruments are exploited so as to create a wide range of effects in terms of timbre and dynamics. In this case the basic numerical structure is not taken from a dodecaphonic series, but from "Fischia il vento", a famous song of the Italian resistance, particularly well known at the time. Nicola Verzina points out that in 1952 Nono had used Andalusian rhythms and "Bandiera rossa" in a similar way in his *Epitaffio per Federico García Lorca*, and in a later article analyzes Maderna's sketches for *Vier Briefe* in order to reconstruct the mathematical mechanism used to derive the pitches and durations of the score from the notes of the song.[37] "Fischia il vento" has sixteen measures and Maderna divided them into four segments of four measures; each of them was then used as the numerical matrix for each of the four songs. For example, the first letter is built on the ten notes of the first line ("Fi-schiail-ven-toin-fu-ria-la-bu-fe-ra"), which involves four pitches (D-E-F-A) and three durations (eighth-note, quarter-note and dotted quarter-note). The notes of the song are transformed on the basis of numerical calculations: Maderna built a square of ten horizontal by ten vertical numbers organized in a sequence. The result obtained from this mechanism changed the familiar order of the notes of the song and destroyed their metrical framework as well as their tonal organization. The song is obviously no longer recognizable, but its presence retained its symbolic value.

Although the *Vier Briefe* could be said to sound like a work of the radical avant-garde, Maderna has allowed himself the privilege of adding certain "subjective" elements to the severity of the fundamental construction. In the first letter, written by a man condemned to death, the instruments alternate

---

[36] Details about the publication of the texts are taken from Nicola Verzina's introduction to the critical edition: *Maderna* 2003.

[37] Nicola Verzina, "Musica e impegno nella *Kranichsteiner Kammerkantate* (1953): il tema della libertà," in *Bruno Maderna. Studi e testimonianze*, cited in note 32, 199-225. Id., "Tecnica della mutazione e tecnica seriale in *Vier Briefe* (1953) di Bruno Maderna," *Rivista Italiana di Musicologia*, 34/2 (1999), 309-345.

between a thick texture and percussive rhythms, while the voice declaims isolated syllables with no apparent association with the words; in the letter of the industrialist, the bareness of the spoken line accompanied by ironic punctuations on the piano, has the effect of underlining the violence of the words; Kafka's love letter deliberately contrasts the previous section with its light timbre and the sweetness of the female voice in its high register; and finally Gramsci's letter concludes the series with the austere rigidity of its construction and the ghostly echoes of a female voice that dialogues wordlessly with the bass.

The cantata is a clear example of what the composer meant when he spoke of New Music being a synthesis between the construction of new materials and the manifestation of human values. On this matter, it is worth pointing out that the influence of politics on musical culture was a particularly Italian phenomenon mainly deriving from the post-war contrasts between the parties on the left and the Christian Democrats; the young generation of Germans tended to avoid any resonances of their recent political past, while French music was perhaps more inspired by an anti-conformist and anti-bourgeois spirit than by political ideals. In this sense Maderna's approach, like that of Nono, reveals a cultural identity that is quite distinct from the general context of the Darmstadt tendencies.

Besides the premiere of the *Vier Briefe*, the courses of 1953 featured various other interesting events. Among these, the conferences and concerts dedicated to the figure of Webern deserve particular mention. It was here that the famous quarrels broke out between Stockhausen (supported by Boulez and Goyvaerts) and Nono about the interpretation of Webern's poetics: the former insisted that he had totally purified music by pushing it far beyond the approach advocated by Schönberg; whereas Nono (and some days later Maderna too expressed the same opinion) believed that Webern was a highly sensitive musician and not a cold calculator. Other memorable moments include Messiaen's conference on his own musical language ("Birds were my first and greatest teachers. I have never abandoned their school") and the performance of Honegger's *Antigone* directed by Harro Dicks and sung by Christa Ludwig. Maderna gave a talk on Radio Frankfurt titled "Positions and possibilities of new music today" during which he clearly pointed out the two directions that young composers could choose between: that of experimentation, mainly supported by Boulez and Stockhausen, and that of expression, as Nono had underlined [*Trudu* 1992, 86-89 passim]. This brief summary of two weeks of concerts and discussions provides further evidence that to speak of a "Darmstadt school" would be totally misleading, since in reality the true "school" was precisely the opportunity to compare, without constrictions or opportunisms, the most diverse variety of positions.

Although it is not clear when Maderna left Darmstadt after the end of the courses (July 30), several clues and reports suggest that he spent some time in Milan, where – among other things – increasing attention was being paid to the radio, its language, and its technical and expressive possibilities, an interest that would soon lead to the creation of the groundbreaking *Studio di Fonologia*. And it was in Milan that Maderna met Luciano Berio, who since 1950 had settled in the city with Cathy Berberian. The romance between Luciano and Cathy was almost novel-like, and was just as intense as it was short-lived. He was from Liguria, and had come to Milan to study composition at the Conservatory; he was penniless and alone like all students far from their family and circle of friends. She was of Armenian origin but was born in Massachusetts; she had started studying History of Theater at Columbia University and while in New York had befriended groups of Armenian dancers; she had come to Milan in 1949 to study singing, attracted by the world of Italian opera. As well as receiving help from her family, she was also supported by a Fulbright scholarship. They were both born in 1925, and were both highly talented and full of enthusiasm. They first met when Berberian asked Berio to become her accompanist, and shortly afterwards (in 1950) they married in Como and decided to settle down in Milan. Their peculiar skills and diverse but converging interests soon made the couple a point of reference for those working in the theater and radio, as well as for critics and writers, whether living in Milan or simply passing through the city. Their wide group of friends and colleagues included such names as Umberto Eco, John Cage, Roberto Leydi and other members of the Milan intelligentsia.[38] Maderna too was fascinated by the couple and all they were involved in, and his friendship with them may well have been among the many reasons why he eventually made Milan his second base for his work, alongside Darmstadt. And his association with Luciano and Cathy would soon lead to the creation of the *Studio di Fonologia* and to a variety of projects involving the radio, a collaboration that lasted throughout the

---

[38] For further details, see A. I. De Benedictis, N. Scaldaferri, "Berberian Cathy" in *Dizionario biografico degli Italiani*, Treccani (2014), sub voce. Here we would like to supplement the "official" portrait of Berberian with a few details dating from her last years of life, when the authors of this book had the fortune of being able to meet her in person. Rossana Dalmonte visited her in the hope of obtaining some first-hand information about Berio and Maderna. "The first thing that struck me about her," Dalmonte recounts in a radio interview, "was her 'cordiality': right from the moment I entered her home in Milan she treated me like a friend, with no hint of any airs or graces. Another trait that soon emerged was her 'generosity' in accepting to share her time and thoughts with me. She tended to avoid any talk of her health (it was autumn 1980) and tried to keep our conversation to lighter matters. At a certain point I happened to mention that we often went to Mantua to visit Mario's family and Cathy seemed to brighten up at the thought of the culinary delights offered by the city, so we decided to go there together to eat with some of Mario's friends at the restaurant 'Il Cigno.' As well as enjoying a couple of excellent dinners, our trip also included a recital at the Teatro Scientifico, during which I presented my book *Luciano Berio. Intervista sulla musica* recently published by Laterza, and Cathy gave an incredible rendition of her *Stripsody* and some songs by the Beatles, as recalled in the obituary that appeared in *La Gazzetta di Mantova* on March 17, 1983."

'50s. His work with Berberian went even further, culminating in the performance of *Ausstrahlung* at the court of the Shah of Persia.

However, Maderna apparently found it hard to stay in the same place for very long and soon left Milan to return to Verona, as we gather from his correspondence with Steinecke regarding *Musica su due dimensioni*. But neither does he appear to have stayed very long in Verona, given that in his previously mentioned letter of October 28, 1953, he fixes an appointment with Steinecke for a concert in the *Musica Viva* series in Heidelberg, which was scheduled for November 23. In the same letter he informs his friend that he would hear a "good piece" on that occasion: the piece in question was certainly *Improvvisazione n. 2*, which was composed while in Verona, as he himself confirms in a curriculum provided for Darmstadt.

The new work was performed in Venice on September 17, 1954 conducted by Nino Sanzogno.[39] Compared to *Improvvisazione n. 1*, written more than a year before, a marked difference in style is quite evident. The earlier piece still contained certain vestiges, albeit vague, of tradition (which also played an important expressive role), whereas in the new work there are no traces of macro-formal repetitions or pseudo-melodies: the whole construction is based on rigorously and minutely atomized and punctiform structures. In other words, Maderna's invention is now more aligned with what was predominantly presented as "new" at Darmstadt. The micro-structures of the work, as Verzina pointed out in his analysis, derive from a basic series to which Maderna applied a process of numerical mutation, giving rise to many dozens of new series which are gradually integrated within the composition to produce the individual instrumental parts.[40] But other aspects (especially the dynamics and the attacks) were added quite freely in the score, and also the agogic and metronome markings retain their independence from the serial calculations. It could therefore be affirmed that also in *Improvvisazione n. 2* the composer has not totally capitulated to a rationale of objectivism or impersonality.

The score contains a series of particularly significant markings: the work opens with an *Impetuoso* (mm. 1-27) followed by an *Andante* and an *Adagio*. A successive *Concitato* and then *Allegro* (mm. 56-101) dissolve in turn into a *Tranquillo* and an *Intimo* (mm. 102 -120). Lastly, after a long pause, there is an episode marked *Solenne*, which starts **ff** and then slowly ebbs into a final *Calmo*. These indications are not, then, purely agogic, but imply well defined expressive

---

[39] Concert program in *Centro Studi Maderna*, Section D 7.4.

[40] N. Verzina, "Procedimenti di costruzione ed elaborazione del materiale in *Improvvizione n.2* (1953) di Bruno Maderna," *Mitteilungen der Paul Sacher Stiftung*, 9 (März 1996), 50-55; and Id., "Improvvisazione n. 2 (1953) de B. Maderna. Technique sérielle dans les esquisses. Génétique intervallaire et élaboration du matérieau," *Les Cahiers du CIREM. Centre International de Recherches en Esthetique Musicale*, 40-41 (1997), 156-161.

characters which correspond to quite specific moments within the elaboration of the serial material. The macro-form of the work (that is to say, the linear organization of the musical time) thus involves three peaks of energy: a strong opening, a quite lively central section and the start of the impressive finale, and these all fade into more reflective zones.

It was again Verona – as Maderna specifically indicates on the score – that saw the birth of the *Divertimento in due tempi per flauto e pianoforte*. This short piece was not published at the time and neither does it appear to have been performed: there is a suggestion that it may have been performed, perhaps in Italy, in November 1953, but this is unconfirmed.[41] The sketches contain evidence of serial calculations that Maderna appears unwilling to renounce even in a work that he conceived as a "divertimento" in the classical sense of the term, but also as a piece (according to tradition) that the performers will enjoy playing and that would not prove too challenging for the listener. The first of the two movements, the longest and lightest, starts with points of isolated notes set within a thin texture, which then gradually thickens and reaches a lively climax in the central section, full of staccato notes and rhythmic patterns. The movement closes with short melodic figures and light chords that the composer asks to be played *delicatamente*. The second movement, is an *Allegro* that opens with a certain harshness, and then light-heartedly – and not without a touch of irony – presents hints of "antique fineries," reduced to minimum gestures. Maderna is evidently making a provocative reference to the past that would probably not have gone down too well in the very serious Darmstadt environment (in which the piece never appeared). Interestingly, a similar evocation of antique fineries reappears, and is systematically exploited, in his later *Serenata n. 2*.

Maderna is clearly working on various fronts, but at the end of the letter to Steinecke of October 28 one can perceive a certain nostalgia for the company of his German colleagues: "I would like to talk to you about many things, and I am happy to be able to do so next month in Germany." In the following letter, after repeating how he is looking forward to seeing him for the concert in Heidelberg, he adds "and maybe for a few days in Darmstadt." In the meantime he was working on a new piece for the coming season of concerts at the summer courses, a *Concerto per flauto* dedicated to Steinecke and to the flutist Severino Gazzelloni, who was enthusiastic about the project. To sum up, Maderna appears to have spent the first part of 1953, up until the *Ferienkurse*, in Italy, and especially in Verona (from where he sent most of his letters) and Milan. In October his letters

---

[41] This information comes from the introduction to the critical edition by Francesca Magnani: *Maderna* 1996. The first certain performance (by Anna Maria Morini and Valeria Cantoni) took place in 1984.

are again sent from Verona, leading us to conclude that it was not until November that he returned to Germany and stayed there for any long period of time.

In 1954 he was frequently in Milan, but also elsewhere, though it is hard to stay for how long. An important date is April 10, when Scherchen – at the invitation of Boulez – conducted the first version of *Serenata* during the cycle of the Domaine Musicale in Paris. The new work is dedicated to Scherchen, who arranged for it to be published that year by *Ars Viva*, the publishing house he himself had founded. The composition was most likely written between the end of 1953 and the start of 1954. The piece was subsequently subject to a long and complicated story that went on for at least two years and finally concluded with a second shorter version, titled *Serenata n. 2*, which was published by Suvini Zerboni in 1957. Since the second version came to be considered the definitive one, we will wait until we reach the year in question before offering a description of the work.

At the end of April he is in Verona for a concert at the Auditorium Montemezzi [*Romito* 2020] and he is there again at the start of July, from where he writes to Steinecke reassuring him about his work on the *Concerto per flauto* and to tell him about his forthcoming engagements: in mid-July he will be recording a concert for the Bayerischer Rundfunk in Munich featuring ancient Italian music by Vivaldi, Scarlatti and Veracini, and "afterwards I might come to Darmstadt" [*Carteggio* 2001, 86-87]. But at the end of July he is back in Verona, from where he writes another letter to Steinecke: he is finding it hard to finish the *Concerto per flauto*, a fact that appears to have caused no small difficulty for those who were waiting for the score so as to begin rehearsing the piece. It also created problems for Steinecke, who wanted to include the work's premiere in the official program of the *Ferienkurse* (that year held from August 12 to 27) and needed to know the exact title and how many parts it was divided into. And poor Ernst Bour, who was due to conduct the work, found himself in desperate straits, as he tells Steinecke in a letter of August 4: "[... so far I have received]: a) a telegram on July 29th: 'score of *Concerto per flauto* sent by express mail letter will follow'; b) 40 pages of score sent on the 30th and that arrived on August 2nd; c) another 16 pages sent on the 31st and that arrived on August 2nd, so a total of 56 pages without the ending" [ibid., 88-89]. The flutist Gazzelloni must have found himself in a similar situation, and yet, almost by miracle, the work was successfully performed on the evening of August 22 in the *Stadthalle* in Darmstadt. It should be added that while Bour was anxiously awaiting the score, in the first days of August Maderna was at the Auditorium in Turin recording a concert with the Orchestra Sinfonica della RAI [*Romito* 2003, 99].

The *Concerto per flauto* marks a culminating point in the experiments with serial techniques that Maderna had long been working on. Indeed, the language of this work not only obeys the principle of calculating pitches and durations applied to previous compositions, but could be defined as radically "pointillistic," to use a term much in vogue at the time. Once again, though, the micro-formal structure, which is based on this type of system, should be distinguished from the macro-form, which follows paths that are partially independent of the procedure. Certainly, Manfred Böhlen, who carried out a meticulous study of the general form of the concerto, observed the presence of an extraordinary quantity of numerical regularities that Maderna adhered to in planning the relation between the number of measures belonging to each section of the piece and the type of time signature assigned to each measure (for example, the 3/16, 5/16, 4/16 with which the piece begins).[42] Of the ten parts that make up the concerto (all distinguished in the score with double bar lines) three are in the form of a "Tutti" for full orchestra, and seven (1 +3 +3) in the form of pieces for flute soloist and instruments. And this "Vivaldian" alternation is not just visible on paper, but is perfectly perceptible to the listener. The "Tutti," in the first third and seventh parts, are characterized not only by the use of the full orchestra, but also by violent dynamic outbursts and a constant alternation between different instrumental groups. The first and third "Tutti" are mostly dominated by a pervasive use of sixteenth-notes, producing a sense of impetuous rhythmic vitality. The seven episodes featuring the flute soloist are marked by a distinct contrast with the parts for orchestra. Although it is too early to speak of the extravagant form of experimentation that would later be known as *Gazzellonimusik*, the constant and delicate interventions of the flute nevertheless exploit a wide range of contrasting effects: long held notes, staccatos, trills, flowing passages and tremolos, in a style of writing that is never ostentatious but always highly sophisticated. The intervention of the orchestra in these episodes is, in general, minutely fragmented, unobtrusive and with refined timbres. The ninth episode (the longest section, lasting for three of the eight total minutes) is characterized by an explicitly slower tempo, almost a sort of concerto-style Adagio, and is immersed in a subdued atmosphere, with particularly rich and exquisitely molded interventions in both the solo and orchestral parts. In the tenth and concluding episode, the rapid sixteenth-notes reappear, almost like an echo of the opening, until finally dying out at the end of the piece; but there is no sense of tension in the solo passages, where a suspended and meditative climate prevails. What distinguishes this work from his previous compositions is the lack of alternation between moments of expectation and of tension, which tended to hold the listener's attention. The linear narration has disappeared and has given way to long, static patches, or to temporal circularity.

---

[42] See M. J. Böhlen, "Nell'incantesimo del numero. Il *Flötenkonzert* di Maderna," in *Studi* 1989, 33-51.

Two days after the end of the *Ferienkurse* in 1954 Maderna is in Rome for a concert at the Basilica di Massenzio [*Romito* 2020], then in September he is in Venice, from where he gives Nono precise details of the Biennale and in particular of the positive critical reception of his *Improvvisazione n. 2* conducted by Nino Sanzogno in the concert of September 17 [*Extraits* 2007, 498]. In the same month, and in part of the following one, Maderna is working hard on his *Composizione in tre tempi*, and in fact on October 25 the publishers Suvini Zerboni urge him to send them the score, as it was needed by Hamburg Radio to prepare for the performance scheduled for the coming December. We have no way of knowing whether he managed to send the score immediately or continued working on it, but we do know that shortly afterwards he went to Milan, as he himself recounts in a letter to his mother. He writes that the plans to create the first Italian studio of electronic music at the headquarters of the RAI in Milan seemed to be going ahead, and adds that the superintendent of La Scala had invited him to compose a one-act opera. He also tells her that Ghedini had promised to help him convince Ricordi to publish the eighteenth century treatise by Padre Martini that he was in the process of editing.[43]

Maderna probably commuted between Milan and Verona, since it was from the latter city that he wrote a letter to Berio on November 13 that begins in a strangely formal manner: "Dear Berio." He goes on to tell him that he was unable to find him at the RAI and arranges to meet him the following Wednesday [*Centro Studi Maderna*, Section L 3]. And in fact, it was not long before they worked together on *Ritratto di città*. But before starting work with Berio in Milan, Maderna left Italy and towards the end of November was back in Hamburg, from where he wrote two very long and affectionate letters to Irma Manfredi. These letters reveal how closely he continued to share all aspects of his very busy life with his adoptive mother. First he gives precise details of the program of the concert in Hamburg: Zehden – *Les Chansons*; Varèse – *The Desert* [*sic*]; Stockhausen – *Kontrapunkte 1*; Maderna – *Composizione in tre tempi*. He then tells her how much he is looking forward to the event and that he will not only write the introduction but will also present it in person on the radio. He goes on to tell her about his life with Christine, who had joined him in Hamburg. Despite being in an advanced stage of pregnancy, Christine had decided to continue her work in the cinema [*Centro Studi Maderna*, Section L 3]. The mention of the town where the film was being shot allows us to identify it as a work by László Benedek, which would be released in March 1955 and was

---

[43] These last sentences offer a great deal of information: we learn that after taking part in the Biennale, Maderna went to Milan, and we also understand that his passion for ancient music was not totally compromised by his work on contemporary music, even though Martini's treatise was never published. See the letter to Irma Manfredi in *Centro Studi Maderna*, Section L 3.

quite well received. The film in question was translated and shown in various European languages, and it was released in the USA under the title *Sons, Mothers and a General*. In Italian it was called *All'est si muore*. It tells the stories of young men that were forced to go and fight on the Russian front during the Second World War, and of their mothers, who tried in vain to stop them. It was the fourth film that Christine had taken part in and her role within the cast seems to have become more important compared to her first appearances as an actress.

In the second letter, probably written not long afterwards, dated November 29, 1954 and written on the same headed paper as the last one, which shows us his address (Hotel Excelsior, Hamburg, An den Alster, 23), he first tells his mother how well the rehearsals are going for the concert, and then he asks her to write to a friend of hers in London who might be able to help with some legal matters concerning Christine. Next, he asks about the radio program *Storia della Dodecafonia* broadcast by the RAI on the 24th of the same month, wanting to know if they had talked about him and whether they had played one of his pieces. He was particularly interested in the program because it was presented by Roman Vlad, whom he would work with if the negotiations with the RAI went as planned. This brief mention seems to imply that Maderna had not completely abandoned the idea of settling in Milan. Finally, he asks Irma to get in touch with the director of the Istituto Musicale in Verona to propose a concert entirely devoted to Mozart, which he describes to her in detail.

At the time when he wrote these very interesting letters, Maderna was preparing for the concert in Hamburg on December 8 in which he would conduct the premiere of his *Composizione in tre tempi*. The work is based on three popular songs, in the same way as in *Vier Briefe*, and is divided into *Allegro – Adagio – Allegro*, following a pseudo-classical structure. The opening *Allegro* is built on a 3/8 meter that remains unchanged for over 200 measures, an incredible feat if we think of the intricate calculations of the *Concerto per flauto* in which the time signatures change from one measure to the next. This stability allows the composer (and especially the performer) to underline the constant presence of a rapid pulsation that continues unchanged throughout the whole movement, making it both vital and nervous. This vitality is further enhanced by the extraordinary range of timbres, mostly light, but made all the more fascinating by the vast array of small percussion instruments (over thirty), in addition to the piano, harp, mandolin and guitar. The movement concludes surprisingly with ironic and diatonic bursts on the trumpets, whose last three notes recall the closing notes of the popular song "Biondina in gondoleta", on which the piece is based. The second movement is an absolutely static *Adagio*, interspersed with very short, almost melodic phases on the strings (many of which on solo instruments and with mutes) and pervaded by the constant presence of the percussion, at first the light clapping of the castanets and *Rumbahölzer*, joined finally by four delicate triangles. The movement calls for a great deal of concentration, like listening to a mysterious nocturnal landscape, and one wonders whether the choice of the song "Splende la luna ciara" ("brightly shines the moon") has something to do with the character of the piece. Also the third movement, like the previous two, has a constant meter (in this case 2/4), apart from in a central episode dominated by the drums, glockenspiel and piano, together with the strings, which are used as percussion instruments. The most notable feature of the third movement, though, is the way the speed of the rhythm is maintained, while the regularity of the pulse is modified, systematically changing the duration patterns of the instrumental groups as they join in one after the other, and constantly introducing asymmetric accents. In the last part of the movement the rhythm accelerates and the mandolins and guitars vaguely allude to the melody of the song "L'alegrie la ven dai zoveni," making fun of the underlying severity of the mathematical structure. In some way, the role of the third movement appears to be similar to that of the lively Giga which often concludes the Suites in ancient music.

The summer concerts in Darmstadt that year also included Nono's *La victoire de Guernica*, based on the Communist anthem "L'internazionale". However, it differs from *Composizione in tre tempi* in that the three melodies used by Maderna have no underlying political connotations, but are simply three popular songs in the Veneto dialect. Nono was always more influenced by his social commitment whereas Maderna seems to have been more inclined towards a broader variety of expression. The character of Nono's piece for voice and orchestra, inspired by Picasso's *Guernica*, was extremely violent and almost expressionist, and the combination of singing and shouting anticipated the stylistic tendencies of his more politically engaged works of the following decade. Maderna's intentions were quite different and he explained them synthetically in the program notes for the concert in Hamburg. He remarks that "making music means living as men and not as vegetables," and he then mentions the "lyrical" power of his music (a term he often used as a synonym for communicative power), and stresses that this power in no way contradicts "the extreme precision of expression." His words are on the whole rather enigmatic, but the score and its excellent performance, of which we fortunately have a recording, may help to interpret their meaning.[44] Maderna seems to have been inspired by the eighteenth century formal model, but this has obviously little to do with neo-classicism and is perhaps linked to what he meant by "precision of expression," that is to say mathematical calculations.

[44] The Italian translation of the program notes was published by Maurizio Romito in *Studi* 1989, 66-67. The recording of the performance was sent to the *Centro studi Maderna* in the 1980s by the NWDR radio.

Such precision nevertheless left space for "living as men" (as he writes in the program notes) and was still able to incorporate a certain element of light irony.

Some days after the concert in Hamburg, Maderna was in Stockholm, from where, on December 14, he wrote a letter to Luigi Rognoni full of interesting details about his life and work. He says he will be staying in Stockholm until December 20 and afterwards can be contacted c/o Köpnik in Darmstadt, until January 8, when he will be leaving for Milan. He also mentions the success of the concert in Hamburg and in particular of his *Composizione in tre tempi*, which he says he intends to dedicate to the orchestra of the NWDR to mark his third year of participation in their concert series *Das Neue Werk*.[45] Also of note is the information he provides about the concerts of "repertory music" he will conduct in Stockholm and Copenhagen. He realizes, in fact, that his particular technical specialization in the contemporary repertory is not enough to fill his calendar as a conductor, so he will also have to look for engagements involving more traditional works. But above all he expresses his genuine disappointment at the delay in realizing the plans for the *Studio di Fonologia*. He urges him to do what he can and reassures him that it would not take too much money to set it up: they would just need four Magnetophons with three or four different speeds and a generator, which the Studio in Cologne could acquire for maximum of DM 5,000 (equal to around 750,000 Italian Lire), "this would really amount to nothing if you think of what we could do with it."[46]

---

[45] In his introduction to the critical edition of the *Composizione in tre tempi*, Edoardo Bruni states that the dedication "does not appear either in the score or in any other documents." See *Maderna* 2008, VI.

[46] L. Rognoni, "Memoria di Bruno Maderna negli anni Cinquanta," in *Documenti* 1985, 148-149. A copy of the letter is kept in the *Centro Studi Maderna*, Section L 8. 4, and was sent to us by the Fondo Rognoni of the Dipartimento Aglaia of Palermo University.

CHAPTER IV
MUSICA EX MACHINA

In following the events in the life and work of Maderna we have already noted that, at certain points in the story and for various different reasons, the changes that took place were so radical that we could speak of a "before" and an "after" with respect to a particularly significant circumstance. This phenomenon might sometimes be due to epochal facts like the end of the war, and at others to the appearance of a landmark composition such as the *Quartetto in due tempi*. Maderna not only put a particular amount of effort into the writing of this work, but he also went on to consider it as a sort of "opus one." So it seems appropriate to resume our account starting from the year of its composition, 1955, as if this marked the beginning of new era for the composer.

Returning to the letter that Maderna sent to Luigi Rognoni (Stockholm, December 14, 1954), we recall that he mentioned how early in the New Year he would leave Darmstadt and go to Milan. This fact is confirmed in an article written many years later by Luciano Berio, with reference to this period:

> Bruno was very often in Milan and we worked together in the same room, on two adjacent tables in an apartment in Via Monteceneri. In those years to make a living we wrote a lot of music for the radio and the theaters in Milan. This was often a joint effort: he worked on the strings, sitting down, and I dealt with the winds, standing behind him – in front of an astonished copyist who was waiting nearby. But Bruno also worked on his *Quartetto per archi* and I on my *Nones* for orchestra. In the *Quartetto in due parti* Bruno enthused about the idea of presenting two different readings of the same system of proportions of durations and intervals. A rigid and objective reading of the original serial structure in the first part, and, in the second part, a reverse reading, more selective and *lyrical* (as he himself said).[1]

By adding just a few extra details we can outline the main activities that occupied Maderna's life during the year 1955: incidental music for the radio, musical research at the *Studio di Fonologia della RAI* in Milan, and the composition of the *Quartetto in due tempi*. We can also add that his stay in Milan (after January 8) does not appear to have lasted very long, since on January 15 he was in

---

[1] L. Berio, "Un inedito di Bruno Maderna," *Nuova Rivista Musicale Italiana*, 12/4 (1978), 517.

Naples to record a concert entirely dedicated to Mozart at the Conservatorio San Pietro a Majella and then he almost certainly returned to Darmstadt in time for the birth of his daughter Caterina (February 28). How long he stayed within the domestic circle is hard to say. However, he was still in Darmstadt on March 11 when he wrote to Nono with news about the composition of the *Quartetto*. Work on the piece was going ahead at breakneck speed because Steinecke had commissioned it to mark the tenth anniversary of the *Ferienkurse*, which that year were being held unusually early: from May 29 to June 6. In April, an engagement in Venice to conduct two concerts, in which he was highly praised (news of which traveled as far as Darmstadt, as Steinecke mentions in a letter to Maderna dated May 8, 1955) and the need to attend to his works for radio, took him to Verona, where he was later joined by Christine – one supposes with their baby – to pay a visit to grandma Irma.

When he returned to Naples on May 16 to 17 to record a very varied program that included, among other things, Webern's *Variazioni per orchestra*, Berio's *Variazioni per orchestra da camera* and an *Ouverture per orchestra* by Donatoni [*Romito* 2003 /1, 100], he presumably traveled alone, but came back to Verona immediately afterwards and then set off with his family to Darmstadt for the start of the courses, stopping off in Ravenna on the way, for a reason that remains unknown. Here, at the end of her husband's letter about work (May 19), Christine tells Steinecke that she is bringing a lovely dress for his wife Hella, made by the tailor Manfredi, a sure sign of the friendship that had grown between the two families, over and above their working relations.[2]

Maderna's most significant role during the *Ferienkurse* of 1955 was the direction of the "International Study Group of Young Composers," which he had also held the year before, but this time he shared the task with Boulez and Henze [*Trudu* 1992, 358]. Another important event was documented by the newspaper *Der Mittag* June 5: Luigi Nono became engaged to Arnold Schönberg's daughter Nuria, who also attended the course in Darmstadt that year. We know that this was not merely an attempt to make news, as the couple were actually married that very year. A further memorable event among the circle of Italians was the performance of Maderna's *Quartetto in due tempi* during the concert dedicated to *Musik der Jungen Generation* given on the evening of June 1 by the Drolc Quartet [*Chronik*, 574].

In the weeks before the performance an intense exchange of letters took place between Maderna and Steinecke, who asked him several times for news about the work. In brief, on April 15 Maderna said he had started writing the parts for the performers and on May 19 he stated that the Drolc

---

[2] The letters cited here are reproduced in *Carteggio* 2001, 90-96.

Quartet had already had the parts of the second movement. Keeping in mind that the work was due to be performed on June 1 and that studying it was certainly no small affair, given that each note (and there were several hundreds of them) had a specific and very detailed performing direction, one can easily understand why the organizer was rather concerned. Maderna, on the other hand, tried to reassure his friend in his letters, adding how satisfied he was with the work he was writing: it was a completely new composition that he defined a "revolution in continuity," and even went as far as describing it as a work that made everything else he had written before seem kitsch. Such strong words were apparently not aimed solely at allaying his correspondent's worries – he appears to have been totally convinced of what he was saying, and this is also confirmed in Berio's previously mentioned article where he describes Maderna's extraordinary enthusiasm for the new piece.

But despite all these various communications, it is still not certain when the work was first conceived and how many months, or even years, it took to complete. Also Markus Fein laments the lack of information about this aspect in his Ph.D. dissertation on the work, which provided material for a long chapter of his book. Certainly, the huge quantity of notes and sketches present in the draft of the work could not have been thought of and written down in any short space of time. Fein has divided the sources he examined into three chronologically distinct groups: the first includes the drafting of the original series and the subsequent large number of numerical tables and graphs on squared paper dedicated to the systems of mutations that modify the forms of the initial series. The second group involves the transformation of the numbers into notes, which is derived from the numbers in two different tables referring respectively to the pitches and durations. The third and final group consists in drafts of the score and the parts, where we find not only the notes and rests but also dynamic and attack markings. These indications, however, do not appear to be based on the numerical calculations, but were chosen by the composer.[3] This particular aspect of the work would continue to be a source of discussion between Maderna, Berio and Nono for several years afterwards. In a letter to Nono of 1957 Berio states that the pitches and durations had been fixed, while the registers and dynamics had been decided case by case, along with the attack markings (pizzicato, frog, *legno*…) on the basis of a sort of "interior automatism."[4] This is obviously a personal opinion held by Berio, who had "felt" the quartet as a remarkable succession of sonorities.   But in trying

---

[3] M. Fein, *Die musikalische Poetik Bruno Madernas. Zum seriellen Komponieren zwischen 1951 und 1955* (Frankfurt am Main: Peter Lang, 2001), 134-136.

[4] Berio's letter is cited in V. Rizzardi, " La 'Nuova Scuola Veneziana' 1948-1951," in *Le musiche degli anni Cinquanta*, eds. G. Borio, G. Morelli, V. Rizzardi (Firenze: Olschki, 2004), 40.

to understand the logic underpinning the work, the use of the term "interior automatism" is extremely revealing. It seems to imply that the mechanism of using numerical series had become almost second nature to Maderna and that it now came automatically, to the extent that he spontaneously applied it to other parameters, such as the quality of the sound produced by the string instruments. Similar thoughts were expressed by Giacomo Manzoni, who claims that the notes chosen by Maderna are without any "particular meaning," but acquire sense only through the modalities of producing the sound. Moreover, he too suggests that the minute specifications given to each note stem from a sort of Freudian "automatism of the unconscious," which is precisely what Maderna, according to Berio, called "interior automatism."[5]

Over and above these undoubtedly authoritative observations, the most far-reaching studies on the *Quartetto*, by Horst Weber, Markus Fein and Christoph Neidhöfer, focus on the disproportionate number of serial calculations that Maderna made for the piece, probably between the last months of 1954 and the first months of 1955, despite the many other engagements that were keeping him busy.[6] Interestingly, all those who analyzed the work came up against the same seemingly unsolvable problem: at a certain point while composing the work, he decided that the quartet would be divided into two parts and that the second part would be the retrograde of the first. But this retrogradation is not so simple to reconstruct, not even with the aid of the most sophisticated analytical tools. It is almost as if Maderna had followed the example of his beloved Flemish composers who, in their days, amused themselves by creating enigmatic canons to test their colleagues.

Although many analysts have found vague and rather enigmatic traces of retrograde procedures in the work, none of them has yet been able to find a convincing answer to the question. The most likely solution is that Maderna had allowed himself some liberty in this phase of the work and had acted on the basis of purely musical considerations, relying perhaps on his "interior automatism." In his article the young Manzoni observes that the process of composition is constantly carried out "with the receptive capacity of the listener" in mind. He does not dwell too much on this point, but the idea of the need to maintain a relation between the structures of a composition and their listeners was taken up again and used

---

[5] G. Manzoni, "Bruno Maderna," *Die Reihe*, 4 (1958), 113-118.

[6] See H. Weber, "Form und Satztechnik in Bruno Madernas Streichquartett," in *Miscellanea del Cinquantenario* (Milano: Suvini Zerboni, 1978), 206-215. Weber's essay, as can be seen, was written shortly after Maderna's death. The two most exhaustive studies on the subject, though, are those by M. Fein (cited in note 3) and C. Neidhöfer, *Vers un principe commun. Intégration de la hauteur et du rhythme dans le Quartetto per archi in due tempi* (1955), *Basalte* 2 (2009), 323-358, who follows procedures similar to those used by Fein, although with slightly divergent results.

as the basis for a study carried out by the *Gruppo Analisi e Teoria Musicale* (GATM). At the start of the 2000s this Italian group of analysts created a subgroup devoted specifically to the analysis of contemporary music. The project involved a dozen or so experts in the field, but the results were then summarized in two articles written by Mario Baroni and Egidio Pozzi.[7] Both essays deal with the problem of how form is organized once the centuries-old principles of tonality are no longer applied. And there is little doubt that the tendency of a good part of the composers involved in the Darmstadt courses was to cancel the basic fundamentals of form, just as the traditional concept of phrasing, harmony and melody had been abandoned. This topic was inevitably discussed many times during the meetings, until it was finally decided to organize a conference specifically dedicated to the question: *Form in der Neuen Musik*, Darmstadt, July 20, 1965, with an introduction by Adorno.

The research carried out by GATM divided the participants into three groups. The first group were assigned the task of making a systematic analysis of the text; the second listened to the quartet while following the score; the third listened to the piece without the score. Baroni's article sets out the results of the study. In brief, the experiment concluded that any connections between the compositional procedures (the structural calculations, the likely segmentations, the reciprocal numerical proportions) and what is actually perceived on listening to the piece are rather tenuous, if not almost totally absent. It goes without saying that Maderna, with his infallible musical ear, was perfectly aware of the divide between his compositional work and the possibilities offered to the listener. It was a problem of aesthetics that at the time had no precise solution, but one that Maderna faced with a certain composure and with the pragmatic self-assurance of one who firmly believed in the value of his music, over and above any theoretical reasoning that he generally distrusted.

As far as offering a guide to listening to the *Quartetto* is concerned, there is no doubt that the first impact is certainly not immediate or easy. But if we approach the task by allowing ourselves to be swayed instead by the ever-changing quality of the sound, we could perhaps come to appreciate the freshness of what the composer's imagination never fails to offer us: very gentle sounds alongside harsh and violent sounds, sparse textures alternated with dense and full-bodied zones, long notes and pizzicatos, moments of ethereal brightness and others of unprecedented gloom, string tremolos and hard non-vibrating sounds, in other words a vast variety of sound qualities that one would not

---

[7] M. Baroni, "The macroform in post-tonal music. Listening and analysis," in *Musicae Scientiae*, 7/2 (2003), 219-240, and E. Pozzi, "Aspetti della multidimensionalità formale e della relatività nella musica del Novecento. Il *Quartetto per archi in due tempi* di Bruno Maderna," in *Con-Scientia Musica. Contrappunti per Rossana Dalmonte e Mario Baroni*, eds. A. R. Addessi, I. Macchiarella, M. Privitera, M. Russo (Lucca: LIM, 2010), 149-193.

usually expect to find in a quartet. Normally the sonorities are marginal, they are means of "pronouncing" a discourse, whereas the essential contents are to be found elsewhere: broadly speaking, it is the musical "themes" that we perceive as the "contents" of the musical discourse. But here this kind of content never arrives: it is simply replaced by ways of pronouncing it. The *Quartetto* is the paradoxical pronunciation of an absent content. Also lacking is the expressive rhetoric of the musical discourse, which normally has a beginning, consolidates, reaches some sort of peak, and perhaps diminishes, then resumes, and finally concludes. Although hints of these elements can be occasionally be perceived, they are always fleeting, not linked in any systematic way, and not such as to form the basis of any structure.

After the end of the *Ferienkurse*, which, as we have said, ended as early as June 6, Maderna remained in Germany for the whole month to take part in various concerts, and then returned to Italy, stopping off in Milan to make recordings (including a concerto by Boccherini for harmonica and orchestra) and to continue his work in the field of radio [*Romito* 2003 /1, 100]. It would be interesting to know whether, in future studies on Maderna's music, the year 1955 will be remembered more for the birth of the *Quartetto in due tempi* or for the flourishing of a new artistic language associated with the growing phenomenon of radio broadcasting. Over and above the "objective value" of these two products (assuming that one can expect to find any sort of "objectivity" in this area), one could say that *Quartetto* is the outcome of individual choices made personally by Maderna, in the context of the most recent developments and trends, while his work for radio has more general traits, one might even say political. The need to create a novel form of art specifically for such a particular medium was a concept that struggled to find fertile ground, despite the exciting new paths of exploration that had opened up already in the decades before the Second World War. And since the radio was, at the time, an instrument of the state, it was inevitable that all that surrounded it – and even more so its possible exploitation in the field of art – would become a political matter. The long discussions that ensued are well documented in the literature and here we will limit ourselves to citing the words of a far-sighted speech on the subject delivered in the lower chamber of the Italian parliament at the start of the 1930s:

> [...there is an urgent need to find a language] aimed at creating a completely autonomous art for the Radio, an art, that is, that considers the Radio a new instrument, as it is indeed, with its own particular characteristics, that takes it into due account, is almost inspired by it, in other words takes advantage of it, with new means, new words.[8]

---

[8] *Discorso di Adriano Lualdi alla Camera dei Deputati* (November 16, 1931), cited in *L'undicesima musa. Nino Rota e i suoi media*, ed. V. Rizzardi (Roma: CIDIM, 2001), 199-204. The topic was widely taken

In 1949, Maderna had been invited to explore the paths of these new possibilities by Alessandro Piovesan, director of the Program Office of Radio Venezia, who had put him in touch with Giuseppe Patroni Griffi, a young playwright who at the time was working in the Prose Office of the same Radio. Already in Piovesan's first letter to Maderna he suggests a theme which they could possibly work together on – "a story of destitution […] set in any southern city, which might be Naples, Marseilles, or New Orleans" – and with the music provided by "a small orchestra of jazz instruments," suggesting they could "compose the text and music side by side."[9] And so it was that Maderna's first important work for radio was born, *Il mio cuore è nel Sud. Ballata in prosa e musica* on a text by Patroni Griffi that the composer was immediately able to identify with. Not wishing to make the setting too popular in style, but also avoiding an over-explicit reference to the language of American jazz, Maderna succeeded in finding the right balance to express the contamination in his own personal way, namely through an equilibrium between the peculiar timbre of the jazz band, the use of rhythms clearly inspired by genres such as Blues or the lullaby, and the use of dodecaphony along the lines that he was experimenting with in his more exacting works. This by no means simple balance was replicated two years later in the sound track to Antonio Leonviola's film *Le due verità* (1951) and, at a distance of more than a decade, in one of his justly most famous pieces: *Don Perlimplin* (1962). The premiere of *Il mio cuore è nel Sud* took place on March 11, 1950 during the *Festival di Opere Radiofoniche in Prima Esecuzione* and the work was repeated several times following its immediate success with the public and critics. Not only was it awarded the *Microfono d'Argento* in Italy, but it was also well-received in a Swedish and German translation until at least the end of the '50s.

But the work that most exemplifies Maderna's contribution to the creation of a genuine language for the radio is *Ritratto di città*, on a text by Roberto Leydi, with music produced, captured and processed by Luciano Berio and Bruno Maderna. This is the work that is traditionally associated with the birth of the *Studio di Fonologia* in Milan, inaugurated in June 1955, although it was almost certainly composed some time before. The exact date of its first broadcast on the radio is not known, but we do know that *Ritratto di città* took part in the 1955 edition of the Premio Italia.[10] And this work could be said to

---

up in the literature not only in Italy but also in many other countries: see A. I. De Benedictis, *Radiodramma ed arte radiofonica. Storia e funzioni della musica per radio in Italia* (Torino: EDT, 2004), 3-60.

[9] Letter of February 1, 1949, cited in *Romito* 2000/2, 235.

[10] A. I. De Benedictis carefully summarizes the different dates regarding the genesis of the work, based on evidence drawn from highly reliable accounts, and from the composers themselves, although the dates do not always coincide. See A. I. De Benedictis, *Radiodramma*, cited in note 8, 192.

seal the friendship between Maderna and Berio and their shared venture, which had already been foreshadowed in various circumstances during the previous months. According to Marino Zuccheri, the technician who was one of the key figures at the *Studio della RAI* in Milan from its very outset, Maderna and Berio worked together on a short piece of electronic music, *Sequenze e Strutture*; and in the same months Maderna unfailingly included a work by Berio in his concerts. But above all the two composers were often together in Milan for meetings with influential figures in the world of radio, pursuing their quest to organize the *Studio di Fonologia*. With *Ritratto di città* they were finally able to reach a cohesive result after the many years of experiments and attempts to find a suitable artistic language for the radio. The fact that they were fully aware of their achievement is reflected in the subheading of the work: *Studio per una rappresentazione radiofonica*. In other words, more than a work with the precise and direct aims of a composition as such, it was considered a "study," a path investigating the means and the possible results.

Unlike his previous works for radio (including *Il mio cuore è nel sud*), *Ritratto di città* has no narrative intention or plot, but is a "representation" – in this specific case of a city – not through images, but through its various sonic features. The work contains some elements that could be considered *musique concrète*, like the direct recording of recognizable sounds of the city, while others derive from electronic sounds that have been purposely produced and processed; some of the effects are clearly intended to describe the text, but others are the result of a more subjective interpretation; a kind of counterpoint is created between the background noises and the "voices" in the foreground, whether they come from the speakers (Nando Gazzolo and Ottavio Fanfani), or from a real instrument (glockenspiel, tubular bells, piano). However, the authors have deliberately avoided the use of "first-hand" instrumental or vocal music, that is to say especially written for the work. The most evident feature that emerges from the various types of treatment is the taste for experimentation and the capacity to re-invent even the simplest of basic materials. Just how much effort the two composer put into this work can also be gleaned from the large quantity of extra material produced in preparation for the composition, but never actually used in the final product. In fact, Maurizio Romito discovered various preparatory tapes at the *Studio di Fonologia* that are self-standing and could well be added to their list of works for radio: *Sottosuolo di città* and *Via Maestra* by Maderna, and *FFSS* and *Tragedia americana* by Berio [*Romito* 2000 /2, 238].

The *Studio* gradually began to attract an increasing number of composers from Italy and abroad, and it soon became – together with the city of Milan

– an important center for the production and diffusion of the most advanced research into the language and form of artistic productions for radio.[11]

At this point one might ask oneself: how exactly was the *Studio* born? And what was the underlying project that led to its creation? Piero Santi and Luigi Rognoni, who, together with Alberto Mantelli and Roberto Leydi, were immediately convinced of the idea proposed by Berio and Maderna, retrace the first steps in the venture:

> At first we thought of calling it the "Club d'Essai," in analogy with the one founded in 1948 at the Radiodiffusion et Télévision Française, then we chose the formula "Centro Sperimentale di Ricerche Radiofoniche." [...The] project for the establishment of a *Centro Sperimentale di Ricerche Radiofoniche* [...] was presented to Filiberto Guala [then director general of the RAI] in November 1954.[12]
>
> Maestro Giulio Razzi supported our proposal; Gino Castelnuovo was hesitant but not hostile. In the meantime at the start of 1954, Berio and Maderna obtained permission to carry out experimental research using the normal equipment available in the studios in Corso Sempione.[13]

However, the project also comprised other interests besides music, a fact that can be deduced from the definitive name chosen for the *Studio*. "Phonology" is a term taken from linguistics, referring to the study of the distinctive and oppositional properties of phonemes, a field in which non musician scholars like Umberto Eco were involved. So in order to underline the participation of both musicians and non musicians, they finally arrived at the name "Studio di Fonologia Musicale," "which was intended not only to be a name, but also to define a project [for experimental analysis] of the sonic continuum."[14] At the same time, issue number 3 of the journal *Elettronica* included an article by Gino Castelnuovo, who placed the stress on the term "phonology," alluding to the fact that the new *Studio* would focus principally on forms of vocal expression, in which language played an important role. The same issue

---

[11] Music for radio became a topic of considerable interest also in France and Germany. In 1954, a very significant book on the subject was published in Paris, which was subsequently translated into German in 1959: A. Silbermann, *La musique, la Radio, l'Auditeur: étude sociologique* (Paris: Presses Universitaires de France, 1954).

[12] P. Santi, "Le nuove tecnologie: musica elettronica e radiodrammi," in *Documenti* 1985, 156.

[13] L. Rognoni, "Memoria di Bruno Maderna negli anni Cinquanta," ibid., 148.

[14] L. Cossettini, A. Orcalli, *L'invenzione della fonologia musicale. Saggi sulla musica elettronica sperimentale di Luciano Berio e Bruno Maderna* (Lucca: LIM, 2015), 6.

of the journal also included an article by Berio, in which he emphasized the combination of words and voice "observed through the possibilities of the electro-acoustic manipulation of the signal recorded on tape."[15] In essence, since sine waves, harmonic partials, impulse generators, continuous-spectrum noises, ring modulations and aleatory variables would soon be a regular part of the theoretical and practical tool-box of musicians, it was necessary to learn to compose using measurable data distributed over time and analyzable also in terms of statistics, and not only musical choices measurable by the ear. Maderna was quick to appreciate the implications of this new way of composing, even though the opportunity to express his thoughts only came two years later during a conference held in Darmstadt:

> [...] the fact that it is possible to set aside a very large reserve of partial material, places the composer in a completely new situation. Time now presents itself as a field offering an enormous number of possibilities for the arrangement and permutation of the material just produced. We now feel strongly oriented towards this type of thought and behavior, also in instrumental music. It is pointless to wonder whether this renovation was provoked by our experience in electronics or whether it was simply the result of a development in this direction already present in the music of recent years. The undeniable fact is, though, that electronic music made it possible to prove the validity of this way of thinking of composition.[16]

The fame of the *Studio* in Milan soon spread, and already in the year following its foundation Steinecke asked Maderna – and through him Berio – to bring some of the works created there to Darmstadt, not only pieces that they themselves had composed, but also ones by Henze, Pousseur and Stockhausen. Besides the effects of electronic elaboration on composition as such, mentioned by Maderna in his speech at the conference, and besides the composition of specific works for this new means (which we will speak of later), one of the most discussed issues at an international level regarded the particular qualities of the radio as a medium, where the relation between music and word – and especially between music and action – could be expressed more explicitly. In a work for theater the music has no need to resort to special means to inform the spectator that the action takes place in the foreground, in the background or even behind the scenes, whereas in a work for radio the listener must be given this information through the use of exclusively musical effects, for instance by

---

[15] See L. Cossettini, A. Orcalli, ibid., 20.
[16] B. Maderna, "Esperienze compositive di musica elettronica," conference held on July 26, 1957 at the *Internationales Musikinstitut* in Darmstadt, in *Documenti* 1985, 83.

playing with the dynamics, through echo, filtering or reverberation. Another aspect to be considered concerned the effects necessary to distinguish when the electronically produced and elaborated music defines the "genre" (for example, a fable or a thriller), or when the music and song belong to a familiar type of music such as a "melodrama for radio," or whether it is the plot itself that foresees the insertion of some kind of music: a song, a serenade, or a dance, in other words in all the cases where the music is "diegetic," that is to say produced by the characters themselves. An interesting example of the "intradiegetic" capacity of music can be found precisely in a work by Bruno Maderna, composed some years later (1959), *Aspetto Matilde*, on a text by Enzo Maurri.[17] And it should also be remembered that in the same period the very first television programs were being produced, a circumstance to which Maderna contributed personally with the music for six episodes of the program *Diapason* broadcast between August and November 1955 [*Romito* 2000/2, 248].

It is not clear how long Maderna remained in Italy, but we do know that on November 14, 1955, in a concert for the *Terzo Programma della RAI* in Turin, he conducted Berio's *Nones*,[18] and on November 29 at the Teatro dell'Arte in Milan, he recorded Goffredo Petrassi's *Morte dell'aria* as part of the RAI's opera season. On December 2 he was back in Darmstadt, from where he sent a letter to Berio in which he speaks of the interest in the *Studio* shown by the organizers of the summer courses and by radio broadcasters in Cologne and Frankfurt. But still more interesting is his description of a project proposed by Steinecke, even though it never materialized:

> Speaking of the journal,[19] he has made a very interesting proposal: to combine the forces of Boulez, with his Domaine Musical, of [Steinecke] himself, with his financial and diplomatic, organizational resources etc…and ourselves, in order to create an international journal in three languages (Italian, French and German, with relative summaries in translation). The expansion of the journal would not mean limiting space for the single sections (Italian, German and French) but would result in a kind of quarterly organ of the most important European composers, without detracting from the key contribution made by you and Ruziscka [the publishing director of Suvini Zerboni] as previously planned. It

---

[17] A. I. De Benedictis, *Radiodramma*, cited in note 8, 128-129. It should not be forgotten that much of the success of the work was due to the participation of Cathy Berberian in the role of the singer.

[18] Maderna appears to have been particularly interested in this work, since he chose it as the object of a course on analysis and performance during the *Ferienkurse* of 1956.

[19] Here Maderna is referring to Berio's plan to found a journal promoting the principles of new music, "Incontri Musicali"; its first issue was published by Suvini Zerboni in December 1956.

would be published simultaneously in Milan, Paris and Darmstadt. As far as the German section is concerned, he guarantees the backing of UNESCO, of publishers (Schott and UE etc…), as well as of numerous respected organizations and institutes of the country. So there would be three directors of the journal: Steinecke, Boulez, Berio. Each would be the editor of the relative national issue. I am sure you understand immediately that this idea needs to be considered without delay. There is no need for me to list the advantages of such a situation both for us and for music in general. So talk to Ruziscka about it immediately. Naturally the journal would have a wide circulation, Steinecke would see to promoting it as necessary. He now has very notable contacts in the USA, in Scandinavia, as well as in Latin America. The journal would act as the mainstay for all the organization of concerts in Paris, Milan and Darmstadt […] All these things would slowly but surely lead to the ever more desirable and hoped for union of the young, or in any case living, forces of music […][*Carteggio* 2001, 97-99].

At the end of this letter, which clearly testifies to how the two musicians were working together in perfect harmony in this period of their lives, Maderna sends the regards of Christine and the young Caterina to Berio and his "female inversion" (Berberian, Luciano's wife, was known in Milan as Caterina, and their daughter was called Cristina), promising to return soon; in fact, just a few days later, on December 15, he is already in Milan, at the Hotel Alba in Viale Certosa, and appears to have stayed in the city until January 8, 1956.

As soon as Christine and their daughter were able to join him, Maderna left the hotel and found an accommodation more suitable for a family, although he is still not sure where it would be best to establish a permanent home. Once again the changes of address in his correspondence bear witness to his wanderings. We know that in February 1956 he was in Milan, at Viale Boezio, 4,[20] while, not far away, in Verona, the home of his mother Irma was always available, as was the Köpnik's apartment in Darmstadt; but not long afterwards we find him back in Milan, at Piazzale Accursio, 12. It was probably from Berio's home that Maderna "dictated" a letter to Cathy Berberian, which she wrote in English to their common friend Edgard Varèse.[21] The letter contains some lighthearted remarks, but also some particularly interesting information. We learn that the plans for the new journal, *Incontri Musicali*, were already going ahead autonomously, irrespective of Steinecke's proposal. Varèse was warmly invited by Berio to write an article that would complete the first issue, but that

---

[20] See Maderna's letter to Steinecke in *Carteggio* 2001, 113-115.

[21] Letter from Maderna in Milan dated January 2, 1956, preserved in the Varèse collection of the Paul Sacher Stiftung [*Extraits* 2007, 500].

would also act as a "spur" to convince the managers of the RAI to invite him to the *Studio di Fonologia*, so that they could start working together: "[...] it's about time you stopped being a solitary creator." Varèse never wrote the article, nor did he ever come to the *Studio*, but at least news of the journal now began to circulate.

The first of the four issues that made up the short series came out at the end of the year. The aims of the journal were clearly set out in the sub-heading – *Quaderni internazionali di musica contemporanea diretti da Luciano Berio* – and in the epigraph: "these notebooks of contemporary music were conceived with the aim of establishing a fruitful dialogue among those composers wishing to clarify to themselves and to others the technical and poetic substance of their work." So the journal was not made by theorists who commented on music written by others, but by composers who wished to reflect upon their own work: the journal therefore succeeded in breaching the "great distance" proclaimed by Guido d'Arezzo between theorists and practical musicians (*musicorum et cantorum magna est distantia:...*).[22]

We have no exact details about the other facet of Steinecke's project, namely the organization of concerts that would accompany the publication of the journal, as mentioned by Maderna in his letter to Berio. But there surely must have been a musical offshoot to the publishing side and we can imagine that Maderna was working on this aspect, perhaps following Boulez's example. Just two years before, in fact, a famous couple of actors from Paris – Jean-Louis Barrault and his wife Madeleine Reinaud – had been particularly struck by Boulez's human and musical qualities, and allowed him to use their theater for four series of concerts, one every month, from January to April 1954, that were innovative both in the way they involved a chamber group especially formed for the occasion, and in the choice of programs. The first concert – conducted by Hermann Scherchen – featured works by J. S. Bach, Luigi Nono, K. H. Stockhausen, Anton Webern and Igor Stravinsky, and the following concerts similarly combined Baroque music with classics of New Music and more recently composed works.[23] And so, shortly afterwards the instrumental ensemble *Domaine Musical* was formed, which Boulez then made famous throughout Europe and which served as a model for similar ensembles, for

---

[22] Berio wrote a short piece in the same spirit to mark the 60th anniversary of the International Society of Musicology, *Ecce. Musica per musicologi*, which was commissioned by the organizers of the conference held in Bologna and was performed by participants of the conference on August 31, 1987 conducted by the composer himself. A reproduction of Berio's manuscript score is introduced by R. Dalmonte in *Atti del XIV Congresso della Società Internazionale di Musicologia*, vol. I, (Torino: EDT, 1990), 739.

[23] D. Jameaux, *Pierre Boulez* (Paris: Favard, 1984), 83-93.

example the *Incontri Musicali* in Milan, directed by Maderna and formed after the *Ferienkurse* of 1958, and the *Darmstädter Musikensemble*, which began its activity in 1960, again under the direction of Maderna.

But the most important event at the start of 1956, one that was destined to become a milestone in the history of theater and music in Italy, took place at the Piccolo Teatro in Milan, where Bertolt Brecht's *Dreigroschenoper* with music by Kurt Weill was staged, directed by Giorgio Strehler and conducted by Bruno Maderna, in an Italian translation (*Opera da tre soldi*) by Ettore Gaipa, Gino Negri and Giorgio Strehler. The principal actors-singers included Ottavio Fanfani, Mario Carotenuto, Giusi Dandolo, Tino Carraro and Milly; a particularly notable component of the small orchestra (nine instruments) was the composer Giacomo Manzoni at the piano. The preparation for the event was long (the actors who had never sung before appear to have started work already in November of the previous year) and the production, which premiered on February 10, had fifty-two repeat performances until March 25.[24] The show was well-received by the press, although certain right-wing commentators could not hide their disapproval at the deplorable mixture of poetry and anti-bourgeois ideology, for instance in the long article written by "Senior" in the Milan newspaper *24 Ore*, published the morning after its première.

As is well known, the text of Brecht's play was inspired, like many other works, by John Gay's eighteenth century *Beggar's Opera*, and the tone of Kurt Weill's version was perfectly in line with its intent to denounce bourgeois society. In the new text the characters express their social criticism not only through direct references to recognizable coeval situations, but also in the detachment from the traditional ways of making theater. In this case the costumes, and also the sets, are those typical of the twentieth century bourgeoisie: "[…] We bourgeois artisans are being swallowed up by the large concerns" comments one character, and Mackie Messer, in all his baseness, is portrayed as the prototype of the despised middle classes, with his shady, disheveled and violent demeanor. The old text now gains fresh vigor, an element that is recaptured many years later in the dramaturgy of Maderna's *Satyricon*.[25] Strehler's stage direction and Maderna's conducting both shared a common approach. In the words of Luigi Pestalozza, who followed the work from the very beginning and never lost sight of the opera throughout its many revivals over the decades, in the first edition "Maderna translates [the intentions of Brecht and Weill] into questions of

---

[24] Details taken from an article by Luigi Pestalozza marking the 60th anniversary of Paolo Grassi and Giorgio Strehler's Piccolo Teatro. See *Il Giornale della Musica*, no. 237 (May 2007), 28. The citation below is taken from the same source.

[25] See S. Pasticci, "La presenza del *Satyricon* sulla scena culturale degli anni Settanta, da Maderna a Pasolini," *Musica/Realtà*, 91 (2010), 102-108.

musical performance, of sonic, vocal and instrumental behavior [...] he inspires the actors in their singing and the instrumentalists in the way they treat their instrument, until in a very short space of time they prove to have assimilated Brecht and Weill's epic alternative to opera, compared to the form of drama predominant until now." News of this extraordinary undertaking spread quickly even while it was still being prepared, and Brecht himself wanted to attend the premiere, later expressing his wish to have it performed in exactly the same form at his theater in Berlin. The situation is summed up in the words of Maderna:

> Lately I have been absurdly busy and haven't been able to leave Milan, always because of the *Dreigroschenoper*. I am obliged to work every day until the end of March. There is a performance every evening and two on Sundays. So the *Dreigroschenoper* is a huge success. Our edition worked out very well and Brecht himself, who came to the premiere, was very pleased."[26]

This landmark event in Milan had its origins in the work of the *Komische Oper* in East Berlin, which was well known in Europe, even beyond the iron curtain. Over 300 productions were taken to thirty different countries, including several tours in West Germany.[27] The *Komische Oper*, as the name suggests, was founded at the end of the nineteenth century as a theater for operetta; after the end of the Second World War it reopened on December 23, 1947 with Johann Strauss's *Die Fledermaus*. The director who managed it for many years and made it famous throughout Europe was Walter Felsenstein, while – in the years we are dealing with here – its principal conductor was Kurt Masur. We learn from the newspapers that the productions of the *Komische Oper* were able to appeal to very wide audience from different social strata.

Despite his heavy commitments with the theater, Maderna never stopped composing. The fact that he was able to work at the *Studio* meant that he could now experiment with a new way of making music that he found truly fascinating. He later spoke of this in an unusually open and detailed fashion:

> My encounter with electronics totally overturned my relations with musical material. At that point I was forced to completely reorganize my intellectual metabolism as a composer. Whereas composing

---

[26] Letter from Maderna to Steinecke dated February 27, 1956, original in German [*Carteggio* 2001, 113-115].

[27] The details given here are taken from the *Jahrbuch der Komischen Oper Berlin*, 1965/66 (Berlin: Henschelverlag, 1966). Articles by Walter Felsenstein, Joachim Herz, Alan Seymour, and Ernesto Grassi.

instrumental music is in most cases preceded by the development of a linear type of thought – precisely because it is a question of developing a thought that is not in direct contact with the material –, the fact that in the electronic studio you can try out various possibilities in realizing the structures of sound, and that by means of continuous manipulations continue you can endlessly renew and change the sonic images thus obtained, and, finally, the fact that it is possible to set aside a very large reserve of partial materials, places the composer before a completely new situation.[28]

And so it was that in the spring of 1956, probably while he was working in the theater with Strehler and Manzoni, *Notturno* was born, a work – according to Luigi Rognoni and confirmed by the technician Marino Zuccheri – that owes its title to the fact that is was composed at night.[29] It is easy to imagine that, once the spotlights of the Piccolo Teatro had been turned off, Maderna had dinner with some night-owl member of the team, and then, instead of making for his home at Viale Boezio 4, he headed to the *Studio* in Corso Sempione, where at that hour he could certainly work in peace without being disturbed by his colleagues. In fact, ever since his years of training in Rome, Bruno had no qualms about working in the small hours, and actually enjoyed it, then going to bed when the noises of the world outside began to intrude. Moreover, apart from Sundays, his work at the theater usually took place in the evening, and so, incredibly, he would also have found some time to rest.

Returning to the title, though, Massimo Mila did not share the opinion of Rognoni and Zuccheri. Indeed, he believed it to be "a programmatic and meaningful title [...] suggesting a poetic and expressive inspiration"; after a brief description of the techniques used and of the effect "like an artificial whistling of flutes in the mist," Mila informs us that "in the words of the composer" (probably spoken during a private meeting) one can note in *Notturno* "an element of continuity between natural bodies of sound and the sonic means of the electronic music" [*Mila* 1976, 19-20].

A careful listening reveals that the basic material seems to be made up of sine sounds – individual sounds with a sound spectrum composed of a single frequency (1 Hertz) – and white noise. Sine sounds do not occur in nature (or might be similar to a kind of whistle) but can be produced electronically and modulated in amplitude (that is, with variations in dynamics). White noise, on the other hand, is the sum of all the components of the spectrum (including those that lie between one frequency and another of the notes of a scale) and

---

[28] Extract from the conference of July 26, 1957, mentioned in note 16.
[29] L. Rognoni, "Memoria di Bruno Maderna," cited in note 13, 149.

its sound is like that of a rustling (perhaps more gray than white). In this case it is possible not only to modulate these components in amplitude, but also to filter them, that is to say reduce them to a more limited band of frequencies. In *Notturno* Maderna works on the superimposition or layering of sine sounds and filtered white sound (sometimes with very limited bands of around 2 Hertz), playing with variations in intensity and duration, and with short pauses or interruptions in the flow of sounds, thus creating fragments of varying lengths. The overall effect of this brief piece, which lasts just over three minutes, is a succession of shifting timbres, further enhanced by changes in the running speed of the tape, without too many contrasts or bursts of sound, but rather with a fairly constant flux in which short units alternate with more continuous stretches of sound.

The first document attesting to the work of the *Studio di Fonologia di Milano* is the concert program of its first ever public exhibition, given on May 8, 1956 at the headquarters of the RAI in Milan: the *Audizione di composizioni di musica concreta e di musica elettronica,* providing an overview of the current tendencies illustrated by works from various European and American composers.[30] Among these we find pieces composed jointly by Berio and Maderna, such as *Sequenze e strutture*. This piece was long considered lost, but today a tape of the work can be found at the *Centro Studi Maderna*.[31] Between 1956 and 1958 his most significant output was, then, created at the *Studio*. During the previously mentioned concert-lecture held at Darmstadt in July 1957, he remarked that the impact of the possibilities opened up by electronics was so great as to change his way of conceiving composition. He also gave some technical details about two of his own tapes (*Notturno* and *Syntaxis*) and two by Berio, who appears not to have attended the lecture (*Mutazioni* and *Perspectives*). His enthusiasm for the new means may perhaps have led him to overstate the limits imposed by the temporal unidimensionality of composing with traditional instruments, which in reality continued to feature in his work, but the multidimensionality of electronic music and the possibility to imagine new types of sound layers began to have a notable effect on certain aspects of his way of composing. In fact, the years between 1957 and 1959 saw a marked slowing-down in his output for written scores, while his work with electronics continued to proceed regularly. Interestingly, the three pieces he produced at the *Studio* in that period (*Notturno, Syntaxis* and *Continuo*) are still conceived as concert pieces (with an aesthetic function), while

---

[30] See P. Santi, "Le nuove tecnologie," cited in note 12, 159.

[31] See N. Scaldaferri, "Documenti inediti sullo Studio di Fonologia della RAI di Milano," *Musica/Realtà*, no. 45 (1994), 153-154.

in the following years the electronic component would begin to take on other "alternative" roles: for example, it was combined with instrumental sounds in the orchestra, or was used for dramaturgical purposes in works for theater or radio; it could even be used to create ambient music to accompany events that were primarily visual.

Syntaxis, presented during the above-mentioned conference in Darmstadt, was written after the short *Notturno* and is substantially the same in terms of its experimental character, apart from certain features perhaps resulting from the use of partially different studio equipment and the use of two tracks for the recording instead of just one. The main difference, however, lies in the length of the piece, which in this case exceeds 10 minutes. This longer duration raises more specifically the question of overall structure, although Maderna appears to have chosen the path of a "non form." While it is true that the work contains some more extensive episodes that might create a certain sense of continuity, it is nonetheless hard to perceive any relations between these moments, such as the rhetorical use of contrast or tension. So it would seem that Maderna was purposely avoiding any kind of macro-form, an approach that was largely in line with the non-formal trends in the figurative arts in the second half of the century.

The structure of the third piece, *Continuo*, is quite different. A description can be found in the concert program for the performance given on April 11, 1959 during the series *Pomeriggi Musicali* in Milan. The program notes are not signed, but were most likely written by Maderna himself, or by someone who had spoken to him in person. The composition is generated "from a single electronically produced sound that passes through twenty-two stages of slow and gradual transformation. The various stages follow one another without a break [...] characterized by a greater or lesser density (pregnancy) of the material." The title therefore alludes to the continuity of a sound, throughout a piece that in this case lasts around 8 miniutes. In his book, Massimo Mila makes no attempt to hide his enthusiasm as a listener: its "magical opening [...] remains one of the most sublime moments of poetry that electronic music has ever reached [...] it is the 'night music' that Bartók would have created if he had known electronics [...] the form, clearly ternary, is determined by the dynamics: it gives the piece a clear line of evolution, which is basically like a parabola, starting from a *pianissimo* and returning to it through a central climax" [*Mila* 1976, 20-21].

The perception of a three-part division is also noted by Giordano Montecchi, who carried out a highly detailed analysis in which he divides the first and third parts into three phases. The second part, though, does not lend itself to any internal division, nor does it reveal any perceptible changes in the quality of the sound material: "the climax of the section – and of the entire piece – is reached at the end [...] in a general fusion marked by a crescendo of deafening and highly reverberant rumbles that overpower everything else. The sensation is one of chaos, of relentless collapse, which then suddenly relents, leaving approximately two seconds of reverberation followed by a liberatory silence." After several pages of analysis Montecchi arrives at the conclusion that the work "seems instead to be open to multiple ways of reading, suggesting the need for not one but perhaps a series of methods of analysis and interpretation at various levels, which should nonetheless be seen as heuristic, non dogmatic tools.32 Taking into account the comments of Mila and Montecchi, it seems legitimate to suggest that in *Continuo* (first performed in Cologne in March 1958, and probably composed between 1957 and '58)[32] Maderna seems to have become quite confident in handling this new form of material, and in understanding its mechanisms of elaboration and construction. One might say that, within this new sonic environment, he has finally succeeded in finding a space open to authorial individuality, a goal he had never completely ceased to pursue.

While he was working on these three electronic pieces, between 1956 and '58, Maderna was also involved in many other activities. Since the beginning of 1956 he had been working in the medium of radio, composing the musical comment for two plays adapted for radio by the director Alessandro Brissoni. The two works could not be more different from one another, but they both share Maderna's taste for *divertissement*. The first piece was written to mark the centenary of George Bernard Shaw's birth and was supposed to be titled – like his famous play inspired by the philosophical ideas of Nietzsche – *Man and Superman* (in Italian *Uomo e Superuomo*), but since the radio play focused only on the third act, Brissoni chose to rename it *Don Giovanni e il commendatore*. The Mozartian characters of the play have become specters in the world beyond, intent on discussing topics of current interest, in a setting that resembles the landscape of the Sierra Nevada. Maderna's score – for harpsichord, flute and tom-tom – is deposited under this title with the Italian copyright society, the SIAE, but it is clearly just an outline of the music that was eventually used for the radio play. The other piece probably composed in the same period is a radio farce titled *Brigida vuole sposarsi* based on Eugène Labiche's comédie-

---

[32] See G. Montecchi, "*Continuo* di Bruno Maderna," *I Quaderni della scuola civica di musica*, nos. 21-22 (December 1992), 51, 52. Part of the program notes mentioned above is quoted on p. 48.

vaudeville *La Cagnotte*. Maderna's score, which provides background music for the play, consists of a single page for drum and solo instrument, a fairly modest sketch with respect to what was actually used for the definitive radio adaptation.[33]

Although we do not know exactly when Maderna left Milan, he was certainly in Rome for the performances of the *Opera da tre soldi* throughout nearly all of May. He then went to Darmstadt for the summer courses, which this year were held from July 11 to 22. He almost certainly attended Adorno's conferences on Schönberg's counterpoint, a series organized by Steinecke to mark the fifth anniversary of the composer's death. During his lectures Adorno also extended the discussion to include some of the points raised in his rather controversial essay, *Das Altern der Neuen Musik*, recently republished in the miscellaneous volume *Dissonanzen* (1956). He returned once again to the question of objectivity in composition, an issue that was no longer as radical as it had previously been, not even in Darmstadt. Maderna, in any case, had never felt himself particularly involved in this matter. While it is true that he went out of his way to ensure that nothing in his music was left to chance (as we saw in the analysis of the *Quartetto*), he always maintained a personal form of musical humanism that persisted, or rather was enhanced, through the modification of the techniques he applied to his work. Just a few days before setting out for Darmstadt, on July 4 he wrote an interesting letter to Luciano Berio from Verona, where, in addition to affirming his friendship and giving news about his work, he expresses some of his thoughts about music and life:

> Before leaving Milan, last Sunday, I listened again to our electronic pieces [probably his *Notturno* and Berio's *Mutazioni*] and Stoki's [Stockhausen's] *Gesang der Jünglinge*. They are fine pieces – they say a lot about all three of us. Differences and identities. But above all they reveal a conscious and sincere position towards life and being alive. I believe that music can really be none other than this. Besides, there is, thanks again to the galaxy principle I mentioned before, a tremendous honesty that comes from our having the courage to free ourselves from the *"humanae" conditions*. In other words from contingencies, seeing that we believe it beautiful and necessary to exist in a state of awareness and, if we can, to live and love this awareness. The era of life for life's

---

[33] *Romito 2000/2*, 238; *Lo Studio di Fonologia. Un diario musicale 1954-1983*, ed. M.M. Novati (Milano: Ricordi, 2009), 184. On pp. 163-187 there is a list of all Maderna's tapes preserved in the *Studio*.

sake has ended. Let us leave this to the various Scherchens, big and small. And it is precisely for this reason that we must aim to achieve ever more, ever better. We must communicate this to others. So we will help them not to be simple biological structures. Even if this seems imposing, we must at least try, so we can die in beauty.[34]

During the courses that year (1956), Maderna held a series of workshops on the theme of "Conducting realization" in which he tackled the wide-ranging question of the relation between writing and interpretation. The series lasted three days and had been carefully planned and discussed with Steinecke in various letters in June. On the first day Maderna talked about Berio's *Nones*, whose first performance he had recently recorded at the RAI in Turin, in the presence of Berio himself,[35] and which would be performed live later that year, during the concerts given by the orchestra of Radio Cologne conducted by Nino Sanzogno. The second day was dedicated to a work of fundamental importance to Maderna, Webern's op. 30. The third day focused on *Kontra-Punkte* by Stockhausen, who also attended the session. During the preparations for the upcoming courses, Maderna urges Steinecke to find lodgings for him and Christine in Marienhöhe, "at least for the three days when I'll be working." This detail is highly significant because it implies that the couple, even though they were now a small family, still had no independent base in Darmstadt.

Besides the workshops, Maderna also played an active role in the discussions about electronic music, which followed the presentation of works composed mainly in the studios of Cologne and Milan. On these occasions he was able to underline the fundamental coherence that guided the work of composers in the Milan studio and in particular his affinity of thought with Luciano Berio, who was at the courses for the first time that year. But the most outstanding feature of the 1956 courses was the chance to hear music from the USA – especially piano music – thanks to extraordinary talents of David Tudor, who played works by Earle Brown, Christian Wolff, Morton Feldman and John Cage (either live or in recordings on tape). It goes without saying that the work of John Cage made a particular impression owing to the violence entailed in using the instrument as an object to produce sounds and noises by exploiting all its various parts and materials. The group from

---

[34] A transcript of the full letter can be found in *Carteggio* 2001, 122-123.
[35] On June 27, Maderna sent Steinecke a letter from Turin, at the end of which there is a short greeting signed by Luciano Berio [ibid.,118-119].

Milan – which also included Luigi Rognoni and Piero Santi[36] – criticized the American composer's total lack of constructive responsibility, which, according to Santi, amounted to an "existential realism" that Tudor illustrated "by punching the keyboard, kicking the piano, hammering inside the soundboard and other similar means."[37] Among the younger participants, a favorable impression was made by the Swedish composer Bo Nilsson, while the already familiar composers, including Maderna, Nono, Boulez and Stockhausen, were now joined by Berio, whose *Nones* met with general approval.

In the same period as his participation in the courses, Maderna was working on a piece that experienced a particularly complex history, the *Serenata n. 2*. On July 4, 1956, in the letter to Berio cited in note 34, he writes: "I'm now cutting my Serenata and then I'll send it to Suvini Zerboni for publication. Scherchen had made no contract for this work so I consider myself free." These few lines offer a second hint at the change in relations between Maderna and his last teacher, with whom he had been closely associated, also on very friendly terms, since 1948. And this may also have something to do with his decision to "cut," that is to say modify, the piece. The original version, dedicated to Scherchen, was published by Ars Viva in 1954;[38] the second version, partially reduced and with no dedication, was published by Suvini Zerboni in 1957, with printed characters.[39] The first version appears to have been already partially written by January 1953,[40] and was premiered by Scherchen during the Domaine Musical series organized by Boulez in Paris, on April 10, 1954. Another two performances were given in 1956, one conducted by Hans Zanotelli in April at the Landestheater in Darmstadt, and the other conducted by Maderna himself, with the Orchestra Scarlatti of Naples, of which a recording exists on a RAI tape kept at the *Centro Studi Maderna*. Giordano Montecchi has made a very careful analysis of the differences between the two versions, and on p. 112

---

[36] In the letter cited in note 35, Maderna suggested that Steineke should invite Massimo Mila, Roman Vlad and Roberto Leydi. Steinecke did not take up his suggestion, maybe because he was concerned about having to contribute in some way to the expenses of these guests; however, the presence of eminent music critics from Milan was assured.

[37] P. Santi, "L'XI Internationale Ferienkurse für neue Musik di Darmstadt," *Aut aut*, no. 36 (1956), 386, cited in *Trudu* 1992, 111.

[38] The title of the edition published by Ars Viva Verlag, Zürich (copyright 1954) is *Serenata. Komposition Nr.3*, with the following dedication on the cover: *Hermann Scherchen gewidmet*.

[39] This is the first time that a work by Maderna was published with printed characters, a system that continued to be rare over the following years. Nearly all of his works subsequently published by Suvini Zerboni still consisted in reproductions of the manuscript.

[40] See M. Fein, *Die musikalische Poetik*, cited in note 3, 29.

of his article there is a table showing how 60 measures (of the original 327) have been cut.[41] The article reconstructs the extremely complex path of its composition, based on a painstaking study of the sketches, tables and magic squares referring to the serial organization of the pitches, durations, timbres, and performing styles. At the end of his analysis Montecchi remarks that:

> the statistical-numerical procedure is able to produce results that are more varied and unpredictable than could have arisen purely from the composer's imagination, results however that are assessed and then accepted or refused on the basis of a faculty of judgment that is by no means subjugated to the rigor of the structure [see note 41, 126].

Further interesting comments about the *Serenata* were written by Berio, Pousseur and Lewinski, who speak of the evocation of ancient Italian serenades. Berio in particular observes that compared to the "austere mutterings" of the avant-gardes of the time, the *Serenata* offers a "seductive and tender" smile.[42] The reference to the eighteenth century perceived by its earliest listeners probably derives from the opening measures of the piece. In effect, the techniques of filtering, or some other mathematical machination, allowed the composer to select the durations, pitches, and harmonic relations between the instruments so as to obtain results that respect the rules of a strictly serial and even vaguely pointillist syntax, while at the same time preserving in some of the instrumental parts (especially in the solo piccolo) melodic fragments made up of small stepwise, or at least neighboring intervals, and daring to allow harmonic relations between the instruments created by an occasional isolated interval of a fourth or fifth, and even moments of unison, producing echoes of distant times. And then there are the long held notes and an unusually sparse texture, which create a suspended atmosphere in which one is not quite sure what will happen next. Certain fragments catch the attention on account of their peculiar structural qualities, unusual for the time. An example worth quoting is the singular *Allegro alla Danza*, a very brief central episode (lasting just over 30 seconds) in which the irregularity of the beats precludes any hint of a dance; but there is nevertheless a reminiscence of a certain kind of lightness: the instruments play *pianissimo* in the upper zone of their registers, constantly passing an identical module from one instrument to the other. The pitches, durations and timbres are still governed by the infallible numerical calculations, but at the same time there is a fleeting sense of disembodiment. In the closing minutes the texture grows more compact, more condensed

---

[41] G. Montecchi, "Il lavoro di precomposizione in *Serenata n. 2*," in *Studi* 1989, 109-137.

[42] See M. Fein, *Die musikalische Poetik*, cited in note 3, 33.

and softer in timbre. But then, at a certain point, the climate becomes similar to that of the start, this time without echoes of the past, but in a suspended atmosphere that slowly dissolves and gently dies away.

At the end of the *Ferienkurse* Maderna was busy with concerts in various parts of Italy, in Florence, in Turin and in Palermo [*Romito* 2020] and with the composition of music for Riccardo Bacchelli's play *Amleto*, first staged in Vicenza that September. But he was most likely also in Milan, working on various electronic pieces and music for radio that would appear the following year. In fact, in a letter to his mother dated January 7, 1957 Maderna tells her he has just finished his new work *Syntaxis* and the electronic incidental music for Euripides' *Medea*, due to be broadcast on television a few days later [*Extraits* 2007, 501].

Bruno Maderna
Photo Album

Fig. 2: Maderna in a typical conducting pose.

Fig. 3: Brunetto Grossato in his father's band.

Fig. 4: Brunetto Grossato conducting the orchestra at the Arena di Verona, 1933.

Fig. 5: Young Maderna with Giacomo Manzoni (left) and Piero Santi (right).

Fig. 6: With Earle Brown in Darmstadt, 1959.

Fig. 7: Maderna during a theory class, 1960.

Fig. 8: At a rehearsal in Darmstadt, 1961.

Fig. 9: Maderna and Nono in front of La Fenice in Venice, 1962.

Fig. 10: Photo with dedication, 1968.

Fig. 11: Maderna in Persepolis with the Empress Farah Diba (right) and Cathy Berberian (left), 1971.

Fig. 12: Bruno Maderna and the tenor Paul Sperry.

Fig. 13: Maderna at the WNCN in New York.

Fig. 14: Bruno Maderna and Han de Vries during rehearsals for the Concerto per Oboe n. 3, 1973.

Fig. 15: Bruno Maderna and Lucas Vis, Amsterdam, 1973.

Fig. 16: Bruno Maderna and Maurice Béjart at La Scala in Milan (P. Boulez's ballet, *Le marteau sans maître*), January 1973.

Fig. 17: Maderna in his home at Darmstadt.

CHAPTER V

THE CRISIS OF TOTAL SERIALISM

Various clues emerging from the late 1950s – after 1956 – would seem to point to a further change in Maderna's way of making and conceiving music, as well as in the techniques he adopted and how he applied them. During the many years of public conferences and private conversations with musicians and critics, especially during the lively weeks of the Darmstadt courses, Maderna had listened attentively to those advocating the annulment of tonality (a concept now widely accepted), but also of any idea of "form." The latter referred not only to form in an academic sense, but to any type of linear structure that foresaw a point of departure and a point of arrival. The new ideology based on numbers was directed increasingly towards the objectivity of "pure material," which inevitably implied excluding to the greatest possible extent any subjective intervention on the part of the composer.

    A very similar move towards objectivity was taking place on the other side of the Atlantic, where the ideology of the so-called "American School" was taken to its extremes in the works and writings of John Cage. Here too the underlying idea was that art should renounce any manifestation of individuality: "The in-the-heart path of music leads now to self-knowledge through self-denial, and its in-the-world path leads likewise to selfishness."[1] In other words, any form of intentional expression was to be avoided: the denial of the self and of individual expression that Cage drew from his reading of Buddhist texts formed the basis for all his criticisms of contemporary music, including that of the European avant-garde. "Curiously enough," he observed, "the twelve-tone system has no zero in it […] a zero musical structure must be just an empty time." The idea of music as "zero" or as "nothing," which often recurs in his writings, implies the need to empty sound of any psychological intrusions: "[…] one must be disinterested to begin with, accept that a sound is a sound and a man is a man, give up illusions about ideas of order and expressions of sentiment, and all the rest of our inherited aesthetic clap-trap."[2] The lack of intentionality almost automatically brought with it the idea of chance: "[…] sounds are to come into their own, rather than being exploited to express sentiments or ideas of order. What brings about

---

[1] J. Cage, *Silence: Lectures and Writings* (Middletown, Connecticut: Wesleyan University Press, 2011), 66.
[2] Ibid., 79-82. These thoughts were originally expressed in an article on Satie published in 1958.

this unpredictability is the use of the method established in the *I Ching* (*Book of Changes*) for the obtaining of oracles, that of tossing three coins six times" and so on.³ Statements of this kind, which were never expressed in the form of rational declarations as in western philosophies, but always in the form of stories, anecdotes and examples, so typical of Zen philosophy, were certainly fascinating, but were open to transversal discussion, and tended to be only partially accepted, without reaching the extreme consequences that Cage implied.

Generally speaking, Maderna preferred to remain detached from this aspect of the avant-garde and had no interest in either refuting it or proposing an alternative theory; he simply continued to apply the new techniques to his work without ever renouncing his commitment to create a dialogue with the listener. In this rather unsettled moment, other "fellow travelers" shared similar doubts. A particularly well-documented example is the case of Boulez. As early as 1954, in an article titled *Recherches maintenant*, he had warned: "All is not going for the best in the realm of the series...." He goes on to speak of how rhythm, timbre and dynamics were all being organized until reaching "a monstrous all-purpose mill."⁴ Boulez ended his essay with a sort of call to arms: "Let us reclaim for music the right to parentheses and italics...," in other words the freedom to experiment with the diverse possibilities of using the numerically prepared material. Some years later, in 1957, the composer resumes the same topic in a long essay, *Aléa*, where he nevertheless does not seem to find a clear balance between his two lines of thought: on the one hand he appears to deplore the inescapable presence of chance even in the most rigorous of constructions ("one desperately tries to dominate the material, but chance finds a thousand ways of creeping in"), while on the other he advocates other forms of probability: "The fetishism of numbers is harmful to music, but one can also consider a proliferation of automatic structures to be organized flexibly, conceding alternative presences and different networks of probability."⁵

Stockhausen, too, gradually introduced the concept of chance into his work, in various stages. The first consisted in leaving it to the performers to freely interpret the tempo markings in a piece like *Zeitmasse* for five woodwinds. This work is based on the "polyphonic" combination of varying time measures,

---

³ Ibid., 57, 69. The citation refers to the composition of *Music for piano*, from an article originally published in *Die Reihe* in 1957.

⁴ P. Boulez, "Current investigations" (1954), *Stocktakings from an Apprenticeship*, trans. Stephen Walsh (Oxford: Oxford University Press, 1991), 15-19, 16. Original title "Recherches maintenant," published in the *Nouvelle Revue Française*, 23 (November 1954), 898-903.

⁵ Pierre Boulez, "Aléa," in *La Nouvelle Revue Française*, 59 (November 1957), 839-57. The essay was read in a German translation during the *Ferienkurse* in July 1957 [*Chronik* 1997, 587].

whereby a sort of "series of tempos" is created, resulting in melodic and harmonic outcomes that the composer is unable to predict. The opening section uses a serial technique, but this is lost when one performer is instructed to play "as fast as possible," another "as slowly as possible" and a third to "start quickly and gradually slow down," etc. The key concept is the "indeterminacy" of the tempos, which each player can choose within certain limits. A similar time framework, though organized in a different way, can be found in his *Klavierstücke V-X*. In other works, and especially in *Klavierstück XI*, Stockhausen introduces a greater percentage of chance, though within the context of a very precise structure. The piece is made up of a set of 19 separate fragments written on a large score (a special frame is needed to keep it open on the music stand), and at the end of each fragment there are instructions about the speed, dynamics and articulations to apply to the next episode, whatever it may be, chosen by the performer. The aleatoric element consists in the fact that the performer should not plan the order in advance, but must play whichever piece happens to catch his/her attention at the time. The composition could therefore be defined "open" as opposed to "aleatory" in the sense used by Cage.

As we have said, Maderna's doubts were shared by other participants of the *Ferienkurse*, and in the second half of the 1950s many composers began to see electronics as a sort of momentary means of escape, or at least of respite, and this could partially explain why he became so readily interested in this new medium. In the meantime, Maderna's two main points of reference continued to be the different musical worlds of Milan and Darmstadt.

"Darmstadt" was neither a faction nor a school. Its initial objective had been to offer young Germans the chance to make up for the time lost during the dark times of Nazism, and hence to stimulate the young generations from all other countries to take part in a renewal of contemporary music. However, after a decade or so, it had become a sort of broad label, almost a convenient way of referring to the "music of today." The most accredited performers of the time held instrumental lessons there, composers held courses on new techniques, and the most sought-after conductors, accustomed to working with orchestras and ensembles in the most important concert halls and theaters in Europe, gave conducting lessons, or else opened their rehearsals to discussion with the participants of the courses; and among the long established theorists and philosophers that now gave conferences in Darmstadt, the name of Adorno stands out, whose thoughts continued for many years to engender both supporters and detractors.

In his characteristically blunt manner and with his usual critical astuteness, Malipiero referred to Darmstadt as the "intestine" city, able to digest everything it was served up.[6] And another voice raised against what was happening in Darmstadt was that of the Austrian musicologist Josef Rufer, well known for his teaching of the "classic" dodecaphonic technique. He openly expressed his disappointment in a letter dated August 1, 1955 to Rognoni, whom he had recently met during the courses: "I often think of Darmstadt: the Tower of Babel…The only thing missing today is 'the genius' who can resolve all these questions, by revealing that they are not really questions but just banter […]. It is truly a pity that this atmosphere in Darmstadt has left us no space for deeper reflection […]."[7] Steinecke, the director of the courses, doubtlessly had his own ideas about the music of today and perhaps of tomorrow, but his main aim was to have as many different languages as possible spoken at Darmstadt.

Milan, on the other hand, had certain aspects in common with, or at least similar to, those of Darmstadt, but also enjoyed its own distinct identity. In the second chapter of this book we quoted Roberto Leydi's vivid evocation of the city in the post-war years. According to the art historian Massimo Martignoni, in the more prosperous 1950s Milan had by then become a national point of reference for the economic, political and cultural rebirth of Italy, even though the Italians (Milanese or otherwise) set out "at a disordered and ineptly joyful pace to gather the mature fruits of consumer society, […] attracted, like bees to flowers, by American-style cuisine, Vespas and Lambrettas […] by Mike Bongiorno and the Kessler twins" [*Pour Bruno* 2015, 45]. But the city also boasted some of the country's finest architects, like Gio Ponti, who in the 1950s "radically changed the skyline of Milan, earning the city a rightful place among the international capitals of modern architecture" [ibid., 50]. As far as music is concerned, the theoretical and practical debate on the exploitation of certain features of the radio centered mainly on the RAI, and benefited from the involvement of specialists from a variety of fields, including linguistics, electronic engineering and music criticism. And it was amid this lively exchange of expertise that the *Studio di Fonologia* was born, an institution that would soon acquire a truly international stature.

But the musical history of the city in this period was also marked by two further events: the publication of the journal *Incontri Musicali: Quaderni internazionali di musica contemporanea* directed by Luciano Berio, the first issue of which came out in December 1956, and the formation of the instrumental group of the same name, directed by Bruno Maderna, which took part in the Darmstadt courses in 1958. In the four years of its existence, the *Quaderni*

---

[6] Letter to Rognoni of July 30, 1956, in P. Misuraca (ed.), *Luigi Rognoni intellettuale europeo*, vol. II, *Carteggi* (Regione Sicilia: edition not commercially available, 2010), 168.

[7] Ibid., 213.

featured articles written by many of the most noted foreign composers involved in the use of serialism: among others, Pousseur, Boulez, Stockhausen and Cage were able to promote their aesthetic views and technical projects in Italy. Also Berio published two fundamental pieces providing details of two his works: *Allelujah* and *Omaggio a Joyce*, while Krenek spoke to the younger generation about the latest trends based on his historical experience in the early phase of dodecaphonic music. Alongside these technical contributions there were also articles by philosophers and critics (including Paci, Eco, Santi, Metzger, and Souris), as well as by engineers that dealt with the equipment used by the radio and the *Studio di Fonologia*, such as Lietti and Righini. Bruno Maderna never wrote any articles for the *Quaderni*, but conducted numerous concerts and presented tapes of electronic music often related to themes covered by the journal.

The newspapers circulating in Milan at the time nevertheless offered contrasting views. Although the principal lines of the press still largely reflected the cultural tastes of the broad Lombard *bourgeoisie*, it was also possible to read the opinions of younger musicians and critics, in many cases participants of the *Ferienkurse*, which appeared above all in the more "progressive" newspapers. At times the coexistence of these two opposing sides reached a point of conflict. For example, in October-November 1955, when Luigi Rognoni's talks about Expressionism, first broadcast in 1952, were repeated on the radio, long articles appeared in the *Corriere Mercantile* by a certain Elfio, with highly explicit titles: *Offensiva d'autunno dei dodecafonici* ("Autumn offensive of the Dodecaphonists"); *Un nuovo assalto dei dodecafonici* ("A fresh assault by the Dodecaphonists"). It is more than likely that the columnist in question had not been able to grasp Rognoni's ideas, which only someone who had completely misunderstood the context could interpret as revolutionary. And shortly afterwards the same Elfio adds a political touch to his musical criticism in an article in praise of an unashamedly tonal work – a genre still being written not only in Italy but throughout the whole of Europe – with the heading: *Finalmente musica vista da destra* ("At last music seen from the right wing"). And Rognoni commented: "I wonder why he speaks of 'right wing'? [...] I must confess that Mr. Elfio's articles are more amusing, in their stupidity, than offensive."[8] These brief examples of the varied and contradictory faces of Milan in the mid-50s may help to explain why Maderna, who had always managed to steer his way through the most contradictory of situations, must, all things considered, have felt quite at his ease.

At the start of 1957 Maderna was in Hamburg to conduct a concert (on January 12) and after a short visit to his family in Darmstadt, returned to Milan,

---

[8] Letter from Luigi Rognoni to Louis Cortese (pianist and composer from Milan working in Paris), Milan, January 20, 1956, ibid., 127-128.

where he arrived on January 16, as we learn from a letter written to Steinecke [*Carteggio* 2001, 124]. Over the next two months, while working at the *Studio di Fonologia*, he found time to carry on an intense correspondence with Steinecke, mainly concerning the two instrumental concerts planned for the coming summer courses. The letters cover a wide range of topics: the program of the concerts would, notably, include a piece titled *Indices* by Earle Brown, an American composer who had recently arrived in Milan; they discuss what sort of instrumental group this would require and whether they should involve the Dresden orchestra; Maderna suggests inviting the students to the rehearsals, which, in a way, would transform them into a "course," during which the conductor and the composer could discuss the fundamental theme of "Realization/Interpretation."

Steinecke discussed Maderna's proposals with the other organizers of the courses, especially regarding the choice of pieces and how much each of them would cost in terms of the number of performers required. And these matters were likely among the topics covered when Maderna stopped off in Darmstadt, around April 20, on his way to a concert in Stockholm. But his visit was short and many issues still remained unresolved. In fact, on June 24, not so long before the opening date of the courses (held that year from July 16 to 28), a distraught Steinecke sent Bruno a brief but earnest telegram: "Please answer all the questions. Best wishes." One of the questions was the pressing need to send the text of a lecture that Maderna was to give on "Composing with electronic means," due to be published in the first issue of the course journal, the *Darmstädter Beiträge*. But more importantly Steinecke urged him to send the tapes from the *Studio* in Milan containing the works that would be presented during the coming *Ferienkurse*: Pousseur's *Scambi*, Berio's *Mutazioni*, and Maderna's *Notturno* and *Syntaxis*. As it turned out, Maderna never wrote the text that his friend had so urgently requested: the lecture he gave on July 26, 1957 (which Steinecke luckily had recorded) has already been discussed in Chapter Four. As far as the tapes of the *Studio* are concerned, they were sent from Milan on July 26 [ibid., 142-143] and arrived just in time for the concert that took place at 8 pm of the same day [*Chronik* 1997, 587].

But between January and July 1957 Maderna's work was by no means limited to the programming of the concerts in Darmstadt. Besides composing works at the *Studio* (to where all his letters are addressed), much of his time was taken up in recording concertos at various branches of the RAI, so much so that he was unable to guarantee he would be attending the whole length of the *Ferienkurse*, even though they lasted just thirteen days. The programs of the RAI concerts were quite varied and tested his ability to tackle all types of repertoire depending on the different radio channels he was working for (although most of his work was with the Third Program of the RAI and involved contemporary music). At the Auditorium of the Foro Italico in Rome he conducted one recording on March 17 and another on May 17 (featuring, among others, works by Varèse and Ives); he was back on the podium in Milan on May 31, and then, on June 17 to 18, he conducted the premiere of a work by Adone Zecchi at the Auditorium delle Celebrazioni in Turin and was there again on July 6to conduct a "Venetian" program which included Torelli's *Concerto* op.8 no.1, Malipiero's *Concerto* no.1 for piano and orchestra, and Renzo Dall'Oglio's *Cinque espressioni*. Still in Turin, on July 17, by which time the Darmstadt courses had already started, he recorded Luciano Berio's "racconto radiofonico" *Waterloo*, premiered at the *Prix Italia* in Taormina [*Romito* 2003/1, 101-102].

This simple list of dates and venues gives a good idea of just how burdensome this aspect of his profession really was, not only on account of the constant traveling but also due to the wide variety of programs he had to prepare, which obviously did not depend on him. Maderna's participation in the 1957 courses in Darmstadt mainly centered on electronic music. For instance, on a single day, July 26, in addition to the previously mentioned lecture, there was also a concert entirely devoted to the work of the *Studio di Fonologia*.[9] However, the only trace of the concert programs discussed at length in his correspondence with Steinecke, is a work by the young Swedish composer Bo Nilsson, in a concert conducted by Maderna. Instead, the courses were notable for the first ever participation of three Italian composers, most probably at the instigation of Maderna himself – Clementi, Evangelisti and Manzoni – as well as for the remarkable success of Nono's *Canto sospeso*, which according to Boris Porena was "by far the finest thing to be heard in Darmstadt this year."[10] But the aspect of the courses that attracted the greatest attention of the public was the decisive move towards the sphere of "alea": rather than increasing the number of totally serial works the organizers made every effort to promote works based on chance, hoping to take advantage of this new trend. The first exposure to the theories of John Cage, in a concert given by David Tudor the previous year, had met with derision and puzzlement, and in some cases even indignation among the listeners and critics. But the theory itself did not go unheeded and various composers, including Maderna, saw it as a way of "breaking down a door" that was already partially open, given that – as we have seen – many of them had already started to have doubts about the future of total serialism.

That year, Maderna's stay in Darmstadt was particularly short. No sooner had the lights of the *Ferienkurse* been turned out, than – probably out of economic

---

[9] Before Darmstadt, *Notturno* and *Syntaxis* were presented in Milan during the concerts of the *Incontri Musicali* on May 24 and 31 of the same year.

[10] B. Porena, "I Ferienkurse di Darmstadt," *Ricordiana* (November 1957), 514-515 [cited in *Trudu* 1992, 119].

necessity – he left the international scene to conduct a concert of opera music for soloists and choir in Milan, which would be broadcast by the RAI on July 29. His engagements as a conductor also kept him busy throughout the second half of the year. Just to give an idea of the variety of the works involved, it is worth mentioning some of these appointments. On September 19 and 20 he conducted two concerts in the cycle "Le Opere di Paul Hindemith" at the auditorium in Turin; on October 18, at the same venue, he gave a concert of recent Italian music that among other things included two important premieres: Nono's *Composizione per orchestra* and Dallapiccola's *An Mathilde*; and on December 2, at the Auditorium in Rome, he conducted an unusual concert titled "I Compositori Moderni e il Jazz" in a program that included *Divertimento per orchestra* jointly composed by Berio and Maderna. This work is particularly significant because it reaffirms the synergy existing between the two composers that Berio later recalls in his previously mentioned article in the *Nuova Rivista Musicale Italiana*. In the article he talks of the time when he was writing his *Nones* and Maderna was working on the *Quartetto*; but their partnership had begun still earlier in *Ritratto di città* and was destined to continue for many years to come. It is also interesting to note that, despite being written by two different hands, it is quite hard to perceive any distinction in the musical language used in the three parts of the *Divertimento per orchestra*. The only noticeable difference lies in the character of the pieces but not their compositional technique. The first part, composed by Maderna, has the enigmatic title "Dark rapture crawl." In an introduction to *Divertimento* Berio states that the fanciful titles of the three pieces were invented by Cathy Berberian and were naturally accepted by the composers. He goes on to say:

> The three parts that make up the work amiably merge into one another without a break. The first and second part [...] were written [...] in 1957. The third part ("Rhumba-ramble") dates from earlier and is taken, unchanged, from my *Mimusique II*. In the first two parts there is a constant reference to the manners and inflections of jazz music in the most symbolic and non literal sense of the word [...]. In the third part, the well known basic rhythm of the *rhumba* is subjected to a constant process of permutations. Therefore, in *Divertimento*, there are constant references to blues, rag and rumba but without ever becoming explicit and are caught up in a network of allusions and transpositions that avoid the *divertissement* suggested by the title and, without openly manifesting or betraying it, hint at the physiognomy of these allusions...[11]

---

[11] Quotation taken from the program notes for the performance of the piece he conducted on November 4, 1989, in *Dialogo con Maderna. 18 concerti. Milano 30 settembre - 20 dicembre 1989* (Milano: RAI Lombardia, 1989), 210.

In Maderna's piece the allusions to jazz can be identified not so much in the rhythm as such but in the timbre of the saxophone quintet that, often in solos, dominates over half of the piece. The broken melodies of these solo episodes are sometimes also given to a trombone or flute, but are always systematically cut short by the intervention of other groups of instruments that obstruct their path. They are mere scraps of melody that are never fully expressed, and seem to be trying to emerge from the dark and apparently disorderly climate of the piece. It is hard to understand the sense at first, but the idea of "dark rapture" suggested by Berberian probably refers to something that gradually finds the strength to impose itself. This interpretation is confirmed by Maderna himself when he inserts two extracts from the same piece under the title "Blues," in *Don Perlimplín*, as a comment to Belisa's amorous advances towards a mysterious being in a red cloak, who is later discovered to have killed himself on her account. After this dramatic start *Divertimento* lifts its mood in the two following parts, the first a "Scat rag" and the second a stormy finale with percussive rhythms, carefully structured, and concluding in an exuberant burst of vitality. There are no records of the work being performed again during Maderna's lifetime, and in fact both composers went on to use material from their respective parts in later works.

Despite the combined efforts put into the writing of pieces like *Divertimento*, the two composers nevertheless retained their own characteristic styles. The difference between the works of Maderna and those of Berio could, to some extent, be put down to their diverse backgrounds and also to the five years separating them in age. While Maderna's first tentative experiments with serialism date from 1948 and the technique always remained deep-rooted in his work, Berio first emerged on the international scene in 1953, and by that time many of the issues surrounding structuralism had reached a fairly common solution. And so, from the outset, his attention was focused more on how he could exploit the technique in his music.

The assumption that 1957 was, for Maderna, the year of music for radio and electronics, is further confirmed by the fact that in December he was awarded the Sczuka Prize by Radio Baden Baden, amounting to the considerable sum of 2000 Deutsche Marks for his contribution to Patroni Griffi's radio play *Il mio cuore è nel Sud* (1949), translated into German as *Stadt im Süden*. Since the few available letters dating from autumn 1957 are addressed to Piazzale Accursio 12, it would be reasonable to assume that Maderna was now based in Milan, presumably with his family, and traveled from there to other parts of Italy. Among the correspondence sent to this address is a letter from Steinecke, dating from early 1958, in which, as usual, he raises the question of the programs for the forthcoming *Ferienkurse*. It was evidently such a large undertaking that he preferred to meet Maderna in person: "Couldn't you stop off at Darmstadt for a couple of hours <u>before</u> you go to Cologne? This would be the perfect occasion to discuss everything." The fact that Steinecke was asking him to fit in a brief meeting while he was on his way to his various conducting engagements would seem to imply that Maderna had no intention of staying in Darmstadt for any length of time, as he certainly would have done had Christine and their daughter been living there. He was planning to be there just for the period of the *Ferienkurse*, which in 1958 were held quite late in the year, from September 2 to 13. So where else would his family be living if not in Milan?

One of the things that Steinecke wished to discuss was Maderna's contribution to the journal *Darmstädter Beiträge*. In particular he was keen that he should write an article about electronic music, a topic the composer had previously dealt with in his lecture of 1957, but something he had never written about. Another issue, one that Maderna found more attractive, was the possibility to organize one or two concerts that would feature the chamber group Incontri Musicali, or even an entire concert dedicated to Italian music, similar to the Italian Evening that had taken place in 1952. Both Maderna and Berio were immediately enthusiastic, but they were nevertheless concerned about the costs involved in moving the whole group to Darmstadt and accommodating them for the entire length of the rehearsals and performance. Steinecke, too, was rightly worried about this aspect, since the economic side of the courses was part of his role as organizer; he repeatedly suggested they should ask the Italian authorities for support, especially the Ministry in charge of cultural exchanges between Italy and other countries.[12] Whether or not they followed his advice is hard to say, but if their previous dealings with financial matters are anything to go by, this appears very doubtful; the fact is that they were unable to obtain any help and Maderna urged Steinecke to find some means of financing the project through the organization of the *Ferienkurse* itself, or if not from some local radio, in exchange for concerts or recordings. Whatever the case, the concert involving the group of ten musicians eventually took place on September 5, during which Gazzelloni played the 1958 version of *Musica su due dimensioni* [*Chronik* 1997, 590-591].

As we have said, Maderna was at the time based in Milan, and it was from here that he set out on his various travels to fulfill the various commitments he had taken on, mostly at the request of the RAI, who invited him to record programs of varying kinds. One of his first appointments in 1958 took him to Naples, where the Associazione Alessandro Scarlatti, one of the oldest concert

---

[12] Steinecke's letter is undated, but he makes reference to a previous letter, no longer traceable, that Maderna and Berio had sent him on February 21.

institutions in Italy (founded in 1919), was particularly active in this period. In 1949 the Scarlatti Orchestra had united with the local ensemble of the RAI in Naples, and in 1956 officially became one of the RAI's several regional orchestras. The orchestra's repertoire had now expanded from its original scope of rediscovering ancient Neapolitan music, to include a rigorous revisitation of "classical" music and a wide range of contemporary and avant-garde music, giving concerts at various venues around the city and especially at the Conservatorio S. Pietro a Majella.[13] Maderna arrived in Naples on January 9 and stayed there several days to record G. Pietri's operetta *Acqua cheta* at the Teatro dell'Arte, later broadcast on TV, and, on January 17, a concert at the Conservatorio San Pietro a Majella dedicated to the wider audience of the association AGIMUS, featuring music by Geminiani, Haydn, Mozart and Schumann.

After Naples he returned to Milan where, from January 24 to 30, he rehearsed and recorded Kurt Weill's musical comedy, *Knickerbocker Holiday* in its first Italian performance. Maderna's well-affirmed eclecticism and his highly versatile skills enabled him to adapt perfectly to the wide range of repertoire covered in his work with the RAI. These programs do not, of course, reflect Maderna's personal preferences as a conductor, but rather the notable variety of performances offered to radio and television audiences in that period. On February 11, in the Auditorium A of the RAI in Rome, he conducted a particularly refined concert entirely devoted to Wolf's Lieder for soprano and orchestra. And no less interesting, but of a totally different genre, were the two concerts given in Cologne in March for the festival *Musik der Zeit*, where he conducted a program that included works by Stockhausen, Berio and Varèse.

On some occasions Maderna was directly commissioned by the RAI to write music for their radio transmissions. He was, for example, invited to contribute to the series *Fiabe Teatrali*, which involved a combination of traditional instruments and voices, and the new tools available at the *Studio di Fonologia*. In April 1958 Maderna composed and conducted the music for *Augellino belverde*, a "philosophical tale" by Carlo Gozzi, a well known eighteenth century writer from Venice, adapted in three parts for radio by Vittorio Sermonti. The text – made up of parts in verse and prose, and others left to the free improvisation of the actors – prompted Maderna to write a soft parody of eighteenth century melodrama, underlined by recognizable quotations from Mozart. A total of seven instrumental and eight vocal pieces from this work are deposited at the SIAE, featuring a quite unusual group of instruments (that also included a glass harmonica) accompanied by strange and novel effects produced by electronic

---

[13] P. P. De Martino, "Scarlatti e Rai due istituzioni per un'orchestra," in *'Appunti di viaggio'. Novant'anni della Associazione Alessandro Scarlatti*, ed. R. Bossa (Napoli: Grimaldi, 2009), 121-133.

devices.¹⁴ The title of one of the last pieces, *Ho bevuto e visto il ragno*, recounting the exploits of the fairy Tartagliona, was used again many years later by Sermonti, in 1999, for a collection of poems, introduced by the words "dedicated to Bruno Maderna, Rome, February 1958." De Benedictis, who edited the score for Edizioni Suvini Zerboni, reproduces a part of the work in her book on radio drama (the *Sinfonia del complotto*) and comments on the relations between music and spoken dialogue.¹⁵ Her remarks leave us in no doubt that this particular branch of his work represented a kind of escape, a game he unashamedly enjoyed, and was not merely a matter of economic necessity. Further evidence came shortly afterwards, in November of the same year, when, together with Berio, he was commissioned by the RAI to write the music for *La scampagnata*, a play based on Eugène Scribe's vaudeville *Le déjeuner sur l'herbe*, freely translated and adapted by one of the most talented radio play directors of the moment, Alessandro Brissoni.¹⁶

Immediately after the transmission of *Augellino belverde*, Maderna was in Brussels where, on 25 April, he conducted an important concert featuring his *Serenata n. 2*, Nono's *Epitaffio* and Berio's *Nones*. He then resumed his collaboration with the RAI, which, among other things, foresaw the first performance of various significant works. On May 17, at the Auditorium del Foro Italico in Rome, he conducted the world premiere of Berio's *Alleluja II per orchestra*, while the concerts of contemporary music organized by the ISCM and held in Naples at the Conservatorio di San Pietro a Majella on June 13 and 16, included the world premieres of Nono's *Incontri* and Berio's *Serenata per flauto e 14 strumenti* [*Romito* 2020].

The same period saw the completion of the second version of *Musica su due dimensioni* (1958), although the sources offer conflicting accounts on this matter. According to *Chronik* 1997 (591) the work was given its first performance on September 5 during the Darmstadt courses, and a recording of the event exists at the *Centro Studi Maderna*. However, the same archive also holds a tape sent by the RAI, which contains a recording of the work made in the great hall of the Conservatorio di S. Pietro a Majella in Naples on June 11, 1958. This was presumably a preview performance in anticipation of the premiere to be given during the *Ferienkurse*. Having said this, it should be pointed out that *Musica su due dimensioni* differs from all his previous works in its being the first of many "open

---

¹⁴ *Romito* 2000/2, 239; *Romito* 2002/1, 82.

¹⁵ For Sermonti's collection of poems, see *Ho bevuto e visto il ragno. Cento pezzi facili* (Milano: Il Saggiatore, 1999). For *Sinfonia del complotto*, see A. I. De Benedictis, *Radiodramma ed arte radiofonica. Storia e funzioni della musica per radio in Italia* (Torino: EDT, 2004), 135-147.

¹⁶ *Romito* 2002/1, 82. Alessandro Brissoni later made it into a film titled *La merenda sull'erba*, in 1991.

works" that Maderna would write over the following years. And so the two recordings (from Naples and Darmstadt) that are discussed below should not be seen as "performances" of the work, but rather as two different "versions".

First of all, let us consider the sense of the word "dimensioni." In those years Maderna used the term to refer to the distinction between the dimension of electronic sounds and that of live sounds. As we have seen, he already used the term back in 1952; six years later, when he returned to the idea of contrasting the two "dimensions," only the title of the former piece remained, whereas the musical substance and structure changed radically.[17] The new part for flute was composed on the basis of the usual serial techniques, while the part for tape owes much to the three electronic works written between 1956 and '58. The score specifies five sections for the flute and five for the tape. The order of the sections is given on the first page, but this is just a kind of index and not an instruction for their performance. In fact, the two versions mentioned above, recorded in the presence of Maderna, both feature a much richer and varied interaction between the flute and tape. The Naples version, for example, contains as many as eleven alternations, in which the flute sections are easily identifiable since they are written in the score, whereas the division of the sections for tape is less clear.

The two versions in question are, then, quite different from one another and almost seem to have been structured on the basis of the differing expectations of the two distinct audiences. In the Naples version the form of the piece seems to be suggested by the predominance of certain expressive characters: the uncertainty and rhythmic ferment of the opening is followed by a sweet, cantabile passage on the flute, which is suddenly contrasted by a much harsher episode; but the piece ends with a consolatory finale. The Darmstadt version, on the other hand, is much more varied and unpredictable, consisting of numerous brief episodes that follow one another with unexpected shifts and contrasts: in other words, the piece does not present any perceptible or memorizable form. The pronounced difference between the two versions highlights the fact that this is not a work as such, but rather a modular construction that can be put together each time in a different manner.

Despite being a significant milestone within Maderna's output, *Musica su due dimensioni* does not seem to have made any notable impact at the *Ferienkurse*. One reason for this could be the great interest stimulated by the presence of new composers and in particular of John Cage, who, together with David Tudor, held as many as four meetings, including both seminars and concerts. However,

---

[17] Interestingly, in the same year Maderna chose to call his course at Darmstadt *Composizione per strumenti e nastro elettronico*.

the 1958 edition of the *Ferienkurse* will also be remembered for another, totally unexpected turn of events. Less than a month before the courses were due to begin Boulez wrote to Steinecke saying he would be unable to attend. This sudden decision on the part of one of the key figures of the annual event was not only a serious blow to the organizers but also disheartening news for "regular guests" like Nono and Maderna. In a letter to Steinecke, undated but probably written near the start of August, in response to one or more letters now lost and to phone calls alluded to in the text, the two composers, who both added their signatures (and perhaps wrote the letter together as it is typewritten and only the signatures are autograph), set out their proposals on how to fill the gaps resulting from the departure of Boulez:

> Together with Gigi [Nono] I have thought long about what would be best to do to allay the effects of Boulez's treachery. We believe there are two possibilities: 1) Stockhausen will hold the seminars in place of Boulez on the same subject;[18] 2) Gigi and I will hold Boulez's ten seminars, and by adding our own three courses we can create one single course [there follows a list of thirteen appointments, often involving meetings both in the morning and afternoon of the same day]. As I mentioned on the phone I am willing to take over the two chamber concerts of the "Domaine Musical." I hope that Bour will be able to do the symphonic concert with the Frankfurt orchestra [*Carteggio* 2001, 164-167].

Maderna and Nono were therefore prepared to take on the task of ensuring that there would be no gaps in the program on account of Boulez's desertion. Even though Steinecke eventually managed to limit to some extent the amount of work Maderna had been willing to take on, the following list prepared by Steinecke, with the relative fees, reveals that his contribution was still considerable:

> So you can see that you won't just be working hard but will also be earning [...]. I can inform you that: from Frankfurt you will receive the fees agreed upon for conducting [in place of Boulez]; again from Frankfurt, the fee for the performance of Schönberg's *Suite*. From Darmstadt [...] for conducting the "Incontri Musicali" concert on September 5 and the "Domaine Musical" concert on September 6 [...], and a payment from Cologne radio for the recording with "Incontri." On top of this there is naturally the accommodation in a hotel in Jugenheim and in the castle of Heiligenberg. Thank you once again, best wishes [ibid., 173].

---

[18] In his imperfect German, Maderna probably meant that Stockhausen's three seminars could cover the same topic that Boulez would have dealt with.

This brief summary provided by Steinecke could prompt various other remarks, but to remain within the theme of this chapter we will limit ourselves to observing that Maderna evidently had no home in Darmstadt (and so presumably his family was not there either). It still remains to understand, though, what exactly led Boulez to his "treachery." Various critics, fully reliable and well informed about the facts, appear to have no doubts that the inclinations of the so-called American school, and in particular of Cage, first presented at the Darmstadt courses in 1956, were so anomalous as to make the simultaneous participation of the two former friends quite incompatible.19 The long association between Boulez and Cage, which had begun during the American's stay in Paris in 1949 and had continued through an intense correspondence until 1954, would appear to suggest that the two musicians initially shared common interests: among other things Boulez was always fascinated by the complex sounds of the prepared piano. But after 1954, and for no apparent reason, they stopped writing to one another. It should also be remembered that in his last letter to Cage in July 1954 Boulez writes: "Clearly we disagree as far as that goes – I do not admit—and I believe I never will admit— chance as a component of a completed work."[20]

Some hints of discordance at Darmstadt had emerged in 1956 during Wolpe's seminar on Music in America and Tudor's performance of pieces by Cage; and yet Boulez does not seem to have been particularly affected by this fact since he had already arrived at a certain element of "indeterminancy" in his own work. In the discussions that followed David Tudor's performance of the first two parts of *Music of Changes*, the positions assumed by Boulez and Stockhausen were divergent, as was their knowledge of Cage's music: Stockhausen was contrary, Boulez was prudent, and in fact, as Piero Santi confirms, the discussions after Wolpe's seminar focused more on technical aspects than on any theoretic-aesthetic principles. Other commentators instead report that the official reason put forward by Boulez – which many consider to be merely a pretext – was of a more practical nature, making it necessary for him to change his plans. In the spring of that year (1958) Boulez had been invited to work at the SWR in Baden-Baden by Heinrich Strobel, director of the Music department and convinced advocate of New Music and promoter of young talent. Strobel considered his presence so important that he not only offered him access to all the highly sophisticated equipment of the Radio, but also invited him to his own home as a fixed guest from June onwards.[21] And in fact,

---

[19] This hypothesis is also put forward in *Trudu*, 1992, 128.

[20] J. J. Nattiez (ed.), *Pierre Boulez - John Cage, Correspondance et documents* (Mainz: Schott, 2002), 242.

[21] D. Jameux, *Pierre Boulez* (Paris: Fayard-Sacem, 1984), 105.

Boulez began working on an ambitious piece on a text by Henry Michaux, *Poésie pour pouvoir*, that called for particularly large forces: two groups of instruments, a group of vocal soloists and a narrator, in addition to electronic sounds on a 5 track tape, for a duration of 18'40". In the end, the impact of the piece was not as great as he had hoped for, maybe due to his inexperience with electronics, and he made a new version in the '80s exploiting the more modern tools available at IRCAM.

Besides the participation of musicians from across the Atlantic, another noteworthy aspect of the 1958 courses was the concert of electronic music given on September 4 that featured works coming from different "schools": that of Cologne Radio and that of the *Studio di Fonologia* in Milan (whose contribution included Maderna's *Continuo* and Berio's *Perspectives*). The Italian Concert promised by Steinecke earlier that spring took place on September 5, when Maderna conducted the newly formed group Incontri Musicali in a program of works by the Italian composers Walter Marchetti, Franco Donatoni, Luigi Dallapiccola and Aldo Clementi, and the Spanish composer Juan Hidalgo. The concert also included Maderna's *Musica su due dimensioni* and Berio's *Sequenza I*, both featuring Severino Gazzelloni, one of the brightest stars of the *Ferienkurse*. In the concerts given on September 6 and 11, Maderna conducted the *Domaine Musical*. Memorable too was the concert held on September 7, in which the choir of the Kölner Rundfunk had to give an encore of Nono's *Cori di Didone* on Ungaretti's *La terra promessa*. Another interesting moment was the class held by Nono and Maderna on September 10 (and then repeated on 12 and 13), made up of a combination of lectures, analysis and performances that covered works by composers of various nationalities, including three Italians – Boris Porena and Franco Evangelisti from Rome, and Antonino Titone from Palermo – which extended the scope to include works by composers from the southern part of Italy.

After the end of the courses Maderna returned to Milan, apparently leaving the city only twice during the next two months, once in September for a concert in Liège and then in October for another in Brussels. The main reason for his prolonged stay in Milan was the continuing success of the Italian version of Brecht's *Dreigroschenoper* at the Piccolo Teatro, which had as many as seventy-six performances between November 15, 1958 and January 19, 1959, and was then taken to Turin, where it was staged at the Teatro Carignano from January 21 to 25. Although only Maderna's name appears as conductor during this long run of performances, he was almost certainly substituted on some occasions, perhaps by Vittorio Fellegara and Gino Negri, mentioned only under the heading "musical collaboration." Maderna could not, for instance, have been at the Piccolo Teatro in Milan on November 21, when he was conducting a concert at the RAI in Turin, nor on December 1 when he conducted at the

Angelicum; while on January 9 and 13 he was back in Brussels for two more important concerts [*Romito* 2020].

Throughout this intense bout of work as a conductor, Maderna was thus able to enjoy a fairly stable period of residence in Milan (most likely with his family), during which he could also concentrate on his involvement in radio plays, as well as starting work on an important new composition, the *Concerto per pianoforte e orchestra* dedicated to David Tudor. The fact that he could devote himself simultaneously to such diverse styles and genres is further proof of his immense versatility, and of the virtually all-embracing nature of his musical creativity: on the one hand he freely used idioms drawn from jazz and popular song in order to satisfy the tastes of a public that "consumed" the radio broadcasts as part of their daily lives, a public that needed to be attracted by something familiar, recognizable and yet able to offer them surprises; and on the other, he effectively communicated with an audience of more attentive listeners, often frequenting the concert hall, who were curious, eager to understand and to be challenged by music they had never heard before, different from the usual repertoire. And we are not speaking simply of differences in musical styles, but also of different routes of communication that required the composer/performer/conductor to have the ability to assume different guises, in other words to become a single figure endowed with multiple facets. Maderna's dual role as composer and conductor remained effortlessly intact until the end of his life. This clearly emerges in an extract from a conversation with Christof Bitter broadcast on the Saarländischer Rundfunk in 1970:

> For me, these two activities are totally compatible; but at times it is very tiring because they require two different approaches: your own composition should be kept inside you, while those you conduct need a great deal of external energy. However, I believe that this direct and constant contact with music, not only as abstract thought in the form of a theoretical formulation, but also as a practical experience, as living sonic material, is very important [*Documenti* 1985, 102].

Maderna had, in fact, been accustomed to tackling a vast variety of different genres right from his very first experiences as a conductor as a child prodigy. And he maintained the same fundamental convictions even in his more mature years, as he affirms in a radio interview carried out in Chicago in January 1970:

> Music is so important: you dance to music, you pray, you die, you dine, you go to a concert. It is a boundless means of communication. When there are no mere words to express what you feel, that's where music begins; and there are many moments when our vocabulary is not adequate [ibid., 96].

Looking at Maderna's activity in this stretch of time towards the end of the '50s, it is often hard to understand whether his greatest need was to write his own music or to interpret the work of others, that of colleagues more or less close to him or of composers of the past, and whether he was more inclined to search for new paths or preferred to re-explore forms of communication that were more simple, but were never, as he himself stresses, "cheap" [ibid., 95]. All in all, one could say that in this period, more than at any other time, it is particularly hard to make out which Maderna is Dr. Jekyll and which is Mr. Hyde. It goes without saying that his more commercial output was in general more short-lived and only fragments have survived in particular archives, but the priceless work of Maurizio Romito on Maderna's incidental music for the RAI, the television and theater, together with Angela Ida De Benedictis' book on radiophonic art and the assorted writings of Leo Izzo on film music, have opened the way to a long overdue reassessment of this group of repertoires.[22]

At the start of 1959, between the end of January and beginning of February, Maderna spent around two weeks recording the musical comedy *Il cavallo di Troia* with the *Orchestra della RAI di Milano*, and so other compositions dating from this time were presumably written during or immediately after the Christmas and New Year period. The text of the American novelist Christopher Morley, freely adapted for radio by Gastone Da Venezia and Ugo Liberatore, is a lighthearted revisitation of various episodes of the Trojan War: the battle field has become a football game, whose events are reported in the newspaper *Evening Trojan*; there is a nightclub where the Mirmidon Boys are performing, who can also be heard on Radio Ilio, and so on. Around fifteen "numbers," still highly enjoyable today, have survived, including songs, marches, types of dance and overtures, all owned by Edizioni Suvini Zerboni [Romito 2002/1, 83]. Proof of the care with which Maderna composed and preserved his more commercial music comes from the fact that one of the Blues pieces used in the radio play, a piano solo, was originally written for Antonio Leonviola's film, *Le due verità*, dating from several years before (1951). At the express wish of the composer, the singers in the radio play were the actors themselves, that is to say the well known and much loved voices of Giorgio De Lullo, Rossella Falk, Romolo Valli, and Anna Maria Guarnieri [*Romito* 2000/2, 240-241].

In April, Maderna is again busy with the recording of another play, *Laure persécutée*, part of a series broadcast on the Third Program of the RAI focusing

---

[22] A. I. De Benedictis, *Radiodramma*, cited in note 15; L. Izzo, "Il commento sonoro realizzato da Bruno Maderna per il film *Le due verità*," in *Bruno Maderna. Studi e Testimonianze*, eds. R. Dalmonte, M. Russo (Lucca: LIM, 2004), 299-341.

on French literature of the seventeenth century, which gave him the chance to work once more with Virginio Puecher, who had been involved in the Italian production of Brecht's *Dreigroschenoper*. In this case, though, Maderna was not only the director of the music and sound effects, but also composed the score. About one month later, from May 19 to 22, he was the composer and conductor of the incidental music to Enzo Maurri's radio comedy *Aspetto Matilde*, recorded for the National Program of the RAI. The work is particularly notable for how he skillfully manages to place the voices, sounds and noises of the play – easily identifiable on account of their sonic characteristics – in different spaces. As in *Ritratto di città*, whose subheading clearly identifies it as a *Studio per una rappresentazione radiofonica*, here too, thanks to the various effects obtained from manipulating the sounds and noises, the audience is able to imagine a reality perceived solely with the ear and not with the eye and ear, as in the theater. Part of the play takes place amid the noises in a bar, where the customers are listening to the voice of a singer (that of Cathy Berberian) on the radio. So those listening to the play can hear Berberian's voice coming from a radio inside the radio. Finally, at the start of July, he recorded Ranko *Marinkovič*'s story for radio, *Mani*, directed by Alessandro Brissoni, who had often worked alongside Maderna in previous radio productions.

But his work with the RAI was not limited to producing incidental music for radio plays. In the same period, for example, he recorded an important concert held at the Auditorium del Foro Italico in Rome on February 28, whose program included two Italian premieres: Messiaen's *Oiseaux exotiques* and Nono's *Due espressioni* for orchestra. Nor was the RAI his only source of work in that particularly eventful year. In addition to the various projects listed above, three important theater productions should be mentioned: on June 25 at the Miramare Castle in Trieste, he conducted the music for Massimo Dursi's play *Massimiliano e Carlotta*, with stage direction by Sandro Bolchi; on June 29 at the Teatro Romano in Ostia Antica, he was musical director for an Italian production of Shakespeare's *A Midsummer Night's Dream*, with stage direction by Mario Ferrero; and on July 4 at the Teatro Romano in Verona he prepared the music for a production of Shakespeare's *Julius Caesar* in a translation by Eugenio Montale, again directed by Sandro Bolchi. Particularly impressive was the staging and lighting of the production at the Miramare Castle, where the audience were seated in a raised stand above the sea in front of the castle and the sounds were transmitted through six loudspeakers, some on the land and some on the sea. The incidental music was a rich blend of effects obtained with electronic technology and pieces purposely composed by Berio and Maderna, performed by the Orchestra dei Pomeriggi Musicali and conducted by Maderna. The performance in Ostia was also held in the open air and in an equally evocative setting. The musical accompaniment was a harmonious combination of music by Mendelssohn, chosen and adapted by Berio and Maderna, and electronic pieces, either composed especially for the event or taken from previous works by Maderna. For *Julius Caesar* at the Teatro Romano in Verona, Maderna prepared an original electronic tape that also contained noise effects. This production was repeated a few weeks later at the Teatro Comunale in Bologna, and was broadcast live on television.[23]

His engagements as a conductor were by no means confined to Italy. In a letter dated April 22, after sending his birthday greetings, Steinecke wonders if Bruno could stop off in Darmstadt for a while before his now habitual visit to Cologne. Maderna had no plans for any performances in Cologne, but was probably going there to work with the city's radio orchestra in preparation for the two concerts scheduled for the *Wiener Festwochen* on June 15 and 17, the second of which would include Stockhausen's *Gruppen* and Nono's *Il canto sospeso*. In the same months Maderna's music for radio received various important recognitions. Among other things, his *Amor di violino* on a text by Ermanno Carsana was awarded first prize in the 1958-59 competition for original works for radio organized by the RAI. In this instance the instruments are personalized and transformed into prototypes of human vices and virtues [*Romito* 2000/2, 242]. A similar blend of human voices and instrumental voices would appear again some years later in *Don Perlimplin* and *Hyperion*, in which some characters "speak" with the voice of particular instruments.

The months leading up to the latest edition of the Darmstadt courses (which in 1959 were held from August 25 to September 5) could therefore not have been more demanding in terms of his commitments as a composer and a conductor, and yet Maderna also found time to write one of his most important works of this period, which was precisely linked to the recent developments at Darmstadt: the *Concerto per pianoforte e orchestra* dedicated to David Tudor. Steinecke seems to have had some notion of the importance of this work, given that in a letter of March 5 he immediately announces he would like to include it in a concert that Maderna was due to give with the Frankfurt Radio Orchestra [*Carteggio* 2001, 182-183]. In a fragment of a letter, not dated but probably written shortly afterwards, in the spring of that year, Maderna makes an interesting comment about the planning of the program for the upcoming summer courses. He is against the idea of including music by Cage "as he only wants his own new things, and these are not good." This scathing judgment leaves us in no doubt as to Maderna's position with regards the wind of "chance" that was blowing from across the Atlantic, one that would have no small influence,

---

[23] The three productions are described in detail in *Romito* 2000/2 and *Romito* 2002/1.

but that would also bring about deep rifts within the European avant-garde. Some time later (letter of July 29) Steinecke comes back to the program for the concert of the Frankfurt orchestra; in particular he asks Maderna to write an introduction for the program notes and to send him the facsimile of a page of the *Concerto* for David Tudor. And he also mentions the work that had been successfully presented the previous year, *Musica su due dimensioni*, which similarly needed a description written by the composer (which never came to be). On this matter, Steinecke adds an interesting remark: he asks him if this time, during the courses of 1959, *Musica su due dimensioni* would include a part for the xylorimba, thus implying that the idea of increasing the contribution of live instruments had not been completely shelved [ibid., 192-194]; in the end, though, the piece was once again performed with the sole participation of Gazzelloni [*Chronik* 1997, 600].

The first thing that strikes one about the *Concerto per pianoforte* is that, contrary to what one might expect, the two most significant stylistic features that had characterized Maderna's output over the previous years (after 1955) are suddenly missing, namely the use of electronics and the introduction of aleatoric elements. According to Maurizio Romito, who examined the numerous surviving preparatory sketches, the *Concerto* is based on a fresh application of the same serial material as used in *Dark Rapture Crawl*.[24] At first glance this would seem to be a return to the techniques he had last used in his *Quartetto* (1955) or, more to the point, in the *Divertimento* written jointly with Berio (1957). But in reality the recourse to this technique allowed Maderna to feel he was working on safe ground, something he considered necessary when his underlying intentions were in line with the experimental aesthetics of the avant-garde (a consideration clearly not applicable to the various pieces of "functional" music mentioned above). However, on listening to the *Concerto* or studying its score, it becomes quite evident that the serial technique is simply used as a starting point: the five dense introductory pages of the score are entirely given over to a set of highly detailed performing instructions not only for the orchestral instruments, but especially for the piano, which is exploited in such a way as to produce an unprecedented range of timbres. When the piano keyboard is played with the fingers the purpose is to create contrasts in timbre with respect to what came before (for example, single notes compared to violent bursts, transparent textures compared to dense groups, low registers compared to high); but the majority of the instructions are not for notes played with the fingers, but rather with the forearm or with the flat of the hand, or else for when the fingers touch parts of the piano other than the keyboard, for example the wood or the

---

[24] See *Documenti* 1985, 228.

inner strings; not to mention the countless instructions regarding the use of timpani mallets or the innumerable forms of glissandos. On top of all this we must add the exceptional dimension of the orchestra, made up of no less than thirty-six wind instruments and forty-two strings, without counting the harps, the keyboards and the percussion.

As far as the overall sonic effect is concerned, the most notable feature is that Maderna avoids creating arches of tension: the listener is instead expected to focus on short, local episodes, momentary forms that alternate with one another, sometimes in contrast but more often featuring a constant shift of colors and timbres. Particular attention to the timbre had already been evident in the *Quartetto*, but in this case one could say that the *Concerto* represents a sort of enormous expansion of what the *Quartetto* had achieved in a more reduced form. The complexity of the score is nothing less than monstrous, in the sense that each of the thousands of notes is always accompanied by extremely precise performing indications, aimed at obtaining very particular timbres. Maderna, of course, was well aware of his own intentions and had no difficulty in realizing them in the performance he conducted on September 2, 1959, skillfully dosing the blends and successions of sounds he had imagined. David Tudor, too, was prodigiously confident in his technique and in his discerning interpretation, and even the small liberties he occasionally took seem to have met with the composer's approval. The listener is never called upon to respond emotionally to the music, but is rather invited to take each episode as a separate entity and to savor the unusual and unpredictable sounds. The only concession to rhetoric appears at the end of the piece, when the music slowly fades away into an entrancing silence.[25]

The extent to which the *Concerto* was influenced, if at all, by the ideas of Cage and of American music at the time, is hard to say. The provocative aesthetic and philosophical stance taken by Cage was met with contrasting, not always favorable responses in Europe. But his prophetic notion of the prepared piano, which dated from the pre-war years, had aroused the curiosity and often enthusiasm of many of those concerned. Maderna's *Concerto* could perhaps be seen as a sort of extension of Cage's idea, most likely combined with his recent experience with electronic timbres (although he never spoke of this aspect explicitly). It should also be added that while Cage's work, when presented by Tudor in 1956, had been met with bewilderment and had even prompted violent protests about the way the instrument was treated, Maderna had no intention of eliciting any form of provocation, his sole aim being to create a world of exquisite timbres.

---

[25] Maderna's performance with the Frankfurt Radio Symphony Orchestra is captured on a tape preserved in the *Centro Studi Maderna*.

The 1959 edition of the *Ferienkurse* also brought with it certain changes of a more practical nature. The event was now shared between two different venues, the recently built Studentenheim in the town center, with a limited capacity, and the Hessischer Rundfunk in Frankfurt where the *Tage für Neue Musik* were held. And some courses started on August 25, whereas the rehearsals in Frankfurt had already begun on August 17. As always, the individual instrumental and composition seminars were led by internationally famous experts, including Maderna, who that year chose as his theme "Composing for instruments and tape," in other words, the "two dimensions" he had explored in his recent work. The lectures, on the other hand, which were traditionally characterized by a wide range of theoretical and ideological perspectives, in 1959 were marked by conflicting lines of thought and attitudes. Indeed, the chapter of Trudu's book covering that year was fittingly titled *Fine di un'amicizia* ("The end of a friendship"), although in reality there were at least two significant clashes of ideals. Boulez's lecture on his *Troisième Sonate* focused almost exclusively on attacking the concept of "open work" as proposed by Cage and Stockhausen. In particular, his criticism of Cage confirms the unbreachable gap that had now opened between the two former friends. On the other hand, although the main target in Nono's provocative lecture *Historical presence in today's music* was undoubtedly Cage, he had no qualms about expressing his objections towards all those who abandoned music to chance, suggesting that they were afraid of freedom and so avoided making personal decisions that were based on a history of music, and of mankind, that had created the conditions of the present. These comments prompted a strong reaction on the part of Stockhausen, both immediately and in the following year.[26]

The styles and forms of the works presented at the courses that year were equally contrasting, and elicited widely differing reactions among the participants and in the articles that ensued. It is interesting, for example, to compare the two different approaches adopted in two works explicitly dedicated to David Tudor: Maderna's *Concerto* and Sylvano Bussotti's *5 Piano Pieces for David Tudor*. While both pieces are inclined towards the pianist's extraordinary technical skills and his adherence to the aesthetics of the American School, the musical substance is highly different, if not decidedly contrasting. Unlike Maderna, who, as we have seen, offered meticulous guidance to the performer's interpretation, Bussotti totally detaches himself from the sonic result of his work, which he had written in the space of just a few months at the start

---

[26] See *K. Stockhausen bei den Internationalen Ferienkurse für Neue Musik in Darmstadt 1951-1996: Dokumente und Briefe*, eds. Imke Misch und Markus Bandur (Kürten: Stockhausen Stiftung für Musik, 2001), 210.

of 1959 at the suggestion of Hans-Klaus Metzger. In place of a score as such, Bussotti provides the pianist with a line drawing made ten years before, apparently leaving its interpretation totally open to the fantasy of the performer, although the lines of the drawing might, perhaps, be seen as a sort of guide for the performer to follow. However, the work was not as provocative as it may have seemed, since during the courses of that year (from August 26 to 31) Stockhausen held five seminars on the theme *Musik und Graphik*, during which, in addition to this own works, he also presented and analyzed live recordings of works by Cornelius Cardew (who also played his own piano pieces) and John Cage, similarly based on graphic scores.

Following his short but intense stay in Darmstadt, Maderna returned to Italy to attend to his multifaceted commitments with the RAI, which took him not only to Milan and Rome but also to Venice, where on September 14 he conducted the Orchestra della RAI di Roma in a concert at La Fenice, held as part of the *XXII Festival di Musica Contemporanea*. The program of the concert – which was recorded live – was entirely devoted to world premieres, and saw the participation of his friend Gino Gorini at the piano. The works in question were mostly by Italian composers, including Roman Vlad, Boris Porena and Mario Peragallo, but the concert also premiered a piece by Hans Erich Apostel, a German composer who had studied with Alban Berg. It was, then, a typical program of dodecaphonic music, closer to its historic form than to that of the new avant-garde.

On October 16 to 17 he was in Rome with the same orchestra to prepare for the RAI's production of Alban Berg's *Lulu*, with Ilona Steingruber in the title role. The choice of this particular opera had been proposed two years before by Luigi Rognoni, who recalls the occasion as follows:

> [Maderna] wanted me to play an active role and suggested I should direct the radio broadcast, helping to make the "contents" of the opera (which was sung in German) comprehensible to the listener. I managed to insert the voice of a narrator, who described the events of the drama, in agreement with Bruno about the points where the voice should intervene without compromising the sense and integrity of the musical discourse [*Documenti* 1985, 150].

And Rognoni was almost certainly present at the *Studio di Fonologia* in Milan when, on November 13 and 14, the spoken text, the announcements and credits were edited; after the lengthy preparations, *Lulu* was finally broadcast on the Third Program of the RAI on December 13. In the meantime Maderna had composed the soundtrack for the radio play *L'altro mondo, ovvero Gli stati e imperi della luna*, on a text by Alessandro Brissoni based on his own *I viaggi di Cyrano de Bergerac in quei lontani paesi* [*Romito* 2002/1, 85]. Maderna's music was prepared at the *Studio* towards the end of October, also incorporating parts of *Continuo*, *Dimensioni* and *Syntaxis*.[27]

To conclude our account of the pivotal events of the 1950s we believe it useful to dwell a moment on some passages from the paper in which Nono announced his dissociation from the Darmstadt on account of his disaffection with the orientations that were emerging at the time. The meetings in Darmstadt held in these years were undoubtedly crucial for the collective construction of the techniques and poetics of New Music, also in the years that followed, but, as we have seen, towards the end of the decade these initial common aspirations dissolved into divergent and conflicting trends. It is important to remember that Maderna and Nono, together with their Venetian pupils, had originally presented themselves as the sustainers of a long and, in a certain sense, "prophetic" historical-cultural tradition which, starting from the Flemish school of polyphony, anticipated the fundamental core of the musical ideas that were destined to evolve in the post-tonal era; at the end of the decade the two composers continued to believe in the need to respect the social and historical legacy of music-making, in opposition to the trends whereby music had assumed a sort of autonomy from its historic context, radically excluding a subjective approach to composition. On this matter, Veniero Rizzardi points out the existence of a significant exchange of opinions and experiences in the correspondence between Nono and Stockhausen between 1952 and '59.[28] This mutual exchange of ideas certainly helped them to find technical solutions to some of the complex issues arising from the serial and compositional structures they were both working on in those years (for example, the extension of serialism to include also the surrounding acoustic space). However, there remained one point on which the divergence between the two musicians proved irremediable: on the excesses of "subjectivism" for which Stockhausen continued to reproach Nono.

A more precise picture of Nono's position can be gained from the famous paper that he read in Darmstadt during the 1959 courses.[29] The focus is no longer on the question of subjectivity as opposed to objectivity as in his discussions with Stockhausen, but is now much wider and more profound:

---

[27] See M. M. Novati (ed.), *Lo Studio di Fonologia. Un diario musicale 1954-1983* (Milano: Ricordi, 2009), 165.

[28] The title of Rizzardi's article is "Karlheinz Stockhausen e Luigi Nono. Teoria e invenzione musicale 1952-59." Available on the web at: *web.tiscali.it/ensemble900/Diastema/Rivista/Vecchia%20serie/07/Rizzardi.pdf*, consulted November 14, 2019.

[29] Our main source is E. Restagno (ed.), *Nono* (Torino: EDT, 1987), 239-245. We also took into account the perceptive comments made in J. Impett, *Routledge Handbook to Luigi Nono and Musical Thought* (Routledge, New York 2019), 185-187.

> Nowadays the predominant tendency, both in the creative field and in that of criticism and analysis, is to not want to integrate an artistic cultural phenomenon within its historical context, that is to not want to consider it [...] in relation to its participation in the reality of today and its efficacy in that respect [...] but exclusively for its own sake and as an end in itself.

In his speech he also rails against those who support the notion of musical language as a *tabula rasa*, he criticizes Schillinger, guiding spirit of the American avant-garde, for reducing art to its structures while ignoring its contents,[30] and accuses Cage of dreaming of a static art, one that is timeless, eternal and immobile, like that of the Celestial Empire. These conceptions, he believes, imply the idea of art seen as an absolute, of an individual artist with no ties to other individuals, and of musical material whose sole purpose is to become the object of a sort of mystical contemplation that Nono defines "stagnant and sterile." Instead, his idea of art presupposes the capacity of an artist to critically observe the social context in which his art is born, and to orient himself towards the present, making decisions that involve agreement or disagreement with prevailing trends.

Maderna, as always, offered no comment on this matter and wrote nothing. However, the direction taken by his works over the following years leaves no doubt as to his sharing the principles set out by Nono. In particular, his cycle *Hyperion* says much about his sensibility towards the socio-historical issues raised by his ex-pupil. Although the styles and ideals of the two composers tended to diverge throughout the '60s (unlike Nono, Maderna did not systematically pursue a politically committed line in his music), his sharing of the belief that art should be placed within its social context and that subjectivity was an essential element of composing (and in the case of Maderna also of performing) is nevertheless undeniable.

---

[30] J. Schillinger, *The mathematical basis of the arts* (New York: Philosophical Library, 1948).

CHAPTER VI

CHANGES IN LIFE AND WRITING IN THE SIXTIES

An overview of Maderna's engagements at the start of the 1960s would seem to suggest a continued variety and accumulation of work rather than any change in direction. He still lived in Milan with his family, he maintained the same close relations with the RAI as he had established over the previous years, and he continued to compose music for a wide range of uses, both commercial and more strictly artistic, with the same enthusiasm as ever. His second daughter, Claudia, was born in 1960.

As far as his associations with other musicians are concerned – in terms of poetics and joint projects – his links with Luigi Nono began to slacken, while the occasions to work alongside Luciano Berio grew steadily. In fact, although he fully appreciated the motivations that had led Nono to distance himself from Darmstadt, Maderna's divergence with the aesthetics and compositional practice of some of the musicians attending the *Ferienkurse* were not so great as to prevent him from helping to organize the programs of the summer courses. He had always worked hard at Darmstadt, but had also held himself aloof from any polemics, cultivating his own aesthetic values through as wide an outlook as possible, while steering clear of any extremist tendencies or musical choices that were not consistent with his own theoretical position. Nor was he able to share Nono's hard line, based on political stances that Maderna acknowledged as valid, but not absolute. He was instead convinced that there existed a wide variety of musical genres that differed from one another just as the circumstances that surrounded them differed. And it was this open-minded view of music that led Berio in the '70s to launch his highly successful television program *C'è musica e musica*, even though in practice the choices of the two composers did not always run along parallel lines and Maderna's work as a conductor remained an important part of his activity. The extent of this side of his work is testified by the detailed list prepared by Maurizio Romito, which reveals that in the period 1960-69 his conducting engagements reached the staggering number of 359, without counting the repeat performances, which in the case of theatrical works were particularly numerous. If we compare this number with that of the 1950s, 144, it is easy to appreciate just how much this aspect of his work had grown within a relatively short space of time [*Romito* 2020].

Already in the first part of 1960 the list reveals how both in Italy and abroad his activity as a conductor covered a wide range of repertoires, not only of New Music. One of his first appointments was in Vienna, and to reach this destination he set out from Milan on January 17, as he tells Steinecke in a letter dated January 1, in which he sends him his best wishes for the New Year [*Carteggio* 2001, 194]. His work in Vienna mainly involved the Wiener Symphoniker, one of the instrumental groups with whom he worked most regularly, and it is perhaps worth dwelling a moment on this special relationship. His collaboration with the orchestra began precisely in 1960 and continued throughout the whole decade and, despite several by no means negligible setbacks, he fostered this association with great and almost obstinate resolve. One of the reasons for the persistence of this relationship was probably their shared interest in presenting and promoting some of the most recent developments in music in an important city like Vienna. Maderna was there again in May to conduct the orchestra during the *Wiener Festwoche*, in a program that included the concert version of the first two acts of Berg's *Lulu*. The outcome could not have been more successful, especially thanks to the singers, who were unanimously praised by the critics and by the orchestra and its conductor.

A detailed summary of the concerts held during the festival in 1961 was provided by the newspaper *Die Furche*: three conductors were invited, and in the space of three days four concerts were given featuring fourteen compositions, half of which had never been performed before in Vienna. In particular, the concerts included Nono's *Due espressioni per orchestra* (1953) and the work of Nikos Skalkottas, a former pupil of Schönberg who had died prematurely in 1949. Three works by one of the three conductors, Winifried Zillig, were also performed, while Italian music was represented by recent compositions by Castiglioni and Dallapiccola. A program, then, rich in new offerings, which were received by the public and critics with a certain surprise and some reserve, but largely without bias. Some of the newspaper headlines were particularly meaningful: "Expressionism has lost its ability to rift" (*Österreichische Neue Tageszeitung*), "Music of the fear and joy of living" (*Die Presse*). One imagines that both the orchestra and Maderna took these comments positively and were all the more determined to go ahead with their plans. The following year, 1962, all the concerts were broadcast on the radio and the audience was notably broadened, but a different, decidedly less open tone began to be used by the press. The conclusion of *Das Kleine Volksblatt* is particularly indicative: "the Wiener Symphoniker have as always been patient and prepared to make sacrifices; Bruno Maderna is and remains a congenial conductor and – as we have remarked on other occasions – a good musician." The first concert ended with a piece by Mahler, which diverged from the main theme of the cycle but was deemed "more alive than the living" (*Kurier*). Two years later (1964), despite the notable deterioration in the reaction of the Viennese public and critics, Maderna – still with the Wiener Symphoniker – conducted the first and third concert in the cycle of six that made up the *Festival Musica Nova* organized by the Viennese radio that year. The concerts were held in the headquarters of the Radio and in the same period the Vienna Music Academy organized a Sunday seminar on dodecaphony.

Already after the first concert the Austrian newspaper *Kurier* sums up the situation – that is, how the cycle was received by the public – with the following sentiment: one must raise one's hat to Maderna, friend and supporter of the Wiener Symphoniker, but, this said, no further words should be added, as they would seem offensive in the face of music. Also the other journalists who reviewed the concerts concurred in affirming that New Music surely began with that of the Viennese School, and yet the young generation of composers seemed unwilling to heed this lesson. The Greek composer Nikos Skalkottas (one of whose works had been quite successful just two years before), as well as the German Konrad Boehmer and the Spaniard Cristobal Hälfter, who Maderna presented alongside Webern, were "grandchildren of the Viennese school, but are only to be pitied." Finally, a review in the *Volksstimme* concluded with the following judgment, which seems irrevocable: "The Wiener Symphoniker, who fear nothing, have taken upon themselves the expression of this non-music." Basically, then, Maderna's first four years in Vienna had a negative outcome; however, as we will see later, Maderna eventually managed to recapture the favor of the Viennese public in the years that followed. This brief diversion on the reception of the most recent music in a city that was traditionally open to new ideas provides us with a better view of the kind of difficulties Maderna had to face even under seemingly favorable circumstances: that is to say, an excellent orchestra who had total faith in him, and institutions willing to present new repertoires, though tackled with caution.

Coming back to our account of Maderna's life during the years parallel to his work with the Viennese orchestra, already from January 1960 we find him involved in various projects with the RAI. Firstly, he composed the music for Eugène Scribe's radio play *Il puff*, directed by Alessandro Brissoni, which he recorded between January 23 and 28. Then, on January 29, he was in Naples, in the concert hall of the Conservatorio S. Pietro a Majella, where he conducted a concert with a highly varied program that included Vivaldi's *Concerto* F.1 n. 13, which he himself had prepared for Malipiero's edition. On an unspecified date he began recording a cycle of three broadcasts, which were aired starting from February 4. The cycle, titled *Arcidiapason*, was curated by Stefano Sibaldi and featured a selection of musical pieces that were broadcast during the months of

February and March. Maderna was in charge of the musical direction and he had also orchestrated many of the pieces, some of which involved the participation of Cathy Berberian. On March 12 he was in Rome to conduct a concert at the Auditorium Foro Italico which featured mainly contemporary music, including Nono's *Epitaffio per Federico García Lorca n. 3: Memento. Romance de la Guardia Civil española*. Two days later he is at the WDR in Cologne, and he then spent two weeks in Paris, where the highly successful production of the *Dreigroschenoper* had been taken on tour. At the end of April we find him in London, for two important concerts broadcast on the Third Program of the BBC [Romito 2020]. The invitation to London came from William Glock, musical director of the BBC and of the summer school in Dartington.[1] Maderna's music for Shakespeare's *Macbeth* was recorded at the RAI between May 5 and 8; and on June 11, in Rome, he conducted *Die Verurteilung des Lukullus*, an opera by Dessau to a libretto by Brecht. Finally, from June 20 to 27, in Milan, he conducted his own arrangements for the musical comedy by Gino Marinuzzi jr., *Scandalo a Sweet Spring*.[2] And in the meantime the *Studio* in Milan had seen a change of hands: Berio left for the USA and Nono made his entrance with the electronic composition *Omaggio a Vedova*.[3]

And so we arrive at the 1960 edition of the *Ferienkurse*, which this year were held from July 6 to 16 and were in some ways similar, and in other ways different with respect to previous editions. Steinecke had wanted to involve Maderna in a novel project, whereby his customary composition/conducting course would be based on a collaboration with a Polish chamber orchestra that would be conducted by Andrzej Markowski, but would also be made available to those attending Maderna's course to practice their conducting and listen to the newly written pieces. Already in the previous year's edition Markowski had been appreciated both as a conductor and as an expert in applied music, in particular music for films. Steinecke was very eager to have Maderna's opinion about the project and his willingness to participate. He was particularly concerned about the economic side of the venture: to accommodate an orchestra of twenty-two musicians for ten or more days would prove extremely costly; furthermore they would only be involved in two concerts (one in Darmstadt one in Frankfurt). Unfortunately Maderna's reply has been lost, but in the end Steinecke's worries about the cost seem to have prevailed, and the Polish orchestra was not invited.

---

[1] See R. Fearn, "Maderna e l'Inghilterra," in *Documenti* 1985, 139.

[2] All details of Maderna's recordings and conducting engagements with the RAI from January to June 1960 are taken from *Romito* 2002/1, 2003/1.

[3] N. Scaldaferri, "Documenti inediti sullo Studio di Fonologia della RAI di Milano," *Musica/Realtà*, no. 45 (1994), 153.

The relation between composition, performance and reception was an issue that held a particular importance for Maderna throughout his whole career. He was, in fact, not just a composer sitting at a desk but also a performer, and as such was always sensitive to the response of the listeners. At Darmstadt, where the audience was for the most part made up of composers or people interested in new music, the problem of reception was perhaps relatively secondary, but the question remained paramount for Maderna, who since his childhood had been accustomed to catering for a wide variety of audiences and felt a strong need to be understood by all. Outside of Darmstadt this issue became even more evident, and numerous dedicated festivals were organized across Europe, as well as radio broadcasts, to promote contemporary music among a wider sector of the public. In particular cases, like that of Nono, the search for new audiences (preferably from the working classes) became one of the essential elements of his approach to composition. As far as Maderna was concerned, we know that he had always been sensitive to the relation with the listeners, both as a conductor and as a conducting teacher in Darmstadt and in other places, and it is easy to imagine that this aspect was always in his mind while he was composing.

Among the events that focused on questions of a more theoretical nature during the courses of 1960 the six lectures given by Boulez were undoubtedly the most significant. He referred to them as *Hauptvorlesungen* ("key lessons") and gave one a day between July 11 and 16. The theme of the series was "Thinking of music today" and it was divided into six parts, clearly defined in the program of the courses: 1. General considerations, 2. Musical technique, 3. Notation and interpretation, 4. Form, 5. Provisional (partial) conclusion, 6. Final discussion. He held the lectures in French, with a simultaneous translation into German by Metzger. According to the testimony of Paolo Castaldi, one of the most attentive participants, in presenting his ideas Boulez indifferently mixed themes and tones, outlining the principles of composition with didactic rigor but also with an unprecedented polemic virulence, especially when inveighing against certain approaches to composition that, in his opinion, bordered on libertinism.[4] Today, many years later, the only way to understand what really happened is to turn to the publications that reproduce the content of the lectures, both in the original

---

[4] In his long essay "Darmstadt 1960," in *Il Verri*, no. 5 (1961), 129-135, Paolo Castaldi openly refers to the tone used by the speaker as being "worthy of Savonarola." As far as the content of the lectures is concerned, he reports, without hiding his disagreement, the following extract: "people believe that in this way they have reached a point of arrival, whereas it is actually, at most, a chaotic confluence of scraps of shipwrecks of many different and equally rigorous systems already irredeemably condemned by time, which they now delude themselves into thinking they can acritically, and without providing justifications, make worthy of cultural realities." [133]

language as well as in various translations. Unfortunately, though, right from the very first publication (Gonthier, 1963), the only parts remaining, besides the title, *Penser la musique aujourd'hui*, are the first two themes, *Considerations générales* and *Technique musicale*. The latter summarizes what the author had originally divided into separate lectures and in some ways is the clearest part, in that Boulez refers to working tools already familiar to anyone involved in new music, especially as composers. However, on reading the text of the lectures, translated into English by Susan Bradshaw and Richard Rodney Bennett (*Boulez on Music Today*, Faber & Faber, 1979), both the sequence of arguments and the contents of the various sections fail to live up to their initial promise.

That year (1960), Maderna limited his participation in the *Ferienkurse* to his customary composition courses. He was not present on the podium and appeared only once as a composer (although selected at the last minute) with *Dimensioni II Invenzione su una voce*, which unexpectedly concluded the concert given on July 16. Curiously, the work in question included an additional part for soprano, performed by Annemarie Jung [*Chronik* 1997, 606], of which no trace has survived. The courses had, in fact, already started when, on July 8, Steinecke wrote to Alberto Mantelli, the managing director of the RAI in Rome, asking for permission to include Maderna's new work in the closing concert of the courses, most likely to replace another work that had been removed from the program. The composition, together with the authorization, arrived on July 12, just four days before the performance, further proof of the frenetic rhythm of the Darmstadt scheduling and of Maderna's promptness in adapting his music (that is, if he really did add the soprano part in just four days).

The story behind the writing of *Dimensioni II* is partly linked to the working relationship that had developed in those years between Maderna and Berio, as already mentioned on various occasions. But besides their joint ventures in composition, and over and above their shared interest in the new musical genre of radio drama, there was another area of culture that particularly attracted Berio: that of semiotics and linguistics. Interest in this peculiar branch of research was growing fast at the time and was destined to have important implications also in the world of music. As we pointed out in Chapter Four, even the new sector of the RAI in Milan, the *Studio di Fonologia*, owes its name to this discipline. Also Umberto Eco, who kept a keen eye on the latest developments in new music, reignited the debate with Lévi-Strauss some years later.[5] Enzo Restagno recalls the evenings Eco used to spend in the home of Berio and Berberian, and mentions that Eco and Berio embarked on reading Joyce's *Ulysses* together and

---

[5] See U. Eco, "Pensée structurale et pensée sérielle (1968)," in *Musique en jeu*, no. 5 (1971), 45-56, where he revisits some of the polemics of the 1950s.

it was their mutual reflections on the book that led shortly afterwards to the idea of *Omaggio a Joyce*, exploiting the voice of Berberian, who declaims words taken from the text.[6] Berio wrote a short but intense article about this piece in which he comments on the phonetic musicality of Joyce's book and how he attempted to expand this element through musical techniques.[7] At the root of this experiment was Berio's conviction that verbal and musical language shared common ground and that the discipline of linguistics could reveal significant insights into the structures and sense of music.

Although Maderna did not follow his friend in his theoretical-philosophical adventures, he was nevertheless fascinated by his explorations of the relation between the musicality of the word and its musical setting. His approach was however very different from that adopted by Berio. The text of *Dimensioni II*, for example, is based on a singular experiment that Maderna proposed to Hans G. Helms, a curious German Jew who was a jazz musician and then a composer of avant-garde music, and at the same time a scholar of linguistics. He asked Helms to provide him with a set of non verbal phonetic sounds that were purely sonic or, one might say, musical. Helms responded with thirty-five consonants, fifteen vowels and a semi-vowel, sounds that existed individually in many languages across the world, but, when put side by side, never formed words present in the lexicon of any real language. Each phoneme of this imaginary language had a statistical presence calculated between 1 and 18. Maderna then asked Cathy Berberian to read the sequence of these phonemes with varying tones as suggested by their sound and according to her fancy. The abstract phonemes thus acquired an expressive character as if they were words recited during a theatrical performance. The result was then processed on magnetic tape and named *Dimensioni II*, with the apt subtitle *Invenzione su una voce*. The tape was sometimes presented as a self-standing work, though in versions of differing lengths, but it was also used as an item of musical material that could be reassembled and was inserted (in separate parts) in the stage performances of *Hyperion*, as well as in other works like *Tempo libero* and *Ages*. The processing of the tape involved a painstaking selection of extremely small fragments that resulted in punctiform sounds, mostly lasting less than a second (probably produced by accelerating the running of the tape). On listening to the tape, some of the contents may seem to resemble extra-musical events: certain very high punctiform sounds might recall small bursts of laughter while, later on, the pseudo words from an inexistent language are read by Berberian as if they made sense. Equally significant are the many sudden silences in which the echo of the

---

[6] E. Restagno (ed.), *Berio* (Torino: EDT, 1995), 18.

[7] L. Berio, "Poesia e musica - un'esperienza," *Incontri Musicali*, no. 3 (1959), 98-111.

immediately preceding sound events seem to be almost refracted. Later in the work the texture becomes gradually and unevenly more complex, thinning out only towards the very end. As we have said, this was Maderna's only contribution as a composer in Darmstadt that year.

In 1960, and in the two following years, Maderna extended his work as a teacher, which till then had been largely limited to the *Ferienkurse*, by accepting an invitation from William Glock, the founder and historic director of the summer school in Dartington, Devon (England), from 1948 to 1978. The school and the associated music festival had originally been held in Bryanston, but was moved to the medieval estate of Dartington Hall in 1953. The summer courses were attended by students, young professional musicians and amateurs, and focused mostly on classical music but also covered other genres, such as jazz and ethnic music. The difference between Dartington and Darmstadt was basically a question of logistics: the German summer school was located in a city with its own autonomous life and facilities, offering historical buildings that could be used as concert venues as and when needed. Dartington was instead the typical English college, self-contained and immersed in the surrounding nature. Here too – and long before that of Darmstadt – an instrumental group had been formed specializing in contemporary music, the Melos Ensemble, active since 1950 thanks to a group of musicians coordinated by the viola player Cecil Aronowitz. The ensemble broke up in 1972, whereas the school and festival are still running today. Another aspect that the two schools shared was the existence of a journal, in the case of Dartington *The score*.

Maderna taught at the Dartington International Summer School from 1960 to '62. His first appearance at the school was on July 31, 1960 when he gave a talk on the possible sense of music "by advancing some tentative hypotheses on what it might mean." The main focus of the lecture was the notion that "when listening to music one realizes that it has two meanings: one objective, in some way inherent to its actual structure […], and the other subjective, which is extraneous to it but pertains to the personality of the composer as a man, craftsman, performer." However, Maderna went on to warn that it was "necessary to overcome the temptation to reduce such a complex matter to any kind of schematism."[8] This uncharacteristic debut – a theoretical paper of the kind that Steinecke had often asked him for, with no result – probably stemmed from the fact that the school and the students in Dartington were very different from those that attended Darmstadt. Suffice it to read the booklet sent by the administration in preparation for the courses in 1961 to gain some

---

[8] An Italian translation of the whole text can be found in *Documenti* 1985, 86-88. A copy of the document can be found at the *Centro Studi Maderna* (Section S) and the original is preserved in the Maderna Collection of the *Paul Sacher Stiftung*.

idea of the rather spartan atmosphere that reigned at the college. Among other things, it gives details of exactly what time the participants should arrive and by which train ("For domestic reasons, no earlier than this time, please"), and then gives details of where to find the offices, the classrooms, as well as other useful details. The last paragraph could even sound a little intimidating: "Finally, please remember to bring a music-stand, a torch, a bar of soap, and – for those who use an electric razor – an adapter." The booklet contains a plan of the first floor showing where the Dance School and Drama School were situated, and there is also a plan of the whole complex.

The school was attended by quite a high number of students, with differing levels of musical experience and interested in diverse topics (including ethnomusicology and jazz); the teaching staff – when Maderna first arrived – was made up of thirty people, mostly unfamiliar English names. In previous years the list had included such famous figures as Nadia Boulanger, Arthur Schnabel and Paul Hindemith. In 1961, Maderna worked alongside Luciano Berio, Luigi Nono and Virgil Thomson, the latter most likely having acted as a liaison between the Italian musicians and the English institution. In the courses of the following year, held from July 28 to August 25, 1962, special mention is given to Nono, who appears to have dedicated a work to the school; and Berio held a course of electronic music, but only for the more advanced students. The works studied during the course included compositions by Berio, Nono and Maderna. On Wednesday August 9, Maderna conducted the Melos Ensemble in a concert featuring works by Mozart, Maxwell Davies and Messiaen.[9] The first meeting between Glock and Maderna in 1960 was particularly fruitful. Glock not only invited him to teach at Dartington, and to conduct the two previously mentioned concerts, but he also managed to procure him a series of as many as eight appointments with the BBC Symphony Orchestra, including concerts and recordings, that lasted almost a month, from October 19 to November 16 [*Romito* 2020].

In a letter addressed to London and dated November 10, Steinecke arranges to meet Maderna in Munich to discuss the program and the financial situation for the 1961 summer courses in Darmstadt, and informs him in advance that he would like to open the season with a concert featuring the Melos Ensemble. And in fact they met on December 1 and 2 while attending the concerts of *Musica Viva*, the cycle directed by Karl Amadeus Hartmann and in which Maderna took part that year. The letter is very similar both in tone and in subject matter to those that Steinecke had always written to

---

[9] Details about Dartington are taken from various documents kept at the *Centro Studi Maderna*, Section S 1.

Maderna ever since their first years of collaboration, as soon as he had drafted the program for the coming year. It usually turned out, though, that during the months leading up to the start of the courses all sorts of unforeseen events intervened, with the result that little actually remained of what they had planned through their correspondence. In this case, however, the general lines of calendar were preserved, although one of the few variations concerned the chamber concerts. Steinecke had originally intended to invite the Melos Ensemble to give the opening concert on August 29, as well as a concert in Frankfurt at the Hessischer Rundfunk. In the end these engagements, along with four additional concerts, were given to the newly formed Internationales Kranichsteiner Kammer-Ensemble directed by Bruno Maderna, often referred to in documents simply as the Bruno Maderna Kammerensemble. Steinecke must doubtlessly have had to overcome considerable obstacles before being able to form a group dedicated specifically to New Music, many years after this had already been achieved by other forward-looking institutions in Great Britain, France and even in Italy.

Immediately after his stay in London, Maderna returned to his commitments with the RAI: on November 23, 1960 he was at the Auditorium del Foro Italico in Rome, for the program *Ritratto di Kurt Weill*, part of the opera season of the RAI, where he conducted and recorded *Der Protagonist* and *Der zar lässt sich photographieren*; and on December 23, again for the RAI, he conducted and recorded a concert of French music. Then, on January 28, 1961, still in Rome, he recorded a concert that among other things included two important Italian premieres: Boulez's *Le marteau sans maître* and Nono's *España en el corazón*.

His many engagements in the first half of the year included a broadcast on Radio Vienna on 11 February featuring music by Schönberg and Nono, and concerts in Brussels on March 17 and 21, with recent works by Italian composers. In mid-April he was at the Biennale di Venezia for the first performance of his *Serenata III* for magnetic tape. The main problem involved in composing this work was the gradual transformation of a passage on the marimba into a piece of electronic music that had the same characters in terms of pitch and rhythm as the original, and to couple it with a similar transformation of the sounds of a flute. The combination of these sounds on the tape was then organized in layers of relatively higher or lower pitches, within thicker or more rarefied textures. Basically, the aim of this composition seems to have been a sort of technical "wager," namely the passage from live sounds to electronic sounds, able to produce interesting results.

Immediately after the end of the Biennale, which that year was exceptionally held in spring, and during which Maderna also conducted Nono's *Intolleranza*, his first journey outside of Europe took him to Tokyo, for the festival East-West Music Encounter. There he conducted five concerts with the Ensemble Européen de Musique de Chambre and the Japan Philharmonic Orchestra. He stayed in Japan until the end of April and then, little more than a month later, he was back in England working with the BBC, on June 1, 5 and 15.

On July 10 he recorded *Don Perlimplin, ovvero il trionfo dell'amore e dell'immaginazione*, with the instrumental ensemble of Radio Roma. In the score published by Suvini Zerboni we read "Adattamento radiofonico di Bruno Maderna." And in fact his role was not limited to the editing of the particular sounds he had created at the *Studio* in Milan, but he also conceived and directed the radio play, which was broadcast in August on the Third Program of the RAI, during its opera season. [Romito 2020]. *Don Perlimplin* therefore differs from his other radio plays in that both the script and the direction were entirely the result of choices he had made himself. But it also stands apart from other similar works on account of its bordering between a work for radio and one for the stage. For the text, Maderna adapted a play by García Lorca (*Amor de don Perlimplín con Belisa en su jardín*). A notable feature of his adaptation is that the main character, Perlimplin, is not represented by a human voice, but by the voice of a flute, while the Suocera (the mother-in-law) "speaks" through a saxophone quartet. Don Perlimplin, an elderly man, "kind and shy, who lived quietly amidst his books," as the Speaker tells the listeners in his introduction to the tale, is encouraged by his enterprising housekeeper Marcolfa to look for a wife, and so he marries "the young and beautiful Belisa, who agrees to the marriage out of personal interest, but already on their wedding night is enjoying delightful affairs. Perlimplin, who was previously reluctant to marry, now loves her tenderly. With the help of his housekeeper, he now has passionate love letters delivered to Belisa, pretending to be a mysterious young man; when she agrees to a meeting at night, she discovers that the secretive lover is actually her husband."[10] At this point the story ends in the space of just a few moments: Perlimplin kills himself with a knife and Belisa, surprised and overwhelmed, suddenly realizes that love does not just have a body but also a soul. The account of love told in the tale is therefore twofold: that of Perlimplin, who had never experienced it before, and that of Belisa, who discovers the profound truth only following the dramatic death of her husband-lover.

In 1961 (after the recording of the tape) Edizioni Suvini Zerboni published a non-traditional score of the work, consisting of a manuscript made by a copyist who put together six portions of the original score, along with

---

[10] The quoted text is taken from the descriptive card in *Documenti* 1985, 239. The card was written by Francesca Magnani and Tiziano Popoli.

some performing notes made by Maderna, and the dialogues from Lorca's play (in Italian translation) that the composer selected for his radio adaptation.[11] The scores that were materially used for the performance (and then edited onto the definitive tape) are preserved in a fascicle (partially incomplete) containing the surviving autograph manuscripts.[12] However, as Sandro Gorli underlines in his introduction to the critical edition (p. VIII), it would be wrong to consider either the scores or the tape as complete and definitive works, since Maderna purposely left many aspects of his text undefined. Some years later, in a short article requested by André Boucourechliev, he remarked that "the performer must intervene on the actual structure of the work [...] Open, mobile works are a necessary adventure for the creative thought of our time" [*Studi* 1989, 68-70]. And in fact his performance of *Don Perlimplin*, as well as his later recording, reveal a certain amount of liberty in its interpretation. It was not just an open work, but also an adaptation of previous "reassemblable" works: besides adapting parts of *Dark rapture crawl* and *Musica su due dimensioni*, the score also re-uses elements of works published in the same year, 1961, namely the flute part of *Serenata IV* and *Honeyrêves*. After Maderna's death, *Don Perlimplin* was performed in Cologne in German in 1975, and in 1984 also in Italy by the orchestra of the RAI in Rome. Gorli performed it in a stage version in Bologna in 1996 and subsequently on many other occasions.

The role assumed by the music in *Don Perlimplin* is quite varied, although always in keeping with the surreal climate of Lorca's text. Throughout the first part, in which the house-keeper insistently tells her employer that he should find a wife, their light and comical dialogues are between Marcolfa's actual voice and Perlimplin's "flutey" replies. Here the flute literally speaks, that is to say it reproduces the rhythm and prosody of human speech, becoming frenzied, for example, when Perlimplin refuses to get married. In other cases the instrumental music (in the episodes marked *Rag tempo*, where Belisa makes her first appearance) provides a rhythmic element to the character's words and to a certain extent also underlines their sense: Belisa's character is "à la mode," her spirit is fashionably American, and the music becomes "jazzy" while still remaining serial. The music takes on another role when it comments on the action: it creates emotional tensions matching those communicated by the words (for example, when Don Perlimplin is lost in ecstatic thoughts at the start of their wedding night) or acts as an external voice (almost like a Greek chorus) that comments on what the

---

[11] The Italian translation was that of Vittorio Bodini, published in 1952 by Einaudi.

[12] Details of the Suvini Zerboni score and Maderna's manuscripts are taken from Sandro Gorli's introduction to the critical edition [*Maderna* 2002]. The printed score, Maderna's autograph manuscripts and the tape recorded by the composer do not always perfectly match. The text of the critical edition is the result of a painstaking comparison between the three sources.

characters are saying and doing (for example, when we hear four bell chimes after Perlimplin's suicide). All the music is written in a serial style, as if it were an instrumental piece, something rarely seen in his previous work for radio; here, though, the writing has a narrative intent, an element till now totally absent from his concert works. The fact that the protagonist's voice is replaced by that of a flute often results in a tendency towards melody, a feature that Francesca Magnani associates with the style of singing in Malipiero's theater works.[13]

Don Perlimplin was presented at the thirteenth Prix Italia in Pisa, but the first prize that year was awarded to Niccolò Castiglioni's radio play *Attraverso lo specchio*, which was similarly composed in 1961.[14] Rather than tackling contemporary themes, both plays are based on internationally known literary works (Castiglioni's model was *Alice in Wonderland*) and use non tonal language for their radio adaptations. The RAI now seems to have been prepared to experiment with more adventurous and less traditional projects, something they had tended to avoid in the past.

In 1961 the *Ferienkurse* were held from August 29 to September 10 and were preceded by a special composition course held by Karlheinz Stockhausen (in collaboration with David Tudor) from August 19 to 29. Around 400 people took part – counting performers, teachers and audience – coming from thirty-seven countries, such a large number that the town's hospitality structure was unable to accommodate them all and it was necessary to involve private families and even a hospital ward! Notably absent were Luciano Berio, who was in the USA, Henri Pousseur and Luigi Nono (although nobody could have imagined that Nono's absence would be permanent). Besides the unexpectedly high attendance, the other novel feature of the 1961 courses was the contribution of the newly formed instrumental group, the Internationales Kranichsteiner Musikensemble, who, as we have said, opened the courses on August 29 and performed on several other occasions, during one of which Ernest Bour premiered Maderna's *Serenata IV*. The ensemble also took part in five seminars on the "Analysis and Realization of New Works" held by Maderna. A document attached to Steinecke's last letter to Maderna [*Carteggio* 2001, 205-206] contains details of the participants enrolled in the seminars: thirty-two composers or composition students of varying age (from the 56-year-old Emile Spira from England to the 17-year-old Joshua Rifkin from the USA), from all over the world: seven from Western Germany, three from Switzerland, and two each from Austria, Japan, Greece, Great Britain and the USA; Italy was represented

---

[13] See F. Magnani, "Il canto nell'immaginario teatrale di Malipiero e di Maderna," in *Malipiero Maderna 1973-1993*, ed. P. Cattelan (Firenze: Olschki, 2000), 185-195.

[14] See A. I. De Benedictis, *Radiodramma ed arte radiofonica. Storia e funzioni della musica per radio in Italia* (Torino: EDT, 2004), 158 & 174.

only by Renato de Grandis (an already established composer whose *Studi per flauto e pianoforte* was performed in the concert of August 31), and only one participant each from Bulgaria, Chile, South Korea, France, New Zealand, the Netherlands, Poland, Portugal, Spain, Russia and Turkey.

As always, the lectures of the 1961 edition were followed with great interest, particularly because in some cases they were linked to the programs of the concerts. For example, "The Development of Form since 1950" – a lecture by Karlheinz Stockhausen – was given a few hours before the concert with music by Schönberg, Ives and Krenek; Stockhausen also described his idea of Moment-form through examples taken from his *Kontakte*. And as in Stockhausen's lecture on form, those given by Boulez – "Taste and Function," and "Discipline and Communication" – similarly looked back to the past and compared it with the present. Against this rich and varied background a clearer picture emerges of the dualism between the concepts of "structure" and "material." The latter term was generally used to refer to the new experimental sonorities of electronic music, and to the serial and numerical schemes applied to organize the successions of notes. The "structures," on the other hand, were the procedures underpinned by logics of an acoustic type, such as successions or superimpositions of pitches, textures or rhythms. By producing an indefinite quantity of possible sound objects, the materials and structures ensured non tonality, but did not envisage any formal application to composition, although the composer could choose the elements of his composition from among these materials (and only these). Hence the prevailing tendency toward non-form, the informal, the instant-form. The two lectures given by Adorno marked the culminating point of the theoretic debate. Returning to Darmstadt three years after his sadly famous verdict on *The Aging of the New Music* (1957), he now focused on aspects of the responsible rethinking of form in the different approaches adopted in New Music, especially by German, but also American composers. Adorno's rationale is not, in fact, so far from that proposed by Stockhausen in his lectures and also his works. Adorno, though basing his argument on essentially theoretical grounds, similarly stressed the need to free music from any pre-established formal constraint that did not derive from the music itself, whatever the basis for this need and whatever the means to achieve it: whether I Ching, Momentform, Indeterminacy (John Cage), Jetztform (Stockhausen) or Alea (Boulez). Although those attending his talks were well aware that the notion of non-form had its origins in oriental philosophies or in Goethe's metaphysics of the instant, Adorno's insistence on the need to free creation from any form suggested or imposed from outside brought him in line with the most commonly held positions in Darmstadt, in spite of being derived from different paths of thought. It should also be mentioned that the notion of non-form was not only limited to music: significantly, the so-called "informal art" movement was consecrated at the Biennale Arte in Venice precisely in 1962, in the works of artists like Fautrier, Hartung, Vedova and Consagra.[15]

Maderna did not take part in the debate directly, but the issue in question was clearly pertinent both to him and to his music. He was, in fact, no stranger to the idea of pieces that were not fully and definitively assembled, but were instead "assemblable." The *Serenata IV* for flute, instruments and tape might appear to be complete and definitive, and not material that could be transmuted and re-used, but its status as a self-standing "work" is nevertheless quite ambiguous. Not only do the solo flute parts use fragments taken from other coeval works (*Honeyrêves, Don Perlimplin, Komposition für oboe und Kammerensemble*),[16] but after its first performance on September 4 it was never performed again or published. As a result, any comments about the contents of the work can be based just on a few surviving sketches and its recording.[17] The general impression one gets on listening to the piece is that in 1961 Maderna was no longer specifically interested in any further exploration of the multi-serial grammar that until then had dominated his composing technique; he seems instead to be attracted by certain aspects of expression not readily obtainable from a system of that type. The whole work is made up of a series of short episodes, each of which investigates, whether in the solo flute part, the orchestral and electronic sonorities or the combination of both, particular situations that interest the composer, notably the blending of timbres, rhythms and intensity. Maderna pays particular attention to the quality of the sound, and appears to have renounced the play of tension and drama that had previously attracted him. One might say that his work dating from the sixties often has a provisional feel about it, or else revives the practice of re-usable material common among composers like Bach or Haydn, which the dogma of originality, typical of the romantic aesthetics, had subsequently tended to reject.

After the *Ferienkurse* Maderna's activity as a conductor was more demanding than ever. Between September and December he took part in at least ten concerts, only one of which was in Italy, at the RAI in Turin. In most cases the concerts featured recent music, although sometimes pieces from the Baroque era were added. Towards the end of 1961 Darmstadt witnessed a tragic, totally

---

[15] See R. Pasini, *L'Informale. Stati Uniti, Europa, Italia* (Bologna: CLUEB, 1995).

[16] See the descriptive card by Francesca Magnani in *Documenti* 1985, 232.

[17] A copy of the recording was sent from the Internationales Musikinstitut Darmstadt (IMD) to the Centro Studi Maderna. De Benedictis has attempted to reconstruct the score from the available material. See A. I. De Benedictis, "Materiali parziali o strutture fungibili? Prospettive filologiche su *Honeyrêves, Don Perlimplin* e *Serenata IV* di Bruno Maderna," *Il Saggiatore musicale* 18/1-2 (2011), 139-172.

unexpected and unpredictable event, one that would have profound implications for the cultural scene of the small town in Hesse and for the destiny of New Music. On December 15 Wolfgang Steinecke, the historic founder and guiding spirit of the *Ferienkurse*, was involved in a car accident and died eight days later at the age of 51. The circumstances of the accident are quite implausible: while he was about to return home with his wife after an evening with friends, he was opening the car door when he was struck by another vehicle that then continued on its way. At first Steinecke's condition did not appear alarming, but subsequent complications had a fatal outcome.[18] The tragic event was reported in all the musical journals and in particular in *Melos*, which contained tributes – among others – from Boulez, Maderna, Nono and Stockhausen, the "young composers" of ten years before and now "maestri" in their own right, and close friends of Steinecke.

Stockhausen's contribution was particularly significant as it revealed plans that had not yet been announced by Steinecke himself, namely to extend the length of the *Ferienkurse* to six months a year and to found an international university of music in Darmstadt [*Trudu*, 1992, 161-162]. Maderna, for his part, projected his own thoughts about music into Steinecke: he "was not just a great promoter of New Music and a magnificent organizer [...] he understood that music is not [...] intellectualism, but a necessary means of communication for mankind, in constant evolution." Considering the musical scene of the post-war years, Maderna points out the difference between the courses conceived and organized by Steinecke and the many festivals promoting new music, whose initiatives were "simply an act of snobbery, or at best 'tourist attractions'," it was necessary to continue along the same lines "otherwise the future of the music of the young and of those to come will depend solely on the whims of the self-styled promoters and the professional seekers of 'new talents'."[19]

Ernst Thomas accepted to cover the role of course director, and the most prominent figures associated with Darmstadt, including Boulez, Maderna and Stockhausen, continued to offer their full support so as to ensure that the absence of the former director would not have too negative an affect on the programs of the courses and the quality of the concerts, and to allow them to proceed along the lines quite clearly advocated by Steinecke. However, already in 1962 the "new course" offered by the school came under varying attacks, and some went as far as to suggest a "moment of stagnation" [*Süddeutsche Zeitung*, July 16, 1962]. But this opinion was not widely shared: Otto Tomek,

---

[18] The driver of the car that struck him is alleged to have been the judge Hanns Mondorf, a member of the anti-alcohol league.

[19] B. Maderna, "In memoriam Wolfgang Steinecke," *Melos* 29/2 (1962), Italian translation in *Studi* 1989, 67-68.

for example, through the microphones of the Hessischer Rundfunk (the main radio of the Hesse region, based in Frankfurt) and of the Westdeutscher Rundfunk (in Cologne), spoke positively about how the courses had turned out and praised the performances of the four compositions commissioned by Darmstadt that year, making particular mention of Maderna's *Komposition für Oboe, Kammerensemble und Tonband* (or the *Concerto per Oboe n.1*). Tomek expressed the same positive thoughts about the piece in an article:

> Maderna's musical language is modern in the best sense of the word: it embraces the whole vocabulary of the stylistic aspects of our time, and besides has no need of any "mysterious keys" to be understood [...]. The particular thing about this work by Maderna is that it does not present anything particular, none of the complicated formal systems. No abstract relation between the single elements [...] substantially music sprung from the vital power of a primordial talent [*Darmstädter Beiträge*, 1962, 4-5].

Besides his involvement in the *Ferienkurse* and the period spent in Dartington, Maderna's list of engagements in 1962 reveals that his collaboration with the RAI was continuing to subside. Records exist of only three concert recordings before Darmstadt and two in the second part of the year. On the other hand, his work abroad continued to grow: in addition to the six appearances in other countries during the course of the year, between November and December he conducted six performances of *Lulu* in Bielefeld and three of *Salome* in Berlin [*Romito* 2020]. What is more, during the *Ferienkurse*, that is in the period July 8 to 20, he conducted the Kammerensemble in eight different concerts, starting with the opening concert dedicated to the memory of Wolfgang Steinecke. Interesting, too, were the courses he held on the theme "Theories of Composition Compared: Medieval and New Music," in which he had the opportunity to relive some of the decisive phases of his own musical training.

In the meantime his activity as a composer showed no signs of slowing down, resulting in at least two important works dating from this period. The *Konzert für Oboe und Kammerensemble* (with the dedication "a Lothar Faber e ai suoi oboi") was premiered at during the Darmstadt courses on July 15, 1962, performed by Faber and conducted by Maderna. The work features a new and complex approach to form and was performed several times during the '60s, as well as being released twice on disk. The composer came back to the work several times with variants and under different titles. For example, a first version was titled *Komposition* (and not *Konzert*) and also included a magnetic tape (*Komposition für Oboe, Kammerensemble und Tonband*), whereas a version from 1963 performed at the Biennale di Venezia, had the Italian title *Concerto per oboe*. The work was published, in the form of a reproduction of the manuscript, by Bruzzichelli: a performance by Faber and Maderna appears in the catalogue of RCA records. To all extents and purposes, it is – three years after the *Concerto per pianoforte* of 1959 – a "finished" work, even though hints of an "assemblable" work can be found here and there: for example, the shared material with *Honeyrêves* and *Serenata IV*, or the pages written in non traditional graphic notation that allow for a wide margin of freedom in its performance. The complexity of its form is not only due the lack of any clear division into parts (and since the *Quartetto* this had been a fairly constant feature of his work) but also, and above all, to the multiple relations that are created between the instrumental ensemble and the oboe and its relatives: the oboe d'amore that plays the first part of the work and the cor anglais that concludes it. Maderna seems to be captivated by the evocative timbres of these instruments, as well as by the bravura of the artist (as the dedication suggests); so rather than concentrating on the brilliance of the solo part and of the performer (as happened with Gazzelloni), he focuses more on the fullness and sweetness of the sound. The complexity of the piece can also be put down to the fact that Maderna seems to avoid the usual formal schemes of a concerto (for example, collaboration or contrast between soloist and orchestra), maybe because they were too obviously linked to tradition. What is certain, though, is that he has also avoided making use of numerical calculations and has preferred to adopt a more perceptive approach. The first five of the twenty or so minutes of the composition are dominated by the presence of the oboe d'amore, with all the characteristics of calm and sweetness commonly assigned to opening adagios. This is followed by a singular episode featuring a "cadenza" that involves not only the oboe, but also the orchestra as a whole. At this point the score has no measure indications, and so there are no regular beats that the conductor can use to guide the performers. This has subtle consequences also at a perceptive level: the "open" notation produces a sense of suspension, as if time were absent or something was expected that never arrives. The absence of time is also confirmed by the timbres of the orchestra: evocative atmospheres are created but with a predominant sense of immobility that often proves quite disorienting. In the central part the music becomes decidedly more animated and oriented in time, with rhythmic situations in which the writing varies between extreme chaos and lighter, more orderly phases. Finally, in the last five minutes we arrive at a sort of concluding adagio, in which the haunting voice of the cor anglais emerges, used mostly in its middle-low register, with melodies that bring us back to the peaceful and gentle climate of the opening, against which the piece gradually draws to a close.[20]

At the same time, or perhaps shortly before, though still in 1962, he wrote *Honeyrêves*, a short piece for flute and piano that has many features in common with the *Konzert*, including the fact that it was given various performances in the following and later years. Although the piece is based on rigorous numerical-serial procedures, particular emphasis is placed on the perceptive-expressive aspects, involving subjective choices of the composer. One of these is the frequent recurrence of moments of sound/silence, where the silence is not simply the absence of sound, but is a space open to the echoes of the previous utterances. The writing for the flute (evidently inspired by the "voice" of Gazzelloni) has two opposing aspects, these too recurring: sometimes it is characterized by quite long held notes (which Gazzelloni was able to perform with great delicacy), in other cases there are short and hurried notes that seem intent on contrasting the nascent pseudo-melodies, with rhythmic flourishes and extraordinary virtuosity (in other words, in the style of the proverbial *Gazzelloni Musik*). In the second case the piano aligns itself aggressively with the flute and reinforces its intentions with intricate rushes of sound. Instead, in the case of the pseudo-melodies, the piano tends to shroud the sounds of the flute in dense swathes of timbre, obtained by moving the fingers across the piano strings, rather than on the keyboard.

Throughout this intense period of conducting and composition, his private life appears to have carried on very much as normal. For the last five years Maderna had lived in Milan with his family and traveled from there to meet his various professional commitments and there is little to suggest that he was contemplating the significant change of life that would take place between 1962 and '63, when he moved definitively to Darmstadt. The first signs of such an intention come from his contacts with the registry office of Verona – where he had been registered since May 17, 1935 as living in Via Anfiteatro 6, care of Irma Manfredi – that led to his being cancelled from their lists. This took place on March 15, 1963 "due to definitive transfer abroad." Shortly afterwards, on May 16 of the same year, his name was also cancelled from the records of the district tax offices of Verona. This leads us to understand that his official link with Verona had not been severed either in 1945 when he went to live in Venice with his wife Raffaella Tartaglia, nor in 1957 when he moved his address to Piazzale Accursio 12 in Milan. As far as his trips to Darmstadt are concerned, we know that he had occasionally stayed with the Köpnik family, but at other times, starting from 1952, his correspondence is addressed to Martinstrasse 125,

---

[20] As in other works mainly based on the effects of timbre, our invitation (expressed in the Introduction) to accompany the descriptions provided here with listening to a performance, will prove particularly fruitful in the case of the *Concerto*.

for reasons that are still unknown, since an authoritative source tells us that he went to live with the family in Adolf-Spiess Strasse.[21] But between 1962 and '63, Maderna began to make the administrative arrangements necessary for his departure from Italy and for his move to Darmstadt.

After his move to Darmstadt (the "emigration" recorded in the registry office in Verona), it became increasingly natural for him to spend more time in the German town. For quite lengthy periods in March, April and May 1963 (apart from a fairly long parenthesis in Milan for a production of Purcell's *Dido and Aeneas* at La Piccola Scala) he was busy at the Landestheater in Darmstadt for the preparation and performance of Darius Milhaud's opera *Esther de Carpentras*. The work was by no means new, having been written in the period between the two wars, but it was the first time it was performed in a production for theater, moreover in a German translation. We do not know who chose to put on the work, but those involved in realizing the production were faced with an extremely challenging task. The narrative approach was very hard to interpret: in the city of Carpentras, in the South of France, against a backdrop of mutual acceptance between Catholics, Jews, French and the people of Provence, the characters are in search of their own identities; but in Milhaud's adaptation, what could have been a source of interior drama or even violent actions, is treated with unconcealed irony and with the aid of ambiguous symbologies, poised between tragedy and humor. Nothing better for stirring the imagination of the director Harro Dicks, who enlivened this *Carnaval hébraïque* (the subtitle of the work) by adding a ballet of fantastic animals and imaginary figures accompanied by complicated dance steps and playful arm gestures in the chorus.

Maderna's contribution was not, however, appreciated by all. "Maderna conducted the performance with his customary command and decision. The richness of the sound was astonishing and the intensity exemplary. A pity...." The reviewer of the *Darmstädter Tagblatt* goes on to criticize Maderna for pursuing his own path without paying attention to the underlying intentions of the director, Harro Dicks. But Maderna's seemingly contradictory interpretation may well have been the result of a deliberate choice made between the conductor and the director, in order to create a sense of heightened confusion, which more than the actual libretto, succeeded in drawing a picture of the interior condition of contemporary man. The audience, like the journalist, perhaps failed to understand the serious implications of the production, but nevertheless dutifully appreciated it as a worthy example of theatrical art [*Centro Studi Maderna*, Section D].

In the months before and after this event Maderna reaffirmed his now

---

[21] See W. Schlüter, "Anmerkungen zum Kapitel 'Darmstadt 1949 bis 1973'," in *Bruno Madernas Biographie*, 21, an unpublished typewritten document kindly made available to us by the author.

habitual relations with various German orchestras in twenty or so concerts, as well as inaugurating a new contact with the public of the Netherlands through concerts in The Hague and Amsterdam [*Romito* 2020]. The *Ferienkurse* of 1963 took place from July 14 to 26, during which Maderna conducted the Kammerensemble on four occasions: in the first and last concerts the whole ensemble were involved, whereas in the other two only small groups of soloists participated. In the last of the series, on July 24, he conducted the second version of his first oboe concerto (*Konzert für Oboe und Kammerensemble*). Maderna had probably decided to repeat the work, despite the success of its first performance, because he was not entirely satisfied with the original version, and in fact he made a very thorough revision of the work before passing it to Bruzzichelli for publication.[22] On the whole, Maderna's contribution to the courses that year was not particularly notable. In reality, his lesser involvement corresponded to a general weakening of the institution itself, which was gradually losing some of the salient points of its identity. In 1963, the historic symbol of the courses (the rising fourths of Schönberg's *Kammersymphonie* op. 9) was replaced with an image of the tower of Marienhöhe, while in 1964 the chamber ensemble lost its reference to the castle of Kranichstein and was renamed as the Internationales Kammerensemble Darmstadt (IKD); and a year later the institution itself was now called the IMD, *Internationales Musikinstitut Darmstadt*.

A few days after the end of the *Ferienkurse*, Maderna spent some time in a clinic in Darmstadt. The letter he wrote to his mother on August 8 gives the impression that he had just recovered from a deep crisis and now wished to give her his news:

> During the first days at the clinic, I didn't want to do anything but sleep [...] now I feel much, much better. [...] All these years of work, worries, concerns about my career and my family, the traveling and the irregular life had almost taken me to the end of my road [*Extraits* 2007, 502].

But even at the height of the crisis he was still thinking of his career more than his health, as we can gather from another letter written on August 1 to Francesco Siciliani, one of the principal managers of the programming at La Scala in Milan:

> I am losing hope of hearing any news about my possible appointment as conductor at La Scala in the forthcoming season 1963-64; [...] in the meantime here in Germany [...] I have conducted various performances

---

[22] A comparison between the two versions by Francesca Magnani can be found in *Documenti* 1985, 236-237.

of Verdi's *Simon Boccanegra* and Mozart's *Zauberflöte* in Cologne [...] and a new edition of *Rigoletto* [...] Besides, I have a great deal of private engagements and I cannot afford to remain on a trial basis at La Scala, perhaps for several more seasons, waiting to be able to conduct maybe one performance a year and jeopardizing all the contacts I have here, in Holland, in England, in France (and from next year in the USA).[23]

Not long afterwards (on August 19) he wrote a letter to Nono in Italian mixed with Venetian dialect, telling him that during the weeks of rest spent at the clinic he had persuaded himself that he should follow his friend's advice and write for the theater, promising him that for the Biennale of the following year he would come up with something interesting for La Fenice [*Extraits* 2007, 502]. Most likely he was referring to the stage version of *Hyperion* which was, in fact, put on at the theater on September 9, 1964.

Despite the worrying descriptions of his state of health, Maderna appears to have recovered fairly quickly given that from September 26 to 30 at the RAI in Turin he conducted and recorded a quite demanding program featuring choral and instrumental music by Stravinsky and Berg. In October he had his first encounter with the Finnish public in Helsinki, and at the start of November, he was back in Italy, again in Turin, to record another program of twentieth century music [*Romito* 2020]; finally, in mid-December, he traveled to Paris, where he performed – among other things – the first version of the orchestral work *Dimensioni III*, which would later become part of the *Hyperion* cycle.

The first part of 1964 similarly saw a wide range of engagements in different venues across Europe. He was at the Foro Italico in Rome on January 11, in Berlin on 22, in Hanover on 25 for the series *Tage der Neuen Musik*, and back at the Auditorium RAI in Turin on 31. From mid-February to mid-May his work was mainly concentrated in Cologne, where he conducted an intense series of theater productions including works from both the traditional repertoire (*Aida* and *Rigoletto*) and the twentieth century (Schönberg's *Erwartung* and *Die glückliche Hand*, and Bartók's *Bluebeard's Castle*). At the end of May he took part in the Maggio Musicale Fiorentino, where he conducted *Die glückliche Hand* again, as well as Malipiero's *Pantea* and Strauss's *Salome* [*Romito* 2020].

During the 1964 edition of the *Ferienkurse*, held from July 12 to 24, Maderna conducted "his" Kammerensemble four times; in particular, the first

---

[23] Autograph letter sold as lot no. 25 at an auction of the antique dealer Gonnelli (Florence, July 2, 2017). Maderna's requests to obtain a fixed position at La Scala continued in vain throughout the sixties; Francesco Siciliani nevertheless succeeded in procuring him a contract as chief conductor at the RAI in Milan. Maderna's correspondence with the various managers of La Scala is preserved in the archives of the theater and in copy at the *Centro Studi Maderna* Section L 5.

concert included a performance of Ligeti's *Aventures*. Much of his time and energy in this period was devoted to composing pieces associated with the idea of *Hyperion*: besides the previously mentioned *Dimensioni III* he now added *Dimensioni IV*, which he himself premiered in the final concert of the courses. On the same day (July 24) he sent a letter to Virginio Puecher, who shortly afterwards would direct the stage version of *Hyperion* for the Biennale di Venezia [*Centro Studi Maderna*, Section L 5]; in the letter he describes *Dimensioni IV* and also tells him, among other things, that he was about to leave for Buenos Aires.

He spent the whole of August in Argentina performing works from the classical repertoire, ranging from Gabrieli to Mozart, as well as Debussy and Ravel, while from the more modern repertoire he conducted pieces by Schönberg, Nono and Ives, and his own *Concerto per due pianoforti e strumenti* [*Romito* 2020]. No sooner had he returned from Buenos Aires than he was in Venice for the Biennale, where, from September 6 to 15, he conducted four concerts, the first of which included the premiere of the first stage version of *Hyperion*, which we will describe in detail in the next chapter. He then traveled to Berlin for three concerts, one of which, on September 28, included the first performance of the electronic piece *Le Rire*, on this occasion with a last minute addition of a flute and a marimba.

The sonorities of *Le Rire* are close to those of French *musique concrète*. The basic material consists of the sounds of metal and glass, of gushing water, of voices speaking either individually or in a group, and strokes on the timpano; their electronic transformation sometimes makes these elements difficult to recognize and their combination at times seems to elicit extra-musical images different from the original sound sources. However, the editing of the sounds was not aimed at evoking any aspects of real life: the tape consists of noises, some very short, others longer, always separated by pauses of varying length, which become elements of a purely musical scheme. Roberto Leydi mentions that sometimes at the *Studio* they jokingly spoke of an ironic portrait of the famous technician Marino Zuccheri, but any such allusions have disappeared from the definitive title. Rognoni insists that the intention was simply to mechanize certain aspects of the real, which, according to Bergson, could lead to effects recalling laughter [*Documenti* 1985, 243]. But any interpretation of the work linked too closely to the title, as proposed by some commentators, finds no justification in the contents of the tape.

The subsequent fortune of *Le Rire* owes itself primarily to the last five minutes of the piece, where the alternation between sounds and pauses gives rise to disconcerting effects similar to the sonority of a bell. In the low part of the sound spectrum the bell-like images are accompanied by strokes on the timpano, whose constant and insistent presence rules out any suggestion of a frivolous or ironic intent, and on the contrary produces a sober, almost dramatic effect. This final part of the work was, in fact, used recurrently in particularly tense moments of the stage versions of *Hyperion*.

Much of his time between October and November was taken up by his participation in the Holland Festival, during which he conducted the Residentie Orkest of The Hague in ten concerts in various parts of the Netherlands. In the same period he was also involved in a new theater production, *Les adieux*, by an unknown playwright favored by the superintendent of the Landestheater in Darmstadt. The stage director Heinz Schirk recalls that neither he nor Maderna liked the play:

> I met Maderna one morning, very early, in October 1964. He seemed a little sleepy and taciturn. I described the noises, the rhythms and musical underscoring I would need. He pressed some buttons on his electronic device and the sounds that I wanted came out. The whole procedure took just a couple of hours [*Romito* 2000/2, 261].

In November and December 1964 he took part in three of the concerts featuring the complete performance of Mozart's twenty-seven piano concertos, with the soloist Yvonne Loriod, Messiaen's wife. The concerts were held in the Salle des Conservatoires in Paris, and in addition to Maderna, were conducted by Pierre Boulez and Louis Martin. Fortunately, between one engagement and the next, Maderna still managed to spend some more relaxing moments with his family. One particular occasion is colorfully described by Wilhelm Schlüter, a regular participant at the *Ferienkurse* who had become a close friend of the family:

> A few months after my engagements at the Musikinstitut in 1964, Beate Köpnik – always a formidable organizer of family life – phoned me to ask if I would accept to take part in their Sanktaklaus party, and more precisely if I would play the role of the Saint. At the arranged time she met me at the cellar door of their home in Adolf-Spiess-Strasse. She helped me put on a splendid costume with all the necessary accessories (beard, stick and a sack for the gifts) which she had borrowed from the stores of the Darmstadt theater. I will never forget my entrance into the family's living-room. After my "Prologue," Caterina, the elder daughter, recited a poem, then Claudia – who was then four – played a piece on Brunetto's small violin. They all received gifts from the sack. Mum and Dad exchanged gifts. I was especially struck by how lovingly the father treated his rather excited daughters. After around twenty minutes my merry theatrical interlude ended. Later, on several occasions, Maderna spoke enthusiastically of my show.[24]

---

[24] See W. Schlüter, "Anmerkungen," cited in note 21, 21.

In 1965, between the countless engagements that continued to arrive without respite, Maderna found the time and concentration to draft one of the most intense articles he had ever written.

At the request of André Boucourechliev, he wrote a piece for the journal *Preuves* on the theme "La musique sérielle aujourd'hui," titled *La révolution dans la continuité*. Not being able to reproduce the whole essay, we report here at least some fragments, which seem to offer a fair idea of his philosophy:

> There can be neither breaches nor fractures in a civilization, it is an ontological impossibility. Cultures are neither abstractions nor things: they are human facts. Even revolutions are rooted in continuity and if they interrupt the course of things, at the same time they confirm this continuity. The rupture that atonal music seems to have provoked and that serial music seems to prolong and deepen, is only an apparent rupture [...] What is serial music today? Above all a *forma mentis*. What yesterday was a grammatical system, an instrument of organization, has today become a concept in the world of music. The notion of serialism comprises multiple and wide-ranging meanings, and yet it must remain. [...] The system – and every composer has his own – must provide a logical basis for thought; it enriches this thought, it does not limit it in any way [...] Then there is a particular field, that of "open forms," in which the performer must intervene on the very structure of the work, reveal through his own judgment this or that possible aspect of the work. It is a great responsibility that I assume with joy and awareness [...] The listener assumes his own! "Open, mobile" forms are a necessary adventure in the creative thought of our time, which logically needed to be reached [...] a glorification of form, therefore, not its negation.

After a very significant excursus about electronic music and how to listen to it, the essay ends with a utopian vision:

> I am thinking of the project of an Argentinian architect, Aparicio Williams, of an elliptical auditorium with six thousand places in which the listeners are seated all around: would this perhaps recreate the ancient magic of meeting in a circle, and would collective communication rediscover its deepest sense, at once archaic and modern?[25]

After four concerts in Vienna and Paris on February 10 and 13, 1965, Maderna was once again at the Foro Italico in Rome with the symphony orchestra of the RAI. On this occasion the programs were quite curious: the first concert combined music by Berlioz and Liszt inspired by the Faust legend

---

[25] See "La révolution dans la continuité," in *Preuves*, 15/177 (1965), 28–29.

with his own transcription of dances by Schubert originally written for piano duet. The idea of transcribing these dances probably goes back many years. Towards the end of 1952, during his first trip with Christine in the north of Germany, we recall that he had been fascinated by these pieces and was so enthusiastic that he mentioned them to Nono and suggested they should write a version for orchestra together. In the end, Maderna appears to have made the transcription alone, dedicating it "to all my friends in the RAI orchestra in Rome," and with a special mention for Severino Gazzelloni [*Documenti* 1985, 323]. The second concert, three days later, featured both the harpsichord and the piano in concertos respectively by Carl Philipp Emanuel Bach and Elliott Carter. Soon after these concerts he set out on his first visit to the USA, where on February 21 in Boston he conducted the American premiere of Nono's *Intolleranza 1960*, which he had already presented at the Biennale di Venezia shortly after its composition. The new production of the opera was particularly sumptuous and prompted high praise for the conducting, but also a certain amount of political dissent.

Before this challenging and in some ways prophetic journey, Maderna, as we mentioned, had continued his collaboration with the Wiener Symphoniker in Vienna. One might think that after the heavy criticisms of the press in 1964 he would have decided to remove Vienna from his schedules. But this was not so. Evidently, and contrary to the whims of the public, the national radio and the concert organizers in Vienna persisted in their resolve to promote modern music and Maderna continued to accept their invitations. However, a certain change in the choice of programs can be noted, since the concerts held in 1965 no longer included the works of young composers, or at least contained very few, and preference was given to composers unlikely to cause any controversy, like Schönberg and Stravinsky. Less than a year had passed since the concert that had been so harshly criticized, but the change in the reaction of the press (and presumably also of the public) was tangible, since, at least in the headlines, they appear to have accepted a program mainly dedicated to the twentieth century. The tone adopted by a journalist from Graz was more or less as follows: the most *courageous* part of the Viennese public who came to hear this *revolutionary* program applauded enthusiastically [our italics]. In reality it was Maderna himself who was courageous, as just a few days later he involved the trusting Wiener Symphoniker once more in the cycle Musica Nova, which again featured a program of well established classics (Debussy's *Jeux* and Mendelssohn's Fourth Symphony) combined with more recent works. The original plan was to include Penderecki's already tried and tested *Threnody for the victims of Hiroshima* (1951) and two freshly written – or at least not yet published – works, both for flute and instrumental ensemble: Kazuo Fukushima's *Hy-Kyo* and his own *Dimensioni*

IV. As it turned out, though, it was not possible to perform the two more recent works for flute owing to the sudden indisposition of Severino Gazzelloni. The critic of the *Wiener Zeitung* did not seem too upset by this fact, and on March 17, 1965 commented: "Two out of three pieces of this 'Musica nova' were dropped, but the one that remained was bad enough for all three!" In the end, Maderna seems to have capitulated to this refusal of the Viennese public to accept the music of the younger generation, and even gave up offering "mixed" programs, instead concentrating on the first part of the twentieth century. And finally, in January 1966, when he reappeared for the sixth year in a row in the Great Hall of the Austrian Radio with a program featuring Borodin, Webern and Stravinsky, the consensus was unanimous and appreciative. The concert was repeated one week later and was again well received by the public and press alike. And so it was that in the years that followed, Maderna did not miss a single appointment with the Wiener Symphoniker in the Great Hall in Vienna, earning himself the reputation of being a sensitive and comprehensible conductor in the Viennese series of "modern classics," without however succeeding in his main aim of allowing more recent music to be understood and appreciated.[26]

At the end of March, to celebrate the twentieth anniversary of the liberation of Italy, Maderna presented a program of anti-fascist music (including works by Schönberg, Berg, Ghedini, Henze and Nono) in Bologna, Reggio and Modena, with the orchestra and choir of the Teatro Comunale of Bologna. At the end of April he made a second journey across the Atlantic, this time to Montréal where he gave two concerts with a mixed program, combining Mozart's *Haffner* with his own first *Concerto per oboe* and *Serenata n. 2*. In May, back in Europe, he took part in five concerts (in Cologne, Munich, Brussels, Paris and Zagreb) which featured performances of Stockhausen's *Gruppen* for three orchestras conducted by Stockhausen, Maderna and Michael Gielen. In June and July he was in Amsterdam, The Hague and Utrecht for five performances of theater works by Dutch composers [*Romito* 2020].

As always, the *Ferienkurse* of 1965 included composition, theory and instrumental lessons held by eminent teachers. Although the courses lasted two weeks (July 18-31), there were notably fewer concerts: two by the Residentie Orkest of The Hague, conducted respectively by Boulez and Maderna, three by the Kammerensemble, two of which conducted by Maderna and one by Boulez, and a single concert of electronic music. Maderna's concert with the Residentie Orkest included a performance of the recent instrumental version of

---

[26] We were fortunate enough to have been in direct contact with the Wiener Symphoniker, who, on learning of the research we were carrying out in Bologna, kindly sent us all the documentary material they had collected over the years about their association with Maderna. We are deeply grateful for their help and interest.

Hyperion, which, according to Antonio Trudu, was met with "genuine ovations." One of the most interesting elements of the courses that year was the series of lectures on "The Form of New Music," which took up eight whole evenings; the transcripts of nearly all the lectures were published in the *Damstädter Beiträge* in 1966. However, the problems that had arisen over the previous years concerning the theory and practice of form were left largely unresolved and found no shared solution; Ligeti even spoke of "Darmstadtian academicism" and questioned the very notion of applying the concept of form to music, which he considered a spatial and not temporal entity. And the courses as a whole also came under criticism: the Spanish composer Tomás Marco remarked that they were no longer as stimulating for young composers as they had been in the past [*Trudu* 1992, 183, 187].

After the end of the courses Maderna was involved in a production of Schiller's drama *Die Verschwörung des Fiesco zu Genua*, which was staged at the Landestheater in Darmstadt from September 18. He wrote the incidental music for the play and conducted the theater's orchestra, although we do not know for how many of the numerous performances. The same can be said of his appearances at the opera house in Kiel, where on September 26 a new production of Mozart's *Don Giovanni* was inaugurated, followed by fifteen further performances that went on until February of the following year. It is unlikely that he managed to conduct many of these, given that between October and the end of the year he conducted as many as thirteen concerts in eight different European cities. Looking through the list of engagements carefully compiled by Maurizio Romito [2020], one is struck by the fact that between March and the end of the year, Maderna appears not to have conducted a single concert in Italy. The programs of those he conducted abroad show a clear preference for music of the twentieth century, often coupled with more consolidated classics and works from the Italian Baroque. The only exception is the concert he gave in Hanover on 8 November – and repeated the following day – which was entirely dedicated to Mahler's Seventh Symphony. Maderna had been familiar with Mahler's works for many years, but until then had, for some reason, only conducted the *Adagio* from the unfinished Tenth Symphony. However, after the concert in Hanover he turned to Mahler's other symphonies and regularly included them in his programs until his last days. The reason for choosing these works are clearly expressed in a conversation with Christof Bitter and Theo Olof broadcast on the radio in 1970:

> In his symphonies – and especially in the Seventh – I believe we find the man in all his complexity, even with his errors and dirtier sides, which were however cleansed by a constantly strong internal tension,

by an inclination towards totality and the absolute. Today I feel how contemporary Mahler is, I feel it is he that represents the poet, the Ideal as I imagine it [*Documenti* 1985, 105].

The year 1966 started with two concerts that, alongside works by other composers, featured two new concert versions of the *Hyperion* cycle: on January 8 at the Foro Italico in Rome, with the soloists Dorothy Dorow and Severino Gazzelloni, and on January 19 in Hamburg, with the orchestra of the Norddeutscher Rundfunk. Another version was presented on March 11, in a concert with the orchestra of the Bayerischer Rundfunk during the traditional Musica Viva season. Before this, in February, he had spent a couple of weeks on tour in the Netherlands with the Utrecht symphony orchestra, with programs that ranged from the Baroque era to the Viennese school, including works by some of his favorite composers, like Mozart, Schubert and Debussy. He had already taken part in the Holland Festival in 1963 and '64, but this year he returned to the country on various occasions. In April he conducted the Residentie Orkest of The Hague in various concerts; in June and July he was back with the Utrecht orchestra for the premiere of Peter Schat's new opera *Labyrinth*, which was given six times at the Royal Theater Carré in Amsterdam, prompting lively discussion and polemics among the public and critics; finally, in November he gave another eight concerts with orchestra of The Hague. Therefore, in what was one of his most intense years of activity as a conductor, more than a half of his appointments were in the Netherlands [*Romito* 2020]. It is interesting to note how a relatively small country like the Netherlands was able to offer such a rich array of musical events, with as many as four large orchestras – those of Utrecht, Rotterdam, Amsterdam and The Hague – that organized cycles of concerts also in smaller towns. Even more surprising is the fact that in a large and culturally important country like France, Maderna only performed in Paris and just a few times in Royan.

That summer he spent some time at a health resort in Königstein, a picturesque town in Hasse not far from Frankfurt. Here he received a letter from Ernst Thomas dated August 1, 1966, inquiring about the solo parts of a new work, titled *Amanda. Serenata VI*, that was due to be performed during the upcoming *Ferienkurse* [*Carteggio* 2001, 213-214]. The autograph inscription on the last page of the score tells us it was composed in Königstein in July 1966; it was eventually performed in Naples during the Autunno Musicale series in October, the performance in Darmstadt having fallen through. The origin of the unusual title is unclear, but from a musical point of view the subtitle *Serenata* is certainly appropriate. Some commentators have suggested a possible derivation from "Alabanda" (one of the main characters of Hölderlin's novel

Hyperion, which we will return to in the next chapter).²⁷ This would help to explain why in a performance in Graz in 1967, Maderna referred to the work as *Amanda, Serenade aus der Oper Hyperion*, and could also justify the decision of Péter Eötvös to include it in a stage performance of *Hyperion* in Paris in 1991. But the mystery remains as to what relation Maderna could have imagined between the light nature of this "serenata" and the dramatic events narrated in *Hyperion* (not to mention the association with the violent inclination of a character like Alabanda). These considerations raise some doubt as to any possible initial link between *Amanda* – over and above the title – and the novel. The score published by Suvini Zerboni in 1967 bears the title *Amanda. Serenata VI*, prompting Massimo Mila to suggest the existence of a *Serenata V*, about which we still know nothing [*Mila* 1976, 29]. A certain continuity can nevertheless be found between the various *Serenate* he composed. The carefree nature of *Serenata n. 2* and its reference to the eighteenth century have already been mentioned, and this characteristic is reaffirmed in the lightness of the third and fourth of the series.

In *Amanda* the reference to ancient, and perhaps also to popular music, is already suggested not only by the presence of the guitar but more especially of the mandolin, which has a particularly prominent role in this work. But, while not neglecting their traditional identity, Maderna now experiments with their timbres in a quite original and free manner. In the opening of the piece, for example, the guitar and mandolin are used to create "points" separated by silences. And in a central episode, despite the thick texture, two overlapping layers can be distinctly heard: one made up of dense chords on the strings, which gradually descend to their lowest, more austere register, the other consisting in groups of stringed instruments (guitars, mandolins, harps) and small keyboards (xylophones, marimbas), which merrily launch into a lively chattering of short, fast notes. Notable too is the virtuoso episode for solo violin – guided by a vast variety of performing instructions such as bow attacks, trills, accents, glissandos, and so on – where the highly imaginative writing proves surprising in its constant liveliness and unpredictability.

Exactly how long Maderna stayed in Königstein we do not know, but he was certainly in Darmstadt for the opening of the *Ferienkurse* on August 21, when he conducted the first concert given by the Kammerensemble. His participation in courses that year was nevertheless quite limited. He held no practical or theoretical lessons and just conducted two more concerts with the Ensemble, whose members, all of them highly qualified musicians, actively supported him in the preparation of the pieces. The second concert included Ligeti's *Aventures &*

---

²⁷ See *Verzina* 2003, 184, and G. Ferrari, "*Hyperion*, les chemins du poète," in *Basalte* 1 (2007), 96.

Nouvelles Aventures, whose first version, simply titled *Aventures,* he had previously conducted in 1964. A curious sequel to this event appears in Wilhelm Schlüter's account. The German record producer Werner Goldschmidt commissioned Maderna to make a recording of the piece to be included on an LP of Ligeti's music. The recording subsequently reached international fame when part of it was used for the soundtrack of Kubrick's movie *2001: A Space Odyssey.* All those who took part in the recording were apparently given an unexpected additional fee by the American cinema production company Warner Brothers. Maderna returned to the work in the first of two concerts he conducted in Berlin, at the Akademie der Künste, on September 26 and 27, again with the Darmstadt Kammerensemble [*Centro Studi Maderna,* Section L. 8].

On January 13, 1967 Maderna inaugurated the new year with five performances at La Scala of his revision of Monteverdi's *Incoronazione di Poppea,* which was well received by both the public and critics. After one of his now traditional concerts with the Wiener Symphoniker (whom he would see again in April and May), he immediately traveled to the Netherlands where he remained for the whole month of February, conducting the Rotterdam orchestra in its home and in various other towns, with programs ranging from the Baroque to the twentieth century. And at the end of his stay he conducted the Concertgebouw Orchestra in Amsterdam in a concert of contemporary music including works by Lutosławski, Nono and the young Dutch composer Jan van Vlijmen. Then, on May 9 he was in Zurich, where he conducted his *Dimensioni III* during the Musica Viva season, which took place in various venues in Bavaria and Switzerland [*Centro Studi Maderna,* Section D 4.3]; and towards the end of the month he gave three concerts in Graz, whose program included, among other things, the work originally titled *Amanda,* but on this occasion referred to as *Amanda, Serenade aus der Oper Hyperion.* In July and August his engagements as a conductor seem to have slackened a little; in fact, some sources tell us that he held a course in advanced conducting at the *Sommerakademie* of the Mozarteum in Salzburg, one of the oldest institutions of its kind that had reopened its courses in the years immediately following the war. His participation from 1967 to 1969 is testified by the Dutch conductor Lucas Vis [*Pour Bruno* 2015, 226-229], and in 1968 also by Francesco Valdambrini, who in a letter of August 18 apologizes for not saying goodbye to him in Salzburg and hopes that the courses that year had gone better than those of the year before [*Centro Studi Maderna,* Section L 7].

In 1967 the *Ferienkurse* were held from August 22 to September 3 and, to a certain extent, were less innovative than those of the previous years. The most interesting contribution came from Karlheinz Stockhausen, whose huge group-composition named *Ensemble* involved twelve young composers who had participated in the writing of the work during a seminar held before the start of the courses themselves. The work was performed on August 29. Maderna, on the other hand, for the first time since 1951, had no role in the courses, neither as teacher, composer or conductor. The reason for his absence from the event – especially in a town where he was actually living – is unknown, but not entirely surprising given the history of the *Ferienkurse* in those years. In 1968, the Kammerensemble, which had been purposely created by Maderna, broke up for economic reasons and in that year he only conducted one concert (which would be his last) with the Residentie Orkest of The Hague. And in 1969 he gave just a few lessons on the New Music Conducting Course. The following year his recent *Concerto per violino* was performed, but was conducted by Michael Gielen. From that year on, the courses were held every two years, although Maderna did not take part in the 1972 edition. His distancing from the *Ferienkurse* was therefore gradual and not only of his own choosing. But he nevertheless continued to play an important role in the cultural life of the town, especially at the Landestheater.

In the meantime, his long association with the Darmstadt courses was reaffirmed in another context, when, on September 9, he conducted a concert at the Biennale di Venezia, to commemorate his friend and former colleague Hermann Scherchen. Then, about ten days later, he set off on a lengthy tour with the Residentie Orkest, encompassing various towns of the Netherlands and lasting almost until the end of the following month. Besides numerous concerts, the tour included five performances of a version of *Tannhäuser* in theaters in Scheveningen and Amsterdam. The next month, on November 10, he was in Cologne to conduct the premiere of his *Concerto per oboe e orchestra n. 2* with the soloist Lothar Faber, and on November 17, he was in Turin for a concert that, alongside pieces from the traditional repertoire (Gabrieli, Händel, Schumann), included his *Konzert für Oboe und Kammerensemble*, again with Faber as soloist [*Romito* 2020].

The *Concerto per oboe n. 2* was, as we learn from the score, commissioned by the WDR (Westdeutscher Rundfunk) in Cologne and dedicated to Faber. In a chapter of his book on Maderna, Nicola Verzina precedes his analysis of the oboe concertos from the '60s with a mention of a technique widely used in the pieces, but already adopted some years before by Stockhausen: the so called "group technique" [*Verzina* 2003, 213 ff.]. Stockhausen's *Gruppen* for three orchestras had been premiered in 1958, when the three orchestras were conducted respectively by the composer himself, Maderna and Boulez, and was performed again in 1965 with Gielen in place of Boulez, when it was taken on tour to various venues in Europe. The technique involved an extension of the four parameters that were initially considered suitable for a serial approach:

pitch, duration, intensity and timbre. While the number of pitches, durations and intensities (dynamics ranging from *pianissimo* to *fortissimo*) can be fixed, and subsequently "serialized," the more complex nature of timbre makes it different from the other parameters. The term timbre can, as we have seen, refer to a wide range of sonic entities: not only the specific sonority of an instrument, but also the way it is played and its high or low registers. Each of these elements will result in a different kind of timbre. However, the situation becomes even more challenging if we consider not only the sound produced by a single instrument, but also the sounds of an orchestra as a whole, a quantity that would be impossible to reduce to a number able to form a traditional row or series. In other words, timbre is a sound parameter that cannot be treated in the same way as the others. The technique proposed by Stockhausen attempts to overcome these difficulties by distinguishing between different sets of groups: the types of instruments used (strings, wind, percussion etc.), the density of the groups (the number of instruments present), the shifts between different zones of the register, and other still more subtle distinctions. The result is extremely complex: the number of groups foreseen by Stockhausen was more than 150, and their possible combinations were calculated on the basis of very precise numerical methods. Verzina suggests that Maderna has consistently applied this technique in his second *Concerto per oboe*, although without going into any minute calculations. He focuses his attention mainly on what he calls the "timbral writing" and provides a detailed analysis of this aspect.

The form of the *Concerto* is decidedly aleatory, although not "open" as in Cage, but well "controlled" by the composer. The aleatory element is represented in two different ways. Firstly, the score includes various separate panels or frames, each of which is made up of a precise group of timbres. These are usually numbered up to 4 or 5. The conductor decides which of them to select, how long to make them last and how to overlap them, usually by pointing to the players during the performance. The second aleatory aspect derives from the fact that the duration of the notes is often represented simply with a horizontal line, which can be interpreted in terms of length, but without being precisely measurable. The panels are occasionally alternated with portions of more traditional writing, marked "battere il tempo" ("beat the time," obviously referring to the conductor). Also the parts of the solo instruments are written with notes of a precise pitch and duration, but these are not divided into measures, meaning that the player must "feel" their actual length, without the guidance of the conductor. The dynamic markings (*piano, forte, crescendo,* accents, etc.) are almost always carefully written, but in both performances kept in the *Centro Studi Maderna* their frequency and the balance between the various instruments are always controlled directly by the conductor.

From the listener's point of view, the whole concerto is perceived as being divided into different sections, depending mainly on the alternation between the various types of oboe prescribed by the composer. There is an introduction for orchestra alone, followed shortly afterwards by a long and elaborate dialogue between the musette and the other instruments. There are then solos for the oboe, and finally for the oboe d'amore. The use of different types of oboe has a strong influence on the expressive character of the concerto. The musette, which has a penetrating sound that Faber renders particularly aggressive, moves in a disorderly and bizarre fashion, and is furiously pursued by the orchestra. Towards the middle of the work this frenzied climate begins to be slightly mitigated by episodes featuring groups of violins and then passages shared between the musette and the oboe. It is only in the closing minutes of the work, when the oboe gives way to the oboe d'amore, that the more "elegiac" finale begins, sustained by the guitars, strings and small, inconspicuous percussion instruments. The piece follows an evident path of expression (from extreme aggression to extreme sweetness), which is clearly confirmed by Maderna's indications in the score. The "assemblable" element of the work is therefore only a technical matter and does not affect the composer's musical choices. Maderna, as always, offers no theories: he simply restored, without telling anybody, the notion that a piece of music should have a beginning, a development and an ending.

Maderna enjoyed a particularly close relationship with his soloists, many of whom became lifelong friends. We have already seen how Severino Gazzelloni, after being assigned prominent roles in a variety of works, was finally rewarded with a special dedication in *Honeyrêves*. Also Lothar Faber became a good friend and both the *Concerto per oboe n. 2* and *Aulodia per Lothar* were dedicated to him. Just how warm the relationship was with these two exceptional artists can be gleaned from the fact that Maderna's son Andrea, born in 1966, was given the middle names Severino Lotario.

Aulodia per Lothar for oboe d'amore and guitar is a clear tribute to the sweet "voice" of Faber, whose name appears in the title. The piece was composed in 1965 when Maderna's interest in Hölderlin's novel *Hyperion*, set in Greece, was at its height. The Greek aulos, like the modern oboe, was a double-reed instrument, while his choice of the guitar was probably aimed at evoking the ancient *cithara*. Basically, the piece well captures the nostalgia that Maderna had for the ideal of beauty held by the ancient Greeks; moreover, it is one of the richest examples of the "melodizing" that all Maderna scholars have unfailingly noted and that we too have pointed out several times in this book and elsewhere.[28]

---

[28] A more technically detailed description of Maderna's melodizing can be found in M. Baroni, "L'archetipo dell'aulos. Echi e reminiscenze melodiche," in *Studi* 1989, 227-240.

A similarly high regard was held for the extraordinary violinist Theo Olof, who would later perform the *Concerto per violino* in 1969, and who in October 1967 premiered *Widmung* for solo violin, a piece commissioned by the curators of a museum of abstract art in the German town of Nüttingen, where it was first heard. The title, in fact, means "Dedication," although it is not clear whether this refers to the performer or to those who commissioned the work. It is a highly virtuosic piece that became popular among violinists and was performed and recorded several times. Generally speaking, the structure could be said to continue along the lines already adopted by Maderna in those years, namely the alternation between two contrasting styles: one that is violent and aggressive in character and the other elegiac and more meditative, with gradients and passages between the two moods, easily perceptible to the careful listener. But here too, Maderna's main interest (further pursuing the investigation of string timbres he had begun in *Amanda*) was to explore the instrument's capacity to produce new sonorities and to experiment with novel techniques.

Returning to Maderna's conducting engagements in 1967, which we had interrupted to dwell a moment on the performances of the oboe concertos in November, it is worth referring once again to the recollections of Wilhelm Schlüter, who recalls with pleasure the two evenings in which Maderna concluded the year with performances of Johann Strauss's operetta *Die Fledermaus* at the Landestheater in Darmstadt. The production was particularly successful and was repeated numerous times in the same theater until the following April. In 1968 his work as a conductor continued at the same lively pace. His preferred destination firmly remained the Netherlands, where he went several times during the course of the year, and where he always stayed for many days, conducting the local orchestras, one of which – that of The Hague – he took with him on a foreign tour. A notable feature of his schedule for this year was his consistent attention to works for theater: besides *Die Fledermaus*, in March he took part in a production of *Moses und Aron* in Berlin, in May he conducted his own *Hyperion en het Gewelt* in Brussels, in June Rameau's *Platée* at the Royal Theater Carré in Amsterdam, in July his *Hyperion-Orfeo dolente* in Bologna, and in November Janáček's *From the House of the Dead* in Düsseldorf; finally, in December, he conducted *Carmen* several times in The Netherlands [Romito 2020].

The same relentless rhythm persisted throughout 1969. In January we find him in one of his favorite countries, Austria, where he conducted the Wiener Symphoniker not only in Vienna but also in Graz, Klagenfurt and Bregenz, in a series of concerts that included Ligeti's *Atmosphères*, although the programs were predominated by Schubert, Mussorgsky and Brahms. In March many of his appointments again involved the theater, including two works by Kurt Weill (*Die sieben Todsünden* and *Mahagonny*) which were staged at the Landestheater in Darmstadt directed by Harro Dicks, one of which appeared to have been particularly successful as it was repeated various times in April, May and June. And in September his transcription of Monteverdi's *Orfeo* was well received by the audience at the La Monnaie Theater in Brussels and was repeated as many as seven times. That autumn also saw two engagements outside of Europe. In September he took part in the Shiraz-Persepolis Festival of Arts, in Iran, where he conducted the French Radio Orchestra in works by Messiaen and Debussy; and in October he returned for a second time to the USA, this time visiting Pittsburgh. Finally, among the numerous concerts he gave towards the end of the year, it is worth mentioning the program of the concert he gave at La Scala, repeated three times between October and November, which combined Manzoni's *Insiemi* with his first performance of Mahler's Ninth Symphony [*Romito* 2020].

But over and above his association with the theater, 1969 also witnessed many performances of his own most recent compositions, something that had not happened for some time. On April 2 *From A to Z*, an experimental play by Rebecca Rass with music by Maderna, was broadcast on Dutch television; on May 13, he conducted his *Suite aus der Oper Hyperion* in Berlin; from June 12 to 14 he recorded the radio play *Ritratto di Erasmo* in Rome; and again on June 14, he gave the first Italian performance of *Quadrivium* at the Foro Italico; on July 4, Shakespeare's *Coriolanus* was staged at the Teatro Romano in Verona, with incidental music by Maderna; on September 12 he conducted his *Concerto per violino* at the Biennale di Venezia; and in the same month his *Serenata per un satellite* was premiered in Darmstadt. Such a wide array of works produced in the space of just one year is certainly to be admired, but a closer look at their content will offer an even richer picture of the extent of his creative activity.

The first work in the list, *From A to Z*, actually comprises three different works: the book written in English by Rebecca Rass, the script based on the book that was used for a play aired on Dutch television in 1969 with music by Bruno Maderna [*Romito* 2002/1, 91-92], and a new video-theater adaptation that was presented in German at the Landestheater in Darmstadt in February 1970. This third version is the only one of which a substantial amount of material has survived, namely the literary text and the audio recording, now preserved at the *Centro Studi Maderna*. The spectacle tells the imaginary tale of prehistoric wars between words, phonemes and punctuations that eventually gave rise to the sounds of human languages. Maderna's tape contains fragments of speech in various languages mixed with electronic sounds, instrumental sounds and an assortment of acoustic materials: bells, shots, bird song, bellowing, etc. There is little doubt that the planning of the initiative owed much to Maderna; he was actively involved in the cultural life of the town, not only with regards music and theater, but also other forms of art: among other things, his friend Wilhelm

Schlüter recalls his involvement in exhibitions on the Secession movement, which had a strong tradition in Darmstadt. Such was the appreciation for all his efforts that on June 8, 1970 Maderna received an honorary award from the mayor of Darmstadt in recognition of his support for the culture of the town [*Centro Studi Maderna*, Section L 7].

Also *Ritratto di Erasmo* is a work on tape, and has the particularity of being the only one without any known collaborators. Maderna, in fact, appears to have done most of the work himself, including the choice of sources for the script and how they were used, the composition or revision of the recorded music, the tape editing and the radio direction. However, the work is surrounded by several issues. The first of these concerns the reason why, despite being specifically commissioned by the RAI, it was not admitted to the Prix Italia, and was broadcast only thirteen years later during Paolo Donati's radio program *Pomeriggio Musicale*.[29] Massimo Mila suggests that it was withdrawn from the competition on account of its text, or rather "the liberty [...] of the historic-religious notions stirred up within it" [*Mila* 1976, 50]. This hypothesis is taken up again by De Benedictis, who speaks more explicitly of "a sort of internal censorship" because the work "could not represent the Italian radio corporation" due to its contents.[30] Neither of these two affirmations is backed up by any documentation. Adriana Anastasia, instead, is more inclined towards the explanation given orally by Renata Bertelli, head of programming of the Third Program of the RAI at the time, who claims that the work was not admitted to the competition for artistic reasons, namely the predominance of the spoken part over the music. Another circumstance that makes any discussion of the work problematic is the fact that the tapes of the intermediate phases of the work have not been preserved, while there are only a few sketches pertaining to the elaboration and composition of the musical part. A reconstruction of the preliminary stages of the work is therefore quite difficult to achieve. It is impossible to know when Maderna started work on the script or the musical part, since no traces have so far emerged in his own correspondence or in that of those close to him regarding the course of this composition. We only know that the recording was made in two different places, in an atmosphere of great excitement, as testified by the actors who were involved in the project. The first part was recorded at the Auditorium della RAI in Rome, in Via Asiago, between June 12 and 14, while the spoken part was made in Darmstadt, as stated on the title-page of the script: "Darmstadt giugno 1969."

---

[29] See A. Anastasia, '*Ritratto di Erasmo*'. *Un' opera radiofonica di Bruno Maderna* (Trento: Università di Trento, 2009), 20.

[30] A. I. De Benedictis, "*Ritratto di Erasmo* di Bruno Maderna," *Musica/Realtà*, no. 73 (2004), 153-154.

Although his time in Rome was very short, he did not spend it exclusively on *Ritratto di Erasmo*. On June 14 at the Auditorium del Foro Italico he conducted a concert that included works by Bach-Webern, Stravinsky and Renosto, as well as his own *Music of Gaity* and the Italian premiere of *Quadrivium* [*Romito* 2003/1, 122], a program that surely needed more than one rehearsal before the event. He then traveled to Milan, where, between June 16 and 29, he put the final touches to the recording of *Erasmo* at the *Studio di Fonologia*, apparently without the precious assistance of Marino Zuccheri, who was probably busy with other work elsewhere. And one must admit that his absence can be felt in the final product. From the start to the finish, our attention is firmly caught by the arguments put forward by the two main characters, Erasmus and Luther: on the one hand we hear the critical reflections and ideals of equality and fraternity, and on the other the remonstrations against the hypocrisy of the powerful in the world of politics and religion. Instead, the music running beneath their voices (and even in the pauses in the speech) remains, despite the variety in style and the wealth of timbre, largely in the background. The choice of texts bears witness to Maderna's vast knowledge of literature and history, and the various sources are so skillfully blended that, in the end, the different texts seem to have been written by a single author, in a crescendo effectively underlined by the different narrating voices and the passing between the various channels. In the last part of the work the voices of the actors are disturbed, in a kind of counterpoint, by the interjections of a more distant group, who describe the appearance and character of a range of demons, forcing the two protagonists to almost shout in order to be heard. Besides the moments of electronic music and effects on the percussion, various pieces of medieval sacred music are interposed: among others, a piece by Gabrieli (in an instrumental version), a madrigal by G. Caimo, and an instrumental arrangement of a piece by G. Binchois. The last piece that can be made out, at 40 minutes, is Francesco Landini's "ballata" *Gram pianto agli occhi*, after which the electronic music prevails until reaching the long concluding pedal. Mila wondered whether this rich reference to ancient music was the fruit of a perfect assimilation of stylistic models or whether it was based on Maderna's transcriptions. Romito, instead, demonstrates that they were in fact accurate transcriptions of original sources [*Romito* 2000/2, 246-247].

This fact brings us back to the question of Maderna's relationship with ancient music, a theme that surfaces regularly from his very first experiences as a conductor and composer until his death. Maderna claims to have loved ancient music ever since he was a child, a passion that was then reaffirmed during his studies with Malipiero:

> One day [Malipiero] came to my home – it was in 1948 – and brought me *Odhecaton A*, the first part, to transcribe [...]. Every day I transcribed a page or two, then we studied it together. He was truly enthusiastic about this music and also tried to have it performed by small instrumental groups of students.[31]

This brief comment tells us not only about Maderna's relationship with ancient music, but also about the resolve – widely shared at the time – to bring this repertoire to the attention of the present. It would appear (though not affirmed explicitly) that the task of transcription came easily to him: the young composer transcribed the ancient notes in a "diplomatic" fashion, that is to say, faithfully to the source, just as his teacher had instructed him.[32] One might wonder what exactly his studies with Malipiero involved. Did they simple study what they found written down or did they also try to deduce the way the music was played? From what Maderna says, it would seem that Malipiero wished to respect the original performing practices by having the transcriptions played by small groups and not by an orchestra. Although we do not know precisely which instruments were involved in these groups, they were most likely modern instruments, given that the players were students at the conservatory. The custom of playing ancient music on modern instruments continued for many years, and not only in Italy. And in fact, the only truly "ancient" instrument involved in the performance of some of Maderna's transcriptions of the *Odhecaton* at La Fenice during the 1967 Biennale was the harpsichord [*Centro Studi Maderna*, Section D 12. 9]. It should also be kept in mind that Maderna's encounter with the *Odhecaton* was fortuitous, as was his transcription of Vivaldi in the late 1940s. In the following two decades, up to his *Music of Gaity* (1969), he specifically chose pieces that he wished to introduce to the modern audience, transcribing and performing them in different ways. Maderna put much effort into these transcriptions and as such they can be considered a not insignificant part of his output. But due to limits of space we will focus mainly on those that received the greatest coverage in the press of the time.

In 1952, much attention was attracted by his transcription of Orazio Vecchi's *Amfiparnaso*, which kept the director Harro Dicks and the vocal and instrumental soloists of the Landestheater in Darmstadt busy for several months and was presented to the public eleven times on different occasions, a sure sign

---

[31] From a radio interview with Bruno Maderna made by George Stone and Alan Stout in Chicago on January 23, 1970 [*Documenti* 1985, 92-93].

[32] See M. Messinis, "Malipiero e Maderna vent'anni dopo (1973 – 1993)," in Cattelan (2000), cited in note 13, 6.

of the positive reception it received. The piece had already been transcribed various times: in one of his letters Maderna mentions the performance that took place in 1938 at the Maggio Musicale Fiorentino, although he did not make use of this transcription, nor did he base his work on the edition by Carlo Perinello (Milano: Bocca 1936), where on p. IX of the introduction the editor comments "any addition of instruments would be an injustice that would destroy the vocal atmosphere of the piece." Maderna had a different scheme in mind, as he wrote in detail to Steinecke: instead of the voices used in what was originally a sort of madrigal, he intended to involve vocal and instrumental soloists, with very particular timbres and positioned as if they were on a theater stage. The subtitle of the piece – *Comedia Harmonica* – had, in fact, supported his idea of transforming Vecchi's music into a theater piece that would be appreciated by a modern audience. He had such a clear picture of how the soloists would be arranged that he even drew a plan in pen to explain it better, and proposed it should be performed alongside two other theatrical works: Luigi Dallapiccola's *Job. Sacra rappresentazione* and Goffredo Petrassi's *Coro di morti. Madrigale drammatico*. "Since I am planning a particular re-elaboration of *Amfiparnaso*, the score must be particular too [and should include] 2 harps, 3 transverse flutes and 3 recorders, a lute and a small string orchestra of violas, cellos and double basses. And on the stage 2 oboes, 1 cor anglais, 2 bassoons, 3 trumpets, 4 horns and 3 trombones" [*Carteggio* 2001, 55-65], as well as drums and timpani for the Prologue presented by an actor, who then invites the audience to enjoy the show "with their ears more than their eyes."[33] The three works were performed during the Italian Evening of the Darmstadt courses on July 15, 1952, but his transcription of *Amfiparnaso* went on to be staged many times at the town's theater. Maderna's idea was clearly not to present the work as Vecchi had written it in his own time, but to "revive" it with the due modifications, and even add some new texts, with a modern audience in mind.

A few years later, Maderna returned to ancient music, this time also in the guise of a fortunate researcher who brought to light two oratorios by Giacomo Carissimi, *Diluvium universale* and *Historia divitis*, which were rediscovered respectively in Hamburg and in the Bibliothèque Nationale in Paris, in a score for voices and organ (*Historia* also had a part for two violins). For the Christmas Concert at the Angelicum in Milan, the two works were "realized with great care [...] and scholarly adherence to the instrumental usage of the time." This brief extract comes from a long article in the Milanese newspaper *L'Italia*; the same tone is used in Franco Abbiati's article in the *Corriere della Sera* [*Centro*

---

[33] C. Vincis, "'Avec l'autorisation du Maître'. Bruno Maderna et la musique ancienne: entre 'reconstruction' et 'recréation'," in *Basalte* 2 (2009), 499.

Studi Maderna, Section D12.1]. Unfortunately the two scores appear to have been lost, but on the surviving title-page we find a list of the vocal soloists, fourteen instruments plus a small string section. Maderna's transcription was undoubtedly recognized as appropriate as well as rigorous, and the same opinion was expressed by the critics who attended the Holland Festival some years later, when *Historia divitis* was performed at the theater in Scheveningen on July 1, 1964. One could in fact say that Maderna's success as a transcriber of ancient music was consolidated precisely in the Dutch theaters, in a country where rigorous studies of performance *praxis* were particularly flourishing. And it was during his customary mixed programs of classical, contemporary and ancient music with the orchestras of Amsterdam, Utrecht and The Hague that Maderna presented his reworkings of Josquin Desprez's *Magnificat quarti toni* (which he had prepared in 1966 during his period of treatment in Köningstein) and Giovanni Gabrieli's *In Ecclesiis*, dating from the same year. According to Claudia Vincis, the reason for Maderna's highly imaginative re-elaboration of these ancient texts was that "these 'arrangements' were born from the need to compensate for a primary function of this music, the liturgical function" for which they were originally conceived.[34] Although this is an interesting hypothesis, it cannot always be applied: for example, his transcription of Gabrieli's *Sonata pian e forte*, which was performed by the Utrecht Orchestra in January 1968, belongs to the instrumental pieces for two groups of four "voices" that Gabrieli mostly wrote for St. Mark's Basilica, but without any strictly liturgical function. In this case his adaptation for modern instruments (groups of brass vs. woodwind) reproduces the ancient sonorities quite faithfully, considering that the practice of constructing copies of the original instruments for this purpose was not yet widespread in the 1960s.

Even freer of any liturgical function were, of course, his transcriptions of secular music, for instance the "new realization and elaboration" of Monteverdi's *Orfeo* presented with great panache from June 17 to 25, 1967 at the Theater Carré in Amsterdam to celebrate the fourth centenary of the composer's birth. Maderna outlines his intentions and his procedures in his own introduction to the score dated "Darmstadt April 23, 1967." Here we limit ourselves to quoting just some of the most salient points:

> There are many editions of Orfeo, old and new, philological and practical. […] Some are philologically splendid but timid and bare, […] others, unashamedly ignoring the history of culture, abandon themselves to gushes of rhetoric and sentiment […]. Certainly, the task of reviving Orfeo in its integral beauty is today hard. […] I embarked on realizing

---

[34] Ibid., 506.

this supreme score with the intention of respecting [...] the emotions and the 'affects' that made Orfeo one of the greatest successes of an époque [...]. The opening 'Toccata' and the final 'Moresca' have been extended [but] the orthodox version will be published in the appendix.

The introduction to the score immediately published by Suvini Zerboni in 1967 also reproduces the page preceding the 1609 print on which Maderna worked. A comparison between Monteverdi's and Maderna's list of characters and instruments reveals that the former are the same, while number of instruments is just a little greater in Maderna's version. The recording of the *Suite Orfeo* performed in Utrecht on May 2, 1969 shows how Maderna's taste for contrasting the sonorities of groups of woodwind, brass and strings still work perfectly well in the moments when Monteverdi himself had foreseen them: for example in the opening Toccata, or in the instrumental accompaniments to the shepherds' choruses. The task of sustaining the recitatives or the grand "ariosi," which in Monteverdi's score were accompanied only by the basso continuo, would have required a thorough knowledge of seventeenth century early Baroque treatises, something that today is commonplace in all conservatories, but in the sixties was not yet universally established. In Maderna the basso continuo is replaced by highly inventive orchestral sonorities. As far as the vocal style is concerned, it should be remembered that at the time there were no singers specialized in this particular repertoire.

Following the success in Amsterdam, the same production was repeated two years later in Brussels during the Europalia Festival, an event that for a whole month (September 1969) featured a wide cross-section of Italian art, including music, theater, painting, songs and cinema. Once again *Orfeo* was performed on six consecutive evenings "before a packed and enthusiastic audience, who never tired of applauding the singers and musicians who had revealed the wonder of this music from five centuries ago." This description was given in an article by Ferdinando Riccardi in the bulletin of *Agence Europe*, who gives a lively account of the most outstanding moments of the Italian exhibitions. But right from the subtitle we also infer that "not all went well. Polemics and discussions among the 'traditionalists'." But the criticisms were not aimed at Maderna's transcription, but rather at another item that had nothing to do with *Orfeo*: "the naivety (or presumption) of the Piccolo Teatro Torinese that came in great pomp to present a regional show, mistaking the capital of Europe for a suburb of Turin." The performances of Maderna's Monteverdi unfailingly met with great acclaim, as they offered the kind of sound that matched the expectations and historical-stylistic knowledge of the audiences, even though some years later more rigorous musical tastes would gradually impose themselves, based on the study of historical documents that laid down the foundation of the so-called "performance practice." On the other hand, Maderna declared in interviews that he had not aimed at historical fidelity, but had rather tried to imagine which instruments and what type of sounds Monteverdi would have chosen if he had had access to an orchestra of our time [*Centro Studi Maderna*, Section D 12.7].

Besides Monteverdi's opera we could also mention his transcription of Domenico Belli's *Orfeo*, which was combined with *Hyperion* at the Feste Musicali in Bologna in the summer of 1968 (more details of this event will be given in the next chapter). Nor were these the only versions of the legend that Maderna encountered during his career as a transcriber and conductor: in 1970 he went as far as proposing a whole season based on the theme:

Bertoni – *Orfeo* (Giazotto) – Belli – *Orfeo* (Maderna) – Monteverdi – *Orfeo* (Maderna) – [...] *Orphée aux Enfers* Offenbach [...] *Malheurs d'Orphée* de Milhaud, l'*Orphée* de Strawinski – e *La favola d'Orfeo* di Malipiero![35]

Quite a different matter is the purely instrumental work *Music of Gaity*, a transcription of items from the *Fitzwilliam Virginal Book* (c. 1560-1610). The work dates from shortly after those previously described (1969), but is not a theatrical piece and there is no attempt to recapture the expressive contents through a stage setting; it is simply a virtuoso display of timbre. The musical grammar (that sounded intriguing to the listeners of the time) is again proto-Baroque, but in this case the contraposition between different groups (woodwinds vs. strings) was joined by other subtle features: melodies on the upper registers of the violins and oboes, at times unaccompanied, duets between string instruments, broad cantabile passages for soloists and moments of fugato counterpoint with constantly shifting timbres. In other words, the ancient grammar was colored by a play of refined and engaging modern sonorities. And the audience appears to have appreciated this bright and delicate writing since the articles that describe the reception of the work all agree on the positive and sometimes even enthusiastic response. Nevertheless, the fact that there appears to be no sign of any critical reaction on the part of the purists does not necessarily mean that Maderna's approach was accepted by all, but simply that the scholars of performing praxis who, especially in the Netherlands, had begun to broach the question of "authenticity" in ancient music, had not yet resolved certain important issues and were not yet forceful enough to level their

---

[35] C. Vincis, "Avec l'autorisation," cited in note 33, 507. Another title could be added to this amusing series, namely Pergolesi's cantata *Orfeo*, which Maderna himself transcribed. The date of his transcription is unknown, but he deposited it with the SIAE, and from there it was published by Suvini Zerboni.

criticisms against those that did not share the conclusions they had reached. In a collection of his essays published towards the end of the twentieth century, Richard Taruskin offers a wide-ranging view of the phenomenon of revisiting ancient music, observing that more than reviving the ancient performing traditions, it was simply the most modern way of presenting this repertoire to the public. He underlines a fundamental problem: there is no way of knowing how ancient music sounded. Even if the use of period instruments can give us an idea of the color of the sound, the overall effect of the music remains hidden because, irrespective of the rules, the result was strictly linked to the interpretation of the agogics and dynamics, as well as to the variations – always possible – proposed by the performer.[36]

But over and above these fascinating and at times problematic transcriptions, the late sixties were notable above all for the three large pieces for orchestra with which he closed the decade: *Quadrivium*, *Concerto per violino* and *Grande Aulodia*. With these three works Maderna not only concluded the long and wholly personal creative path that had evolved following his years of immersion in the novelties of Darmstadt, but also concluded his phase of composition in Europe. The pieces are quite long (each lasting around thirty minutes) and are quite different from one another in terms of their sonority, while sharing certain stylistic features.

Quadrivium, as Maderna states in the program notes for its first performance, which he conducted in Royan in April 1969 [*Centro Studi Maderna*, Section D 9], owes its title not only to the medieval science that combined arithmetic, geometry, music and astronomy, but above all to his fascination with the number four, which provides the basis for the organization of the sonorities of the work: four groups of percussion and four physically separate orchestras.[37] The work itself could also be divided into four parts. There is a first broad episode in which the vast set of percussion is introduced either in minimum (individual instruments) or maximum form (raucous groups), gradually joined by the various orchestras, especially the winds, sometimes violently, sometimes more gently. This is followed by a second, more meditative part, in a very slow tempo, dominated by the strings. In the third part the orchestras and the percussion groups little by little unite in a long, highly charged crescendo, until reaching a stormy climax. In the final part a reduced number of instruments gradually extinguish the previous sounds. Laura Cosso and Ernesto Napolitano [*Basalte*

---

[36] See R. Taruskin, *Text and Act. Essays on Music and Performance* (New York: Oxford University Press, 1995), 164 ff.

[37] Our description is not based on its first performance by the Orchestre National de l'ORTF, of which unfortunately no documentary recording exists, but on the one that took place in June of the same year, with the orchestra of the RAI in Rome, again conducted by the composer.

2, 2009, 34-39] similarly suggest a four-part division which is quite close to our own, and that concludes as follows: the extreme instrumental registers (bass clarinets and very high violins) prepare the final phase, an "auratic [moment] that offers a synthesis of Maderna's instrumental art." Alessandro Solbiati too speaks of two formal zones each divided into two parts.[38] Instead, ignoring the presumed sacrality of the number four, Maurizio Romito proposes a division into seven parts, where our suggested first part is divided into three episodes, and our third part into two.[39] Another division, proposed by Frédéric Durieux [*Basalte* 2, 2009, 143-176] consists of four parts, but divided in a different way to ours. The only constant feature shared by all the various proposals is the significance of the central episode, meditative and slow, with respect to the episodes that surround it. These differences clearly highlight how the idea of the division of a piece (when not objectively established in the score with incontrovertible evidence) always risks being somewhat forced by the person offering an interpretation or analysis, and might often reflect the intentions of the analyst more than those of the composer, especially when dealing with an even more tenuous grammar such as that of New Music.

Over and above these various hypothetical divisions, we can affirm that much of *Quadrivium* is conceived in aleatory form, as the performing instructions leave considerable space to the initiative of the conductor and players. All this reinforces the idea that in this work, and in the other two of his last compositions in Europe, Maderna's greatest concern as a composer (and especially as a performer) was to create music based mainly on successions of different sonorities, that is to say, on evocative combinations of timbres, as well as on shifts in intensity and speed. And it is these successions that provide the basis for the form of the pieces. In his above mentioned article, Durieux distinguishes two different meanings of the word "form." In the classical tradition, and also beyond, the idea of form was linked above all to the recurrence of fragments, or of whole episodes, that reappeared either in identical form or else modified (developed) in some way. This approach played with the memory of the listener, the recognition of formal recurrences and their modifications. The author refers to this practice as "memorial structure." But the word "form" also has another meaning, and this is the one we find in *Quadrivium*. Each part of the work "evolves towards a tension, a relaxation or a break, which allows the music to pass from one section to another." In this case Durieux uses the term "evolutive structure," a definition we believe highly

---

[38] A. Solbiati, "*Biogramma*. Projet et modalité de réalisation d'une Weltanschauung," in *Basalte* 2 (2009), 126.

[39] See *Dialogo con Maderna. 18 concerti. Milano 30 settembre - 20 dicembre 1989* (Milano: RAI Lombardia, 1989), 128-132.

appropriate to describe Maderna's last European works.

Back in 1980, Armando Gentilucci wrote some words about Maderna's last orchestral works (*Quadrivium, Aura, Biogramma*) that are still interesting today, commenting that the complex sonic structure of these pieces reveals "a pleasure in sound and an invention free from any puristic taboo [...]. The profound authenticity of Maderna's work lies in its total lack of any leanings towards or concessions to fashion." In other words he sees Maderna as a model of the composer who is "multifarious" and "beyond the avant-garde," as evoked by the title of his book.[40]

The *Concerto per violino*, which he conducted at the Biennale di Venezia on September 12, 1969, confirms a practice that had become almost a tradition in Maderna's concertos: adapting the structure of the work to the abilities of the soloist who would perform it. Maderna had already done so with the astonishing virtuosity and theatrical qualities of Gazzelloni in mind, as well as the exquisite sonorities of Faber. Now, in this concerto, he exploits the unprecedented sonic capacities of Theo Olof's violin. Other aspects similarly reflect tendencies already encountered in other works: the score, for example, is nearly always accompanied by performing indications that leave the conductor wide choice in terms of the "expression." And the concept of expression also transpires in Maderna's own words when he happens to describe his music. For example, in July 1964, in a letter to Virginio Puecher accompanying the tape for *Dimensioni IV*, he speaks of "long mysterious chords," of "brilliant, mechanical" rhythmic developments, of the "sad, persuasive, almost amorous" nature of the flute melody, and the "cold, almost grotesque, maybe a little comical structures."[41] In other words, when searching for the "expressive" character of his music we can also turn to Maderna's own thoughts and the words he uses to describe it. When commenting on this concerto, Laurent Feneyrou refers to the words of the conductor Péter Eötvös: this music is to be "sung like a Lied," to be conducted "with lyricism," while certain polyphonies, within the groups of timbres, should be treated "like the humming of bees." He goes on to say that the relationship between the soloist and the orchestra is different from usual: the strings tend not to dialogue with the solo part but rather emanate from it, as if the border between the individual and the world had become indistinct. On other occasions, though, the entropic disorder of the orchestra, deriving from serial matrices, brutally interrupts the flow of the soloist with hostile gestures. Feneyrou also points out that some parts of the concerto are taken

---

[40] A. Gentilucci, *Oltre l'avanguardia. Un invito al molteplice* (Fiesole: Discanto, 1980), 71.
[41] The letter is reproduced in *Documenti* 1985, 253.

from previous works (*Amanda, Stele per Diotima, Entropia III*).[42]

As far as the virtuoso writing for the violin is concerned, it is interesting to consider the words of the two protagonists, the performer and the composer [*Documenti* 1985, 103-104]. Olof comments:

> there are many things in this concerto that I had never seen or heard before. The fascinating aspect of this work is that everything that Maderna writes or prescribes is absolutely "possible"; whoever is familiar the techniques of today's music will find plenty to do here.

And Maderna adds:

> with regards the solo violin part, I don't believe it to be so "possible" [...]. The great violinists, the virtuosos, would not have stooped to perform a piece made up for the most part of pitiful noises, almost imperceptible sounds etc. while instead Olof, who is first a musician and then a virtuoso, has understood the sense of the whole, and there is no doubt that only a true musician can understand this concerto.

In September 1969, while he was in Venice to conduct, among other things, his *Concerto per violino* at La Fenice, Maderna received some news that, while not "life-changing," must certainly have come as a pleasant surprise. The newly formed Centro Internazionale Ricerche e Strutture Ambientali "Pio Manzù" in Verrocchio (Rimini), in its very first year of activity, had decided to assign him a special award, and invited him to attend the ceremony. Maderna, who was totally caught up in his commitments as a composer and conductor, thanked them for their invitation but apologized that he would be unable to attend the ceremony due to his engagement "at the Teatro La Monnaie Theater in Brussels to conduct a series of performances of my new version of Claudio Monteverdi's *Orfeo*." He suggested, instead, that they might invite his wife Christine to receive the award on his behalf. And so it was that on September 28, 1970, Christine received the Pio Manzù Award in Bruno's name for his "outstanding contribution to musical culture."[43] Pio Manzù was neither a musician nor a music historian, so why was it that the Center named after him, located in one of the most beautiful areas of the Rimini hillside (even though Manzù was not from Romagna) had decided to offer Maderna this award? The story may seem a little strange, but in reality it

---

[42] L. Feneyrou, "*Solo / tutti*. Introduction à cinq concertos de Bruno Maderna," in *Basalte* 2 (2009), 221-224.

[43] Copies of the letters from the Centro Pio Manzù to Maderna and to Christine can be found in the *Centro Studi Maderna*, Section L 7. The letters are signed by Felice Battaglia, jurist, philosopher and chancellor of the University of Bologna, and by the art historian Giulio Carlo Argan.

highlights the particularly lively attitude towards modernity prevalent in Italian culture at the time. Pio Manzù was born in Milan in 1939, and after graduating at high school he went to Germany to complete his studies at the Hochschule für Gestaltung in Ulm, under the guidance of the Argentinian philosopher and designer Tomás Maldonado, soon becoming his assistant. After a few years, in 1963, his automobile designs earned him his first recognition in the international competition Ars Viva, in the section Industrial Design. His rapid and brilliant career came to a sudden halt in 1969, when he was killed in a car accident just outside of Turin, where he was on his way to present the designs of his revolutionary Fiat 127. The Centro Pio Manzù, founded in the same year as his death, was based on a philosophy of modernity that endorsed a constant quest for a deep and close relationship between humans and the environment, between scientific and technological innovation. This brief portrait of Pio Manzù may help to justify the choice to offer the award to Maderna, stressing the affinity between the two artists who, though operating in two different worlds, had followed similar paths and shared a common notion of modernity.

In gratitude for the award, Maderna dedicated his *Tempo libero* to the center, a piece that was then used as ambient music for the first International Biennial of Global Design Methodology (Rimini-Repubblica di San Marino, September 20 to 30, 1970). This was probably the first version of the piece, which was later modified and assumed different durations and forms. The basic material comes from the *Studio di Fonologia* in Milan (at a certain point we hear the voice of Marino Zuccheri), but this is not necessarily the place where it was composed, as Maderna insinuated when explaining his compositional philosophy to Christof Bitter during an interview broadcast on Radio Saarbrücken, in May 1973, before the transmission of the piece:

> I thought that the behavior of a man who uses his free time should, at least in principle, be different from that of his normal life. [...] I imagined what would happen if someone took pleasure in listening to the noises, the distant voices, the wind, the memories of music heard the evening before or that he would like to hear, and then decided to have fun putting all these experiences together and turn them into a collage [...] but not in the sense of surrealism. It is more like the experience of musical composition known as open form, comparable in practice to Calder's *mobiles* [...]. The piece is on four tracks and it is possible to choose different proportions, so – in different combinations – it could even last many millions of years. [...]. My intention was to give listeners the chance to begin when they want and to stop when they tire of listening. [In the exhibition hall where the work was first heard there were] curious chairs, strange and fanciful pieces of furniture by fashionable designers, conceived for free time,

where one could sit and daydream beyond the dimension of normal life. Inside this vast space the music, transmitted through large loudspeakers, blended with the chatting of people. They could notice the music or else not be aware of it [...].[44]

In other words, Maderna tells us that this work should not be listened to in the concentrated and attentive way we usually adopt for works of art, because it has a different aim, namely to provide a background for the observation of artistic objects that have practical functions, like seats, furniture, decorations, automobiles. In reality the music too could be said to have a practical function, that of supplying an acoustic background. Obviously he is not implying that all music should have this sort of function, but he is simply saying that music can serve various purposes: something he has suggested many times in the various declarations we have previously reported.

The circumstances surrounding the composition of *Serenata per un satellite* were also quite exceptional. In this case the inspiration came from nothing other than the launching into orbit of a satellite that took place on the night of October 1, 1969 in Darmstadt, where a European Space Center was located. And this work too has personal associations. The composition is dedicated to the director of the Center, Umberto Montalenti, who was a close friend of Maderna's. He also wished to celebrate the occasion with a concert that involved some of his most esteemed performer friends, an event that was covered by both the German and Italian press. Maurizio Romito, after listening to the recording of this first performance, commented:

> On that occasion Sweekhorst, Faber and Gawriloff inserted – just like in the 'jam sessions' of jazz – three sections not specified in the score and taken from other works by Maderna (*Musica su due dimensioni, Concerto per oboe n. 2, Widmung*). Evidence of the flexibility with which the performers, who were very familiar with Maderna's music, interpreted the indications provided by the composer, when the score and the felicitous inspiration of the theme-based evening suggested it. There is one more curiosity about the writing of this very successful piece: the first performance, in fact, used a version that is slightly different from the one we know today, titled *Serenata per un missile* for flute, oboe, clarinet, marimba, harp and violin. When the piece was due to be published, Maderna 'redesigned' the score, extending or changing the position of portions of music, sometimes altering the pitches and dynamic markings, also giving the work greater impact from a graphic point of view.[45]

---

[44] The complete interview can be found in *Documenti* 1985, 115-118.

[45] See *Dialogo*, cited in note 39, 208.

This was the first of a long series of versions in which the highly successful work was, and continues to be, performed. In reality, its success is in some ways paradoxical: the score (which was then printed by Ricordi) is written on a small page containing a fanciful series of musical fragments whose graphics appear to have clear aesthetic intentions. This is a unique case in Maderna's output, since it is the only score in which the graphics assume some sort of artistic significance. During the Darmstadt courses in 1959, Stockhausen had held as many as five lectures on the theme *Musik und Graphik*, and Bussotti had also turned one of his own drawings made ten years before into a score. But the participants of the course, perhaps including Maderna, had remained largely indifferent to such an extreme approach. And so it seems quite justifiable to suggest that *Serenata* was intended as a playful homage to his friend Montalenti. What is more, in line with this probable self-irony, Maderna also added very precise performing indications (to be taken in a semi-serious way), from which we gather that anyone could use the notes he had written in any way they wished. And this too is a unique case, because, as we have pointed out on various occasions, his aleatory instructions were normally aimed at obtaining a sonic result that was consistent with the stylistic intentions of his music. The invitation to the game was evidently too great to resist: several, also prominent, composers have written pieces in their own well recognizable style using the notes provided by Maderna in the most fanciful ways.

The last work of the decade was *Grande Aulodia*, presumably composed in the very last months of 1969 and, as the score tells us, was finished in Darmstadt in the first days of 1970, not long before he left for Chicago. Once again it was written with specific performers in mind, in this case Severino Gazzelloni and Lothar Faber, to whom the work is dedicated and who gave its first performance in February at the Auditorium della RAI in Rome. This work too could be said to be free of the strict aesthetic restraints of the Darmstadt tradition and consists of a series of temporally successive episodes whose formal rhetoric is based mainly on expression. This aspect is easily perceived when listening to the performances that took place in 1970, but was destined to become the object of heated – and even bitter – debate at the Royan Festival in 1971, between those that appreciated Maderna's new ventures and the supporters of the more inflexible applications of serial techniques.[46] To describe the form we could turn once more to Durieux's definition "evolutive," that is to say it pays attention to the logic of listening as well as (or perhaps more than) to that of constructive serialism. Put briefly, one could speak of two wide arches of tension concluded by two peaks, and followed by a long final appeasement in which the two soloists

---

[46] See M. Garda, "Rilevamenti sulla ricezione della musica maderniana," in *Studi* 1989, 92.

make use of the deep, soft and persuasive tones of a cor anglais and an alto flute. However, given that the work is quite long, these three principle moments obviously contain numerous sub-parts in which the play of contrasts between the instrumental soloists and the orchestra is given wide scope. Without going into too much detail, we will limit ourselves to pointing out some of the most notable features of the work. Starting the instrumental parts, Maderna's writing shows traces of the friendly terms existing between the two artists. The piece starts with two long *A*s alternated between the instruments, as if the oboist were "passing" the opening note to his friend the flutist, who accepts it and imitates it. But immediately afterwards the oboe overlaps the flute with a dissonant *B* flat. The other responds by moving to a *B* natural, then there is a *C* on the *B*... all in a simple, playful manner. Another similar exchange, though broader and more complex, occurs in the first measures of the long final part (m. 184 ff.). After vying and competing with one another, the two soloists, for some time, play the same notes, and then shift to neighboring notes, creating dissonances similar to those of the opening. This "camaraderie" between the two players continues in different ways throughout the whole of the final episode. Apart from these moments when the two soloists take part in this sort of amicable game, in the broader arches of tension that characterize the first part of the work they tend to contrast one another, to abandon themselves to unpredictable whims, using irregular and broken phrasings, contradictory rhythms, opposing dynamics, and switching to instruments with a more aggressive sound like the musette, indicated by the composer to be played with a "portavoce duro" ("hard mouthpiece"). As far as the orchestra is concerned, the instruments are often treated in an aleatory fashion, in other words the focus is more on the final listening outcome. This, as we have seen, is a characteristic typical of Maderna's approach to aleatory writing. And while it is true that the composer decides on this aspect at the moment of writing the score, and when the serial calculations inevitably make their presence felt, their transformation into concrete sonorities is deferred to a later moment, that is when the sound is rendered perceptible and its expression can be interpreted (and here Maderna is undoubtedly also thinking of his role as a conductor). Maderna had acquired the habit of writing these parts in frames or panels, leaving any decisions about their order of performance and their duration to the conductor; in the case of the percussion instruments, graphic symbols are provided suggesting the way they should be played. Finally, we should add that in every type of writing, whether aleatory or precisely written out, the blend of instruments is incredibly complex, although their expressive intent is always clear, testifying to Maderna's remarkable ability to invent ever new combinations of sound. In the finale, the instruments are reduced to three small string orchestras, spatially differentiated. Maderna writes on the score that the two soloists must play their parts without any strict tempo prescriptions, "as in an interior ecstasy" and stipulates that the orchestra should simply be "a mysterious halo." Maderna did not use this finale at the first performance in Rome: he replaced it with an equally effective dialogue between the soloists, against an evocative orchestral backdrop.[47]

---

[47] See Francesca Magnani's descriptive card in *Documenti* 1985, 292.

CHAPTER VII
THE HYPERION CYCLE

Between 1963 and 1970 much of Maderna's activity as a composer and conductor was devoted to a cycle of works inspired by the figure of Hyperion, the young Greek protagonist of an epistolary novel that Friedrich Hölderlin wrote in various versions between 1792 and 1799. In the novel the young Hyperion corresponds with Bellarmin, a German friend he had met on a previous trip to Germany and with whom he shares his ideals, tribulations and disappointments. Hyperion had escaped death during the Greek proto-revolution against Ottoman rule in 1770, but the experience had left him disgusted by the inhuman behavior of the Greek rebels: the moral decline was not just that of the Turks but appeared to involve the whole of contemporary humanity. The only things saved from this desperate vision are the contemplation of nature, always intact in its beauty, his sublime love for Diotima, who waits for him in their native town (but dies before his return) and, lastly, his nostalgia for classical Greece, where he believes an ideal and almost divine balance had been achieved between the ethical values of the individual and those of the collectivity. Both he and Diotima hoped he would become an educator of his people, but the naivety and incomprehension of his contemporaries prevented him from realizing his plans. The story may perhaps reflect Hölderlin's own experiences as a young rebel: in order to survive he had worked as a tutor in conservative-minded households, and this led to his disillusionment with the revolutionary ideals he had once believed in, but also to a fierce aversion towards the German populace that surrounded him.

Various traces of the "Greek dream" can also be found in the works of Maderna. Apart from his frequent recourse to the Greek lyrics translated by Quasimodo, and his elaboration of the *Seikilos epitaph* that forms the basis for his *Composizione n. 2*, there was also an element of ancient Greece in his passionate attempts to find the key to a possible new melodic model: the term he used for many of his solos for flute and oboe, always present in the various versions of *Hyperion*, is aulodia, clearly referring to the Greek aulos – a distinctly Hölderlinian reference to an unattainable beauty, to an ideal evasion from a difficult, or even despicable world.[1] Indeed, throughout the Sixties, Maderna's consciousness was troubled by a constant stream of rebellion and socio-political

---
[1] See also F. Magnani, "L'Hyperion di Maderna: quale poeta per quale canto," in *Studi* 1989, 177-194.

tension that would remain deep-rooted and was also reflected in his creative output. Maybe only circumstances of this sort could explain his astonishing passion for the figure of Hyperion and for his musical version that, in its various forms, spanned at least seven years. It should also be added that in terms of artistic language, both Hölderlin and Maderna contributed to a radical renewal; however, contrary to the case of Hölderlin, this adventure did not leave Maderna isolated from the rest of the world, but instead gave him the sensation that he was at the center of a process of change in which other composers were wholeheartedly participating.[2]

It is also significant that all three of the major scores of the cycle (*Dimensioni III*, *Aria* and *Stele per Diotima*) are fundamentally derived from transformations of the same basic material. The presence of this internal unity and the calculations used in the composition of the various episodes have been carefully studied by Borio and Rizzardi (and later by Verzina) through an examination of the scores, and more especially of the countless sketches left by Maderna.[3] The materials used for *Hyperion* derive from twenty-one serial forms of twelve notes (forms applied differently in terms of their numerical permutation) that all have in common the initial E flat, and from a series of twelve durations, these too permutated, that derive from another reading of the same series. From a graphic point of view, Maderna organized these series in a star-like form with E flat at the center and twenty-one "rays" around it. One can infer from this arrangement of the basic material that Maderna was no longer concerned with just a numerical series, but was interested in a broader, more flexible structure that could be adapted to sequences of parameters that were not automatically produced, but that were conceived, instead, on the basis of the overall sonic result they could generate.

It would therefore seem reasonable to suggest that the numerous parts that made up the whole cycle were, in a sense, variants of the same underlying structure. Moreover, Borio and Rizzardi observe that the "concretization" of the numerical scheme (the transformation of the numbers into notes) depends on a quantity of very flexible local rules. In the last part of their article they provide examples of constructive models that are quite free and in some cases even close to structures belonging to previous traditions (we too have mentioned aulodies).

---

[2] Verzina (*Verzina* 2003, 167) rightly reminds us that not all the texts set in the cycle came from Hölderlin. Between 1968 and 1970 Maderna also exploited more modern sources (e.g. Claus, Auden, Lorca) which partly modified the sense of his relationship with the figure of Hyperion.

[3] G. Borio, V. Rizzardi, "Die musikalische Einheit von Bruno Madernas *Hyperion*," in *Zwölf Komponisten des 20. Jahrhunderts*, ed. F. Meyer (Winterthur: Amadeus, 1993), 117-148. See also *Verzina* 2003, 138-156.

Basically, then, the "freedom" which was often a source of discussion among the protagonists of the Darmstadt avant-garde, is applied here in ways that, with respect to the initial numerical order, appear arbitrary, although they are not at all arbitrary if we consider an implicit order of a purely musical nature. Giordano Ferrari, in turn, points out, besides the numerical materials studied by Borio and Rizzardi, other aspects of the mysterious internal unity discernible in the "dimensions" relating to the figure of Hyperion: at times he is presented in instrumental form (Gazzelloni's flute, but also the oboe and the violin), at others in the form of words, spoken or sung, or transformed into gestures by the actors, or else in the form of the relation between the single and collective characters (a chorus, an orchestra), and also between the various poetic voices, given that at a certain point García Lorca and Auden join the sources referred to by Maderna. Hölderlin's message is thus expanded "onto different cognitive levels [...] allowing the listener to enter the work, in other words into the spirit of Hyperion, alias Maderna."[4]

Nevertheless, the preparation of the many works that make up the cycle (at least seventeen, including the instrumental works and those for theater) did not prevent Maderna from continuing to take part in the musical life of Darmstadt. As we mentioned in the previous chapter, his contribution to the summer courses, after the death of Steinecke, had become less significant and to some extent even monothematic in the sense that it was practically limited to the conducting of the chamber group, which he also shared with Pierre Boulez. His lesser involvement had been anticipated by the decision taken by his friend Luigi Nono to abandon the courses. Neither of them were able to hide their disillusionment with the loss of the purposeful vitality that had characterized the early years of Steinecke's direction, an aspect that had aroused not only the dissent, but also the wrath of Nono, which he expressed in a letter to Thomas (December 2, 1963) full of exclamation marks [*Trudu* 1992, 175]. By now it had become difficult to hide from the world the fact that the sun was setting on the "heroic" season of the *Kranichsteiner Musikinstitut*. At the end of his letter Nono justly pointed out: "If a new era was to be had, it should have been invented": it was not enough to change the name, on the contrary, this has the opposite effect. Maderna obviously shared his friend's disillusionment, but, from 1964, tried to take advantage of the fame of the courses to allow the various versions of his *Hyperion* to be known at an international level. At this point, though, it could be said that the primary role that Darmstadt had once played in the composer's life was beginning to give way to an ever-dwindling interest.

---

[4] G. Ferrari, "*Hyperion*, les chemins du poète," in *Basalte* 1, 2007, 113.

To introduce the reader to the numerous works that make up what we have called the "Hyperion cycle" it seems helpful to start by outlining its seven-year path, dividing it into three main phases. The first concludes in 1964 with the stage performance of the work at the Biennale di Venezia, the second reaches its peak in '68 with the other two stage performances in Brussels and Bologna, while the third and last phase coincides with the presentation in Berlin in '69 of a completely new version titled *Suite aus der Oper Hyperion*. During the course of these three phases Maderna composed and modified the three major scores previously mentioned (*Dimensioni III*, *Aria* and *Stele per Diotima*), while at the same time reacting to cultural and political events that in some way affected his imagination and the musical materials he was working on. Suffice it to think of the significance of the '68 movement in terms of the poetics and music with which, inspired by the ideals of Hölderlin, the composer attempted to present his view of the world. This is the main reason why we decided to devote an entire chapter to Hyperion.

To complete this preliminary overview more details need to be given about the seventeen works that make up the cycle. Three instrumental compositions preceded the first version for stage (Venice 1964). Then, between 1964 and 1967, nine distinct instrumental versions were performed: five titled *Dimensioni*, three *Hyperion* and one *Stele*. In 1968, as previously mentioned, two new versions for theater were presented, and finally, in 1969, the *Suite* was performed in Berlin and then in Vienna. In the following pages we will attempt to describe the most important features of this complex affair. To help the reader we have provided a list of all the different versions, divided into the three above-mentioned phases (see Table 2).[5]

Of the three major scores in the cycle, *Dimensioni III* is not only the one that re-emerges most frequently, but in several cases it is so characterizing as to give its name to a self-standing version.

Joachim Noller wondered what reasons Maderna had for using the term "dimensioni" so widely.[6] In the 1950s the noun was used to indicate the combination of electronic and live sounds (in *Musica su due dimensioni* or in *Dimensioni II*, where Berberian's voice was processed electronically), but in *Dimensioni III*, where there are no electronics, why should he have used this term? Noller suggests that perhaps in the Sixties the meaning of the word had changed and had broadened its semantic area to include "contrast" or "contraposition." But from among all the possible "musical dimensions" existing, Maderna, when

---

[5] For further information and details of the sources, see Table 1 in *Pour Bruno* 2015, 67-69.
[6] J. Noller, "*Musica su due dimensioni*, e l'unidimensionalità della musica nuova," *I Quaderni della Civica Scuola di Musica*, nos. 21-22 (1992), 65-69.

introducing a concert at Darmstadt in 1959, seems to prefer one in particular: after illustrating the by now traditional contrast between live and electronic sounds, he adds that "the concatenations of musical ideas reduced to numbers, to graphic symbols and technical indications are by no means the same thing as the resulting sound." And speaking of music with a score, he adds: "as a composer I often come face to face with myself as a performer [...]. A synthesis of both existing roles, which I call 'dimensions', seems particularly fruitful" [*Documenti* 1985, 85].

Dimensioni III is divided into three parts, referred to in Table 2 as *Dimensioni III*/1, *III*/2 and *III*/3. Part III/2 contains what Maderna called "cadenza per flauto," that is, a long piece for solo flute that became a *pièce de résistance* for Severino Gazzelloni, while in the manuscript score of III/3 there are visible traces of successive compositional phases that, even at the moment of publication, had not yet reached a definitive form. These additions include five brief but significant episodes for solo piccolo that were not included in the body of the score, but were added at the bottom of the page, when the score had already been written.

TABLE 2: The seventeen versions of *Hyperion* in the Sixties, divided into three phases

TITLES	PLACES AND DATES	NOTES
FIRST PHASE		
Dimensioni III	Paris, November 1963	First incomplete draft
Dimensioni III	Hanover, January 1964	New incomplete draft
Dimensioni IV	Darmstadt, July 1964	*Dimensioni III* + *Aria* for flute (version for chamber group)
Hyperion	Venice, September 1964	First stage performance
SECOND PHASE		
Dimensioni IV	Darmstadt, September 1964	Repeat performance of July version
Dimensioni III (1-2-3)	The Netherlands, October 1964	Version for large orchestra
Dimensioni III (3-1-2 + *Aria*)	Cologne, November 1964	First complete performance of *Aria* for large orchestra
Hyperion II	Darmstadt, July 1965	Repeat performance of the Netherlands '64 version (with a different name)
Hyperion	Rome, January 1966	Repeat performance of the Cologne '64 version (with a new name)
Stele per Diotima (+*Dimensioni III*, 3-2)	Hamburg, January 1966	First performance of *Stele*
Dimensioni III (1-2-3)	Munich, March 1966	Repeat performance of the Netherlands '64 version
Hyperion III	Baden Baden, 1966	Recorded on vinyl, Wergo 60029; *Stele* inserted in *Dimensioni III* /3, *Aria* (flute) inserted in *Dimensioni III* /1-2
Dimensioni III	Zurich, May 1967	Tape lost
Hyperion en het Geweld (Hyperion and violence)	Brussels, May 1968	Stage performance

TITLES	PLACES AND DATES	NOTES
Hyperion/Orfeo dolente	Bologna, July 1968	Stage performance
	THIRD PHASE	
Suite aus der Oper Hyperion	Berlin, May 1969	New orchestral version
Hyperion Suite	Vienna, February 1970	Tape lost

As we have said, the piece had its first public performances in November 1963 and January 1964, respectively in Paris and Hanover, in two similar but not yet definitive versions, and in a third version, performed in Darmstadt. Basically, Maderna "tried out" the composition three times before including it in the stage version of *Hyperion* (Venice, September 1964). In October of the same year, he performed another new version of *Dimensioni III* in the Netherlands, before it was finally published by Suvini Zerboni in 1965.

Setting aside its diverse variants, we would now like to point out a feature of the work that we consider particularly novel and meaningful: the division of *Dimensioni III/1* into small, secondary episodes that the conductor was expected to highlight during the performance, so that the listeners could distinguish them. We could also add that this new dialogue with the audience was not limited to simply facilitating the perception of the succession of the parts, but also offered elements of expressive signification through the creation of contrasts in timbre and dynamics: *Dimensioni* III/1, for example, opens with a homogeneous group of instruments that produce a static band of sound, played ***pp***, evoking a calm atmosphere. After some seconds, forty or so different instruments suddenly play a disordered myriad of incoherent lines, ***ff***, that create a sort of sonic chaos.[7] The approximately four minutes of *Dimensioni III/1* are constantly marked by dramatic changes of this kind. The second and third parts of the piece (*III/2* and *III/3*) offer the listener a similar situation, though differently formulated: the division into small, contrasting fragments creates moments of anticipation, tension and relaxation, a sort of constantly mobile stream of consciousness.

---

[7] Our use of the term "disordered" is not casual: it corresponds to the term "entropy" (as a physical measure of disorder) that Maderna deliberately used as the title for some of the pieces of the cycle.

In *Aria*, the second large score of the *Hyperion* cycle, the relationship with Hölderlin is more explicit and direct, if nothing else because the work is written for voice and orchestra, and the voice sings the words of the German poet. However, the composition passed through various phases. The version for voice probably dates from the early months of 1964, but at its first performance on July 23 during the *Ferienkurse*, Maderna presented the vocal part of *Aria* in a transcription for flute, inserting it within a broader instrumental context that also included *Dimensioni III* transcribed for chamber ensemble; the combined work was named *Dimensioni IV* and was well received. The following day Maderna sent a letter to the director Virginio Puecher in which he described the piece as "a sort of large concerto for flute" [*Centro Studi Maderna*, Section L 5]. The Biennale di Venezia had already scheduled a stage performance of *Hyperion*, directed by Puecher, for that September, and the instrumental part of the work would be played by the Darmstadt *Kammerensemble*. For this reason also *Aria* was reduced to a chamber ensemble. The first performance of *Aria* in its version for voice therefore took place in Venice during the theatrical performance of *Hyperion*, even though the last part of the piece (not yet completed by the composer) was not sung, and the words were only recited.[8] The first complete performance, with voice and large orchestra, took place in Cologne in November of the same year, during the series *Musik der Zeit*.

This account of the various versions of *Aria* and the first performances of the works belonging to the *Hyperion* cycle confirms how, in this phase of stylistic change, Maderna was rethinking the concept and practice of "openness," not limiting it to the internal structure of a single work (where the score was not presented in a strictly prescribed form, but was open to different arrangements), but also extending the concept to multiple versions of the same work and to a set of different works all linked to the same common idea. On this matter, Giordano Ferrari points out that the theme of Hyperion embraces a large number of different titles (the Hyperion "constellation"), including instrumental works (*Aria, Dimensioni III, Dimensioni IV, Entropia I, II, III, Stele, Gesti, Amanda*), magnetic tapes (*Dimensioni II, Le rire, Battaglia I, II, Contrasti, Valzer, Intermezzi 1-4*), and compositions for choir (*Psalm, Zombieschorus, Schicksalslied*).[9] Viewing the concept of "openness" in a broader sense, the question becomes still more complex. The issue is discussed extensively by De Benedictis, who among other things recalls that Pascal Decroupet attempted to systemize the concept and established eight

---

[8] Only 14 measures were missing, but Maderna was evidently unable to complete the work in a satisfactory way.

[9] G. Ferrari, *Les débuts du théâtre musical d'avant-garde en Italie. Berio, Evangelisti, Maderna* (Paris: L'Harmattan, 2000), 126-127.

different types of openness.[10] Therefore, the Hyperion cycle could also be seen as a sort of vast extension of the idea of openness in an artistic work.

Returning to *Aria*, another novel and significant aspect needs to be mentioned. Ever since the time of *Vier Briefe*, that is in the course of more than ten years, Maderna had not composed any works for voice. In the meantime some of his fellow adventurers, like Nono and Boulez, had tried to tackle the task by establishing new types of relations between the semantics and syntax of words and music. The aesthetics in vogue at the time had created a certain suspicion and diffidence towards the association between music and words to be sung, especially concerning the seemingly most obvious approach, whereby vocal music should be modeled on the verbal prosody, on the pronunciation of the words. Nono and Boulez believed that the meaning of the words should remain implicit and hidden, and their pronunciation should be reduced to pure sound, just like other notes. After *Vier Briefe*, Maderna had remained silent on this matter: he neither said nor wrote anything on the topic, and (apart from his radio dramas) had not set any words to music. But the first time he comes back to it, he does so unreservedly: the verbal prosody, even in the context of the non tonal grammar that governed the relations between the notes, is scrupulously respected not only in terms of the syntactic relations, but also in the way the music could sustain the pronunciation of the words and their meaning. This practice evidently came "naturally" to Maderna and was never placed under discussion. On this issue there is a critical "topos," initiated by Mario Bortolotto and then taken up, among others, by Mila, who suggests that *Aria* had succumbed to the "irresistible call" of the Viennese school, and in particular of Alban Berg and his concert aria *Der Wein* [Mila 1976, 56-57]. This affirmation has always been readily accepted, but does not seem to be backed up by any arguments that go beyond Mila's initial intuition. In reality, the only actual reference to Viennese writing is the use of *Sprechgesang*, which appears in some episodes of the work. The musical language adopted by Maderna, his multi-serial grammar, is very different from that of the Viennese school, and the extended vocality of *Der Wein* does not appear to have many points in common with that (somewhat more "extreme") of *Aria*. And so it is likely that the "call" of the Viennese school is not reflected in the structure of the language, but rather in the expressive relation with the word, which moved in the opposite direction to the more abstract and less involved approach that tended to prevail in New Music.[11]

---

[10] A. I. De Benedicts, "Opera aperta: teoria e prassi," in *Storia dei concetti musicali. Espressione Forma Opera*, eds. G. Borio, C. Gentili, (Roma: Carocci, 2007), 324-325.

[11] Giorgio Colombo Taccani, while not ruling out references to expressionism, underlines how the language of *Aria* differs from that of Berg both in the orchestral texture and in the vocal line. See G. Colombo Taccani, "Aria: una proposta di analisi," in *Studi* 1989, 165-166.

In Maderna's piece the words are pronounced according to the rules of their language, care is taken to make sure they are understood and their sense is underscored. For example, in the first episode of *Aria* the instruments sustain the low, calm, almost resigned tone of the soprano when the past is likened to a desert ("The past lay before me like a huge, frightening desert"). The *Sprechgesang* in the second episode ("I then rose with a fierce laugh of derision for me and for everything") resumes the pronunciation techniques adopted by Schönberg in *Pierrot Lunaire*, but differs in its instrumental bursts and the high, almost shouted notes of the singer. The "mortal calm" of the third episode is assigned to the spoken voice, with no singing and no dramas, although the fact that the voice is left to emerge against the virtual silence of the orchestra becomes a drama in itself, the only orchestral comment to these words being the deep and disconcerting voice of the bass flute. The fourth episode, which speaks of pointless questioning ("I search without finding, I question the stars and they remain silent") is unexpectedly characterized by high surges of sound and bold vocalizations by the singer. The following episode, the longest and most complex part of the text, is marked by a series of "wie ich" ("like me") that highlight with increasing intensity the protagonist's gradual loss of identity ("she was not parched, like me, because she still carried heaven in her heart, and had not yet lost herself, like me"). Maderna sets this to music with an increasingly rapid diction and with intervals of pitch always varied in a disorderly fashion and often moving upwards. The disorder, or if you like, the existential irrationality evoked by the words, spreads throughout the orchestra, which gradually increases the violence of the sound until reaching a climax on the last, shouted "wie ich." In the two concluding episodes the preceding desperation gives way to the theme of twilight. In the tormented philosophical organization of Hölderlin's thought, the idea of twilight (*Dämmerung*) is associated with the ambivalence between love as an eternal cosmic force and subjective love nourished by human deviations and contradictions.[12] However, the words chosen by Maderna ("My whole being falls silent and listens attentively, when the light mysterious breath of twilight brushes me") lend themselves to a musical setting of great emotional impact. After the first measures that Maderna had already composed in July, the conclusion, amply and solemnly embellished on the word "Dämmerung," must be performed "dolcemente perdendosi" ("gently vanishing") by the voice and in the mysterious melodies of three instruments: the bass flute, the cor anglais and the clarinet in its low register.

Finally, it should be added that Maderna compiled the verbal text of *Aria* specifically with the Venice stage version in mind. The text does not exist as

---

[12] This Hölderlinian concept of *Dämmerung* is illustrated by G. Scimonello, *Hölderlin e l'utopia* (Napoli: Istituto Universitario Orientale, 1976), 92-96.

such in the works of Hölderlin, as Maderna also took into account various other materials related to *Hyperion*, including those that Hölderlin had published before the two definitive volumes of the novel (for instance, the so-called *Thalia Fragment*, or the other fragment titled *Hyperions Jugend*). He therefore made a collage of the assorted fragments and decided on their order on the basis of the musical setting.[13] In reality, the task of selecting the texts by Hölderlin appears to have been even more arduous. The text provided in the concert program for the production of *Hyperion* at the Biennale di Venezia in 1964 is, in fact, considerably longer than the one that was actually heard, and Maderna had most likely sent it in advance to the organizers of the concert before deciding to stop where he did. At this point he had probably already chosen to divide the work into two distinct parts: the first more complex, varied and dramatic, the second slower and more reflexive. Four years later (when *Aria* was incorporated within the second stage version of *Hyperion* at the La Monnaie theater in Brussels), the distinction between the two parts was further sealed, as they were presented in two different moments of the performance, clearly differentiated as *Aria 1* and *Aria 2*.

In preparation for the first stage version of *Hyperion* Maderna sent Virginio Puecher a letter in which he describes the musical parts he had already composed and adds some ideas about the dramaturgy based on Hölderlinian thought. One of the main problems to be resolved was how to dialogue with an audience slightly different from the one Maderna was used to, given that the people who attended concerts were not always the same as those who frequented the theater. On this matter, we quote the words of Virginio Puecher :

> Opera as it is perceived today in our country is one of the categories most resistant to the corrosive action of reality; it is a category that admits no exceptions or betrayals. Those few official *betrayals*, when the name of a contemporary composer is allowed to appear in the program of an opera house, are carried out in the name of the bureaucracy that governs the game of government funding […] Some particularly alert critics, it is true, occasionally call for clarification, but the pact of silence is so vast as to not to permit even a minimum of discussion.[14]

So the programs of the opera houses only rarely matched the aesthetic intentions prevalent among the most enlightened musicians. The question of the reception of recent music in theaters caught the attention of many composers, who approached the question through the twofold attempt to contribute to the definition of a new musical language and at the same time

---

[13] For details of the various sources, see R. Dalmonte, "Scelte poetiche e letterarie," in *Studi* 1989, 21.

[14] V. Puecher, "Diario di un'esperienza," *Sipario*, no. 224 (December 1964), 46.

convey particular contents (often political) through the use of languages with a greater degree of semanticity compared to music. They naturally made use of sung/spoken texts, alongside props and gestures, as narrative tools for the dramaturgy. Many of them pursued the idea of creating an audio-visual, multimedia spectacle, distinguishable from traditional musical theater, whose main distinctive feature, probably due to the influence of Brecht, was to avoid seeking the emotional involvement of the public, and hence the tendency to present the facts with a logic that was not immediately consequential.[15] In his article, Puecher goes on to comment on his first encounter with Maderna's suggestions:

> With *Hyperion* I am back with Maderna. It is his first opera. Bruno is immediately clear: he has various pieces on paper that are separate, but derive from an identical creative climate. It will be up to me to give a sense of unity to these fragments and so I will become a sort of author myself. Besides, I decide to become the set designer as well. This seems to be the right upshot of an experience as a director that can no longer afford the luxury of working outside the initial creative process [...] We believe, Maderna and I, that opera should in some way find a new way of recounting through images [...]. As musical material Maderna offers me everything: electronic tapes, a concerto for flute, a great lyrical work by Hölderlin almost in the form of a Lied. [....] We then decide that Severino Gazzelloni should become the protagonist of the work. [...] The outcome is a work in which the flute soloist enters a theater almost by chance and, not by chance, each of his sonic images is blocked by a technical-theatrical entity that is the exact opposite of every poetic idea. I think that this need for pure sound, just like the pure song that concludes the work, is the poetic core of *Hyperion* [see note 14].

The musical materials used in the stage version are the same as those described above for the scores of *Dimensioni III* (in its chamber version *Dimensioni IV*) and *Aria*, as well as the two electronic tapes of *Dimensioni II* (1960) and *Le rire* (1962), which we described in the previous chapter. The two scores (written between 1963 and 1964) clearly originated from the idea of a work for theater that Maderna had been contemplating for some time. A record of the performance in Venice has survived through an audio tape and some documentary photos. It was broadcast live on radio by the RAI on the evening of September 9, accompanied by a discrete commentary on which we have

---

[15] Giordano Ferrari recalls that Puecher imposed a similar style in his direction of Giacomo Manzoni's *Atomtod* and *Per Massimiliano Robespierre*. See G. Ferrari, "Le théâtre d'aujourd'hui, un théâtre musical toujours en prise sur l'actualité," *Analyse Musicale*, no. 45 (2002), 6.

based the following description of the eight scenes conceived by the composer together with Virginio Puecher and Rosita Lupi.[16]

I (duration 1'45"): curtain opens: voices of the prop masters at work;

II (duration 1'45"): an assistant brings cases containing various flutes, sheets of score and a table on which everything is placed. Also the flutist enters, a symbol of the character Hyperion and maybe of Hölderlin himself (the flute-poet, as Puecher calls him), who looks around disoriented: he seems to have something to say because he asks for silence, but sees a strange and uncertain world around him, and also looks at the audience, to whom his message should be addressed;

III (duration 8'): the flutist slowly arranges the sheets on the music stand, but the silence is broken by various types of noise (metallic and percussive strokes, continuous metallic sounds): this is the electronic "backing tape," taken from *Le rire* (from minute 11 onwards). After a while, shiny metal partitions begin to lower, enclosing the flutist within a narrow space;

IV (duration 6'20"): the electronic tape stops and orchestral sounds start to be heard. The flutist tries to join in as well, but manages only when the orchestra stops. He seems happy to do so, but at first his way of playing is unusual and tense (this is the solo from *Dimensioni III /2* which lasts around 4'50");

V (duration 5'10"): after the flutist has stopped playing, for the first four minutes the tape can be heard again, this time taken from *Invenzione su una voce* (the voice of Cathy Berberian processed electronically). The tape starts with punctiform sounds, very similar to strange snatches of laughter, and then introduces the imaginary "Helms phonemes," which Berberian was asked to pronounce and record. During this phase a phantasmagorical machine enters the stage (the "whore machine," as Puecher liked to call it) full of alluring and vulgar lights. The pseudo-laughter and the meaningless pseudo-words of the tape provide a background to the scene. In the last minute the orchestra recommences while the machine gradually leaves the stage;

VI (duration 13'30"): the machine's exit has left behind it a wake of indistinct bodies on the ground, dressed in dark suits, which start to move. After a silent opening the tape from *Invenzione su una voce* resumes with its phonemes and its mysterious quasi-laughter, joined by short

---

[16] A copy of the recording was sent by the RAI to the *Centro Studi Maderna*.

comments on the orchestra and some flute sounds. During this long phase the human "remnants" perform a grotesque and disturbing ballet;

VII (duration 14'): after the ballet another machine enters the scene. This time it carries the "woman" (maybe an allusion to Diotima), who sings *Aria* on words by Hölderlin.[17] During the song the flute in the orchestra intervenes with particularly graceful melodies. The last lines of the aria (not yet set to music) are recited by the soprano;

VIII (duration 2'): after the woman has left the stage, together with the machine, also the metal partitions disappear, and the situation returns to that of the opening scene. The flutist slowly exits, playing gently and calmly the last of the piccolo solos Maderna had added to the score of *Dimensioni III/3*.

Throughout the opera the two electronic tapes and the two scores are variously linked to the dramaturgy, and sometimes assume a specific meaning. For example, the metallic sounds and the dark drum beats from *Le rire* "become" the sound of the metal partitions and add to the nightmarish and threatening climate. And the mysterious "laughs" from the start of *Invenzione su una voce* and the pronunciation of the meaningless phonemes acquire new connotations: when they accompany the "machine" they become the perverse qualities (inviting and irrational) of technology; instead, when they accompany the ballet of human remnants the connotations are tragic: they become an insulting and derisive comment on the loss of humanity. On the other hand, the flute solo from *Dimensioni III/2*, after the protagonist has obtained the silence he was looking for, becomes gradually more serene and even quite cheerful: Gazzelloni casts his doubts aside and instead focuses on the sweetness of the sounds he is producing. And this happens again in the last episode of the opera, after the woman's intense and powerful human voice of protest has finally been heard, and the flute-poet decides to quietly leave the stage.

The totally spontaneous applause that concluded the performance in Venice clearly shows that the opera had marked an important point of arrival for Maderna, also in terms of the acknowledgement of the public, to whom he was particularly sensitive. However, the fact remains that, over and above the function they had acquired in the opera, *Dimensoni III* and *Aria* continued to be presented in different instrumental versions. While the differences between the various

---

[17] Here Maderna and Puecher do not specify that the woman represents Diotima. However, *Verzina* 2003 (201) reveals that this association is explicit in the concert program for the performance of the *Suite Hyperion* in Vienna in 1970.

versions doubtlessly bear witness to the composer's adhesion to the aesthetics of the "open work," one cannot exclude that the changes may, in reality, have been symptomatic of a dissatisfaction with his attempts to search for new stylistic paths.

In October 1964 in the Netherlands, one month after the production in Venice, he conducted the orchestra of The Hague in a performance of the complete version of *Dimensioni III*, no longer for chamber ensemble but now for large orchestra. Then, in November, he performed the same version with the orchestra of Cologne Radio, now concluding with *Aria*, performed in its entirety for the first time (see Table 2). However, the arrangement of the sections was different in the German performance: it began with the turbulent disorder of the third part, followed by part 1 and then Gazzelloni's flute solo; it then concluded with *Aria*, which had the same soothing effect as in the stage performance in Venice. The following year, the orchestral version heard in The Hague was performed again during the Darmstadt courses (under the allusive title *Hyperion II*), where it was met "with spontaneous ovations" [*Trudu* 1992, 185].

Following our description of the circumstances surrounding the first two major scores of the cycle (*Dimensioni III* and *Aria*), we will now turn to the third: *Stele per Diotima*. As we mentioned above, Borio and Rizzardi have shown how the three works are all based on the same serial matrix, but we should add that they differ considerably in their expressive characters. *Stele* was composed in 1965 and was inspired by a crucial theme in Hölderlin's novel: the death of the female protagonist. This theme was not covered in the Venice production of *Hyperion*, as *Stele* had not yet been written, nor in Brussels, because the composer had a different narrative in mind, nor in Bologna, where out of practical necessity the structure used in Venice was adopted again. In reality the death of Diotima elicited a strong emotional reaction in Maderna's imagination, but the fact that it was not represented on stage probably suggests that it never achieved its full potential within the cycle. According to Nicola Verzina, the score of *Stele per Diotima* can be divided into four quite distinct parts.[18] This is a new approach to form compared to the compositions written in the Fifties (*Serenata*, *Quartetto*, *Concerto per pianoforte*), which embraced the aesthetics of "non form," in other words, avoiding any separations between one zone of the work and the next. But the choice is not new if we compare it to *Dimensioni III* and *Aria*. All three works therefore anticipate what would happen in the last three works of the decade: *Quadrivium*, *Concerto per violino* and *Grande Aulodia*. The four parts of *Stele* are as follows:

---

[18] See *Verzina* 2003, 200-211. The tape we used for our description of the work, preserved at the Centro Studi Maderna, is that of the first performance conducted by Maderna in Hamburg, with the radio orchestra of the city in January 1966.

1) The piece starts with fifty or so violent orchestral strokes alternated with silences: these could be defined as "chords," that is to say strong and decisive instrumental aggregates, often sustained by the percussion. Such a powerful statement would have little formal sense were it not inspired by an "external" image (that of a funerary stele), which motivated and generated it. Of course, the music does not "describe" or recount anything, but as a musical idea based on the relation between percussive violences and mysterious silences, it generates a novel musical form, which Maderna in fact called "stele."[19] The first part lasted less than 5 minutes.

2) In the second part (3 minutes) the relentless series of funereal "chords" continues, but between one stroke and the next, comments by carefully chosen groups of timbre are gradually inserted.

3) The third part prevalently features one of those solo pieces (in this case on the violin) that Maderna used to call "cadenze" and that, like the various cadenzas for flute previously described, alternate between long cantabile phrases, almost nostalgic for melody, and sudden more impetuous and disorderly sections.

4) The conclusion (lasting around 3 minutes) opens with a peculiar set of small percussion instruments (claves, bamboo, ratchet and reco-reco), which are gradually joined by the brief murmurs of different instrumental groups. But in the last seconds the orchestra suddenly launches into a violent crescendo, finally concluding with the sounds of the cymbals and drums.

One might wonder why, even though the score finishes at measure 98, that is, at an apparently conclusive point (also musically speaking), Maderna almost never performed the work in its entirety: the only other occasion appears to have been in Hamburg on January 19, 1966 (see note 18), when it was followed by two parts of *Dimensioni III*. For the moment, there seems to be no plausible reason to explain Maderna's decision. We can only add that the work was recorded on a disk in 1966 (Wergo 60029), but interspersed with passages from *Aria* (transcribed for flute) and *Dimensioni III*; and that *Stele* was also included in various later compositions (even those not belonging to the cycle, such as the *Concerto per violino*). This appears to comply with the "provisional" nature of some of his works that we have already discussed, but does not explain

---

[19] The "funereal" conception of *Stele* was underscored by Verzina, who, in the pages cited in the previous note, shows how the chords also derive from rigorous schemes of numerical material. Ferrari, for his part, describes the opening chords of *Stele* as "sonic pillars" of Diotima's tomb; see G. Ferrari, "*Hyperion*, les chemins," cited in note 4, 100.

the contradiction between the publication of the score and the lack of any autonomous performance.

It is curious to note that on January 8, about ten days before the performance in Hamburg, Maderna repeated the version of *Dimensioni III*/3, 1, 2 + *Aria* he had given in Cologne in '64, this time in Rome with the orchestra of the RAI, perhaps suggesting that he may have considered this version particularly satisfactory. This hypothesis is confirmed by a tape that Maderna called *Quarta versione di Hyperion* and had kept at home without having ever used it publicly. Alongside a unique assembly of episodes of the cycle (some of them new, including two unaccompanied choruses), much of the tape (over 20') is taken up by an almost complete copy of the concert given in Rome on January 8.[20]

Before moving on to what we have indicated as the culminating point of the second phase of the *Hyperion* cycle, namely the stage performance that took place in Brussels in 1968, it is worth setting aside the cycle for a moment to examine some aspects of the artistic, cultural and political climate that could be considered a sort of preamble to the realization of the new production. The fact that this climate had no small influence on the choices made by important composers during the Sixties was stressed by one of the most outstanding figures of twentieth century music, György Ligeti. During a seminar held at Darmstadt in 1970, when various musical features from the Fifties and Sixties could already be viewed with a certain impartial detachment, he attempted to identify the alternative paths that had likely influenced the work of musicians in different parts of Europe and the USA during that period.[21] Ligeti points out that, besides the positive shock produced by the presence of Cage in Europe, a powerful drive toward innovation came from a group of artists – architects, literati and musicians – who shared a common precept, which was more or less as follows: we do not produce objects of art, but transform life into art, and for us art is a game. The provocative views of this group, which Ligeti referred to as "Situationists," can also be in some way linked to the politically motivated happenings that took place in Amsterdam, Copenhagen and Brussels already before the revolts of '68. The same could be said of the "Fluxus" movement, which in the same period spread across Europe starting from Scandinavia, and

---

[20] For details of this tape, see *Documenti* 1985, 261. On the restoration, see F. Bressan, S. Canazza, G. De Poli, "Restauro e falsificazione: potenzialità e rischi delle pratiche di restauro sonoro," in *Pour Bruno* 2015, 129-150. For a comment on the unaccompanied choruses, see G. Ferrari "*Hyperion* les chemins," cited in note 4, 112.

[21] The text of the lecture can be read in an anthology edited by F. Hommel and W. Schlüter, *New music in Darmstadt 1950-1960* (not on sale, November 1987). The texts, listed in the index, have no page numbering. Ligeti's text has twelve pages. The book can be consulted at the *Centro Studi Maderna*.

whose declared purpose was to annul all systematic methods in the arts and in literature. Its main advocate was a Lithuanian emigrant to the USA, Georges Maciunas, who in 1962 organized a festival titled *Après Cage: Kleines Sommerfest* at the Städtliches Museum in Wiesbaden (not too far from where Maderna lived). The festival had something of a Dada flavor about it, a sort of Dadaism refound, and was not lacking in some interesting ideas. But although Maderna was surely aware of the movement, he does not appear to have been influenced by their irrationalistic outlook, unlike certain other Italian composers, including Giuseppe Chiari and Sylvano Bussotti. His attention must nevertheless have been caught by some aspects that, despite their blatantly or superficially transgressive forms, helped New Music to exit from the blind alley of generalized serialism.

In the previous chapter we already mentioned how, in those years, one of Maderna's most important points of reference as a conductor was the Holland Festival. Here he encountered particularly difficult conditions as far as musical theater was concerned. The organizers of the events as well as the musicians involved in the Festival, were conscious of the fact that the Netherlands had no historical tradition of opera and so the young generation had nothing to free themselves from or to struggle against: they had to start from scratch. This could explain why preparations for operas due to be staged in June-July 1965, and often commissioned by the Festival, began as early as 1962-63. We do not know whether Maderna was in some way involved in the preliminary preparations for the two operas he conducted that year, but the close relations he established with the composers of the works would seem to suggest that he may have had some influence in their choice.

Ton de Leeuw's opera *De droom* ("The Dream"), is a short piece lasting 45-50', divided into three parts, the second of which being devoted to a dance scene. The libretto, written by the composer himself, is in Flemish, but the choruses are settings of Japanese Haikus, translated into English. It tells of a young man who sets out from his home town in search of fortune in a large city; at the start of his journey he meets a woman who gives him a cushion that will allow him to dream of his destiny if he sleeps on it. Most of the opera is taken up by the boy's dreams. As we will see shortly, the concept of dream will also play a significant part in the second version of *Hyperion*, staged in Brussels in 1968. The other opera presented at the Holland Festival that year (1965) was by Guillaume Landré, and was titled *Jean Lévecq*. The composer states that it is based on a short story by Guy de Maupassant that recounts the tragedy of a man believed to have died at war, who returns to his home town after many years only to find himself alienated and refused by his fellow citizens and especially by his wife, who in the meantime has married another man and is raising their children. The outcome of the protagonists' encounter with the civil and religious authorities is not dealt with specifically and is left open to the interpretation of the audience, but the music assumes an important "intermediating" role.

In the same season, Maderna also conducted the Amsterdam Concertgebouw Orchestra in a mixed program similar to those he habitually presented in Vienna. Alongside "safe" works by Schönberg, Mendelssohn and Mozart, he included a piano concerto written the year before by Kees van Baaren, director of the conservatory of The Hague and "father of an entire generation of Dutch composers" [Hans Heg in *Documenti* 1985, 134). The Dutch audience, apparently more open to new ideas than that of Vienna, applauded the recent work with great enthusiasm. Maderna worked with the Dutch orchestras not only in the Netherlands, but also at the Biennale di Venezia and in Darmstadt, where, on July 19 and 20, 1964, he presented his *Hyperion II* with the flutist Koos Verheul as protagonist. From what we have said, it is evident that New Music and the young generation of composers were quite favorably received in the Netherlands, even outside of the Festivals specifically dedicated to this repertoire. However, there also existed strong opposition to innovation, in some cases resulting in violent clashes.

Robert Adlington describes the somewhat complex situation of the young Dutch composers who were embarking on their musical career in the Sixties. Peter Schat, Louis Andriessen, Reinbert de Leeuw, Misha Mengelberg and Jan van Vlijmen all studied at the conservatory in The Hague where Kees van Baaren taught, who, at the start of the decade, was the first to have introduced the knowledge of serial techniques in the Netherlands. However, their development was not limited to music. During the Sixties in Amsterdam a climate had been created among the younger generation who on the one hand sympathized with the struggles being carried out by the movement of the workers and the political left, and on the other asserted the need to find different solutions also in the arts, with new aesthetic ideas with regards music, architecture, graphics and theater. New models of life were also proposed, ranging from the anarchic inclinations of the so-called Provos to the counterculture of the hippies: political, aesthetic and existential revolutions therefore lived side by side in an often contradictory fashion, though with a shared anti-institutional objective, even if attempts were also made to involve the actual institutions in their quest to transform society. A significant and extreme example was that of the *Labyrinth* project, which began to be developed in the early Sixties and derived from the idea to build a sort of alternative city within the Museum of Modern Art in Amsterdam, a New Babylon whose fundamental aim was to foster the "enormous creative potential of the young masses" in a multimedia performance that would also involve various young composers, in particular Peter Schat. The scope of the project was to create a substantial effect of disorientation among the participants: the principle was not to propose a Brechtian type of "didactics," but to exclude it, to present materials without suggesting any solution, so as to stimulate the creativity of those taking part. The organizers of the project also tried to involve the Holland Festival, but the idea was shelved on account of the excessive complications and costs entailed.

In the end the *Labyrinth* project appears to have elicited more bewilderment than creativity. But the attempt to involve the major institutions in youth projects surfaced again in 1966, when Peter Schat's opera *Labyrinth* was conducted by Maderna at the Theater Carré in Amsterdam and when a group of young composers wrote an "open letter" to the management of the Concertgebouw Orchestra, asking that Bruno Maderna should be appointed as a second principal conductor of the orchestra, at the time led by Bernard Haitink, thus inaugurating what Adlington calls the "Maderna campaign." Maderna never appears to have taken part personally in this campaign, and the open debate in the newspapers seems to have become mixed up with the disruption caused by the protests of the Provo group against authoritarianism and consumerism (which even affected the heir to the throne Princess Beatrix).[22] As it happened, though, Maderna found himself inadvertently drawn into one of these protests. On this matter, we prefer to pass the word to someone closer to the facts, the composer Rob Zuidam, who in March 2010 gave the second in a series of three lectures at Harvard University, during which he spoke of the conflicts surrounding New Music that occurred in the Netherlands in that period:

> On the Monday evening concert of the 17th of November 1969, just when conductor Bernard Haitink had lifted up his arms for the first downbeat of the Concerto for Flute by the eighteenth-century composer Joachim Quantz, the intense and silent concentration that got hold over the Amsterdam Concertgebouw, was suddenly disrupted by alarming noises emanating from the foyer and the hallways. Sounds of whistles, drums, rattles, toy clicking frogs and a sporadic klaxon baffled the soloist Hubert Barwahser and prompted Bernard Haitink to slowly lower his arms again, a gesture that displayed a genuine sadness, which was tangible for the audience. When Haitink turned around to see what was the cause of this turmoil, he saw a group of about forty activists storming into the hall, performing what they proclaimed to be their "Notenkrakers-Suite," the Nutcracker-Suite. The word "noot" in Dutch means both "note" and "nut." The group was led by five composers: Peter Schat, Louis Andriessen, Reinbert de Leeuw, Misha Mengelberg

---

[22] R. Adlington, *Composing Dissent: Avant-garde Music in 1960s Amsterdam* (New York: Oxford University Press, 2013), 21-96.

and Jan van Vlijmen. Pamphlets were handed out to the audience and members of the orchestra, stating that the deliberate disturbance of this concert was an act to bring to the attention the deplorable situation of Dutch composers of contemporary music, and their difficulties to have their works performed. With the aid of a megaphone, Peter Schat 'invited' conductor Bernard Haitink for a "public discussion about the programming policy and the undemocratic organizational structure of the Concertgebouw Orchestra." The reaction of the audience and orchestra members was of a strongly emotional nature and there was a vehement disapproval of the action of the Nutcrackers, which was considered to be some form of sacrilege. There was however also some hilarity, when the orchestra was accused of being "an instrument to defend the interests of the ruling class." Some skirmishes and fistfights broke out, and the protesters were evicted with force from the Concertgebouw by stewards and the police. After a brief intermission, the performance of the Quantz Flute Concerto in G major could finally take place, preceded by a long, standing ovation for the orchestra, its conductor and the soloist. [...] So, even though the immediate effects of the manifestation were quite limited, the Nutcracker-action can be seen as a turning point.[23]

Zuidam goes on to recall that for a number of years Dutch composers had been looking for alternatives to the established musical practice. The idea, he says, was not only to create a positive relation between the public and contemporary music, but also to familiarize them with the music of more distant centuries, trying to respect the most authentic way possible of performing it. He also paints a detailed picture of musical life in the Netherlands in the years following the war, underlining in particular the beneficial effects of the "Gaudeamus music week," which took place in a villa owned by Walter Maas, a German Jew who had emigrated to the Netherlands in 1933, an annual meeting that, although somewhat more limited in scope, could be compared to the Darmstadt courses. The guest lecturers included Messiaen, Cage and Stockhausen. On the other hand, this influence of this oasis of contemporary music on the choice of programs among orchestras and public theaters was limited: the main problem was how to prevent recent music from being marginalized and heard only within seasons devoted to this area. The debate went on for over a decade and had a healthy outcome for musical life in the Netherlands, stimulating the birth of numerous ensembles specializing in contemporary music, often conducted by the composers themselves.

---

[23] R. Zuidam, *Erasmus Lectures on the History and Civilization of the Netherlands and Flanders*. http://www.robertzuidam.com/essaysErasmusLectures%20II.htm. Last accessed: July 7, 2019.

The question of the relation between the standard repertoire, ancient music and New Music, which is particularly problematic when dealing with musical theater, not only made reference to situations shared with other arts, as mentioned above, but surfaced at a moment of historical change that involved the whole of the western world, namely the student protests which, starting from the USA, had broken out across Europe and reached their peak in '68. And the contestation described above has all the features typical of this kind of protest. Moreover, the year '68, which became symbolic irrespective of the different national contexts, was also associated with a manifest desire to find a solution to past evils and new contradictions. As far as music is concerned, the student movement was not specifically interested in the language of New Music, but had its greatest effect on the world of popular youth music, creating spaces, styles and audiences different from those of the bourgeois tradition. However, despite the many changes in thought encompassing all aspects of the intellectual world, this traditional line was among the hardest to move, also because the public it catered for was certainly not that of the new rebellious generations.

In retrospect, it could be said that, more than John Cage's *I Ching* philosophy, it was the euphoric boldness of the "flower children," of the American university hippies, that began to infect some of the musical institutions. Moreover, some of the more spectacular actions of the protestors – the construction of barricades in the streets, the occupation of public buildings, especially the university halls, but also the Odéon in Paris – stimulated a constant debate that affected every important moment of life and of cultural organization. The struggle against socio-political prejudice, against the principle of authority, and against the established centers of power was also transmitted to concert institutions and theaters, whose former self-assurance was now – albeit marginally – shaken. Slogans such as "forbidden to forbid," "power to the imagination," "ask the impossible" not only challenged the ruling powers in the academic and industrial world, but had the merit of prompting some substantial rethinking also in the field of music.

Against the backdrop of this turbulent yet stimulating situation, the second stage version of *Hyperion*, commissioned by the Théâtre Royale de La Monnaie in Brussels, represents a significant moment in the scheduling of the theater. The opera was staged (in Flemish) precisely in that famous month of May 1968, and was repeated five times, from May 17 to 25. Maderna conducted the theater's orchestra and choir, and the soprano soloists were Liliana Poli and Beverly Bergen. Already two years before, the director of the theater, Maurice Huisman, had commissioned the poet Hugo Claus to write a libretto that would highlight the institution's position with regards contemporary opera, in other words he asked him to write a text that would involve all the expressive means now available to music and theater.[24] The first version of the opera, titled *Morituri*, was completed in just a few months, but was then substantially modified in the very midst of the struggles of the '68 movement. The idea, already manifest in the title, made reference to the violence suffered by the ancient gladiators and compared it with the suffering inflicted on modern American soldiers, at the time involved in a ferocious war: the conflict between two cultures, between two worlds extraneous to one another that was taking place on the battle grounds of Vietnam, a situation already at the center of polemics among the students of Berkeley University and more or less openly criticized worldwide. The title given to the spectacle was *Hyperion en het Geweld* ("Hyperion and violence"). The theme of violence, the core issue of Claus's libretto, was therefore associated with the name of Hyperion. In Hölderlin's novel the protagonist, in fact, witnesses episodes of violence that fill him with bitterness and mistrust in humanity, even though in the end the mythical ideals of classical Greece still remain his deepest source of inspiration. Maderna, along with the director Deryk Mendel, helped to modify some aspects of the libretto so as to incorporate some elements of Hyperion. In truth, when Maderna was first invited to take part in the project in 1967, he was enthusiastic about the libretto, and agreed that the theme of violence should be central to the work. But it should be noted that at least the beginning and the end of the opera nevertheless followed in the steps of the previous production in Venice: some press reviews speak of an attractive flute solo at the opening and the evocative singing at the conclusion, perhaps the only two moments not centered on the otherwise pervading theme.

Unfortunately there is no way of knowing the exact format of the production, given that, for some inconceivable reason, there is no video or audio recording of the event. We know that at various moments Maderna used parts of tapes coming from previous works (*Le rire*, *Invenzione su una voce*), as well as tapes specially prepared at the studios in Darmstadt[25] and Milan, which bear titles linked to the events narrated: for example, *Battaglia I-IV*, *Contrasti*, *Intermezzi I-IV*, *Castor et Pollux*, *L'Amour maternel*, *l'Amour sexuel*, *Rêverie*. A typewritten document used by the sound engineer (*Klangregie*: see note 24) mentions parts for solo flute and Maderna's autograph scores of *Entropia I* and *Entropia II*, as well as those of *Aria 1* and *Aria 2* made by a copyist. *Stele per Diotima* is performed from m. 51 to the end, with the addition of instrumental sounds superimposed by a recorded tape. Thirty-three copies have survived of a spoken chorus written purposely for the work (*Zombieschorus*), which was probably not initially conceived as an exclusively vocal piece seeing that a small part of it

---

[24] See the concert program for this production and other related documents at the *Centro Studi Maderna*, Section D 6.

[25] As recounted by Wilhelm Schlüter, who witnessed the editing of the tapes.

appears in a fragment of autograph score together with six violin parts and a different spoken chorus. Fortunately, Maderna kept the original tapes and the individual scores used for the production.

This somewhat summary and incomplete description of the materials used in *Hyperion en het Geweld* is mainly aimed at giving an idea of the variety of timbre and form of the music, much of which had been heard at the Biennale di Venezia and in other concerts, while some of it was written or prepared specially for the occasion. The eighty-five minutes of the work featured a wide array of sonorities characteristic of New Music, including the vocal parts of the protagonists, always "shouted" in Flemish, a language that – as the critics who attended the performance point out – could only be understood by around 30% of the audience, although probably what counted was the way they shouted, not the contents of the words. The concert program of the evening includes a brief synopsis of the work (in Flemish, French, English and German):

> Lost in a hostile jungle, some soldiers from an army of invaders are surrounded by the invisible troops of the people they oppress. They are induced into sleep, and dream of figures from their childhood: characters from cartoons and movies. During the night they are all massacred, but at dawn they are born again in the form of mummified specters of their fantasies. As a counterpoint to this somber tale, we hear the noble song of love and human fraternity.

More details about the production can be gleaned from the reviews: the soldiers are tall and handsome, wearing white and golden uniforms and with a transparent helmet on their head. They do not sing, but speak, and more often than not shout. They are "calmly" prepared for battle by a priest and the commander, who attempt to convince them of the values they are fighting for (but the soldiers seem scared and neurotic). The outpost where they are stationed is furnished with objects made of plastic, seemingly "sterilized." This latter term, which the author of libretto appears to underline with particular emphasis, encapsulates an aspect of the "civilized" world, a world of plastic, and discloses its futility. The invisible enemy, on the other hand, are described by the sentries (Castor and Pollux), as small, yellow-skinned, and crawling like rats. The soldiers are given tranquilizers to help them sleep; they sing a Hymn to Slumber, and in their sleep they see stories that reassure them of their strength (videos are projected of Popeye and his spinach, Dracula, Superman and dolls). After being massacred by the rats (this is not shown, but must have been quite brief as it only takes up two pages out of the twenty-nine of the libretto) the soldiers are resuscitated like mummies and sing (in rhythmic speech) the *Zombieschorus*, "in march time" on the words of the dolls in the dream: "One day the world of the rats will be like a desert, with no beginning and no end...." The whole work concludes with the pacifying song of the woman, most likely *Aria 2*, which all the reviewers associate with the gentle flute melody of the opening. The only Italian review, after pointing out the differences with the production in Venice, adds that "the various pieces are open, with no start and no finish, blended into the spectacle through a constant passage from word to sound to action [...] an orchestra of fifty-six instruments, with few strings and a large number of vibraphones and winds."[26]

On the whole the reviews are not particularly enthusiastic, but one of them declares that "the music is of an infinitely superior quality [...] Maderna is the most classical composer of the serial school."[27] However, this observation about a presumed "classicism" fails to take into account a much more significant aspect of the work, its political engagement, something that Maderna had expressed on various occasions over the past years: in 1960 he conducted the premiere of Luigi Nono's *Intolleranza* in Venice, and conducted it again in '65 during his memorable debut in the USA. And he was also very familiar with other works with a political connotation, such as Manzoni's *La sentenza* and *Atomtod*, both dating back to the early Sixties.

Still in 1968, and over and above any issues strictly related to politics, Maderna continued to devote himself actively to musical theater. Just two months after the performances in Brussels he conducted a new version of *Hyperion* in Bologna on July 18 and 19. As had happened in Brussels, the initiative was again the result of a commission from the city's opera house, the Teatro Comunale. Every summer, in collaboration with the theater, the conductor and musicologist Tito Gotti organized a series of events known as the Feste Musicali, which had the added merit of being held in some of the most evocative settings in the city. On this occasion the idea was to juxtapose a work from the early seventeenth century (when the "genre" of melodrama did not yet exist) with one from the second half of the twentieth century (when melodrama no longer existed): more precisely, Maderna's *Hyperion* and a series of "intermezzi" (*Orfeo dolente*) by an almost unknown composer from Florence, Domenico Belli, who had written the pieces in the style known as "rappresentativo," in other words conceived for the theater, a concept that had been expressed some years before in Peri's *Euridice* and Monteverdi's *Orfeo*. The upshot was *Hyperion-Orfeo Dolente*, in which Maderna not only used the music by Belli that he himself had transcribed, but also material from the Venice production of *Hyperion*, once again with the stage direction of Virginio Puecher. However, the overall result was totally different.

---

[26] Unfortunately the author of this review is unknown and we have no other details.

[27] Nicolas Koch-Martin, in *Buenos Aires Musical* (August 1968). The article was translated (with some license) in *Il Mondo lirico*, 4/12 (June 1969).

One of the main challenges, of course, was to justify, from a cultural point of view, this rather singular choice. In the program of the Feste Musicali that year, Gotti wrote that in both works one can perceive "echoes of a profound and suffered crisis of culture and values" of the respective times: Orpheus's unheeded singing in the underworld, and the flute that people of today refuse to listen to, are linked by an "impossible dialogue between two metaphorical extremes, the poet and a reality that shuns his humanity." In fact, at the start of the seventeenth century, the Baroque rhetoric was destroying the ideal perfection of Renaissance beauty, while in the mid-twentieth century, after two World Wars, machines, the market and the slogans of the mass media were putting the final touches to the destruction of the ideals in which the European bourgeoisie had long trusted.

In an interview with Gotti, Maderna upheld, once again, that "music is always a communication with the public [...] and in the future should always have one purpose: to reach the public as directly and immediately as possible."[28] How, then, could the sense of this complex visual and aural experience be conveyed to the public? Puecher's solution was to provide a list of characters in the concert program (*Un itinerario di rara suggestione*) that included not only the "flute-poet" (naturally, Gazzelloni again) and the "woman" (in this case Liliana Poli) who sings the compelling *Aria*, and the characters from Belli's work (Orpheus, Calliope, Pluto, the Graces), but also other "characters" such as the interventions of the orchestra, the sounds recorded on electronic tape, the images prepared by Cioni Carpi to be projected cinematographically, and all the other associated "materials," in particular the "illustrious ruins" that constituted the venue and stage of the spectacle, that is to say the austere courtyard of the counter-reformist Palazzo Bentivoglio, which with its double loggia offered a somewhat unsettling backdrop to the performance.

In brief, the story of Hyperion, which in Venice had conserved some sort of quasi-narrative plot, was now portrayed mainly through sonic and visual images that interacted with one another, often with startling contrasts. Domenico Belli had originally composed his *Orfeo* as a set of five musical "intermezzi" to be performed between the various acts of Torquato Tasso's *Aminta*: they were now inserted between one piece and another of Maderna's *Hyperion*. "Set side by side, strophe against strophe," Puecher continues, "the single parts of the two works can give rise to more than one stimulating discussion about the ultimate, poetic and ideological meanings that they convey." At the start, for instance, the lament of Orpheus, who pleads with the inflexible Pluto, is juxtaposed with the disorientation of the flute-poet, whose attempts to speak are continuously

---

[28] T. Gotti, "Colloquio con Bruno Maderna," in *Pour Bruno* 2015, 155.

interrupted by the violent interventions of the orchestra and by the sinister echoes of the electronic tape. Later, the choruses of the Nymphs and the Graces that try in vain to hearten Orpheus, are paired with the contrasting unease of Maderna's *Aria*. Finally, the composer could not resist ending the work with a gradual extinction, as was often his habit. After the Graces' sad farewell to Orpheus, the last word is therefore left to Gazzelloni's flute, who leaves the stage without provocation, but also without desperation. Why the performance was not video-recorded is hard to say. However, we have integrated our account of the event with our own personal memories (as local journalists) of a faithful replica of the work, conducted by Gotti in 1972, of which a video-recording exists.[29]

The last phase of the cycle is represented by the *Suite aus der Oper Hyperion*, which the composer presented in Berlin in May 1969 and then repeated in Vienna in a partially different form.[30] In this case we are dealing with a total rethinking not only of the Hyperion project, but also of Maderna's fellowship with Hölderlin. The work now features settings of other parts of the novel, as well as poems by Auden and Lorca inspired by the Spanish civil war.[31] Basically, Greece and Spain are symbolically linked as places exposed to the same ideals and the same delusions that had troubled the German poet's conscience, and that unfortunately Maderna could still bemoan more than 150 years later. The *Suite* is divided into five parts, each with a title and a more or less explicitly narrative content. In some episodes the composer re-uses fragments of previous works, but all the rest of the *Suite* has been newly composed, in particular the choral pieces on texts by Hölderlin, Auden and Lorca. There is no narration of the events as such, but a large number of extracts from Hölderlin's novel are recited by a speaker, focusing mostly on the protagonist's state of mind. Maderna takes it for granted that the spectators are familiar with some of the basic events of the novel and the existence of a particular character, the beloved Diotima, who dies before she can see Hyperion again. So the music of the *Suite* is mainly a comment on the states of mind expressed poetically in Hölderlin's subtle prose. The five parts that make up the composition are as follows, with titles chosen by the composer himself:

---

[29] On August 10, 1972 Gotti sent Maderna a letter in which he describes the success of the new production in Bologna, and in particular mentions the spontaneous applause for *Aria* [*Centro Studi Maderna*, Section L 3].

[30] We have no recording of the performance in Vienna, which is likely lost. The concert program nevertheless proves to be an important source as it provides some valuable details: the concert was held on February 20, 1970 in the Grosser Konzerthaus-saal and the work, titled *Hyperion*, consisted of *Message, Psalm, Aria* (in place of *Klage* and sung by Dorothy Dorow) and *Schicksalslied*.

[31] See A. Giubertoni, "Fonti poetiche dell'*Hyperion* di Bruno Maderna," *Nuova Rivista Musicale Italiana*, 15/2 (1981), 197-205. All the texts (either translated into French or in the original language), as well as details of the sources, can be found in *Verzina* 2003, 185-189).

1. *Message*

The contents of the first four passages read by the speaker are all dedicated to the young Hyperion's happiness and his joyful immersion in nature. The flute solo that regularly appears between one reading and the next is again that of the flute-poet that opened the Venice production in 1964. In this case, though, it is not the lost and disoriented sound of Gazzelloni's flute: the piece is performed by two flutists of the Berlin Radio Orchestra, who calmly dialogue with one another, taking turns in playing phrases of the famous solo.

2. *Solo*

This episode too derives from a dramaturgical model already previously employed: that of the contrast between the voice of an individual and that of the collectivity. The musette (the new solo instrument) tries in vain to begin a discourse, but each time is interrupted by the orchestra. Hyperion's initial naive happiness has now been radically transformed into its opposite. But the last contrasting episode concludes in an unexpected way, since the orchestra leaves the solo instrument free to express itself for the very first time. At that point the musette no longer emits just short phrases or "words": it plays a single interminable note, with a pure physical presence whose function is to transport the protagonist into the next episode.

3. *Psalm*

Hyperion's attempts to change the world have now failed and Diotima is dead: *Psalm* is at once a funeral celebration and a prayer. The long-held note of the musette is immediately assaulted by the harsh clusters of *Stele per Diotima*, and given the context, it is not hard to interpret these in terms of death and funeral rites. The prayer alluded to in the title is instead assigned to the choir. Maderna selected words by Auden that are as biting as the funereal clusters themselves: "Not, Father, further do prolong Our necessary defeat […] Illume, and not kill";[32] and he chose to set them with full vocal power. Lorca's lines taken from *Y después*, a poem that Maderna was particularly fond of, serve to interpose Auden's violence with images of sudden sweetness. The episode ends *pianissimo*, with a homophonic chorus: "*Solo queda el desierto, un ondulado desierto*" ("Only the desert remains, a rolling desert").[33]

4. *Klage*

Passages from Hölderlin are again recited. One of these reads: "I kept

---

[32] From *The Orators*, part three (Ode vi).

[33] *Y después* is a poem that appears in the collection *El Cante jondo*, published in Madrid by Ulises in 1931.

seeking until I vanished and looked again at these vestiges until I became blind – and now night lies before me, night like a tomb." After these invocations, the protagonist's "lament" (*Klage*) is taken up by Lothar Faber's oboe, responding to the words with an almost diatonic melody, and a phrasing that strives to appease. But after the third extract, the voice of the oboe is joined by a final, relentlessly violent appearance of the orchestra, performing *Entropia III*, which Maderna wrote expressly for the *Suite*. The conclusion of the lament leads into the final episode.

5. *Schicksalslied*

The final "song of destiny" is a setting of the hymn that, in the novel, the young Hyperion sings before the sea at the end of his existential journey: the happy gods "breathe without destiny, like a slumbering infant... in placid, eternal clarity," while men falter "like water from cliff to cliff impelled." There are no musical allusions to the Song of Destiny set by Brahms at the end of the nineteenth century: the orchestra, prevalently with pizzicato strings and keyboards, seems instead to evoke the lute that Hyperion used to accompany his song,[34] and the choir echoes hints of the imitative polyphony of Venetian composers of the late sixteenth century. The piece ends with a soft unison note in all voices.

In conclusion, we would like to add a final word about the nature of this work. We are dealing with a unique musical genre: it is neither an opera, an oratorio, or a symphonic poem, nor is it experimental music, or a Lied for voices and orchestra. It is simply a new, unprecedented form that not even Maderna was able to define, other than speaking of a "succession" of musical events. The title *Suite* may well reflect this idea.

---

[34] As suggested by Giordano Ferrari. See G. Ferrari, "*Hyperion* les chemins," cited in note 4, 101.

Chapter VIII

THE AMERICAN YEARS

This chapter is mainly devoted to Bruno Maderna's last years of life – the early Seventies – and his relations with the musical world in the USA. However, as will have become clear from the previous chapters, it is hard for our account to proceed in a linear fashion or to limit itself to one particular geographical area: on the one hand, many of the themes covered here have their roots in the Sixties, and on the other, even during his "American" years Maderna continued to have close ties with Italy, Germany, the Netherlands, France, Great Britain and the countries of Northern Europe. We will nevertheless focus our attention predominantly on his experience in the USA during his last– highly intense – years of life, especially because it represents the most important occasion for Maderna – who Mila rightly defines a "European musician" – to express himself and leave a deep mark outside the old continent, even though he had already had other significant opportunities to exhibit his skills "live" in more distant countries, for instance in Tokyo in 1961, in Buenos Aires in '64 and in Persepolis in '69.

Maderna's first contacts with the USA came through Virgil Thomson, who, as we mentioned in the first chapter, immediately appreciated Maderna's work and tried to arrange a performance of his *Requiem* in America. And Maderna's name must surely have been mentioned by the more attentive American press in their coverage of the various festivals and international music meetings already flourishing in Europe in the years following the Second World War. His qualities as a composer were first made known through two quite exceptional events: the performance of the *Quartetto per archi in due tempi* by the Parrenin Quartet, during their tour in Los Angeles in 1959, and – in the same year – the world premiere of the *Tre liriche greche*, conducted by Harold Decker in Kansas City, with an ensemble of the University of Illinois, a performance that has been preserved thanks to a recording on disk.[1] These two moments were obviously not sufficient to spread the fame of his compositions throughout the USA; this first started with works that could be presented without performers specialized in the field of contemporary music, in other words his compositions on tape.

---

[1] The extensive and scrupulously documented work of Maurizio Romito has been an invaluable aid in our account: *Romito* 2018, 2019.

With regards these occasions, mostly occurring in concerts organized by universities, we can mention that *Continuo* was heard in San Francisco in 1959 and was played again, in the same year, in Los Angeles together with *Notturno*. The following year the same two pieces were featured at a concert in Tanglewood, and two years later, were also heard in Ann Arbor, during the Festival of the First Unitarian Church.

In the same year (1962) Maderna's music began to appear quite frequently in programs involving live performers, for instance in Los Angeles, where the flutist Jacques Castagner, a member of the Berio Ensemble, played the second version of *Musica su due dimensioni*. Then, the following year in Seattle, it was the turn of *Invenzione su una voce*, while in same year Severino Gazzelloni played *Serenata n. 2* and *Musica su due dimensioni* in Washington. But it was not until February1965 that Maderna first flew to the USA, where, at the Back Bay Theater in Boston, he conducted a production of Nono's *Intolleranza 60*, an event that remained memorable for various reasons. The performance, which among other things directly involved the audience through the filming of live images and their immediate projection, provoked intense reactions, which only "Bruno's bullish musical and human power" managed to sustain, as Nono himself wrote in a letter that appeared a few days later in *Rinascita*.[2] A recording of the performance was broadcast on the major American television channels, laying the foundations for Maderna's success in the States [*Romito* 2018, 118].

After this, Maderna appears not to have thought too much about America, seeing that he was busier than ever in Europe, with a packed agenda shared between composing, teaching and conducting. It should not be forgotten that, besides his participation in Darmstadt and at the school in Salzburg, he had appointments almost every week with some of the most important European orchestras, and at the same time was still fully involved in preparing the extensive *Hyperion* cycle and in composing his last three orchestral works. While Maderna received numerous recognitions in Europe, in the USA his fame was still not consolidated until 1967, when two important managers from New-York – David Schiffmann and Sheldon Soffer – declared they were interested in representing him in the States, where, they believed, he was too little known. Following an intense exchange of letters with Sylvio Samama, who from 1961-62 had managed Maderna's conducting schedule on behalf of the agency De Koos, and subsequently on his own account, it was decided to assign the task of representing him in the USA to Soffer, who succeeded in organizing what

---

[2] The letter is reproduced in A. I. De Benedictis, V. Rizzardi (eds.), *Luigi Nono. Scritti e colloqui* (Milano-Lucca, Ricordi-LIM, 2001), 177-181.

might be considered his second debut in the States, this time conducting the Pittsburgh Symphony Orchestra in October 1969.[3]

Maderna arrived in the USA in the wake of the notable success obtained in September by his production of Monteverdi's *Orfeo* at the conclusion of the Europalia Festival in Brussels. On the other side of the Atlantic, however, he chose one of his usual "mixed" programs, which also featured his *Amanda, Serenata VI*, a work, as we have said, readily appreciable even by an audience not well versed in the language of contemporary music. During his stay he visited the recently inaugurated electronic music studio and accepted to give interviews for the press and the radio; he was also homaged by an unscheduled performance of *Musica su 2 dimensioni*, played by the principal flutist of the orchestra. Press reviews soon appeared that gave a foretaste of how Maderna's qualities would be generally acknowledged by American newspapers and journals: accomplished conducting, sensitivity, cordiality towards those he worked with, innovative programming. But once again his stay was very brief and would have left only local traces had his manager, Sheldon Soffer, not had the foresight to procure him a quite prestigious engagement for the coming January, namely two concerts with the Chicago Symphony Orchestra. Maderna nevertheless had little time to feel nostalgic about the brevity of his stay in Pittsburgh, although it must surely have left him with fond memories. In fact, no sooner had he returned to Europe than he found himself caught up in a tight schedule that included appointments in Milan and Zurich, respectively in November and December.

At the start of 1970 he flew back to the States, where on January 15 and 22, he conducted the Chicago Symphony, an orchestra that enjoyed an excellent reputation at the time, also thanks to the guidance of their music director Georg Solti. Typically, for both concerts he chose a variety of very different works from diverse periods of the history of music, ranging from Gabrieli to contemporary works, and passing through Mozart, Schubert and Stravinsky, a formula well tried and tested over the previous years, which did not fail to captivate the audience in Chicago and attract the interest of the press and radio broadcasters. Not only did numerous newspapers of varying provenance publish detailed reviews of the different pieces and the way they were conducted, but it was also decided to give Maderna wide coverage in a radio interview lasting around an hour made by George Stone and Alan Stout and recorded at the WEFM in Chicago, a conversation that was considered so important that the programmers were asked to avoid any commercial breaks so as not to interrupt the broadcast!

---

[3] This is what appears to emerge from Maderna's correspondence [*Centro Studi Maderna*, Section L 5]. However, according to Sylvio Samama's son, it was his father himself who invited Soffer to be Maderna's agent in the USA. See Leo Samama's account in *Pour Bruno* 2015, 221-224.

In answering the precise questions of the interviewers, Maderna described the main stages in his professional training as a composer and a conductor, adding now and then some amusing anecdotes about certain idiosyncrasies of his teachers, like Hermann Scherchen and Gian Francesco Malipiero, who were also well known in America. Particularly detailed and informative – almost a sort of statement of his poetics – is the long part dealing with his experience with dodecaphony and his relations with the music of the three great Viennese composers, which he interprets in the light of his own ideas. After openly declaring that the greatest of the three was undoubtedly Schönberg, he justifies his choice by recalling, among other things, an episode he had experienced in first person:

> Shortly before his death, that is after the war, [Schönberg] was surprised by the success that the dodecaphonic technique had obtained. He also wrote a beautiful letter that was read out during a conference organized by Malipiero junior in Milan; in the letter he said that he was not sure it was necessary to hold a conference about the serial technique and urged them not to be too fanatic, to try to develop his idea, because any theory unable to grow is dead.

During the long interview much space is devoted to the topic of conducting ancient operas and especially those most frequently appearing in the repertoire, and the danger – succumbed to by even the most well-intentioned of conductors – of maintaining (and maybe enhancing) an interpretative tradition already deep-rooted in the orchestras and in the expectations of the audience. At this point he airs his views, with no apparent inhibitions, in a quite uncharacteristic fashion: French conductors always perform Debussy too softly, German conductors always perform Wagner too slowly, "we, in Italy, are not capable of performing Verdi well: too many pauses, too many holds and exaggerations of every type," while everyone plays Beethoven on the model of Toscanini "the archetype of this terrible genre of conductors […] Performing Mozart is always very risky; it would almost be better to leave him alone, but when you decide to do it, you must always study his indications very carefully and carry them out precisely." Maderna uses this point to move on to other matters extremely important to him, like the need for the conductor to have a good knowledge of the historical background of the period in which a given piece of music was written and its relation with other arts that were flourishing at the time: in other words the conductor should not only have the skills to guide the orchestra and the audience, but should also have a deep awareness of the historical and artistic context in which a work was composed.

> I have conducted many orchestras whose principal conductors were veritable stars; in these cases the orchestra is simply able to put on a

show, it is hard to make them go more deeply into the music because they are not used to doing so. Orchestras, like horses, assume the prevalent characters of their principal masters.[4]

This is why the Chicago orchestra, molded under the musical direction of Solti, represented a true challenge. Gianfranco Vinay speaks at length about the "poetics" of Maderna's conducting: Maderna's ideal – he comments – was that of a "humanist" conductor, able to declare war on the star system and uncover new facets of the music he performed. His idea of "uncovering" was based above all on the principle of clearing away the incrustations accumulated over the years by tradition. Rediscovering a work implied finding new, unexpected musical meanings, which lie within the music but are usually overlooked. It implies dialoguing between the past and present with "Gadamer-like" hermeneutics, that is to say approaching a work in terms of today's values, uncovering aspects that are still currently meaningful. This, then, is the "humanistic" mediation that Maderna often spoke of.[5]

One of the most successful and highly praised works among those featured in the two concerts in Chicago was his recent *Quadrivium*, performed alongside Berio's *Epifanie*, which was already known in the USA and was again masterfully executed by Cathy Berberian. A tangible sign of how much Maderna was appreciated is the fact that he was subsequently commissioned to write a piece dedicated to the Chicago Symphony Orchestra, an invitation readily accepted by the composer, resulting in the composition of *Aura*, his first American work. His stay was again quite brief, but only a few months would pass before his next visit, when, on May 15, he made his debut in New York.

Between his two visits Maderna was kept busy with an intense series of engagements that took him to various parts of the world. On February 7 he was at the Auditorium of the Foro Italico in Rome for a concert in the cycle *I Concerti di Roma*, during which, among other things, he presented the last work in his "European trilogy," the *Grande Aulodia*, with the RAI orchestra, Gazzelloni and Faber [*Centro Studi Maderna*, Section D 12]. Then, from February 22 and 24, he was at the Landestheater in Darmstadt where he worked alongside Harro Dicks in a curious double bill consisting of a stage version of Ligeti's *Aventures et Nouvelles Aventures* and his own *From A to Z*, a program that was subsequently repeated in March and April. Between February and March, he was at the Deutsche Oper in Berlin for a production of Schönberg's *Moses und Aron*, two

---

[4] The two extracts are based on the partial Italian translation of the long conversation that took place in Chicago on January 23, 1970. See *Documenti* 1985, 89-101, pp. 95, 91. An abridged recording of the original interview can be heard on the Stradivarius disk *Bruno Maderna. L'ultimo concerto. The Last Concert* (STR 10071, 1993).

[5] G. Vinay, "Maderna, chef d'orchestre *humaniste*," in *Basalte* 2, 2009, 536-553.

years after he had previously conducted the work in the same theater, which was now directed by his ex-colleague in Darmstadt Gustav Rudolf Sellner, who also acted as stage director of the new production. He then took the same piece to Osaka and Tokyo, where he stayed from mid-March to early April. On returning to Italy he continued to work in the field of theater, first with Mozart's *Così fan tutte* in Bologna and Ferrara, and then Valentino Bucchi's *Il coccodrillo* at the Maggio Musicale Fiorentino [Romito 2020]. At the end of these hectic three months of highly varied appointments, he finally took a plane back to the USA.

The nature of Maderna's New York debut on May 15, 1970 was quite different from his previous appearances in the USA. On this occasion the program was not the usual blend of ancient, classical and contemporary pieces, a formula successfully adopted for some years now, but rather an opera – Mercadante's *Il Giuramento* – prepared at the Juilliard School, with the orchestra, soloists and choir of the Juilliard American Opera Center to celebrate the centenary of the Italian composer's death; in other words Maderna conducted a performance given by a group of students. According to Soffer, who gave details of the preparations in a letter to Samama, Maderna had quite a hard time putting things together, but in the end the result was excellent, to the extent that he was immediately invited to come back the following year. The event was met with some surprise by the press, who expressed their astonishment at the fact that the "modernist" Maderna, previously introduced to them as the composer of the *Quartetto in due tempi* performed by students of the school on May 7, 1968, had been able to put so much effort into preparing a decidedly outdated score, and that a composer so much in demand for his new works, could devote his attention so assiduously to coaching a group of young musicians. He was warmly received by all concerned and Peter Manning (a well known British conductor then teaching at the school) invited him to the party that, as was the custom at the Juilliard School, would be held after the last performance of the opera.

The surprise expressed at Maderna's commitment in preparing Mercadante's opera with a group of students would seem to imply that his image in the USA had not yet taken into account a very important aspect of his work: his activity as a teacher, which had always been much appreciated and in great demand in Europe. As we have seen, in the post-war years he had first earned his living as a teacher in Venice. Subsequently, his role at Darmstadt had included the teaching of composition and conducting, as well as the preparation of instrumental ensembles, even before the formation of the Internationales Kammerensemble (1964). While other protagonists of the Darmstadt courses like Boulez, Stockhausen and also Nono, had integrated their more "practical" roles as conductors with lectures and introductions to concerts, Maderna often accepted the invitations of Steinecke, and later of Thomas, to hold public talks on the subject of theory or poetics, although more often than not these remained on paper. On the other hand, his work with small groups of young musicians – concerning composition and the performance of pieces they had just composed – was one of his most typical and sought-after activities. In England, in the years when he was invited to the Dartington Summer School (from 1960 to '62), his lessons with young, still inexpert students had achieved excellent results, as had his recent work at the Mozarteum in Salzburg (from 1967 to '70), which had produced several successful conductors including Gustav Kuhn, winner of the Radio Salzburg award in 1969 and Lucas Vis, who immediately in his first year had won the best student award, after which he assisted Maderna as "second conductor" in various important performances.[6]

With all this experience behind him, when he arrived in New York in May 1970 and found himself working with an orchestra made up of students, there was no reason for him to feel daunted, and on the contrary he showed how it was possible to take them to a high artistic level. This "miracle of Bruno," as Soffer wrote in a letter to Samama, immediately resulted in an invitation to return to New York in 1971 to conduct Mozart's *Clemenza di Tito* and two concerts with the Juilliard orchestra; it also prompted him to write a work especially for the school, titled *Juilliard Serenade. Tempo libero II*.

Shortly after his return from New York, Maderna spent a long period in Germany, almost until the end of June, where he shared his time between Saarbrücken, and, one presumes, his home in Darmstadt. The appointment in Saarbrücken was organized by his friend Christof Bitter, who had already invited Maderna as early as 1968.[7] His first engagement was a concert at the Kongreßhalle in which he conducted the Radio Symphony Orchestra in a new version of his *Concerto per violino*, performed by Theo Olof, followed by Mahler's Seventh Symphony. After that he took part in three recording sessions at the Saarländischer Rundfunk, during which he recorded orchestral works by Mozart, Schumann and Schönberg. Between June 26, the date of his last session, and August 30, when Maderna was in Hamburg for a production of *Wozzeck*, there are no records of any concerts [*Romito* 2020], but an important source tells us that he held his usual course at the Mozarteum in Salzburg. The conductor Gustav Kuhn recalled the fact in a recent interview with Valerio Tura:

> In 1970 [...] Bruno came back to Salzburg for the summer courses at the Mozarteum [...] I suggested he should let me play a Mozart piano concerto with him and the course students [...] In Salzburg we spent much of the days talking about everything, with his irregular

---

[6] See Valerio Tura's interview with Lucas Vis in *Pour Bruno* 2015, 226-229.

[7] See Bitter's letter to Maderna dated August 11, 1968, at the *Centro Studi Maderna*, Section L 5.

and erratic hours, his eighty cigarettes a day and his other excesses [...] For Bruno, the most important thing in music was the expression both as a composer and conductor ... everything was always based on great clarity, on musical precision, on depth of analysis, on the perfect knowledge of the structures ... this is why Maderna's sound always had an extraordinary limpidity [*Pour Bruno* 2015, 208].

After his courses in Salzburg we find him in Überlingen on Lake Constance, where the natural peace and beauty provide a perfect setting for particularly well-equipped health resorts. The treatments available there mainly concerned nutritional problems, and various sources suggest that Maderna had gone there to try to lose some weight. In a letter to Christine, Bruno's mother expresses her hope that the "treatment had not left him too weak." From Überlingen Bruno wrote two letters to her, full of affection and describing his plans for the coming months, but also expressing his concerns about the hectic schedule that awaited him:

> It appears that a wonderful career is opening up for me in America. I'll be leaving here on August 12: on the 14th I have to be in Hamburg to start rehearsing for *Wozzeck* [...] Mother dear, I hope, and am right in hoping, that this year will bring me many fine things. [But] I can't always be traveling around the world (even though I am a "first-class itinerant musician"). I want to have more time with my children and more calm to compose.[8]

Even while he was at the resort, and in any case between the months of June and August, Maderna managed to combine his treatment with the organization of conducting engagements and probably also the composition of works that would take on fuller shape the following year, a year that would turn out to be one of the busiest of his already intense career. On August 14, just two days after leaving Überlingen, he was already in Hamburg for the rehearsals of Berg's *Wozzeck*, due to be staged at the Staatsoper at the end of the month and repeated again in October. On September 6 at the Biennale di Venezia he conducted the Stuttgart Radio Orchestra in works by Ligeti, Pennisi, Stockhausen and Schönberg, with Christiane Edinger as soloist in the piece by Schönberg, a young violinist he would continue to work with until the end of his days. Immediately afterwards (on September 20) he was at the *Studio di Fonologia* in Milan to edit the tapes for *Tempo libero*, which needed to be ready for the Festa di San Marino on the 28th of the same month [*Centro Studi Maderna*, Section D 17.6].

After four important concerts in Berlin, Turin, Prague and Vienna, and after the Christmas festivities, presumably spent with his family, on January 3,

---

[8] Letters dated July 21 and 31, 1970, in *Extraits* 503-504.

1971 Maderna was on a plane back to New York. During the flight he wrote a long and affectionate letter to his mother in which he gives her good news about his situation and tells her that he will be returning to Italy in February for a meeting with the lawyer Devoto, in the hope of resolving the question of divorce once and for all and finally putting their family affairs in order.[9] Lastly, he again expresses the wish, as in many other letters, that she could be at his side during this exciting American adventure, which, though tiring, he was facing with youthful vigor.

During the course of 1971 Maderna stayed in the USA for three entire months: he spent all of January in New York, the whole of July in Tanglewood, and in November he was in Philadelphia and Miami. He arrived in January full of hope and trust for the future, a spirit that was noted by all, and especially by his agent Soffer, who, after meeting him in New York on January 8, 1971, wrote to his European counterpart, Samama:

> Bruno arrived on Sunday in great physical and mental form. He seems twenty years younger [...] He is rehearsing like crazy at the Juilliard and is composing lots. Next Monday the SERENADE will be ready [*Romito* 2018, 127].

And in fact the *Juilliard Serenade* was duly performed at the Lincoln Center in the concert of January 31, in which Maderna himself conducted the Juilliard Ensemble. The program also included the tape of *Tempo Libero*, and this addition was considered so significant that the title appearing in the concert program was *Juilliard Serenade (Free Time I)*. And a note by the composer exists in which he states that the *Serenade* can also be performed ad libitum along with the recording on tape, and indeed all the performances conducted by Maderna were integrated by the tape. When dealing with *Tempo Libero* in Chapter Six we mentioned how, in an interview with Bitter, he spoke of the difference between "normal" time (that is, our routine way of living) and "free" time, in which we could enjoy listening to the sounds that surround us. He stressed that this electronic composition is a sonic narration with no beginning and no end, to be listened to not in the "contemplative" manner of a concert, but rather "freely": the listener should not look for any sort of sequential logic but should form mental associations that are wholly personal. Cage, too, had exploited the presence of environmental sounds, albeit in different ways. But the fact that this new work, the *Juilliard Serenade*, could be performed alongside *Tempo Libero*, suggests that

---

[9] The definitive divorce was finally granted in a document dated December 9, 1971. The lawyer Devoto had supported Maderna ever since the early '50s: the records of the first hearing for his separation from Raffaella Tartaglia are in fact dated September 15, 1952. Both documents are filed in the lawyer's office.

the composer believed the two works should be listened to in a similar way. We should keep in mind, though, that a physical score of the *Juilliard Serenade* does exist and it was not conceived as ambient music, but as music for a concert. Its nature, however, implies that it should be listened to "for enjoyment," without necessarily interpreting its structures in a symbolic way, that is to say as vehicles of communication: it can be listened to as a pure and simple sequence of sound objects, like the song of a bird, or other forms of everyday listening.

One might wonder, at this point, whether Maderna had intentionally written something completely different from his previous works, let us say a sort of non-music. But this question is rather futile, because Maderna knew very well what he was doing: the answer given implicitly in his interview with Bitter is that his latest output (including *Tempo Libero* and thus even more so the *Juilliard Serenade*) continues to be "music," although music that needs to be listened to in a different way. What changes is not the nature of the music, which continues to be composed, presented at a concert and heard, but rather the underlying musical aesthetics, that is the different functions that music can have from an aesthetic point of view. However, Maderna is clearly not trying to turn this idea of diverse functions into a philosophical issue: when Bitter asks him about Stockhausen's aesthetics, Maderna bluntly replies: "Stockhausen has turned to metaphysics [but] I am not a metaphysicist […] I am a lover of music." And in fact, in line with this statement, he immediately afterwards returned to writing works to be listened to as "music," in the most traditional sense of the term. Maderna evidently enjoyed musical and intellectual adventures: his curiosity led him to explore the limits of the nature of music, he went beyond the Pillars of Hercules, he admired the new panorama and that was enough for him. This particular state of mind coincided with a moment of good physical health and even a change in his appearance. The difference compared to the previous year was so remarkable that in an article in the *New York Times* the journalist Raymond Ericson commented that the slimmer Maderna looked much less like Fiorello la Guardia than the year before [*Romito* 2018, 127]. And other members of the press soon took up the theme and – on being compared to the much loved mayor of New York – Maderna became increasingly seen as a friend, a household figure that you look forward to seeing again soon.

His month in New York was mostly spent preparing the Juilliard orchestra and choir for the three consecutive performances of *Clemenza di Tito* (January 21, 22 and 23), and rehearsing for the two concerts at the Lincoln Center (January 29 and 31). The review of the opera in the *New York Times* underlined the "unusual clarity and refinement" of the Juilliard Orchestra conducted by Maderna, who had added two arias by Mozart to the usual Bärenreiter edition. Maderna received particularly positive comments from the press, especially as a composer of new music. In an interview with Raymond Ericson, again for the *New York Times*, he made some light-hearted comments about the pieces that would feature in the two concerts. Speaking of *Music of Gaity*, a suite based on old English melodies found in the *Fitzwilliam Virginal Book*, he remarked: "I chose the title because it was the function of music in the sixteenth century to provide gaiety in the form of serenades, dances, and chansons." He goes on to describe his *Quadrivium* as a sort of joke: "it was commissioned for the festival at Royan for a concert dedicated to Berio and me. My piece came between two by Berio [*Questo vuol dire che...* and *Sinfonia*]. I was like the filling in a sandwich, and I decided to write something very brilliant. It is a concerto for percussionists with the orchestra divided into four groups."

Both the opera and the two concerts were warmly received, and not only by the local press. One journalist even went so far as to say that his performance of *Pierrot lunaire* achieved a greater balance between words and music compared to Schönberg's recorded version on disk [Columbia, 1940]. Such openness towards Maderna's contemporary work also came as a pleasant surprise to Soffer, who wrote to Christine: "In the first place New York is not well disposed towards modern music and in the second the critics are basically ignorant about the subject. So they must have studied for a great number of hours to learn about and appreciate Bruno's talent!" [ibid., 130].

During the intervening five months before his next visit to the States, the bulk of Maderna's conducting work involved operas rather than concerts: two works by Offenbach, *Les contes d'Hoffmann* (in Darmstadt, on February 17, 19 and 24), and *Orphée aux enfers* (in Rome, with six repeat performances in May); *Wozzeck* again at the Staatsoper in Hamburg, each month from February to June; and Kurt Weill's *Der Jasager* and Stravinsky's *Histoire du soldat* at the Pergola theater in Florence, with three repeat performances in June. Besides these opera productions, which all received wide coverage in the press, he also conducted several important concerts, including one in London in March (*Quadrivium* and Mahler's Ninth), one at the Royan Festival in April (which included his *Grande Aulodia*) and another in Rome in May including the Italian premiere of his *Juilliard Serenade* [Romito 2020].

In between these important engagements he found time to write various compositions, which included not only *Ausstrahlung*, but also four pieces for solo instruments, whose scores are all dated 1971: *Pièce pour Ivry*, *Solo*, *Y después* and *Viola*. These are highly original works with particularly stimulating parts for the performers, whom Maderna surely had in mind when he wrote them. Over and above the specific features that characterize each piece, they all share the fact of having no well defined structure: two of them (*Pièce pour Ivry* and *Solo*) are made up of separate units labeled with letters or numbers, and the performer must decide the order in which to play them, and in *Solo* (for musette, oboe, oboe d'amore and cor anglais) the performer must even decide which instrument to use. In *Viola* the notes are fully written out, but the performer must choose which sections to play, which to leave out, how to start and how to finish. In *Y después* the first part is written in a traditional way and only the final part has an aleatory element, with no instructions as to the sequence of events. None of the four pieces have any time signatures or measure divisions. The composer has basically chosen to avoid any definition of the form, and gives the performer no guidance on how to create their own: he simply ignores its existence. This choice seems to contradict his care for the formal rhetoric, for the expressive sense of the sequence of events (introductions, contrasts, developments, conclusions) characteristic of his more recent instrumental works. One could wonder what led him to this choice. To find a possible answer we must consider that his main purpose in writing these "minor" works for solo instruments was to try out new instrumental, and perhaps also compositional techniques, aimed at stimulating the performers. Such techniques are particularly notable in the two pieces for strings, *Pièce pour Ivry* (for violin) and *Viola*, which have always presented challenging but highly satisfying opportunities for the outstanding players that have tackled them. In *Y después*, for guitar, the performer is given particular responsibility in the final part, which is totally aleatory. Lastly, *Solo* is a piece for oboes, in which each of the often short fragments already has its own autonomy sustained respectively by the cantabile, brilliance, passion or even eccentricities of the internal themes. Its singular characteristic seems to be how it manages almost miraculously to keep on its feet despite the repetitions of its themes, no matter how numerous they are and in whichever sequence they reappear. The lack of any predetermined form therefore has unpredictable and highly stimulating consequences. It comes as no surprise, then, that many artists have responded positively to the ideas implicit in these four pieces, above all because each of them lends itself perfectly to eliciting sometimes previously unexplored aspects of the performer's skill and creativity.

  Soon after these four works a fifth piece was added, which was given its first public performance in 1971, for flute and oboe, as an episode of *Ausstrahlung*. It later appeared as an independent piece under the title *Dialodia*, perhaps meaning "double aulodia." The title itself conjures up a wealth of associations and allusions: first and foremost to his *Grande Aulodia* written the previous year, again for flute and oboe, and secondly to the Greek instrument, the aulos, which had an important symbolic role in the Hyperion cycle. While this opening episode of *Ausstrahlung* ("radiance") has no strictly Greek connotations, the melodies they share are set in a climate of intense meditation: the light of the word that gave birth to the world. Unlike the other four pieces, *Dialodia* does not appear to have been conceived with the aim of stimulating the virtuosity of the soloists, but rather to highlight their capacities for melody and the luminous harmony that could ensue from their concordance. The parts of the two instruments are, in fact, often homorhythmic, while at other times they vie with one another, sometimes in imitation, at other times trying to differentiate themselves, or else they toy with the consonant or dissonant intervals they produce; finally, they launch into a sort of high-spirited duel of rapid notes in what seems more like a challenge than an agreement, but at that point the piece comes to an end. *Dialodia* could also be played as a chamber duo for other combinations, and this version became particularly popular among performers. Its success also stemmed from the freedom to choose, ad libitum, the instruments to be used from among those listed by the composer in the introduction to the score.

Returning to our account of this highly eventful 1971, we find Maderna once more on a plane to the USA on June 27, when he wrote another letter to his mother, full of enthusiasm and trust in his future plans. And he wrote to her again after the festival in Ravinia, "a lovely place close to Chicago," where, in an open-air auditorium for 7,000 people, he gave a very successful concert with the Chicago Symphony Orchestra "that is currently truly the best in America – which means in the world!" The press reviews continued to be enthusiastic. The occasional criticisms arose mainly from the fact that Maderna never included any of his own works in the programs. The review of the concert in the *Chicago Daily News* included a significant comment about his transcription of Gabrieli's *In ecclesiis*: "No matter what today's purists might think, Maderna's practice would have come as no surprise at the time of Gabrieli when the purely instrumental performance of vocal works was a widespread occurrence." The work had already been performed in January of the previous year and the *Chicago Tribune* had commented that Maderna's transcription helped one imagine the sonorities of the instruments at St. Mark's in Venice.[10]

On July 11 Maderna debuted at Tanglewood with the Boston Symphony Orchestra in a concert well received by both the public and critics, and began an important association with the school of theater and musical composition at the Berkshire Music Center. Maderna had accepted to join the team of guest teachers after learning what his precise duties would be from a letter sent to him personally by the principal organizer of the school, Gunther Schuller. He would have six to eight students to whom he would have to give an hour a week of private lessons, or else he could teach small groups of two or three students together, even though the lessons were traditionally carried out on an individual basis. We know how Maderna loved to let his students work together,

---

[10] Both reviews (dated June 30, 1971 and January 23, 1970) can be read at the *Centro Studi Maderna*, Section D 12. 4.

so he most likely chose the latter option. He would also have to hold two-hour seminars every week for three consecutive weeks, covering topics suggested by the students themselves. Finally, he would have to supervise the creation of a theater piece with music, based on group improvisation.[11]

During his long stay in Tanglewood Maderna was a guest at the summer residence of Serge and Natalie Koussewitzsky, and throughout the whole period was able to enjoy the relaxing atmosphere afforded by the pleasant setting and an easygoing relationship with his colleagues and students. His pupils included Lucas Vis, who had also attended his conducting course in Salzburg in 1967 and had been his assistant there in the following two years. Vis would remain close to Maderna until the end, both as his assistant, and also as his substitute, as happened for the performance of *Satyricon* in Amsterdam. And there was also a young pianist-composer from Buffalo, Rocco Di Pietro, who took an active part in Maderna's lessons and would attend his courses again the following year. At first the students, who had been raised with the prescriptions of dodecaphony deriving from the teaching of Babbitt, found Maderna's idea of working with just a few pitches, elaborated according to their own fantasy, "very strange indeed," but they soon realized that this way of composing offered exciting possibilities.[12]

His main task, though, was to supervise the theatrical and musical improvisation scheduled for August 8, 1971, which the newspapers already anticipated with some interest. The piece in question was the banquet scene from Petronius's *Satyricon*, translated by the director Ian Strasfogel, which Maderna used as a stimulus for his pupils' improvisations, and for which he also made some musical sketches of his own. However, according to recent accounts collected by Maurizio Romito and published in *Musica/Realtà*, the students were not at all keen on the idea of producing a "collective work," because, as novice composers, they preferred to make themselves known through their own works at the Composers Forums organized during the course. The piece created by the group, under the guidance of Maderna and Strasfogel, involved the participation of singers and a piano, and lasted around fifteen minutes. Despite the "open" nature of the work put together by the students, the sketches that Maderna had made for the project eventually found their way into the score of *Satyricon* that he presented two years later in the Netherlands, in what would be his last work for theater.

In the final concert of the Festival of Contemporary Music held on August 12, and repeated on the 17th, Maderna conducted, among other things, Gunther

---

[11] Letter from Gunther Schuller to Maderna dated June 14, 1971 [*Romito* 2018, 136, 139].

[12] All particulars are taken from *Romito* 2018, 136-139.

Schuller's *Double Quintet*, while Schuller, in turn, conducted the American premiere of Maderna's *Concerto n. 1 per oboe e orchestra*. Before leaving Tanglewood he received an invitation from Paul Fromm to write a piece for chamber ensemble that would be performed the following year, again in Tanglewood, to mark the twentieth anniversary of the Fromm Music Foundation; in stating his reasons for the request Fromm added: "We need the imprint and impact of your creativity, professionalism and broad musical horizon."

Back in Europe, most of his short stay was probably spent in The Hague rehearsing for the premiere of *Ausstrahlung* with the Residentie Orkest. The new piece was the outcome of an invitation he had received in 1970 from the organizers of the Festival of Arts in Shiraz, who had asked him to write a piece to celebrate the 2500th anniversary of the death of Cyrus the Great, founder of the Persian empire. The commission to write a celebratory composition was likely the upshot of an initiative by his agent Sylvio Samama, but most probably was also thanks to the highly favorable impression Maderna had made during his previous visit to Iran in September 1969.[13]

Starting from May 1971 Maderna had embarked on a lively exchange of correspondence not only with the directors of the Festival to discuss the work and the texts he was thinking of setting, but also with expert linguists who suggested a large number of writings in Sanskrit, Tamil and Persian, and who translated them and helped him to understand their contents.[14] Various clues in his letters seem to indicate that Maderna made a thorough study of the literary material linked to the Persian empire and had gathered a vast and varied corpus of texts from which he extracted the materials to be used in the work. Angela Ida De Benedictis has traced the sources of the ancient texts he set to music.[15] They are *Kâvyâdarça* (a collection of poetry from the seventh century CE written by the poet Dandin), *Bhagavad Gîtâ* (a text on the doctrine of Krishna, contained in the epic Indian poem *Mahâbhârata*, from the third century BCE), *Atharva Veda* (one of the four collections of hymns of the Indian Vedic religion, whose rites date back to the second millennium BCE), and *Avesta* (a book of mystic wisdom of the Zoroastrian religion, written in ancient Persian). Alongside

---

[13] See the review of the concert preserved at the *Centro Studi Maderna*, Section D 12.

[14] Details of his contacts with the organizers of the festival and with the literary experts are taken from A. I. De Benedictis, "Scritture e supporti nel Novecento: alcune riflessioni e un esempio (*Ausstrahlung* di Bruno Maderna)," in G. Borio (ed.), *La scrittura come rappresentazione del pensiero musicale* (Pisa: ETS 2004), 237-291.

[15] In A. I. De Benedictis, "*Ausstrahlung* ou la textualité brisée d'un hymne à la vie," in *Basalte* 1, 2007, 287-317 (a partial repetition in French of the 2004 article).

these are pieces written by poets from Islamic Persia: Omar Khayyâm (eleventh century), Saadi (born in Shiraz in the thirteenth century), Nezâmî Arûzi (twelfth century), and Rudaghi (tenth century). De Benedictis comments on the Indian and Persian texts, making reference to the hypothesis that Indians and Iranians had shared primordial "Arian" roots in their language and culture. Maderna's homage therefore spans crucial periods in the national identity of Persia: the ancient traditions of the Vedic civilization, those of the Zoroastrians and those of the Muslims. It should also be added that his interest in this area of ancient literature did not stem solely from his exceptional cultural curiosity and the allure of such texts coming from a distant past, but also from the fact that, right from the outset, he had a clear idea of how these words (recited or sung) could be used as a basis for his work.

The structure of *Ausstrahlung* is totally different from all those he had adopted till then and is novel also with respect to the musical trends of the European avant-garde. Among the drafts preserved at the *Paul Sacher Stiftung* in Basel (and in the *Centro Studi Maderna* in Bologna) there are schemes in which the sounds are equally divided and mixed among the four different sonic sources that Maderna indicates as "Tape / Voce / Soli / Orchestra." The real "score" of the work therefore contains the sum of these simultaneous sonorities. More precisely:

– "Tapes": Maderna created tapes in which he superimposed various male and female voices who recite the texts (in Sanskrit or Persian), sometimes with the addition of echo effects or resonance;

– "Voce": a female voice recites or sings the texts in English, French, Italian or German. In the Shiraz performance the voice was that of Cathy Berberian. In the final episode (in German) we also hear the voices (recorded on tape) of his wife Christine and their young son Andrea;

– "Soli": melodies, often superimposed, on the flute and oboe (the flutes were of various sizes and the oboes – in Lothar Faber's performance – also included a cor anglais, musette and oboe d'amore);

– "Orchestra": sections for orchestra are written in the score, played at its premiere by the Residentie Orkest conducted by Maderna. The score specifies seven groups of timbrally defined instruments, which intervene sporadically during the different episodes that make up the work: Maderna refers to these groups as "Ausstrahlungen" ("radiances"), since they "radiate" sonorities suitable for each given situation. Even though there are also seven episodes (or "Sections"), there seems to be no relation with the number of radiances. The Ausstrahlungen numbers 1 and 6 feature string instruments, number 3 brass, number 4 winds, marimbas and harps, number 7 percussion, and Ausstrahlungen 2 and 5 a singing part with orchestra.

Another important element of this highly singular work is the poetic sense of the words, which has a substantial influence on the tone of the setting. A typical example can be found in the second episode, where the voice recites the text of the *Bhagavad Gîtâ*, which Maderna divides into two parts: in the first part the spoken voice narrates the doubts of the hero Arjuna, who notices members of his own family inside the army he is about to fight. He is deeply troubled and is moved to pity; he will not try to defend himself if they want to kill him. The episode is introduced first by the percussion of *Ausstrahlung 7* (in one of his sketches Maderna specifies: "the percussion breaks in brutally and dramatically") and then by violent interventions of *Ausstrahlung 3* (trumpets and horns) and a solo featuring the bitter voice of the musette. The general tone then becomes gradually softer in the second part, when Krishna declares it is an error to be afraid of killing or of being killed, since the human soul is invulnerable: so nothing is more admissible than a righteous combat.

Another equally characteristic example of how the text is reflected in the music can be found at the start of episode 3, when an ancient Vedic prayer is invoked in English: "Power art thou, give me power […] May I have voice in mouth and breath in my nostrils…." Here the singing is full of wide dissonant leaps, from high notes to low notes, and Maderna stresses that the expression must be "always strong and impassioned." Also the voices recorded on tape help to create unexpected forms of music. A particular example is that of *Avesta*, a Zoroastrian hymn that marvels at the sun in the sky and the stars at night that follow their silent paths: "Wie geschieht uns so wunderbar." Here Andrea's childish voice intermittently repeats the amazed words "so wunderbar," transforming the prayer into a sort of mysterious and fascinating rondò. A further example of a particular association between the text and its musical setting comes at the end of the third episode, when part of another Vedic hymn extolling the value of togetherness ("Let's walk together, speak together") is recited by the singer (Maderna specifies "enthusiastically") with full orchestra. At a certain point the hymn is transformed into a shifting interplay of different words (both sung and recited), with alternating instruments, fixed and aleatory texts, and even combining different authors (the ancient poet Omar Khayyâm intervenes with the words – sung in Italian – "sulla mia tomba il vento del nord farà piovere fiori"). All in all, a combination of elements constituting a peculiar language that becomes an extraordinary multimedia amalgamation.

Maderna's contact with such a stimulating cultural source had therefore inspired him to explore unprecedented paths of creativity. Unfortunately, we cannot say what alternative solutions may have developed from this unique experience: the only performance of the work, while Maderna was still alive, was the one he gave in Shiraz on September 4, 1971. His stay in Iran may have been brief, but the news of his success preceded his return to Italy and spread rapidly throughout Europe and America.

On September 26, after a quick trip to Hamburg for yet another performance of *Wozzeck*, Maderna was in Saarbrücken for a radio broadcast, and was there again on October 31 at the invitation of Christof Bitter, who interviewed him during the interval between the two parts of a concert with quite an unusual program: the first part started with Gabrieli's *In ecclesiis*, and was followed by Josquin's *Magnificat quarti toni* transcribed for choir and three groups of instruments; the second part featured Stravinsky's variations on Bach's *Vom Himmel hoch* and a version of Bach's *Magnificat* that included the same chorale. The program had apparently been suggested by Bitter, and Maderna had found the idea "splendid." During the interview he took the opportunity to express his views about what he believed made an ideal conductor: one who was not content to simply perform pieces he loved and were loved by the public, but who was also musicologically aware of what he was conducting. The conversation also turned to the issue of transcriptions and gave Maderna the chance to declare his admiration of the "happy and amiable way" that Stravinsky enjoyed playing with the music of Bach.

Between one concert and the other in Saarbrücken he was at the RAI in Milan and also took part in the *Journées de musique contemporaine* in Paris, where he gave a concert entirely devoted to the dodecaphonic works of Stravinsky. Then, at the start of November, he set off once more for the USA, this time headed for Philadelphia. As we can see, his geographical range was gradually expanding also in America, and slowly included most of the cities where the most famous orchestras were based. And in fact he was not always able to keep up with the demand: for instance, just before leaving Europe, on November 1, he received a letter from Eugene Ormandy – who was then in charge of the Philadelphia orchestra – saying how disappointed he was that Maderna was unable to conduct their orchestra in Washington and Baltimore as well, due to the engagements he had already accepted in Florida [*Centro Studi Maderna*, Section L 7]. On the same date, while on the plane to Philadelphia – as on many other occasions during his Atlantic crossings – Maderna wrote a letter to Irma Manfredi, speaking of the things he had on his mind at that moment. As we have seen, these letters sometimes offer an insight into an otherwise hidden side of his biography, taking us beyond the list of concerts, the reviews and his meetings with famous people. In this case what Maderna was eager to tell his mother is that the following month, he would begin work as principal conductor of the RAI orchestra in Milan. For the moment it was just a contract for six months, but there were all the signs that this would be extended for three or four years. And here Maderna starts to fantasize about how much time this would give him to be close to his children and to compose in peace and quiet [*Centro Studi Maderna*, Section L 3]. This "dream" persists for some time, and is still alive in the following February, when he writes to Francesco Siciliani – an important member of the programming board of the RAI – to talk about his proposals for the 1972-73 and '73-74 seasons. Alongside the detailed list of the composers he intends to promote, the most important events he wishes to cover and other related activities, he also expresses his joy at accepting "the task of educating and polishing the orchestra you have personally entrusted to me."[16]

But returning to his latest trip to the USA, the concert he conducted in Philadelphia on November 4, 5 and 6, 1971 – substituting for Claudio Abbado – included Mozart's Piano Concerto K 466 with Vladimir Ashkenazy and Mahler's Fifth Symphony. This second piece was a new entry in Maderna's programs. For many years he had only performed the *Adagio* from the Tenth Symphony, and it was not until 1965 that he began to discover Mahler's other symphonies, starting from the Seventh and then the Ninth. Instead, the programs of the two concerts he conducted in Florida with the Miami Philharmonic Orchestra on November 21 and 22 were of a very different kind, especially the first, which took the form of a Viennese-style "Promenade Concert."

The two sets of concerts and rehearsals were separated by a week with no engagements as such, and Samama had sent Christine pre-paid plane tickets so she could join her husband in the USA. During this week Bruno and Christine were able to make a brief visit to New York, where they met the tenor Paul Sperry to discuss the work the singer had recently commissioned from him. In an interview with Valerio Tura, Sperry told a curious story about how things went. Around 1969 he had decided he would like to sing a piece of contemporary music, though not – as he specified – serial. With this in mind he asked his agent Sheldon Soffer (who, by chance, was also Maderna's agent) to find something that suited both his voice and his tastes. Without hesitation Soffer replied: "There's a composer whose music you'll like: he's an Italian who's been living some time in Germany, his name's Bruno Maderna... why don't you commission him to write a piece tailor-made for you?" This said and done, the project soon materialized: " ... I paid him a fee for the commission [...] I called one of my writer friends, Jonathan Levy, and asked him for some suggestions. He came up with an idea inspired by the travel journals [...] of James Boswell." Maderna was enthusiastic about the idea and on meeting the singer in New York he immediately asked him to read the piece using various different inflections,

---

[16] The complete letter can be read in *Studi* 1989, 70-73.

and with certain pauses, as if he were already singing the piece, while Maderna recorded the singer's "improvisation".[17]

The work that ensued from this meeting could almost be said to mark a historic turning point in Maderna's career. It is hard to say just how much Sperry's unwillingness to sing "serial music" influenced the composition. The fact is that in *Venetian Journal* Maderna's attitude towards serialism, a language he had contributed to in no small way, seems suddenly to have changed direction. This may also have been occasioned by Levy's theatrical text, in which the protagonist of the story, the famous Scottish traveler, writer and diarist James Boswell, is treated in a decidedly unceremonious manner. The playwright's intention was to spotlight the somewhat hypochondriac side often attributed to the character, and to do so in a light-hearted manner. And so in this sort of small-scale comic opera Maderna makes Boswell sing tonal melodies (e.g. the popular "Biondina in gondoleta" and the opera aria "O infelice mia sorte") accompanied in a ridiculously shambling way by unlikely combinations of instruments such as the harp, horn and marimba, or a trumpet and bass clarinet. In other cases Boswell sings vulgar waltz tunes or vocalizes exaggeratedly on the word "amour," or else prompts coarse remarks from the instruments when he recalls how he has witnessed ill-mannered and rowdy scenes from the audience during the performance of an opera. And the instruments likewise comment on the "dolorosa" ("painful") situation he complains of using the Italian word, with an explosion of rapid and impulsive fragments on the four strings of the small orchestra, followed by cries from the brass and flurries on the celesta and other keyboards. All in all, the post-tonal language, with all its disarray and irregularities, is exploited to draw an ironic and cynical musical portrait of the protagonist's disordered and unsettled mind. In the end, confronted by the beauty of St. Mark's and accompanied by a strict fugue, reminiscent perhaps of the music typically associated with that church, Boswell is forced to confess his utter ignorance and he despairs of the vainness of his libertine ways.

The contents of the magnetic tape, which now and then interrupts the protagonist's monologues, is similarly bizarre and absurd, combining the seventeenth century timbres of the harpsichord with various kinds of noises, sometimes nightmarish, and with aquatic sounds, spoken voices, echoes of songs and female laughter. There is little trace, then, of the ideological enthusiasm and unbending stringency around which Maderna had built his name as a composer, first in Italy and then in Darmstadt: his unfailing trust in the future of music seems to have vanished into thin air. Maybe the milieu in which he was now working and which provided the backdrop for his most recent works had

---

[17] From Valerio Tura's interview with Paul Sperry, published in *Pour Bruno* 2015, 224-226.

different expectations and lacked the faith that was still prevalent in Europe. The American intellectuals were doubtlessly curious to hear the latest novelties from the old world, especially if they came from one of its most authoritative representatives, but it is quite likely that their aesthetic values were influenced, in such a substantial and natural way as to become almost imperceptible, by the multiplicity of tendencies that existed in their own world, in other words a sort of relativism that allowed the countless different possibilities to peacefully coexist. And so a theatrical text such as the one proposed by Levy provided the ideal chance for Maderna to willingly distance himself from his past and feel free to explore new avenues, in addition to taking an unprecedented ironic view of the classical tradition, a tradition that Maderna loved unreservedly and precisely on this account could allow himself to take such liberties.[18]

Back in Europe, Maderna had an important commitment at La Scala involving a program of ballets by Stravinsky, with the choreography of Maurice Béjart (*Pulcinella*, *Apollon musagète*, *Petrushka*). The last engagements of this eventful year were the concert with the Wiener Philharmoniker on December 17, with Christiane Edinger as soloist in Schumann's Violin Concerto, and another with the RAI Symphony Orchestra in Milan, in which he once more conducted Mahler's Seventh Symphony.

The year 1972 began with as many as nine appointments in New York, from January 13 to 24, this time not with the youthful ensembles of the Juilliard school, but with the prestigious New York Philharmonic Orchestra, whose musical directorship had been taken over by Pierre Boulez just the year before. Once again Maderna's visit received wide media coverage and in an interview published in the *New York Times* on January 9 he was asked about his thoughts on the current state of orchestral conducting [Romito 2019, note 2]. Boulez was obviously praised for his extensive culture and for his experience as a composer, while other illustrious conductors – notably, but not only, Toscanini and von Karajan – came in for harsh criticism, seasoned with American-style "bon mots": one conductor makes a "chocolate Beethoven," another creates "Verdi for old women" and so on. Certainly not all readers shared his opinions, and the contrasting positions were inevitably reflected in the reviews of his performances. The programs of his concerts in New York that year were influenced by the preferences of Boulez, who insisted on including a symphonic

---

[18] In her careful analysis of Maderna's ironic forays, De Benedictis (2000) has identified several references to classical works which he clearly enjoyed toying with. A. I. De Benedictis, "Qui forse una cadenza brillante. Viaggio nel 'Venetian Journal' di Bruno Maderna," *Acta Musicologica*, 72/1 (2000), 63-105.

poem by Liszt, despite some objections from Maderna. One of the concerts featured the American premiere of his *Concerto per violino*, which was well received, though without any particular enthusiasm. Another program, performed twice on the same evening, was entirely devoted to contemporary music by American composers, including works by Murray Schafer and Earle Brown. This took place in Greenwich Village during the series Perspective Encounters, which featured debates between the composers, performers and the public, and in the case in question each piece had to be performed twice – before and after the discussion with the composer.

His short but active stay in New York was followed by a European tour that began, in February, with a further performance of *Wozzeck* in Hamburg, and also included two closely scheduled concerts in Vienna, neither of which involved the Wiener Symphoniker, and both devoted to the twentieth century, with three Austrian premieres of works by Ives, Brown and Maderna himself (*Quadrivium*). His second trip of the year to the USA, again very brief, was in the second half of March and was shared between New York and Chicago. At the Lincoln Center in New York Maderna gave the world premiere of his *Venetian Journal*, the theater piece commissioned by Paul Sperry, who took the lead role in the performance. Since the score was largely aleatory in nature, the rehearsals were particularly crucial. Sperry recalls:

> When we met for the first rehearsal of *Venetian Journal* he said to the players, "you play how you like." At the second rehearsal it became clear that what he had really meant to say was, "you play <u>when</u> you like," and that they definitely had to play how <u>he</u> liked. He had definite ideas about the style of every phrase. The result was that at the second rehearsal, which was the final one before the dress rehearsal, we only got through half the piece. This was my first experience doing new music, and I was terrified that we would go on unprepared. I begged him at the dress rehearsal, which was on the morning of the performance, at least to do a run-through and to make some choices for the players about when to come in. He said, "Oh, is that bothering you? OK." And then he proceeded to assign what each player should do on each page and ran the piece through three times. That's when I discovered how remarkably incisive a conductor he was.[19]

Just a few days later Maderna was already in Chicago, where he conducted two concerts (each repeated three times) with the Chicago Symphony Orchestra, which was celebrating its eightieth anniversary with three specially commissioned works. Maderna's return was warmly welcomed by the critic of the *Chicago Daily News* as a "fresh and stimulating breeze." The same newspaper, in its review

---

[19] Personal communication from Sperry to Romito, published in *Romito* 2019, 184.

of the first concert, compared his interpretation of Debussy's *Jeux* with that of Boulez some months before: "Maderna's conception of the piece is much more physical than Boulez's highly abstract reading" [see Romito 2019, 184]. The second concert featured Maderna's *Aura*, one of his large-scale American instrumental works and one of the three works that had been commissioned by the orchestra.

In *Aura* the orchestra is divided into six groups of strings (labeled with the letters A to F), a group of "Corde e Tastiere" (harps, guitars etc. and keyboards) and one of percussion, besides the two usual groups of winds (woodwind and brass). The prevailing idea that dominates the whole work is the exploration of what can be obtained by combining these different groups in the most varied and mobile way possible. This was obviously not a new idea, as Maderna had often treated instrumental sounds as agglomerates in order to experiment with the expressive potential of their different combinations, but in this case he seems intent on doing so in a much more systematic fashion. The very structure of the work seems to be based on this procedure. Against a background of long and evocative swathes of sound created by the six string orchestras, it is possible, in fact, to identify a succession of episodes featuring at least three quite distinctive zones, each characterized by a series of specific instrumental combinations.

How might we interpret this form? The guide offered by Maderna in the program notes for the work's premiere remains open to discussion: the title "refers to the radiations of all the possible consequences emanating from a central musical object [...] aura was the essence of things, the essence of sounds and something like the smell coming from the room where a chicken is cooking in the pan" [*Documenti* 1985, 307]. The intention behind this final whimsical remark was probably to suggest a type of musical communication analogous to that of *Ausstrahlung*, that is to say "radiance."

Alessandro Solbiati reaches a similar kind of interpretation in an article dedicated mainly to *Biogramma* but that can also be extended to Maderna's other "American" works for orchestra (*Juilliard Serenade*, *Aura*, *Giardino religioso*). The works he wrote in his last years, Solbiati believes, are in some way prophetic as they move in the direction that New Music was destined to take during the following decades: "the replacement, so aptly expressed by Enzo Restagno in an essay of 1985, of the concept of "structure" with that of "event" became an axiom for the majority of composers of the new generations [...] who were increasingly more diffident towards any way of composing that was not linked directly and immediately with *sound*."[20] We nevertheless need to specify what is meant by "event" and how an event differs from a "structure." Restagno suggests that an event is characterized above all by aspects of timbre, by timbral "polarities" that create "tensions" which do not derive from mathematical calculations, but from a sort of "magnetic field." Solbiati accepts and expands on this concept: at the basis of all the large orchestral works that Maderna wrote in his final years there is always a "sonic idea" that takes shape both through its macro-formal architecture and through the micro-forms of the groups of instruments with which the musical syntax is defined. The micro- or macro-formal structures can be described in technical terms (e.g., long held chords in the violins, string pizzicatos together with small percussion instruments, and so on), but the inherent musical sense cannot be described simply, because it has to be interpreted, and this interpretation, if put into words, could be expressed through a metaphor (e.g. the "sonic body" mentioned by Solbiati is at first "hesitant," then it becomes "propulsive" and gradually acquires greater "solidity," etc.). Basically, the music becomes an "event" depending on the extent to which it is able to "speak," or communicate, even though its "words" are only implicit in the sound and they form a "sonic idea," as Solbiati calls it, which cannot be directly translated into words, except, as we have seen, through a metaphor. Throughout the Sixties a numerological approach to structure still strongly persists in Maderna's work, as evidenced in the studies by Borio and Rizzardi on the *Hyperion* cycle, but at the start of the Seventies the sonic idea of "event" begins to prevail.

His American period in 1972 was interrupted by a fleeting visit to Saarbrücken, where for some years now he had been regularly invited by his friend Christof Bitter. But exactly one month after his first concert in Chicago, on April 16, he was back in the USA, this time in Rochester, a small town on the southern shore of Lake Ontario whose University housed the Eastman School of Music. The director of the school had written to Maderna on January 12, 1971, asking him to write a work for orchestra that would be performed the following year during the Festival celebrating the school's fiftieth anniversary; he had readily accepted the commission (the school's archives still have his letter) and he now kept his promise by conducting his new work titled *Biogramma*.

The work was probably composed in early 1972 and was performed shortly afterwards in a concert on April 16, in which Maderna conducted the local Eastman Philharmonia. The first thing that strikes one about this work is that, unlike his previous orchestral pieces, which abounded in "aleatory" techniques, the score of *Biogramma* is fairly straightforward. The work is explicitly divided

---

[20] See A. Solbiati, "*Biogramma*. Projet et modalité de realization d'une *Weltanschauung*," in *Basalte* 2, 2009, 124. The article cited by Solbiati is E. Restagno, "L'ultimo Maderna dalla struttura all'evento," in *Documenti* 1985, 163-167.

into three sections which are separated by evident pauses and are marked A, B and C. The first and third sections are in turn divided into subparts separated by pauses. The particular novelty of this new work is the constant presence of numerous silences that break it up into short distinct elements, each of which appears to be self-contained, with no relation to the others. However, if we look at the work in terms of its macro-form, it becomes clear that the underlying intention is, in fact, to differentiate the three broad sections and their sonic and expressive contents, given that each section is markedly different from the others. The function of section A seems to be that of an introduction, as if it were saying to the audience: "Here are my sonorities and my identity." Equally characteristic are the seven subparts of section C, in which Maderna returns to one of his pessimistic readings of the contemporary world in the period of cold war: a portrayal of the violent disorder that had previously characterized his interpretation of Hölderlin. Here, then, Maderna has left his indisputable mark. Section B, instead, is a zone of exploration (in three phases), quite new for those familiar with Maderna's work. The first phase features a succession of melodic fragments, in long dialogues unobtrusively accompanied by the strings, in a general atmosphere reminiscent of a sort of traditional *Adagio*, quiet and thoughtful. In the third phase we hear a long and very dense polymelody, slow and highly expressive, once again creating a climate of mysterious calm. The transition from one phase to another offers a brief aleatory zone, where the performer plays ad libitum. Curiously, though, in his first performance of the piece Maderna began with Section B, and what is more, totally reinvented its first four minutes [*Romito* 2019, 188-189]. In his above-mentioned article Solbiati concludes by suggesting that, despite its apparent scientific connotations, the title *Biogramma* could be interpreted as "bio / gramma," that is to say a "diagram of life [...] in other words a genuine *Weltanschauung*, a vision of the world with unexpectedly bitter reactions," such as those that prompted the violent treatment of some of the "sonic ideas" that make up the work, especially in part C.

The local press and the students and teachers of the school were unanimous in praising Maderna's new work as well as his style of conducting. But his stay in Rochester was of necessity very brief, since a long-hoped for event awaited him in Europe: his marriage to Christine was finally legalized in Darmstadt on April 28, 1972, in a celebration attended by their three children, the Köpnik family and numerous friends. The happy occasion allowed him to spend some precious, albeit limited time with his family. Just a week later, on May 5, he was already back in Italy for a concert with the RAI orchestra at the conservatory in Milan, and then in June he took on the more demanding task of conducting *Moses und Aron* at the Deutsche Oper in Berlin.

Looking at Maderna's tightly-packed schedule in the last period of his life, one has the impression that the label "American period" now routinely used in the literature, should take into account not only the time he was physically present in North America, but also his constant flights across the Atlantic, the many famous orchestras he conducted there and the important works he wrote on commission from his new friends. This is particularly true of 1972: after New York, Chicago and Rochester, he spent part of July and August in Tanglewood, and then returned to New York in September; another flight took him to Canada for two concerts in Montreal at the start of November, immediately followed by a production of *Don Giovanni* in Los Angeles.

Of all these equally important appointments, the most significant was undoubtedly the period he spent in Tanglewood, where he not only taught composition but also had a role in the organization of the event due to the absence of Gunther Schuller: among other things, he was asked to supervise the two Composers Forums that were held on July 22 and August 15, which included the performance of works by some of his students. The two concerts with the Boston Symphony Orchestra (on July 7 and 21) prompted a lively debate in the press. While maintaining a generally positive view of Maderna's conducting, there was no shortage of criticism, especially regarding two points. As had previously happened at the Ravinia Festival, his transcriptions of works by Giovanni Gabrieli came under attack, but also his choice of tempos in the symphonies by Mozart and Brahms was placed in doubt, as they evidently did not match the image of these works favored by the Americans: measured and classical in the first case, and vigorously late-romantic in the second.

Given the large number of concerts that Maderna conducted in the USA between 1971 and '72, and the exceptional attention devoted to his performances in the press, much of which has been described in detail by Maurizio Romito, we will now try to add some further remarks about the "humanism" associated with his conducting as underlined by Gianfranco Vinay [see note 5]. A critic from Boston observed how, during the rehearsals, Maderna was able to communicate the very precise intentions he had in mind, in a friendly but clear manner, thus winning the respect of the members of the orchestra, who were not always so well disposed towards their guest conductors. Another commentator confirmed this aspect, adding that he never imposed his ideas in an authoritarian way, but always managed to persuade the players in a perfectly natural manner [*Romito* 2018, 143]. As far as his "precise intentions" are concerned, many observations focus on his singular interpretations of various composers. Regarding Mozart, one journalist was struck by the "unabashedly lush" manner of certain performances, quite unlike the "lean, crisp" interpretations to which audiences were accustomed [ibid., 134]; and listeners were surprised by his unusually fast performance of Bruckner's Seventh Symphony, while another critic observed that, despite the lack of the customary solemnity, Bruckner's music emerged in full relief, with its "Wagnerian breadth and epic dimensions."

Speaking of Bruckner, a curious observation comes from Lucas Vis, who recalls that at first Maderna really found it hard to stand the composer, and during the rehearsals he urged the orchestra (in that case the Boston Symphony) to overplay certain aspects of the work's expressive tone, believing that it was necessary to exaggerate in the rehearsals to obtain a good result during the performance. At the end of this laborious process, Maderna confided to Vis in private that he was starting to like the composer's music [135]. And turning to Mahler (with whom Maderna in his later years had fallen "madly in love"), the focus was placed mainly on the complexity of his music and the extraordinary contradictions found in his symphonies. When he conducted the Fifth Symphony in Philadelphia in November 1971, one critic remarked on the diversity with which Maderna had presented the various episodes of the work: while the first two movements were "outwardly implacable," in the following movements he stressed "the cries and sorrows of the voices of single instruments" and in particular the inventive and visionary aspects of the marches and dances [143].

Having made these few observations, it should nevertheless be added that the question of forming an adequate definition of Maderna's standing as a conductor is still totally open. One could certainly say that his position among the most outstanding figures of the time was quite original. In the face of the relentless drive for success that stardom and the media urged in all realms of human activity, Maderna was miraculously able to maintain his steadfast and often ironic demeanor, together with an exemplary personal reserve, almost uncaring of what current values seemed to be inexorably imposing.

At the start of August, Maderna allowed himself a brief "vacation" when he accepted to conduct a concert at the Blossom Music Center, the Cleveland Orchestra's summer home for some years now. The outdoor theater was set in a pleasant and inviting location among the hills of Ohio, about twenty-five miles to the south of Cleveland, surrounded by the Cuyahoga Valley National Park. The concert season had been running since 1968 and aimed to encourage the public – and especially young people – to listen to symphonic music, with some particularly attractive deals: youngsters under seventeen entered free-of-charge and those who subscribed to the whole season had discounts to visit Cuyahoga Falls and on the cost of the picnic basket; in addition, parking was free for everybody. With this audience in mind Maderna offered a program of music for piano and orchestra by Liszt and Stravinsky, and Schumann's Second Symphony, avoiding any risky encounters with more recent works. He was welcomed as "a refreshing non conformist," but it was above all his interpretation of Schumann's symphony that won the favor of the critics, who appreciated the "sense of spontaneity and life, tastefully tempered with logic and control," adding "Not a star conductor, Maderna was nonetheless a sunny performer and a welcome guest" [ibid., 195]. But even in this haven of peace Maderna's stay appears to have been short, since on August 8 he was at the Festival of Contemporary Music in Tanglewood to conduct a concert celebrating the twentieth anniversary of the Fromm Music Foundation, during which – alongside pieces by Gunther Schuller, Roger Sessions and Charles Wuorinen – he premiered a work commissioned for the occasion one year before, his *Giardino religioso*.

According to various accounts that have never been refuted, Maderna originally wanted to call the work *Fromm's garden*, inspired by the garden of Paul Fromm's house which he considered a true spectacle (the performing instructions specify, among other things, that at a certain point the conductor must walk among the instruments and select sounds that reflect the flowers of a garden). But following certain objections from Fromm, he decided to "translate" the name of the patron with the adjective "religious" (in German "fromm" means "pious"). And so the composition eventually took on the rather strange Italian title "Giardino religioso" [*Documenti* 1985, 309]. This ingenious and light-hearted association with Mr. Fromm might provide a subtle clue to the work's contents and could perhaps help today's listeners to interpret the composer's actions while conducting the performance. This rather singular tale of the work's origins might also offer a clue as to why, unlike his two previous orchestral works, the score contains a great deal of aleatory material to be improvised, and is written for a fairly small orchestra: ten strings and four brass (without trombones and with no woodwind), but with abundant percussion, keyboards and other stringed instruments. And finally, it explains Maderna's careful instructions about the positioning of the instruments and the movements of the conductor who, at a certain point, must play some of them.

Like *Aura*, but still more explicitly and decisively, the work was conceived as a sort of bountiful anthology of the countless sonic possibilities that the modern orchestra, using carefully chosen compositional and conducting techniques, is able to offer music today. It is an assembly of sounds that clearly has little to do with the tonal tradition, but also with the experiments of Cage, who had placed in discussion the very concept of music and its aesthetic functions, in other words its communicative functions. Maderna has chosen sequences of sounds able to reflect the inner workings of the human soul, at times unusual, but certainly discernible to the careful listener: for instance, the restless swathes of sound on the strings, the ambiguous calls of the trumpets, the percussion strokes left to vibrate at length, and the mysterious silences, the inventive solo melodies, the astral echoes of the crotales, harps and celeste, or the dense turbulences and sudden flairs of the orchestra. All in all, Maderna has created a careful blend of textures, registers, timbres and dynamics that are not ends in themselves, but have expressive properties. And there is no traditional type of rhetorical logic in their sequence – they are organized in a free manner, offering the same expectation of wonders experienced by someone who wanders through a garden and discovers surprises in every flowerbed.

During the first performance of *Giardino religioso*, Maderna did not limit himself to guiding the players in their interpretation of the score in the aleatory sections, but he actually left the podium and moved among the instruments, playing the triangle, the congas, the celesta and the strings of the piano, just as if he were gathering different flowers in a "religious" garden. The audience were captivated by the music and the actions, and this sentiment was also reflected in the reviews that followed and even in a letter of congratulations from Mr. Fromm himself. Applauded for around 5 minutes, *Giardino religioso* was acclaimed as "a genial work," a "fascinating piece of music" [*Romito* 2019, 197].

Equally stimulating and original was Maderna's last contribution to the Tanglewood Festival, a production in English of Monteverdi's *Coronation of Poppea*, presented during the Music Theatre Project, which as in 1971 was stage directed by Ian Strasfogel. The opera was taken out of its Baroque setting, and was transformed into a timeless piece depicting a court in decadence, with grotesque characters that suitably reflected the end of a great empire. The score was drastically shortened by Maderna, who made further changes to the well known reconstruction carried out some years before by Alan Curtis. Maderna conducted the first two performances, while the third, on August 16, was entrusted to his assistant Bruce Hangen, who fortunately kept the score and some of the solo parts prepared by Maderna. The arrangement of the opera provoked mixed reactions among those involved: Strasfogel judged the accompaniment to Ottavia's two important arias ("Disprezzata regina" and "Addio Roma") "very lush" and almost Respighian, while Hangen found the orchestration of the ritornelli particularly interesting [*Romito* 2019, 199-201].

From Tanglewood Maderna moved to Rochester to conduct two concerts at the town's music festival on August 17 and 19. The concerts featured two different programs and included a quite unusual selection of works compared to those generally chosen by Maderna. Apart from Schumann's Second Symphony and one or two other pieces, the choice of compositions by Berlioz, Gounod and Boito inspired by the figure of Mephistopheles, alongside arias by Verdi and Mozart, seems quite out of the ordinary.

In a letter written to his mother on August 18, he repeats the concerns he had already expressed on April 10 while flying from Frankfurt to New York. He complains that he is tired of the hectic rhythm of this American tour, a pace he could still tolerate for no more than two or three seasons [*Extraits* 2007, 508]. On September 6 he gave a concert in Washington in which the most anticipated moment was Charles Ives's Fourth Symphony for three conductors, adapted by Gunther Schuller for just one. The critic of the *Chicago Tribune* particularly appreciated Maderna's ability to beat one time with his left hand and another with his right [*Romito* 2019, 205]. Then, on September 15, before returning to Europe, Maderna conducted a discutable and much discussed edition of Mozart's *Don Giovanni* at Lincoln Center in New York, in a production that did not respect the ethical questions underlying the original work and that transformed the two main male characters – Don Giovanni and Leporello – into two villains from a crime story; and Maderna's performance apparently failed to capture the spirit of Mozart's music. Just how important the organizers had considered this production can be gleaned from the fact that they had not only planned ten performances, but had even combined the original edition with one in English. The premiere of the opera was met with boos, and due to his poor condition of health, mentioned in a letter of Samama and also hinted at by the press, Maderna was only able to conduct five out of the ten contracted performances. He left for Europe and never returned to the USA, not even for the inauguration of the opera season in Los Angeles already scheduled for November [ibid., 206-208].

From October 1972 onwards, our account can rely not only on the amply documented concert appearances that Maderna was able to make, but also on details fortunately supplied by two new sources: a diary initially kept by Maderna (and in 1973 probably by Samama) and a personal notebook in which he listed the professional commitments he was due to fulfill [*Centro Studi Maderna*, Section D 18].[21] The collation of all the various documents reveals that the appointments mentioned in the *Diary*, and even less so those listed in the *Notebook*, do not always correspond to the activities he actually carried out. The supplementary details provided by the two new sources allow us to fill in many of the gaps that sometimes appear between one concert and the next. While these pauses between the various concerts could perhaps point to a lack of engagements in this period, they could also suggest a gradual decline in Maderna's legendary physical resistance during this final phase of his life.

But despite his sudden retreat from the USA, Maderna seems not have been unduly concerned about his state of health. His last performance of *Don Giovanni* had been on September 26, and already on October 5 he was in Milan to record a concert for the RAI; he then left for London, where he conducted two concerts,

---

[21] From here on the two sources will be referred to respectively as *Diary* and *Notebook*.

on October 16 and 19. The next concert we know of was again in London, about a month later, on November 22. We learn from the *Notebook* that in this period he had planned a few days of rest followed by two concerts in Montréal, which did not take place; and two of the three concerts originally scheduled for London in the second half of November were also missed. A possible explanation could be that in the meantime he had gone back to Darmstadt, maybe for some form of treatment. We know, in any case, that on November 22 he took a plane to London, where he conducted Mahler's Seventh Symphony and pieces by Webern at the Royal Festival Hall. His stay in England was nevertheless brief, as on the following day he was already on a return flight from London to Frankfurt. Once again he took advantage of his time on the plane to write to his mother, on this occasion to tell her about his recent success in London and to speak of his immediate departure for Milan [*Extraits* 2007, 508]. There, on November 30 and December 6, he recorded two concerts with the RAI orchestra, and then stayed in the city for the whole of December to conduct six concerts at La Scala, which featured two works by Stravinsky: *Oedipus Rex* (directed by Giorgio De Lullo, with costumes by Pier Luigi Pizzi) and *Le Sacre du Printemps* (choreography by John Taras and costumes by Marino Marini). And between one show and the next he even found the time and energy to go to Turin, where, on December 22, he conducted Mahler's Ninth Symphony.

The last months of 1972 – maybe the most intense year of his life – also witnessed the events involved in the preparation, broadcasting and subsequent performances of *Ages*, his last work for radio. We know that in September the work won the Twenty-Fourth *Premio Italia*, and had therefore been conceived, written and recorded prior to that date (and in fact the tape had been recorded in Milan in May 1972). We also know that while he was still in the USA, Maderna had received an invitation from the RAI in Rome to attend the first broadcast of the work, but had been unable to accept it on account of the excessive number of commitments in that period.

The narrative framework of *Ages* derives from Shakespeare's *As you like it*. Following a practice dating back to Maderna's earliest electronic works, this work too represents a sort of deposit of sound materials combining elements already used in previous pieces and others that could possibly be included in later works: there are fragments with female voices already heard in *Ausstrahlung* and particular effects present in *Invenzione su una voce*, while part of a tape prepared for *Ages* supplies the background of female sighs in a scene of *Satyricon*. The official title of the work is *Ages. Invenzione radiofonica di Giorgio Pressburger e Bruno Maderna*. It seems only right, then, that we should leave the word to Pressburger, a well-established stage director of Hungarian origin, who gives his own account of how the work was born:

One gray afternoon in 1945 in Budapest, […] an autumnal afternoon, I remember it well, an actor came into the courtyard of the house where we lived, an old actor who had no work because the theaters were not working, and he was dressed in rags […] I can still clearly see this image, which has never left me, and he began to recite "*All the world's a stage*, and all the men and women merely players," the lines spoken by Jaques in Shakespeare's *As you like it*, which tell of the seven ages of man […] as only Shakespeare knew how to, that is in a light-hearted but moving way. And this actor, so disheveled and tattered, concluded with these words : "sans teeth, sans eyes, sans taste, sans everything," almost in tears. […] I tried on various occasions to repeat these lines to the audience with all the same dramatic and grotesque impact but was unable to find a way […] At a certain point the idea came to me of composing for the radio […] and so I proposed this work for the Premio Italia […] I tried to think of who might be able to do this musical composition […] and someone mentioned the name of Bruno Maderna, who I didn't know personally. So I made a call to Germany, to Darmstadt, where he lived, and I heard, behind that odd voice that Bruno had due to the effect of 100 Gauloises a day, a person who was incredibly jovial, open, genial […] Afterwards, when I met him in person […] I grew very fond of him and I felt a sincere, great human respect for him because he had an incredible moral and intellectual integrity that is very hard to find, especially among artists, writers and intellectuals, where it is much easier to find facades and mannerisms. He had none of this, and so he was a great lesson of life for me.[22]

The tape editing and the electronic processing was made (almost always at night, as Pressburger recalls) at the *Studio di Fonologia della RAI* in Milan with the assistance of Marino Zuccheri, while the live music was recorded with the RAI Symphony Orchestra and Choir in Milan, naturally conducted by the composer. The verbal text of *Ages* is, as we have said, taken entirely from Jaques' monologue in *As you like it* (Act II, Scene VII), and is an ironic and cruel description of the destinies of man: the world is a theater and human life is divided into seven scenes, passing from helpless infancy to decrepit old age. The tape starts with a broad introduction of around 5 minutes which presents an evocative synthesis of the main sound materials of the work.[23] We then hear various parts loosely based

---

[22] G. Pressburger, "La mia collaborazione con Maderna," ed. N. Verzina, in *Pour Bruno* 2015, 165-167.

[23] The times indicated here refer to an authorized version of the piece that can be found at the following link:
https://www.youtube.com/watc h?v=ImQn9CXngI

on Shakespeare's text, without strictly following the order of the seven scenes. The first part is a sort of ode to infancy, in which children's voices recite words taken from the English text, embedded in hasty flurries of punctiform sounds, both instrumental and electronic. Each short phrase of the text was written on a piece of paper and each child had to choose, at random, a certain number of pieces and read them in front of the tape recorder. The editing process then superimposed the voices, incorporating echoes and reverberations, so that only minimal fragments of Shakespeare's lines can be recognized. In the second part, which starts at 11 minutes 50 seconds, a female voice enters, who proceeds to read the whole text in rich tones, building a lengthy and amiable duet with the elegant melodies of the two wind instruments: "At first the infant [...] And then the whining school boy [...] And then the lover [...] Then a soldier [...] And then the justice [...] The sixth age shifts into the lean and slipper'd pantaloon [...] The last scene of all [...] is second childishness and mere oblivion, sans teeth, sans eyes, sans taste, sans everything." In the third part, which starts at 17 minutes 15 seconds, we hear the overlapping voices of actors, mature men, who read intelligible fragments of the text, key-fragments of each of the seven stages of man. At 23 minutes 20 seconds, some of the voices start to dialogue with the instruments of the orchestra and shortly afterwards with a choir, which quietly in the background, almost like a prayer, sings its comment to the "strange eventful history" of human lives. In the conclusion, particular importance is given to the final line: "sans teeth, sans eyes, sans taste, sans everything."

After the flurry of events in the previous year, there seems to be no sign of any slackening in his pace at the start of 1973. On January 12 Maderna conducted for the first time Mahler's monumental Third Symphony at the Milan Conservatory, with the orchestra and choir of the RAI, and immediately afterwards he was back at La Scala for five performances of the ballets by Stravinsky, with the choreography of Béjart, that he had already conducted just over a year before. In February the details of his work become more vague. He was definitely back at the Conservatory in Milan on February 23, where he conducted Mahler's Fifth Symphony and arias by Mozart sung by his friend Paul Sperry, but according to his *Diary* and *Notebook* he should have given another concert in Milan on February 9, which was instead cancelled. The same sources reveal that he was supposed to start rehearsals for his new chamber opera *Satyricon* in the Netherlands on February 23, but this seems highly unlikely.

The new opera debuted in Scheveningen on March 16 and the rehearsals, according to a more credible entry in both the *Diary* and *Notebook*, took place between February 26 and March 15. The same sources tell us that after its premiere (and until March 29) he was due to take the opera to various other cities in the Netherlands, but in reality these performances were conducted by Lucas Vis, who substituted him at the last moment, as confirmed by the conductor's own account [*Pour Bruno* 2015, 227]. The reasons for the substitution become clear on reading Strasfogel's letter to Maderna, informing him of the great success of *Satyricon*, right up to the very last performance. The letter, dated March 26, was addressed to the Städtische Klinik in Darmstadt. And according to the harpsichordist René van Arenbergh, Maderna was not even able to conduct the work in Brussels on April 7, when he was again replaced by Lucas Vis [both letters in *Centro Studi Maderna*, Section L 3]. Maderna conducted the opera just one more time, in an "oratorial" version recorded in March by the Dutch radio, which also interviewed him in the same days [*Documenti* 1985, 111-114].

Satyricon is his last work for theater, and his penultimate work of all. We have already mentioned how the idea of setting Petronius' novel to music came from Ian Strasfogel, who in 1971 had worked with Maderna in the theater section of the composition course in Tanglewood. On that occasion Maderna had, in fact, helped his students to write some melodies that could be aligned with some of the characters of the novel, and it is not hard to imagine that the lightness and spontaneity of the singing, totally unlike anything he had written before, were the outcome of this collaboration between the group of young composers and a teacher who was always open to welcoming and guiding the initiatives of his pupils. Now the Holland Festival gave Maderna the opportunity to bring the idea to a conclusion by composing an opera true and proper. Both initiatives had been largely influenced by the international fame of Fellini's homonymous film, which, among other things, corresponded with the ideology of sexual liberation widespread at the time among the younger generations in the USA and Europe.

Commenting on the wide success of *Satyricon*, Susanna Pasticci speaks of a sort of "Petronius Revival" that broke out after the events of 1968 and suggests that this aspect may have heightened the interest in Fellini's project: the Italian director announced he was making the film in spring '68, and the more it progressed, the more attention it drew from the press, with "articles about its making, interviews [...] cultural debates," and even after the release of the film, despite its not entirely brilliant success, the initiatives persisted.[24] In an interview with the Dutch national radio made in March 1973, immediately after the premiere of the opera, Maderna stresses how his approach differed from

---

[24] See S. Pasticci, "La presenza del *Satyricon* sulla scena culturale degli anni Settanta, da Maderna a Pasolini," *Musica/ Realtà*, no. 91 (2010), 112. The article also points out how, especially in Italy, this interest immediately led to the production of various popular and comedy films, starring actors like Tognazzi, Franchi and Ingrassia, while numerous publications were made on the subject and new editions of the novel appeared; but she adds that eminent intellectuals, like Sanguineti and Pasolini, were similarly prompted to produce literary works and in-depth discussions on the subject.

that of Fellini's film [*Documenti* 1985, 111-112]: the film revisited the ancient images of Petronius in a manner that commentators defined "oneiric," a view broadly shared by Maderna ("an imaginative, almost legendary portrayal of decadent Rome"), whereas his own intentions were more realistic ("I believe it would be hard to find an image so close to our reality, as the one offered by Petronius"). And we should not overlook the fact that in the same interview Maderna defined his work as "political." But to have a clearer idea of what sort of communication (also "political") the work aims to establish with its audience, we first need to speak of the plot.

In truth, it is not really correct to use to word "plot" to describe the narrative contents of the opera, as it is not "linear" and has no beginning and no end. It is probably more useful to describe the contents of the fifteen or so "episodes" that make up the work, each of which Maderna gave a title in the score. Below we have listed some of them, following the order that Maderna gave in a typewritten note dated September 3, 1973, that is six months after its premiere.[25] It should be remembered that the score, published posthumously by Salabert, was made up of separate parts whose sequence was left up to the performers; in the "oratorial" version recorded for the radio Maderna chose a different order, while the sequence proposed, in the same year, by Lucas Vis in the version of the work recorded for Dutch television was different again.[26] Here, then, are the episodes:

Love's Ecstasy: (Criside I & II) the only words pronounced are those of the title: the character Criside sings them twice with vague bewitching melodies accompanied by a solo wind instrument;

Fortunata: she starts by declaring, in jazz-like tones, that she has "Trimalcione" in her hands, then concludes by listing, in an unrelenting rhythm, all the possessions her husband has at home: you can even find hen's milk;

Trimalchio e le flatulenze: the master has some digestive problems: he complains of them in an operetta-like motive, which then expands into broader phrases with frequent comments on the trumpet and other winds;

La matrona di Efeso: Habinnas tells the story (sometimes singing, more often speaking) of an inconsolable widow who has followed her husband into his tomb and for days has refused to eat or drink. In the meantime three thieves

---

[25] The typewritten document is preserved at the *Centro Studi Maderna* and has been attached to the score. Some of our observations about this work derive from Raymond Fearn's monography *Bruno Maderna* (Chur, Switzerland: Harwood Academic Publishers, 1990), which devotes over sixty pages to *Satyricon*, with comments on the style that have provided the basis for many subsequent publications.

[26] In her previously mentioned article (see note 24) Pasticci defines the form it assumed on that occasion as "radical extremism."

have been crucified near the tomb and a soldier has been charged with watching over their corpses. The young man hears the laments, sees the beautiful widow in tears and persuades her to eat some of his ration, and then also manages to persuade her to take comfort in him during the following nights. But without the night-watch, one of the corpses is stolen. The soldier decides to kill himself to avoid the terrible punishments that await him, but the widow resolves the problem: it is better to hang her dead husband on a cross than lose a living lover;

Carriera di Trimalchio: is a sort of atonal recitative closer to speech than singing. His tale begins from when he was a young slave whose owner was so fond of him that he left him all his fortune. The episode ends with a triumphant crescendo dominated by the word "millions," repeated excessively in various languages, with the number of millions getting higher and higher;

Fortunata e Eumolpus: Trimalchio's wife tries in vain to seduce the philosopher Eumolpus, with a passionate tango sung in French, while Eumolpus replies with quotations in Latin;

Eumolpus fuga: a piece performed very seriously by the Philosopher in an academic style on a complex fugue theme, obviously in Latin, which also receives a rigorous tonal answer from the bassoon;

Trimalchio e il monumento: a solemn, affected and confidential speech in which the protagonist tells his story while constantly changing the expressive tone of his voice; and the changes are matched by vocal and instrumental melodies with mischievous quotations from Puccini's *La Bohème*, Wagner's Tetralogy, and Gluck's *Orfeo*.

Within these episodes Maderna uses five electronic tapes, in which pure electronic sound is often replaced by "natural" sounds like the voices of animals or humans, and sounds of everyday life [*Documenti* 1985, 317]. In the previously mentioned interview [*Documenti* 1985, 112] he states that he "tried to render in music what today is implied in pop-art," and this somewhat enigmatic declaration caught the interest of Geneviève Mathon, who thought about this statement and tried to explain it. He suggests that also in that particular genre of figurative art, the word collage, the putting together of things, has the sense of accumulation, but not of a unified whole, and it is quite sure that Maderna, too, in composing his *Satyricon*, had in mind a process of accumulation.[27] We fully agree with Mathon on this point: in his work, Maderna sets himself the task "of taking into account the world in which we live," he invents a form with mobile elements that intermingle with one another without ever reaching a systematic solution, and does so not simply for reasons of structure, but because this is how the world is today. Not everyone, of course, agrees with the "pop"

---

[27] G. Mathon, "À propos du *Satyricon*," in *Basalte* 1, 2007, 82.

interpretation of the "political" function of *Satyricon*. Pasticci, for example, is more inclined towards a Brechtian influence.[28] But here we prefer to stop our analysis and content ourselves with having pointed out certain problems that need to be further investigated in future studies.

After the cancellations of the performances of *Satyricon* scheduled for March, in April too Maderna was forced to renounce other previously planned appointments that had been duly noted in the *Diary*. The first of these was supposed to take place in La Rochelle, near Paris, from April 12 to 15, with rehearsals in the first part of the month; two more engagements were similarly cancelled, one at the RAI in Milan and another in Orléans. It was not until May 6 that he was he able to respect an appointment in Saarbrücken, where he rehearsed and conducted a program entirely devoted to Schumann. From mid-May, his work as a conductor appears to have returned to schedule. On May 15 he was in Hamburg for a performance of *Aura*, and on June 1 and 16 he conducted two concerts, respectively in Milan and Amsterdam, with programs mainly featuring contemporary music. Then, on July 6 he was back in Amsterdam where, alongside works by Bussotti, Boulez and Zimmermann, he conducted the premiere of his *Concerto per oboe n. 3*, with Han de Vries as soloist.

In an interview with Valerio Tura [*Pour Bruno* 2015, 191], Han de Vries recalls that it was Jo Elsendorn, director of the Holland Festival, who suggested to Maderna that he should write another concerto for his instrument. The work was commissioned by the same festival that had staged *Satyricon* in March, highlighting just how important the Dutch music scene was for Maderna until his very last months of life. At the bottom of the score he added the date of its composition, the last he would ever write: all the facts point to the assumption that the work was born precisely in that year. The premiere was an immediate success.[29] A few days before, the Dutch broadcasting company, the NOS, had filmed a rehearsal performance with Maderna and de Vries, which is also the last visual image of Bruno as a conductor. The oboist recalls, in another interview, how each time he visited Darmstadt before this performance, he was happy to come away with a page of the concerto so he could study it.[30]

The *Concerto per oboe n. 3* is not just Maderna's last testimony as a composer, it also represents a sort of unique synthesis of what his musical fantasy had led him

---

[28] This aspect was already mentioned in note 25 of Chapter IV.

[29] William Mann, in an article published in *The Times* on July 13, asserted that Maderna's composition was by far the most exciting of the five pieces featured in the concert, which concluded a "glorious" cycle for the Holland Festival, but one that was now no longer economically sustainable. The other compositions were by Boulez, Bussotti, Zimmermann and De Leeuw. A copy of Mann's article can be found at the *Centro Studi Maderna*, Section D 3.3

[30] Interview with Han de Vries by Kasper Jansen [*Centro Studi Maderna*, Section D 3.3].

to create over the last two decades. In the 1950s he had focused on elaborations and modifications of the numerical-serial technique; his attention had then turned to experimenting with the countless ways in which controlled aleatory can raise the player to the rank of collaborator in the composition; and after this, two other elements gradually found their way into his writing: the micro experimentation with subtle blends and doses of timbre and sound, and the exploitation of expressive aspects in the phase when the score is transformed into sounds and catches the attention of the audience. The most surprising feature of the new concerto is that it manages to concentrate all these aspects and find a miraculous balance that is hard to identify in any previous single work. Just one page will suffice to illustrate what this means. The opening consists of a single note, an E that arises from the silence and lasts for an unspecified length of time.[31] The instrumentation is typical of the peculiar timbral invention that Maderna often searched for: it consists of four groups that play the same note either *piano* or *pianissimo*, constantly modulating it with small crescendos or diminuendos that make it mobile. The groups are made up of four piccolos, four muted trumpets, four mallet instruments (xylophone, vibraphone, etc.) and a small number of strings (not more than eight) that play the note with the delicate sound of a harmonic. Which of these should play and when? This Maderna does not say, he leaves it to the random choice of the conductor. Neither does he specify which other instrumental parts should appear around this E: something must happen, but he again leaves it to the conductor. In his own performance of the concerto Maderna chooses to let the soloist enter even before the fateful E emerges; and the soloist does not enter with the first notes of its "solo" but with fragments chosen at will, even from the last page of the score, provided they can be played sweetly, in other words compatibly with the mysterious note arising from the silence. The performer can therefore "interpret" the score, not only playing the written notes, but also exploiting the freedom of behavior it allows, as long as the expressive intention is respected.

After this evocative opening, the piece continues with non-tonal procedures deriving from its serial set, and includes episodes where the sweet cantabile of the oboe predominates, or where denser and more gloomy knots of sound assert themselves, or on the contrary thinner and lighter textures – and this is also true in interpretations that differ considerably due to the choices afforded by the aleatory freedom.[32] In particular, Sanzogno's performance is more vital,

---

[31] The performers make it last a considerable length of time in all three recordings considered here, namely: the premiere in Amsterdam conducted by the composer, with the oboist De Vries, a performance given in 1974 in Milan by his friends Nino Sanzogno and Lothar Faber, and another later performance conducted by Gary Bertini, with the oboist Heinz Holliger. The first two recordings are preserved at the *Centro Studi Maderna*, the third can be viewed on YouTube.

[32] For example, that of Bertini-Holliger lasts almost twice as long as that of Sanzogno-Faber.

with more evident contrasts, while Maderna's is more homogeneous and has an intensely contemplative character, but the general sense of the work remains substantially the same.

There is also another aspect that distinguishes this *Concerto* from all his previous ones, a feature opportunely pointed out by Laura Cosso. While in the other concertos the orchestra had the role of frequently interrupting the exhibitions of the soloist, and often did so in a knowingly brutal manner, in this last work this practice has vanished, and "the lyrical voice of the oboe [...] seems to flow free from any obstacle or latent threat."[33] And if we combine the listening with the wonderful images of the video made by the Dutch television during the rehearsals, one might almost say that Maderna feels his performance to be a sort of farewell to life, without nostalgia, but with an incredible aura of serenity.

Following the premiere of the *Concerto per oboe* we read in the *Diary* that on July 18 the rehearsals began for the Salzburg Festival, during which, on July 29, he conducted works by Messiaen, Stravinsky, Boulez and Lutosławski. The next entry in the *Diary* does not refer to any concert engagements, but to an appointment from August 1 to 20 in "Ueber ...mit Carolina und Silvio," where the first word probably stands for Überlingen, the health resort on Lake Constance where he had stayed in the summer of 1970, and similarly after the courses at the Mozarteum in Salzburg; the name Silvio most likely refers to Sylvio Samama, whereas the other person mentioned remains unidentified. Following this break we find him at the Royal Albert Hall in London where, on August 31, he conducted Mahler's Ninth Symphony and Schumann's Violin Concerto, with Christiane Edinger as soloist. According to Lucas Vis, his performance of Mahler was so extraordinarily careful and evocative that one could almost suppose he was identifying himself in this last work of the great Viennese composer and conductor.[34] His final two appointments are a month apart: on October 3 and 5 at the RAI in Milan to record works by Mozart, Mendelssohn and Bartók, and on November 5 back at the Royal Festival Hall in London to conduct Bartók and Schönberg, with Alfred Brendel as soloist. Nobody could have imagined that this would be the last concert of his life, which came to an end just eight days later, on the 13th of that month.

Over the following days all the leading Italian and foreign newspapers carried long articles announcing the news of Maderna's death and commemorating his figure, whose fame must clearly have been exceptional in those years. The archives of the *Centro Studi Maderna* in Bologna holds a particularly large number of detailed articles in Italian, Dutch and German, but

---

[33] L. Cosso, "La forma concerto in 'Aulodia' di Bruno Maderna," *Nuova Rivista Musicale Italiana*, 25/3-4 (1991), 437, 439.

[34] Interview with Lucas Vis by Kasper Jansen [*Centro Studi Maderna*, Section D 3.3].

there are also some in French, English (the news appeared immediately in the *New York Times*) and Polish [Section D 19.1]. Some of them give particulars of his eventful life and his character, by and large mostly accurate, but in certain cases somewhat fanciful, seeing that some episodes of his life had readily lent themselves to journalistic scoops, to which Maderna himself remained calmly indifferent. In the majority of cases he was depicted as an extremely vivacious and generous man, and his figure as a conductor was compared to that of the most outstanding living conductors, though differing on account of his lack of any airs or affectation. The passion with which he conducted had the purpose of highlighting the qualities of the music he loved, rather than displaying his personal qualities as a conductor.

Although in writing their routine and "perfunctory" obituaries journalists are obliged to celebrate the deceased in a positive light, in this case it should be said that the musicological level of the best Italian music critics of those years turned out to be excellent. Those who had followed the vicissitudes of the avant-gardes of the post-war years with interest and passion, and had publicly expressed their enthusiasms, but also their reserves, continued to do so with dignity also on this occasion. Eminent figures such as Fedele d'Amico, Massimo Mila, Rubens Tedeschi, Mario Messinis and Duilio Courir, drew an accurate picture (as we can confirm today at a distance of almost fifty years) of the aesthetic trends fervently pursued at the time, and also well known to the public at large. We might say that in those years the destiny of new music lay not only in the hands of those who made it, but was also shared by those who listened to, commented on and wrote about it.

To conclude our book we have chosen to quote the words of Pierre Boulez, who knew how to comment on music as well as how to make it. On this occasion he seems to have miraculously cast aside all convention and has been able to translate the images that had settled in his mind over the twenty years of experience shared with Maderna, into a vivid description of Bruno's character in an extraordinarily sincere and elegant manner:

Our careers ran parallel. We debuted in Germany, we went to Great Britain one after the other and we met up again in the United States. In 1958 we conducted the first performance of Stockhausen's Gruppen *together. Later we took turns on the podium of the* Residentie *orchestra of The Hague.*

In the heroic era in which Wolfgang Steinecke had founded the Darmstadt ensemble, it was we who shared the task of conducting the countless premieres that had to be presented throughout the summer. The rehearsal schedule was a nightmare. For his part, Bruno was not too concerned. He even took the liberty of arriving late sometimes. He took life as it came and always coped.

In reality, to get a quite faithful idea of the man, we cannot separate the conductor from the composer, as Maderna was a pragmatic man, equally close to the music when he performed it and when he composed. I first met him in Darmstadt when he was rehearsing a piece that needed a percussionist, but there wasn't one. So he sat at the tom-toms and bongos himself and effortlessly played and conducted at the same time. He was like a monkey that could nimbly jump from one musical tree to the other with incredible ease.

This direct and profound contact with the substance of music impregnated all his interpretations. Physically Bruno looked like a small pachyderm but, paradoxically, this good-natured mass seemed to exude an extraordinary lightness. He was all intelligence, finesse, humor and fantasy. The pachyderm was an elf.

His meeting with Scherchen was certainly decisive. He always had a boundless admiration for the elderly maestro who had trained him. But this didn't stop him from telling us, for nights on end, all sorts of affectionately disrespectful anecdotes. For example, the time when they were bathing in the Adriatic at the Venice Lido: the two mammoths blew like two whales, because while they were swimming they started discussing the right way to conduct the "Eroica symphony" and the maestro taught his pupil some surprising but infallible mnemotechnical methods, such as mentally placing the words "Das ist Napoleon" against the theme and variations!

Maderna was a man who knew about rigor, but never decided to apply it to himself simply because he didn't like it. One day, while conducting a new work that had very precise metronome markings and tempo changes like: "from eighth-note at 118 to eighth-note at 80.5" he turned to the composer and to me who were in the hall and exclaimed "eighth-note at 80.5? Are we kidding?".

He did have rigor inside him, but not the rigor of numbers, but rather the certainty that his character could only express itself beyond the bounds of strict obedience. This immediate, irrational sense of musicality is also what gave the composer his best moments, his best discoveries. And so his most successful works are those that leave the player the greatest possibility of initiative. At the end of his last score, a concerto for oboe and orchestra, he wrote:"I hope I have provided material that will allow the soloist, conductor and players to reach some sort of agreement and enjoy playing what I have written." In a certain way, then, he freed himself of the music he carried inside him, and in which he had absolute trust.

While he was composing his Satyricon *on commission from the Dutch* Opéra, *a work that – one might say – combines new music with the best of tradition, he learned of his illness and his closeness to death. This stroke of fate, in that given moment, concorded with the contrasts of his existence. Personally, I prefer that he died swiftly: there is nothing more pitiful than the decline of a being full of life.*[35]

---

[35] From Maurice Fleuret, "Salut à Bruno Maderna par Pierre Boulez," *Nouvel Observateur* (November 26, 1973).

BIBLIOGRAPHY

Abbado, Michelangelo. "Antonio Vivaldi nel nostro secolo con particolare riferimento alle sue opere strumentali." *Nuova Rivista Musicale Italiana* 13/1 (1979): 79-112.

Addessi, Anna Rita, Ignazio Macchiarella, Massimo Privitera and Marco Russo, eds. *Con-Scientia Musica. Contrappunti per Rossana Dalmonte e Mario Baroni.* Lucca: LIM, 2010.

Adlington, Robert. *Composing Dissent: Avant-garde Music in 1960s Amsterdam.* New York: Oxford University Press, 2013.

Adorno, Theodor Wiesengrund. "Das Altern der neuen Musik." Italian translation in *Dissonanze*, 155-186. Milano: Feltrinelli, 1974.

Adorno, Theodor Wiesengrund. *Filosofia della musica moderna.* Torino: Einaudi, 1960.

Adorno, Theodor Wiesengrund. *Dissonanze.* Milano: Feltrinelli, 1974.

Anastasia, Adriana. *'Ritratto di Erasmo': Un'opera radiofonica di Bruno Maderna.* Trento: Università di Trento, 2009.

Auden, Wysthan. *Poesie.* Parma: Guanda, 1952.

Baroni, Mario. "L'archetipo dell'aulos. Echi e reminiscenze melodiche." In Baroni, Dalmonte 1989, 227-240.

_____. "The macroform in post-tonal music: Listening and analysis." *Musicae Scientiae* 7/2 (2003): 219-240.

Baroni, Mario and Rossana Dalmonte, eds. *Bruno Maderna Documenti (raccolti e illustrati da).* Milano: Suvini Zerboni, 1985.

_____. *Studi su Bruno Maderna.* Milano: Suvini Zerboni, 1989.

Bayle, François, ed. *Pierre Schaeffer, l'oeuvre musicale: Textes et documents.* Paris: INA-GRM, 1990.

Bellon, Stefano. "Il *Concerto per due pianoforti e strumenti* di Bruno Maderna verso Darmstadt: un'analisi della partitura." In Cattelan 2000, 335-354.

_____. "Maderna, entre improvisation et jazz." In Mathon, Feneyrou, Ferrari, 522-533.

Berio, Luciano. "Un inedito di Bruno Maderna." *Nuova Rivista Musicale Italiana* 12/4 (1978): 517.

Berio, Luciano. "Luciano Berio e Bruno Maderna, *Divertimento per orchestra (1957)*." *Dialogo con Maderna. 18 concerti. Milano 30 settembre-20 dicembre 1989*, 210. Milano: RAI Lombardia, 1989.

_____. "Poesia e musica – un'esperienza." *Incontri Musicali* 3 (1959): 98-111.

Böhlen, Manfred Johann. "Nell'incantesimo del numero: Il *Flötenkonzert* di Maderna." In Baroni, Dalmonte 1989, 33-51.

Bonomo, Gabriele and Fabio Zannoni, eds. *Maderna e l'Italia musicale degli anni '40*. Milano: Suvini Zerboni, 2012.

Borio, Gianmario. "La tecnica seriale in *Studi per "Il Processo" di Franz Kafka* di Bruno Maderna." *Musica/Realtà* 32 (1990): 27-40.

_____. "Influenza di Dallapiccola sui compositori italiani del secondo dopoguerra." In De Sanctis 1997, 357-387.

_____. "Sull'interazione fra lo studio degli schizzi e l'analisi dell'opera." In Borio, Morelli, Rizzardi 1999, 1-21.

_____. *La scrittura come rappresentazione del pensiero musicale*. Pisa: ETS, 2004.

Borio, Gianmario and Veniero Rizzardi. "Die musikalische Einheit von Bruno Madernas *Hyperion*." In Meyer 1993, 117-148.

Borio, Gianmario and Hermann Danuser. *Im Zenit der Moderne. Die Internationalen Ferienkurse für Neue Musik Darmstadt 1946-1966*, 4 vols. Freiburg im Breisgau: Rombach, 1997.

Borio, Gianmario, Giovanni Morelli and Veniero Rizzardi, eds. *La nuova ricerca sull'opera di Luigi Nono*. Firenze: Olschki, 1999.

_____. *Le musiche degli anni Cinquanta*. Firenze: Olschki, 2004.

Borio, Gianmario and Carlo Gentili, eds. *Storia dei concetti musicali. Espressione Forma Opera*. Roma: Carocci, 2007.

Bortolotto, Mario. *Fase seconda. Studi sulla Nuova Musica*. Torino: Einaudi, 1969.

Bossa Renato, ed. *'Appunti di viaggio': Novant'anni della Associazione Alessandro Scarlatti*. Napoli: Grimaldi 2009.

Bossini, Oreste, ed. *Milano laboratorio musicale del Novecento. Scritti per Luciana Pestalozza*. Milano: Archinto, 2009.

Boulez, Pierre. *Note di apprendistato*, translated by L. Bonino Savarino. Torino: Einaudi, 1968.

_____. *Stocktakings from an Apprenticeship*, translated by Stephen Walsh. Oxford: Oxford University Press, 1991.

Bressan, Federica, Sergio Canazza and Giovanni De Poli. "Restauro e falsificazione: potenzialità e rischi delle pratiche di restauro sonoro." In Dalmonte, Baroni 2015, 129-150.

Bruni, Edoardo. Introduction to Bruno Maderna, *Composizione in tre tempi per orchestra (1954)*, critical edition. Milano: Suvini Zerboni, 2008, V-XXXIII.

Cage, John. *Silence*. Middletown, CT: Wesleyan University Press, 1961.

Canetti, Elias. *Il gioco degli occhi. Storia di una vita (1931-1937)*. Milano: Adelphi, 1985.

Castaldi, Paolo. "Darmstadt 1960." *Il Verri*, no. 5, (1961): 129-135.

Cattelan, Paolo, ed. *Malipiero Maderna 1973-1993*. Firenze: Olschki, 2000.

Cattelan, Paolo and Rossana Dalmonte. Introduction to Bruno Maderna, *Concerto per pianoforte e strumenti (1948-1949)*, critical edition. Milano: Suvini Zerboni, 2006, I-XXX.

Cattin, Giulio and Patrizia Dalla Vecchia. *Venezia 1501: Petrucci e la stampa musicale*, Atti del Convegno. Venezia: Edizioni Fondazione Levi, 2005.

Colombo Taccani, Giorgio. "Aria: una proposta di analisi." In Baroni, Dalmonte 1989, 156-175.

Conti, Luca. "Le *Tre Liriche greche* di Maderna e la prima dodecafonia italiana." In Dalmonte, Russo 2004, 275-286.

Cossettini, Luca and Angelo Orcalli. *L'invenzione della fonologia musicale: Saggi sulla musica elettronica sperimentale di Luciano Berio e Bruno Maderna*. Lucca: LIM, 2015.

Cosso Laura. "La forma concerto in 'Aulodia' di Bruno Maderna." *Nuova Rivista Musicale Italiana* 25/3-4 (1991): 427-440.

Dalmonte, Rossana. "Scelte poetiche e letterarie." In Baroni, Dalmonte 1989, 13-32.

Dalmonte, Rossana. Introduction to *Luciano Berio, Ecce, Musica per musicologi*. In Pompilio, Restani, Bianconi, Gallo 1990, 739.

―――. "Tracce di Malipiero e Maderna nei registri e negli schedari della Marciana." In Cattelan 2000, 197-205.

―――. Ed. *Bruno Maderna - Wolfgang Steinecke Carteggio Briefwechsel*. Lucca: LIM, 2001.

―――. "Letture maderniane de "Il Processo" di Franz Kafka." In Dalmonte, Russo 2004, 9-40.

———. "Introduction to Bruno Maderna." In *Studi per "Il Processo" di F. Kafka* (1959), critical edition, I-XLI. Milano: Suvini Zerboni, 2010.

———. "Prima della serie: Orientamenti stilistici di Maderna negli Anni Quaranta, Le opere con testo poetico." In Bonomo, Zannoni 2012, 129-139.

Dalmonte, Rossana and Marco Russo, eds. *Bruno Maderna: Studi e testimonianze*. Lucca: LIM, 2004.

Dalmonte, Rossana and Mario Baroni, eds. *Pour Bruno: Memorie e ricerche su Bruno Maderna*. Lucca: LIM 2015.

De Benedictis, Angela Ida. "Qui forse una cadenza brillante: Viaggio nel 'Venetian Journal' di Bruno Maderna." *Acta Musicologica* 72/1 (2000): 63-105.

———. *Radiodramma ed arte radiofonica: Storia e funzioni della musica per radio in Italia*. Torino: EDT, 2004.

———. "*Ritratto di Erasmo* di Bruno Maderna." *Musica/Realtà*, no. 73 (2004): 153-182.

———. "Scritture e supporti nel Novecento: alcune riflessioni e un esempio (*Ausstrahlung* di Bruno Maderna)." In Borio 2004, 237-291.

———. Introduction to *Bruno Maderna: Composizione n. 1 per orchestra (1948-1949)*, critical edition. Milano: Suvini Zerboni, 2007, I-LXV.

———. "Opera aperta: teoria e prassi." In Borio, Gentili 2007, 317- 334.

———. "*Ausstrahlung* ou la textualité brisée d'un hymne à la vie." In Mathon, Feneyrou, Ferrari 2007, 287-317.

———. "Gli esordi dello Studio di Fonologia Musicale: 'Il risultato di un incontro fra la musica e le possibilità dei nuovi mezzi'." In Novati 2009, 7-24.

———. Introduction to *Bruno Maderna: Concerto per pianoforte ed orchestra (1942)*, critical edition. Milano: Suvini Zerboni, 2011, I-XLVIII.

———. "Materiali parziali o strutture fungibili? Prospettive filologiche su *Honeyrêves, Don Perlimplin* e *Serenata IV* di Bruno Maderna." *Il Saggiatore Musicale* 18/1-2 (2011): 139-172.

———. "Oltre il Primo Congresso di Dodecafonia. Da Locarno a Darmstadt." *Acta Musicologica* 85/2 (2013): 227-243.

De Benedictis, Angela Ida and Veniero Rizzardi, eds. *La nostalgia del futuro: Scritti scelti di Luigi Nono*. Milano: il Saggiatore, 2007.

De Benedictis, Angela Ida and Giordano Ferrari. "Extraits de la correspondance." In Mathon, Feneyrou, Ferrari 2007, 459-517.

De Benedictis, Angela Ida and Scadaferri, Nicola. "Berberian Cathy." *Dizionario biografico degli italiani*, Treccani 2014, s.v.

De Martino, Pier Paolo. "Scarlatti e Rai due istituzioni per un'orchestra." In Bossa 2009, 121-133.

De Sanctis, Mila, ed. *Dallapiccola. Letture e prospettive*, Atti del Convegno. Milano: Ricordi, and Lucca: LIM, 1997, 357-387.

Donati, Pino. "Colloquio con Arrigo Pedrollo." *Il Brennero* (5 giugno 1935).

Eco, Umberto. "Pensée structurale et pensée serielle (1968)." *Musique en jeu*, 5 (1971): 45-56.

Fearn, Raymond."Maderna e l'Inghilterra." In Baroni, Dalmonte 1985, 137-141.

_____. *Bruno Maderna*. Chur, Switzerland: Harwood Academic, 1990.

Fein, Markus. *Die musikalische Poetik Bruno Madernas: Zum "seriellen" Komponieren zwischen 1951 und 1955*. Frankfurt am Main: Lang, 2001.

Feneyrou, Laurent. "*Solo/tutti*. Introduction à cinq concertos de Bruno Maderna." In Mathon, Feneyrou, Ferrari 2009, 179-228.

Ferrari, Giordano. *Les débuts du théâtre musical d'avant-garde en Italie: Berio, Evangelisti, Maderna*. Paris: L'Harmattan, 2000.

_____. "Le théâtre d'aujourd'hui, un théâtre musical toujours en prise sur l'actualité." *Analyse Musicale* 45 (2002): 5-22.

_____. "*Hyperion* les chemins du poète." In Mathon, Feneyrou and Ferrari 2007, 89-121.

Garcia Lorca, Federico. *El Cante Jondo*. Madrid: Ulises, 1931.

Garda, Michela. "Rilevamenti sulla ricezione della musica maderniana." In Baroni, Dalmonte 1989, 74-94.

Gentilucci, Armando. *Oltre l'avanguardia. Un invito al molteplice*. Fiesole: Discanto, 1980.

Gerberding, Elke. "Darmstädter Kulturpolitik der Nachkriegzeit." *1946-1996, Von Kranichstein zur Gegenwart. 50 Jahre Darmstädter Ferienkurse*, 31-33. Stuttgart: DACO, 1996.

Giovannini, Marina. "Il linguaggio armonico del giovane Maderna." In Dalmonte, Russo 2004, 257-274.

Giubertoni, Anna. "Fonti poetiche dell'*Hyperion* di Bruno Maderna." *Nuova Rivista Musicale Italiana* 15/2 (1981): 197-205.

Gorli, Sandro. Introduction to *Don Perlimplin, ossia il trionfo dell'amore e dell'immaginazione (1961)*, critical edition. Milano: Suvini Zerboni, 2002, VII-LI.

Gotti, Titto. "Colloquio con Bruno Maderna." In Dalmonte, Baroni 2015, 153-162.

Heister, Hanns-Werner. "La musica contro le ombre della politica fascista. L'opera e la vita di Karl Amadeus Hartmann." *Musica/Realtà* 7 (1982): 25-44.

Hommel, Friedrich and Schlüter Wilhelm. *New music in Darmstadt 1950-1960*, not commercially available. Darmstadt: Internationales Musikinstitut Darmstadt, November 1987.

Impett, Jonathan. *Routledge Handbook to Luigi Nono and Musical Thought*. New York: Routledge, 2019.

Izzo, Leo. "Il commento sonoro realizzato da Bruno Maderna per il film *Le due verità*." In Dalmonte, Russo 2004, 299-341.

Jameaux, Dominique. *Pierre Boulez*. Paris: Fayard-Sacem, 1984.

Leonardi, David Giovanni. "Il Festival internazionale di musica contemporanea di Venezia (1946-54)." In Salvetti, Antolini 1999, 137-158.

⸻⸻. "Cronologia del Festival internazionale di musica contemporanea di Venezia (1946-54)." In Salvetti, Antolini 1999, 159-174.

Maderna, Bruno. "In memoriam Wolfgang Steinecke." *Melos* 29/2 (1962). Italian translation in Baroni, Dalmonte 1989, 67-68.

⸻⸻. "Esperienze compositive di musica elettronica." In Baroni, Dalmonte 1985, 83-85.

Magnani, Francesca. "L'*Hyperion* di Maderna: quale poeta per quale canto." In Baroni, Dalmonte 1989, 177-194.

⸻⸻. Introduction to *Bruno Maderna, Divertimento in due tempi per flauto e pianoforte (1953)*, critical edition. Milano: Suvini Zerboni, 1996, II-XI.

⸻⸻. "Il canto nell'immaginario teatrale di Malipiero e di Maderna." In Cattelan 2000, 185-195.

Malipiero Gian Francesco. *Vivaldiana*. Milano: Ricordi, 1953.

Malipiero, Riccardo. "La dodecafonia come tecnica." *Rivista Musicale Italiana* 55/3 (1953): 277-300.

Mangini, Giorgio. "Filmographie commentée." In Mathon, Feneyrou, Ferrari 2007, 229-240.

Manzoni, Giacomo. "Bruno Maderna." *Die Reihe* 4 (1958): 113-118.

Materassi, Marco. "Il Civico Liceo Musicale (1927-1967)." In Och 2008, 75-100.

Mathon Geneviève. "À propos du *Satyricon*." In Mathon, Feneyrou, Ferrari 2007, 69-86.

Mathon, Geneviève, Laurent Feneyrou and Giordano Ferrari, eds. *À Bruno Maderna* I. Paris: Basalte, 2007.

_____. *À Bruno Maderna* II. Paris: Basalte, 2009.

Messinis, Mario."Malipiero e Maderna vent'anni dopo (1973 – 1993)." In Cattelan 2000, 3-9.

Meyer, Felix, ed. *Zwölf Komponisten des 20. Jahrhunderts*. Winterthur: Amadeus, 1993.

Meyer, Leonard B. *Style and Music" Theory, History and Ideology*. Chicago: The University of Chicago Press, 1989.

Micelli, Sergio. "La musica nel film e nel teatro di prosa: l'avvento dello specialismo." In Salvetti, Antolini 1999, 283-300.

_____. *Norme con ironie. Scritti per i settant'anni di Ennio Morricone*. Milano: Suvini Zerboni, 1998.

Mila, Massimo. "Disorientamento dell'arte." *Rinascita* no. 6 (dicembre 1948): 500-501.

_____. *Maderna musicista europeo*. Torino: Einaudi, 1976.

Misuraca, Pietro, ed. *Luigi Rognoni intellettuale europeo* II, *Carteggi*, not commercially available. Regione Sicilia, 2010.

Montecchi, Giordano. "Bruno Maderna e la musica leggera." *Musica/Realtà*, no.10 (1983): 51-61.

Montecchi, Giordano. "Il lavoro di precomposizione in Serenata n. 2." In Baroni, Dalmonte 1989, 109-137.

_____. "*Continuo* di Bruno Maderna." *I Quaderni della scuola civica di musica* 21-22 (dicembre 1992): 43-53.

Morricone, Enio. "Un compositore dietro la macchina da presa." In Nattiez 2001, v. 1, 664-674.

Nattiez, Jean-Jacques, ed. *Enciclopedia della Musica*, v. 1-5. Torino: Einaudi, 2001-2005.

———. *Pierre Boulez - John Cage. Correspondance et Documents*. Mainz: Schott, 2002.

NeidhÖfer, Christoph. "Vers un principe commun. Intégration de la hauteur et du rhythme dans le *Quartetto per archi in due tempi* (1955)." In Mathon, Feneyrou, Ferrari 2009, 323-358.

Nicolodi, Fiamma. "La riscoperta di Vivaldi nel Novecento." *Nuova Rivista Musicale Italiana* 13/4 (1979): 820-844.

———. *Musica e musicisti nel ventennio fascista*. Fiesole: Discanto, 1984.

Noller, Joachim. "Dimensioni musicali: Le composizioni di Bruno Maderna nel primo dopoguerra." In Baroni, Dalmonte 1989, 95-108.

———. "Malipiero: una poetica e un'estetica." *Rivista italiana di musicologia* 26/1 (1991): 35-57.

———. "*Musica su due dimensioni*, e l'unidimensionalità della musica nuova." *I Quaderni della Civica Scuola di Musica* 21-22 (1992): 65-69.

Novati, Maria Maddalena. *Lo Studio di fonologia: Un diario musicale 1954-1983*. Milano: Ricordi, 2009.

Och, Laura, ed. *Il Conservatorio di musica "Evaristo Felice dall'Abaco" di Verona. Gli edifici, la storia, il presente*. Verona: Conservatorio E.F. dall'Abaco, 2008.

Och, Laura. "Bruno Maderna a Verona: istituzioni e protagonisti dell'ambiente musicale fra le due guerre." In Bonomo, Zannoni 2012, 29-44.

Palandri, Cecilia, ed. *Gian Francesco Malipiero: Il carteggio con Guido M. Gatti 1914-1972*. Firenze: Olschki, 1997.

Palazzetti, Nicolò. "Italian harmony during the Second World War: Analysis of Bruno Maderna's First String Quartet." *Rivista di Analisi e Teoria Musicale*, 21/1 (2015): 63-91.

Pasini, Roberto. *L'Informale: Stati Uniti, Europa, Italia*. Bologna: CLUEB, 1995.

Pasticci, Susanna. Premessa a: Bruno Maderna, *Fantasia e fuga per due pianoforti (1948)*, critical edition. Milano: Suvini Zerboni, 2000, IV-XV.

———. "'Una musica di facile ascolto': sulla *Composizione n. 2* di Bruno Maderna." In Dalmonte, Russo 2004, 117-147.

———. "Memorie di Petrucci a Venezia, quattro secoli dopo." In Cattin, Dalla Vecchia 2005, 683-737.

———. Introduction to *Bruno Maderna: Composizione n. 2 (1949-1950)*, critical edition. Milano: Suvini Zerboni, 2006, I-XLVIII.

———. "La presenza del *Satyricon* sulla scena culturale degli anni Settanta, da Maderna a Pasolini." *Musica/Realtà* 91 (2010): 77-126.

Pestalozza, Luigi, ed. *La Rassegna musicale. Antologia*. Milano: Feltrinelli, 1966.

———. "Mila, Togliatti, la verità." *Musica/Realtà* 64 (2001): 21-22.

———. "Grande Sinfonia Piccolo Teatro." *Il Giornale della Musica* 237 (maggio 2007): 28.

Piccardi, Carlo. "Tra ragioni umane e ragioni estetiche: i dodecafonici a congresso." In Micelli 1998, 205-269.

Pompilio, Angelo, Donatella Restani, Lorenzo Bianconi and F. Alberto Gallo, eds. *Atti del XIV Congresso della Società Internazionale di Musicologia*, v. I. Torino: EDT, 1990.

Porena, Boris. "I Ferienkurse di Darmstadt." *Ricordiana* (novembre 1957): 514-515.

Pozzi, Egidio. "Aspetti della multidimensionalità formale e della relatività nella musica del Novecento: Il *Quartetto per archi in due tempi* di Bruno Maderna." In Addessi, Macchiarella, Privitera, Russo 2010, 149-193.

Pozzi, Raffaele. "Classicismo Romano. Maderna allievo di Bustini." In Bonomo, Zannoni 2012, 45-82.

Pressburger, Giorgio. "La mia collaborazione con Maderna" edited by N. Verzina. In Dalmonte, Baroni 2015, 163-170.

Puecher, Virginio. "Diario di un'esperienza." *Sipario* 224 (dicembre 1964): 46.

Restagno, Enzo. "L'ultimo Maderna dalla struttura all'evento." In Baroni, Dalmonte 1985, 163-167.

———. Ed. *Nono*. Torino: EDT, 1987.

———. "Un'autobiografia dell'autore raccontata da Enzo Restagno." Restagno 1987, 3-73.

———. Ed. *Berio*. Torino: EDT, 1995.

Rizzardi, Veniero, ed. *L'undicesima musa. Nino Rota e i suoi media*. Roma: CIDIM, 2001.

———. "La 'Nuova scuola veneziana,' 1948-1951." In Borio, Morelli, Rizzardi 2004, 1-59.

———. Introduction to *Bruno Maderna: Requiem per soli, cori e orchestra, 1946*, critical edition. Milano: Suvini Zerboni, 2006, I-XLII.

———. Ed. *Esumazione di un Requiem*. Firenze: Olschki, 2007.

_____. "Quasi perduto, quasi ritrovato. Nota sulla riscoperta del giovanile *Concerto per pianoforte* di Bruno Maderna." *Atti dell'Istituto Veneto di Scienze, Lettere ed Arti* 166 (2007-2008): 62.

_____. *Karlheinz Stockhausen e Luigi Nono. Teoria e invenzione musicale 1952-59.* Accessed 14 November, 2019. web.tiscali.it/ensemble900/Diastema/Rivista/Vecchia%20serie/07/Rizzardi.pdf

Rizzardi, Veniero and Angela Ida De Benedictis, eds. *Esperienze allo Studio di Fonologia musicale della RAI di Milano 1954-1959.* Roma: CIDIM-RAI, 2000.

Rognoni, Luigi. "La musicologia filosofica di Adorno." In Adorno 1960, VII-XVI.

_____. "Memoria di Bruno Maderna negli anni Cinquanta." In Baroni, Dalmonte 1985, 146-151.

Romito, Maurizio. "Il balletto 'Das eiserne Zeitalter'." *Musica/Realtà* 10 (1983): 63-69.

_____. "Lettere e scritti." In Baroni, Dalmonte 1989, 52-73.

_____. "I commenti musicali di Bruno Maderna: Radio, Televisione, Teatro" (part one). *Nuova Rivista Musicale Italiana* 35/2 (2000): 233-247.

_____. "I commenti musicali di Bruno Maderna: Radio, Televisione, Teatro" (part two). *Nuova Rivista Musicale Italiana* 37/1 (2002): 79-98.

_____. "Cronologia delle Registrazioni e dei Concerti: 1935-1973." *Nuova Rivista Musicale Italiana* 38/1 (2003): 89-126.

_____. "Da *Intolleranza 1960* a *Don Giovanni*" (part one). *Musica/Realtà* 117 (2018): 115-148.

_____. "Da *Intolleranza 1960* a *Don Giovanni*" (part two). *Musica/Realtà* 118 (2019): 177-224.

_____. *Bruno Maderna direttore d'orchestra (1932-1973). Cronologia, discografia, testimonianze.* (in press).

Salvetti Guido. "Ideologie politiche e poetiche musicali nel Novecento italiano." *Rivista Italiana di Musicologia* 35/1, (2000): 107-134.

Salvetti, Guido and Bianca Maria Antolini, eds. *Italia millenovecentocinquanta.* Milano: Guerini e Associati, 1999.

Sanguineti, Edoardo. *Giuoco del Satyricon.* Torino: Einaudi, 1970.

Santi, Piero. "Le nuove tecnologie: musica elettronica e radiodrammi." In Baroni, Dalmonte 1985, 156-162.

_____. "L'XI Internationale Ferienkurse für neue Musik di Darmstadt." *Aut aut*, no. 36 (1956): 386.

Scaldaferri, Nicola. "Documenti inediti sullo Studio di Fonologia della RAI di Milano." *Musica/Realtà* 45 (1994): 151-166.

Schaller, Erika. "L'insegnamento di Bruno Maderna attraverso le fonti conservate presso l'Archivio Luigi Nono." In Dalmonte, Russo 2004, 107-116.

Scherchen, Hermann. "Die Kunst des Dirigierens" in *Werke und Briefe* I., 225-230. Bern: Peter Lang, 1991.

Schillinger, Joseph. *The Mathematical Basis of the Arts.* New York: Philosophical Library, 1948.

Schlüter, Wilhelm. *Bruno Madernas Biographie* (unpublished typescript).

Scimonello, Giovanni. *Hölderlin e l'utopia.* Napoli: Istituto Universitario Orientale, 1976.

Sermonti, Vittorio. *Ho bevuto e visto il ragno: Cento pezzi facili.* Milano: Il Saggiatore, 1999.

Silbermann, Alphons. *La musique, la Radio, l'Auditeur: étude sociologique.* Paris: Presses Universitaires de France, 1954.

Sità, Maria Grazia. "I Festival." In Salvetti, Antolini 1999, 117-136.

Shenton, Andrew. *Olivier Messiaen's system of signs: Notes towards understanding his music.* Aldershot: Ashgate, 2008.

Solbiati, Alessandro. "*Biogramma*: Projet et modalité de réalisation d'une Weltanschauung." In Mathon, Feneyrou, Ferrari 2009, 123-142.

Taruskin, Richard. *Text and Act: Essays on Music and Performance.* New York: Oxford University Press, 1995.

Togliatti, Palmiro [Roderigo di Castiglia]. "Orientamenti dell'arte."*Rinascita* (novembre 6, 1948): 453-454.

Trudu, Antonio.*La "Scuola" di Darmstadt: I Ferienkurse dal 1946 a oggi.* Milano: Ricordi-Unicopli, 1992.

Tura, Valerio. "'Mon vieux', un ritratto a più voci." In Dalmonte, Baroni 2015, 171-234.

Verzina, Nicola. "Procedimenti di costruzione ed elaborazione del materiale in *Improvvisazione n. 2* (1953) di Bruno Maderna" in *Mitteilungen der Paul Sacher Stiftung* 9 (März 1996): 50-55.

_____. "Improvvisazione n. 2 (1953) de B. Maderna. Technique sérielle dans les esquisses. Génétique intervallaire et élaboration du matérieau." *Les Cahiers du CIREM . Centre International de Recherches en Esthétique Musicale* 40-41 (1997): 156-161.

_____. "Mutazioni storiche intorno a tre testi inediti di Bruno Maderna." *Studi musicali* 28/2 (1999): 495-527.

_____. "Tecnica della mutazione e tecnica seriale in *Vier Briefe* (1953) di Bruno Maderna." *Rivista Italiana di Musicologia* 34/2 (1999): 309-345.

_____. *Bruno Maderna. Étude historique et critique.* Paris: L'Harmattan, 2003.

_____. Introduction to *Bruno Maderna: Kranichsteiner Kammerkantate (1953)*, critical edition. Milano: Suvini Zerboni, 2003, V-XXIV.

_____. "Musica e impegno nella *Kranichsteiner Kammerkantate* (1953): il tema della libertà." In Dalmonte, Russo 2004, 199-225.

Vinay, Gianfranco. "Maderna, chef d'orchestre *humaniste*." In Mathon, Feneyrou, Ferrari 2009, 536-553.

Vincis, Claudia. "'Avec l'autorisation du Maître'. Bruno Maderna et la musique ancienne: entre 'reconstruction' et 'recréation'." In Mathon, Feneyrou, Ferrari 2009.

Weber, Horst. "Form und Satztechnik in Bruno Madernas Streichquartett." *Miscellanea del Cinquantenario*, 206-215. Milano: Suvini Zerboni, 1978.

WÖrner, Karl H.. *Stockhausen: Life and Work.* London: Faber and Faber, 1973.

Zuidam, Robert. *Erasmus Lectures on the History and Civilization of the Netherlands and Flanders.* Accessed July 7, 2019.

http://www.robertzuidam.com/essaysErasmusLectures%20II.htm

SOURCES

1946-1996, Von Kranichstein zur Gegenwart: 50 Jahre Darmstädter Ferienkurse. Stuttgart: DACO, 1996.

Dialogo con Maderna: 18 concerti, Milano 30 settembre-20 dicembre 1989. Milano: RAI Lombardia, 1989.

Jahrbuch der Komischen Oper Berlin, 1965/66. Berlin: Henschel Verlag, 1966.

Miscellanea del Cinquantenario. Milano: Suvini Zerboni, 1978.

BIBLIOGRAPHICAL ABBREVIATIONS

Basalte 1, 2007 – *à Bruno Maderna*, vol. 1, eds. G. Mathon, L. Feneyrou, G. Ferrari. Paris: Basalte, 2007.

Basalte 2, 2009 – *à Bruno Maderna*, vol. 2, eds. G. Mathon, L. Feneyrou, G. Ferrari. Paris: Basalte, 2009.

Borio-Danuser 1997 – G. Borio, H. Danuser, *Im Zenit der Moderne. Die Internationalen Ferienkurse für Neue Musik Darmstadt 1946-1966. Geschichte und Dokumentation.* Freiburg im Breisgau: Rombach, 1997, 3 vols.

Carteggio 2001 – R. Dalmonte, ed. *Bruno Maderna - Wolfgang Steinecke Carteggio Briefwechsel.* Lucca: LIM, 2001.

Centro Studi Maderna – Centro Studi Bruno Maderna per la Musica contemporanea, Università di Bologna.

Chronik 1997 – G. Borio, H. Danuser, *Im Zenit der Moderne. Die Internationalen Ferienkurse für Neue Musik Darmstadt 1946-1966. Geschichte und Dokumentation.* Freiburg im Breisgau: Rombach, 1997, vol. III, 513-638.

Documenti 1985 – *Bruno Maderna Documenti raccolti e illustrati da M. Baroni e R. Dalmonte.* Milano: Suvini-Zerboni, 1985.

Extraits 2007 – A. I. De Benedictis, G. Ferrari, "Extraits de la correspondance", in *Basalte* 1, 2007, 459-517.

Maderna followed by a publication date – indicates one of Maderna's works in the series of critical editions published by Suvini Zerboni, edited by Mario Baroni and Rossana Dalmonte.

Mila 1976 – M. Mila, *Maderna musicista europeo.* Torino: Einaudi, 1976.

Pour Bruno 2015 – *Pour Bruno. Memorie e ricerche su Bruno Maderna*, edited by Rossana Dalmonte and Mario Baroni. Lucca: LIM, 2015.

Romito 2000/2 – M. Romito, "I commenti musicali di Bruno Maderna: Radio, Televisione, Teatro." *Nuova Rivista Musicale Italiana*, 2000/2, 233-247.

Romito 2002/1 – M. Romito, "I commenti musicali di Bruno Maderna: Radio, Televisione, Teatro," second part. *Nuova Rivista Musicale Italiana*, 2002/1, 79-98.

Romito 2003/1 – M. Romito, "Cronologia delle Registrazioni e dei Concerti: 1935-1973." *Nuova Rivista Musicale Italiana*, 2003/1, 89-126.

Romito 2018 & *Romito* 2019 – M. Romito, "Da *Intolleranza 1960* a *Don Giovanni.*" Article published in two parts in *Musica/Realtà*, no. 117 (2018),115-148, and no. 118 (2019), 177-224.

Romito 2020 – M. Romito, *Bruno Maderna direttore d'orchestra (1932-1973). Cronologia, discografia, testimonianze*. In press.

Studi 1989 – M. Baroni, R. Dalmonte, eds. *Studi su Bruno Maderna*. Milano: Suvini Zerboni, 1989.

Trudu 1992 – A. Trudu, *La "Scuola" di Darmstadt. I Ferienkurse dal 1946 a oggi*. Milano: Ricordi-Unicopli, 1992.

Verzina 2003 – N. Verzina, *Bruno Maderna. Étude historique et critique*. Paris: L'Harmattan, 2003.

INDEX OF CITIES AND RELATIVE INSTITUTIONS

(THEATERS, FESTIVALS, ORCHESTRAS, RADIOS, SCHOOLS, NEWSPAPERS, PUBLISHERS)

Amsterdam
    Concertgebouw and Concertgebouw Orchestra, 193, 195, 205, 235, 236, 237

    Labyrinth Project, 235, 236

    Theater Carré, 193, 199, 205, 236

    Gaudeamus Music Week, 237

    Festival of the First Unitarian Church, 248

Baden Baden
    Orchestra of the SWR, 59, 153

    Sczuka Prize, 147

    Südwest Rundfunk Radio (SWR), 70, 147

Basel
    Sacher Foundation, x, 39, 262

Bayreuth
    Bayreuth Orchestra, 67

Berkeley
    University of California, 239

    Warner Brothers, 195

Berlin
    Akademie der Künste, 195

    Deutsche Oper, 89, 251, 271

    Komische Oper, 117

    Orchestra of Radio Berlin, 244

Bologna
    Feste Musicali, 207, 241, 242

    Teatro Comunale, 62, 65, 158, 191, 241

    University of Bologna, ix, 65, 211

Bonn
    Institute of Research for Phonetics and Communication, 74

Boston
    Back Bay Theater, 248

    Boston Symphony Orchestra, 259, 272, 273

Brussels
    Festival Europalia, 206, 249

    Théâtre Royale de La Monnaie, 200, 211, 227, 238

Buenos Aires
    187

Cambridge (Massachusetts)
    Harvard University, 236

Chicago
    Chicago Daily News (newspaper), 259, 268

    Chicago Symphony Orchestra, 249, 251, 259, 268

    Chicago Tribune (newspaper), 259, 276

    Ravinia Festival, 259, 272

    WEFM Radio, 2, 26, 155, 249

Cleveland
    Blossom Music Center, 273

    Cleveland Orchestra, 273

Cologne

Cologne Radio, Westdeutscher Rundfunk (WDR), 74 , 113, 123, 152, 154, 168, 181, 196

Electronic Music Studio, 74, 84, 102, 123

Festival Musik der Zeit, 67, 149, 224

Orchestra and Choir of the WDR, 123, 158, 231

Darmstadt

Akademie für Tonkunst, 59

Darmstädter Beiträge (periodical), 144, 148, 192

Das Neue Forum (periodical), 86

European Space Center, 213

Ferienkurse, 71, 75, 82, 83, 86, 88, 91, 96, 97, 99, 104, 108, 113, 116, 126, 141, 143, 144, 145, 147, 148, 150, 151, 152, 154, 161, 165, 168, 170, 172, 177, 179, 180, 181, 185, 186, 188, 191, 193, 194, 195, 196, 224

Internationales Kammerensemble Darmstadt (IKD), 116, 174, 177, 181, 185, 186, 191, 194, 195, 196, 224, 252

Internationales Musikinstitut Darmstadt (IMD), 58, 59, 62, 91, 112, 179, 185, 188, 219

Landestheater, 82, 83, 86, 87, 89, 124, 184, 188, 192, 196, 199, 200, 203, 251,

Kranichstein Castle, 58, 89, 91, 185

Marienhöhe, 59, 60, 64 91, 123, 185

Music Conservatory of Hesse, 59

Orangerie, 59

Stadthalle, 97

Dartington

Melos Ensemble, 172, 173, 174

Summer School, 168, 172, 253

Diano Marina (Imperia)

Chiosco di Piazza Dante, 3

Donaueschingen
    Contemporary Music Festival, 70

Dresden
    Dresden orchestra, 144

Düsseldorf
    Der Mittag (newspaper), 104

Ferrara
    Teatro comunale, 252

Florence
    Editore Bruzzichelli, 182, 185
    Gonnelli (antique bookstore), 186
    La Nazione (newspaper), 19
    Maggio Musicale Fiorentino, 35, 186, 204, 252
    Teatro Comunale, 23
    Teatro della Pergola, 257

Frankfurt
    Frankfurt Radio, Hessischer Rundfunk (HR), 67, 85, 93, 113, 161, 174, 181
    Orchestra and Choir of the HR, 59, 152, 158, 159, 160

Hamburg
    Das Neue Werk Festival, 67, 70, 102
    Norddeutscher Rundfunk Radio (NDR), 99
    Nordwestdeutscher Rundfunk Radio (NWDR), 67, 70, 101,
    Orchestra of the NDR, 193, 231
    Orchestra of the NWDR, 67, 102
    Staatsoper Hamburg, 254, 257

Hanover
    Festival Tage der Neuen Musik, 186

Hochschule für Musik, Theater und Medien, 59

Hilversum
Radio Nederlandse Omroep Stichting (NOS), 280, 283

Innsbruck
Il Brennero (newspaper), 6

Kassel
Bärenreiter Editions, 38, 256

Kiel
Oper Kiel, 192

Leipzig
Eulenburg Editions, 36

London
BBC Orchestra and Radio, 168, 173, 175

Royal Albert Hall, 285

Royal Festival Hall, 277, 285

The Times (newspaper), 283

Lucerne
Radio Beromünster, 87

Magdeburg
Volksstimme (newspaper), 167

Mainz
Schott editions, 9, 36, 38, 114

Wergo recording company, 222, 232

Mantua
Gazzetta di Mantova (newspaper), 94

Teatro Scientifico, 94

Miami

    Miami Philharmonic Orchestra, 265

Milan

    Angelicum, 155, 204

    Aprile Milanese, 35

    Castello Sforzesco, 3

    Conservatorio G. Verdi, 6, 8, 94, 271, 279

    Corriere della Sera (newspaper), 35, 204

    Edizioni Bocca, 204

    Edizioni Mondadori, 92

    Edizioni Ricordi, 36, 37, 38, 67, 99, 214

    Edizioni Suvini Zerboni, 29, 42, 43, 97, 99, 113, 124, 150, 156, 175, 176, 194, 206, 207, 223

    Il Sole 24 ore (Newspaper), 116

    Orchestra and Choir of the RAI, 156, 264, 267, 271, 277, 278, 279

    Orchestra dei Pomeriggi Musicali, 157

    Piccola Scala, 184

    Piccolo Teatro, 116, 118, 154, 206

    Pomeriggi Musicali, 90, 120

    RAI Broadcasting, 186, 276, 283, 285

    Società del Quartetto, 67

    Studio Boggeri, 65

    Studio di Fonologia della RAI di Milano (Corso Sempione), viii, 65, 86, 94, 99, 102, 103, 190, 110, 111, 112, 113, 115, 117, 118, 119, 123, 142, 143, 144, 145, 149, 154, 162, 163, 168, 170, 175, 187, 202, 212, 239, 254, 278

    Teatro alla Scala, 30, 67, 90, 99, 137, 185, 186, 195, 200, 267, 277, 279

    Teatro dell'Arte, 113, 149

Munich
- Bavarian State Opera, 52
- Münchener Philharmoniker, 87
- Musica Viva Festival, 51, 52, 67, 95, 173, 193, 195
- Orchestra of the BR, 193
- Radio Bayerischer Rundfunk (BR), 87, 97
- Süddeutsche Zeitung (newspaper), 180

Naples
- Associazione Musicale Alessandro Scarlatti, 148
- Autunno Musicale, 193
- Conservatorio San Pietro a Majella, 104, 149, 150, 167
- Orchestra Scarlatti (e della RAI), 124, 149
- Teatro dell'Arte, 149

New York
- Columbia Records (CBS), 257
- Columbia University, 94
- Instrumental and choral groups of the Juilliard School, 252, 253, 255, 256, 267
- Juilliard School of Music, 252, 255
- Lincoln Center, 255, 256, 268, 276
- New York Herald Tribune (newspaper), 26
- New York Philharmonic Orchestra, 267
- New York Times (newspaper), 256, 257, 267, 286
- RCA Records, 182
- WNCN (radio), 134

Nuremberg
- Orchestra of the Nürnberg Theater, 19

Nüttingen
Museum of Abstract Art, 199

Ostia Antica
Teatro Romano, 157

Padua
Sala della Ragione, 3
Teatro Garibaldi, 3

Paris
Bibliothèque Nationale, 204
Centre de Documentation de Musique Internationale (CDMI), 85
Domaine Musical, 97, 113, 115, 124, 152, 154
Éditions Basalte, ix
Éditions Salabert, 281
Ensemble Intercontemporain, 70
Journées de musique contemporaine, 264
Institut de Recherche et Coordination Acoustique/Musique (IRCAM), 154
Orchestre National de Radio France (ORTF), 208
Radio France, 74, 84, 85, 200
Salle des Conservatoires, 188
Théâtre de l'Odéon, 238

Persepolis (Shiraz)
Festival of Arts, 200, 261

Philadelphia
Philadelphia Orchestra, 264, 265, 273

Pittsburgh
Pittsburgh Symphony Orchestra, 249

Rimini-Repubblica di S. Marino
    International Biennial of Global Design Methodology, 212

Rochester
    Eastman Philharmonia, 270

    Eastman School of Music, 270

Rome
    Accademia di Santa Cecilia, 14, 24, 52, 55, 87

    Auditorium del Foro Italico, 145, 150, 157, 168, 174, 186, 189, 193, 200, 202, 251

    Auditorium della RAI, 146, 149, 201, 214

    Augusteo, 14

    Basilica di Massenzio, 55, 99

    Casa Pensione S. Carlo, 7, 8

    Cineteca Nazionale, 41

    Conservatory of Santa Cecilia, 7, 8

    Edizioni De Santis, 9

    Orchestra Sinfonica della RAI, 67, 162, 176, 189, 190, 208, 233, 251

    RAI broadcasting company, 38, 42, 67, 83, 89, 99, 100, 111, 113, 115, 124, 142, 144, 146, 148, 149, 150, 156, 157, 158, 162, 165, 167, 168, 170, 174, 175, 177, 181, 201, 228, 229, 265, 277

    Società di Cinematografia Scalera, 40

    Società Italiana autori ed Editori (SIAE), 41, 121, 149, 207

    Teatro Adriano, 9

    Teatro dell'Opera, 10, 83,

    Villa S. Francesco, 7

Rotterdam
    Philharmonisch Orkest, 193, 195

Royan
    Royan Festival, 214, 257

Saarbrücken
    Orchestra of the SR, 253
    Radio Saarländischer Rundfunk (SR), 155, 212, 253, 264

Salzburg
    Mozarteum, Sommerakademie, 195, 253, 285
    Salzburg Festival, 6, 285

Scheveningen
    Kursaal (Theater), 196, 205

Siena
    Accademia Chigiana, 17, 32
    Festival Vivaldi, 36

Stuttgart
    Orchestra of the Stuttgart Radio Südwest Rundfunk (SWR), 254

Tanglewood
    Berkshire Music Center, 259
    Festival of Contemporary Music, 274, 275
    Fromm Music Foundation, 261, 274

The Hague
    Residentie Orkest, 188, 191, 193, 196, 199, 205, 231, 261, 262, 286
    Royal Conservatory, 235

Tokyo
    Festival East-West Music Encounter, 175
    Japan Philharmonic Orchestra, 175

Turin
    Auditorium della, RAI 97, 146, 186
    Auditorium delle Celebrazioni, 145
    Editore Einaudi, 91, 92

Library, Fondo Foà Giordano, 36

Orchestra of the EIAR, 13

Orchestra Sinfonica della RAI, 47, 67, 97

Piccolo Teatro Torinese, 206

RAI broadcasting company (EIAR), 5, 14, 113, 123, 154, 179, 186

Teatro Carignano, 154

Trieste

Castello di Miramare, 157

Teatro Verdi, 3

Ulm

Hochschule für Gestaltung, 212

Utrecht

Symphonie Orkest, 193, 205

Venice

Autunno Musicale Veneziano, 52

St. Mark's church, 27, 205, 259, 266

Biblioteca Marciana, 17

Biennale Arte, 179

Biennale di Venezia, 26, 35, 36, 50, 52, 56, 87, 99, 174, 182, 186, 187, 190, 196, 200, 203, 210, 220, 224, 227, 235, 240, 254

Biennale Musica, 35, 89

Ca' Giustinian, 15, 16

Conservatorio Benedetto Marcello, vii, 2, 15, 22, 31, 32, 35, 36, 52, 67, 87,

Gruppo Strumentale Benedetto Marcello, 35

Happy Grossato Company, 2, 41, 129

Il Gazzettino di Venezia (newspaper), 3, 4

Istituto Italiano Antonio Vivaldi, 36

Orchestra del Teatro La Fenice, 3, 26, 41

Radio Venezia, 109

Teatro La Fenice, 3, 23, 162, 186, 203, 211

Teatro Malibran, 3

Videoteca Pasinetti, 41

Verona

Arena di Verona (theater), 3, 4, 13

Arena di Verona (newspaper), 19

Auditorium Montemezzi, 97

Castelvecchio, 15, 19

Civico Liceo Musicale, 6

Istituto Musicale, 100

Library of the Accademia Filarmonica, 19

Teatro Filarmonico, 3, 5, 13

Teatro Nuovo, 20

Teatro Romano, 157, 158, 200

Verucchio (Rimini)

Centro Internazionale Ricerche e Strutture Ambientali "Pio Manzù," 211, 212

Vienna

Das Kleine Volksblatt (newspaper), 166

Die Furche (newspaper), 166

Die Presse (newspaper), 166

Festival Musica Nova, 167, 190

Great Hall of Radio Vienna, 191

Grosser Konzerthaus-Saal, 243

Kurier (newspaper), 167

Österreichische Neue Tageszeitung (newspaper), 166

Radio Vienna, 174

Universal Edition (UE), 114

Vienna Music Academy, 167

Wiener Festwochen, 158, 166

Wiener Philharmoniker, 267

Wiener Symphoniker, 166, 167, 190, 191, 195, 199, 268

Wiener Zeitung (newspaper), 191

Weimar

Allgemeine Thüringische Landeszeitung (newspaper), 18

Staatskapelle, 19

Thüringer Gauzeitung (newspaper), 18

Wiesbaden

Après Cage: Kleines Sommerfest, 234

Breitkopf & Härtel, 36

Städtliches Museum, 234

Zurich

Ars Viva (orchestra), 51

Ars Viva (publishers), 38, 97, 124, 212

Zürich Radio, 62, 85, 87

ASSOCIATIONS, EVENTS AND PUBLICATIONS NOT LINKED TO CITIES

Associazione Giovanile Musicale (AGIMUS), 149

Berio Ensemble, 248

Casabella (periodical), 65

Elettronica (periodical), 111

Ensemble Européen de Musique de Chambre, 175

First International Congress of Dodecaphony, 53, 55, 56, 61

"Fluxus" (Aesthetic movement), 233

Gruppo Analisi e Teoria Musicale (GATM), 107

Holland Festival, 188, 193, 205, 234, 236, 280, 283

Il Diapason (periodical), 90

Il Politecnico (periodical), 64, 66

Il Ponte (periodical), 90

Incontri Musicali: Quaderni internazionali di musica contemporanea (periodical), 113, 114, 115, 142, 143

Incontri Musicali (concerts), 116, 145, 148, 152, 154

International Society for Contemporary Music (ISCM), 54, 70, 150

La Rassegna musicale (periodical), 67, 89, 90

La Ronda (periodical), 11

Melos (periodical), 180

Polyphonie (periodical), 72

Preuves (periodical), 189

Prix Italia, 145, 177, 201

Pro Familia (periodical), 4

Radiocorriere (periodical), 6, 13

Rinascita (periodical), 248

The Score (periodical), 172

INDEX OF NAMES

Abbado Claudio, 265
Abbiati Franco, 35, 204
Adlington Robert, 235, 236,
Adorno Theodor Wiesengrund, 74, 75, 76, 83, 107, 122, 141, 178
Alighieri Dante, 19
Anastasia Adriana, 201
Andriessen Louis, 235, 236
Angius Marco, 23
Apostel Hans Erich, 162
Arenbergh René van, 280
Argan Giulio Carlo, 211
Aronowitz Cecil, 172
Arûzi Nezâmî, 262
Ashkenazy Vladimir, 265
Auden Wystan Hugh, 218, 219, 243, 244
Baaren Kees van, 235
Babbitt Milton, 73
Bacchelli Riccardo, 126
Bach Carl Philip Emanuel, 190
Bach Johann Sebastian, 14, 24, 45, 46, 47, 88, 115, 179, 202, 264
Ballo Ferdinando, 35, 89, 91
Barblan Guglielmo, 90
Baroni Mario, 19, 21, 107
Barrault Jean-Louis, 115
Bartók Béla, viii, 25, 27, 42, 43, 65, 91, 120, 186, 285
Barwahser Hubert, 236
Bassani Giovanni Battista, 15
Battaglia Felice, 211
Beatles (The), 94
Beatrix, Queen of the Netherlands, 236

Beethoven Ludwig van, 4, 13, 14, 88, 250, 267
Béjart Maurice, 137, 267, 279
Bellandi Nazario, 9
Belli Domenico, 38, 207, 241, 242
Bellini Vincenzo ,19
Bellon Stefano, 42, 43
Bellucco (Don,) 4
Benedek László, 64, 99
Bennett Richard Rodney, 170
Berberian Cathy, 94, 95, 113, 114, 133, 146, 147, 157, 168, 170, 171, 220, 229, 251, 262
Berg Alban, 36, 53, 60, 65, 69, 72, 162, 166, 186, 191, 225, 254
Bergen Beverly, 238
Bergson Henri, 187
Berio Cristina, 114
Berio Luciano, viii, 52, 94, 99, 103, 104, 105, 106, 109, 110, 111, 112, 113, 114, 115, 119, 122, 123, 124, 125, 142, 143, 144, 145, 146, 147, 148, 149, 150, 154, 157, 158, 159, 165, 168, 170, 171, 173, 177, 251, 257
Berlioz Hector, 26, 27, 189, 275
Bertelli Renata, 201
Bertini Gary, 284
Bertoni Ferdinando, 207
Betti Laura, 41
Bettinelli Bruno, 90
Bianchini Guido, 7
Binchois Gilles, 202
Bitter Christof, 155, 192, 212, 253, 255, 256, 264, 270

Boccherini Luigi, 108
Bode Harald, 84
Bodini Vittorio, 176
Boehmer Konrad, 167
Boepple Paul, 26
Böhlen Manfred, 98
Boito Arrigo, 275
Bolchi Sandro, 157
Bongera Giuseppe, 19
Bongiorno Mike, 142
Borio Gianmario, ix, 80, 218, 219, 231, 270
Borodin Alexander, 191
Bortolotto Mario, 76, 225
Boswell James, 265, 266
Boucourechliev André, 176, 189
Boulanger Nadia, 173
Boulez Pierre, viii, 72, 76, 78, 82, 89, 93, 97, 104, 113, 114, 115, 124, 140, 143, 152, 153, 154, 161, 169, 170, 174, 178, 180, 188, 191, 196, 219, 225, 252, 267, 269, 283, 285, 286,
Bour Ernest, 97, 152, 177
Bozzoni Aurelio, 19
Bradshaw Susan, 170
Brahms Johannes, 87, 199, 245, 272
Brecht Bertolt, 60, 65, 116, 117, 154, 157, 168, 228
Brendel Alfred, 285
Bressan Giuliana, 19
Brissoni Alessandro, 121, 150, 157, 162, 167
Brown Earle, 73, 123, 130, 144, 268
Bruch Max, 19
Bruckner Anton, 272, 273
Bucchi Valentino, 35, 252
Busoni Ferruccio, 65

Bussotti Sylvano, 161, 162, 214, 234, 283
Bustini Alessandro, 7, 8, 10, 11, 14, 16, 22
Cage John, 53, 72, 73, 76, 94, 123, 139, 140, 141, 143, 145, 151, 153, 158, 160, 161, 162,164, 178, 197, 233, 237, 238, 255, 274
Cagol Laura, 19
Caimo Giuseppe, 202
Calamandrei Piero, 90
Calandri Max, 40, 41, 90
Caldara Antonio, 15
Calder Alexander, 212
Canetti Elias, 51
Caniglia Maria, 13
Cantoni Valeria, 96
Capuozzo Raffaele, 19
Cardarelli Vincenzo, 11, 12
Cardew Cornelius, 162
Carducci Giosuè, 10, 12
Carissimi Giacomo, 204
Carlino Emilia, 19
Carotenuto Mario, 116
Carpi Cioni, 242
Carraro Tino, 116
Carsana Ermanno, 158
Carter Elliott, 73, 190
Casella Alfredo, 9, 17, 18, 32, 33, 37
Castagner Jacques, 248
Castaldi Paolo, 169
Castelnuovo Gino, 111
Castiglioni Niccolò, 166, 177
Catunda Eunice, 32
Char René, 72
Chavez Carlos, 88
Cherubini Luigi, 4
Chiari Giuseppe, 234

Chigi Saracini Guido, 18
Chilesotti Oscar, 38
Chiosso Leo, 20
Chopin Frédéric, 11
Claus Hugo, 218, 238, 239
Clementi Aldo, 145, 154
Colombo Taccani Giorgio, 225
Consagra Pietro, 179
Conti Luca, 46
Corgnati Maurizio, 90
Cortese Louis, 143
Cosso Laura, 208, 285
Courir Duilio, 286
Crosara Policarpo, 3, 5, 6, 8, 11, 21, 28, 29
Curtis Alan, 275
Cyrus the Great, 261
D'Amico Fedele, 286
D'Annunzio Gabriele, 10, 11, 12, 67
Da Venezia Gastone, 156
Dall'Abaco Evaristo Felice, 15
Dall'Oglio Renzo, 31, 83, 88, 145
Dalla Libera Francesco, 24
Dalla Libera Sandro, 24
Dallapiccola Luigi, viii, 10, 32, 35, 42, 44, 45, 53, 54, 70, 83, 146, 154, 166, 204
Dalmonte Rossana, 55, 94
Dandin, 261
Dandolo Raspani Giusi, 116
De Benedictis Angela Ida, ix, 21, 22, 47, 56, 109, 150, 156, 201, 224, 261, 262
Debussy Claude, 33, 67, 187, 190, 193, 200, 250, 269
Decker Harold, 247
Decroupet Pascal, 224
De Grandis Renato, 178

De Leeuw Reinbert, 235, 236
De Leeuw Ton, 234, 283
De Lullo Giorgio, 156, 277
De Vries Han, 135, 283, 284
Desderi Ettore, 90
Desprez Josquin, 205
Dessau Paul, 168
Devoto Luigi, 255
Di Pietro Rocco, 260
Dicks Harro, 59, 61, 82, 83, 86, 87, 93, 184, 200, 203, 251
Donati Paolo, 201
Donati Pino, 4, 6, 13, 14, 15, 16
Donatoni Franco, 104, 154
Dorow Dorothy, 193, 243
Drolc (Quartet), 104
Durieux Frédéric, 209, 214
Dursi Massimo, 157
Eco Umberto, viii, 94, 111, 143, 170
Edinger Christiane, 254, 267, 285
Eimert Herbert, 74, 83
Elfio, 143
Elsendorn Jol, 283
Éluard Paul, 65
Eötvös Péter, 194, 210
Ephrikian Angelo, 36, 37
Erasmus of Rotterdam, 202
Ericson Raymond, 256, 257
Euripides, 126
Evangelisti Franco, 145, 154
Faber Lothar, 181, 182, 196, 198, 210, 213, 214, 245, 251, 262, 284
Fabris Gastone, 31
Faccio Franco, 5
Falk Rossella, 156
Fanfani Ottavio, 110, 116

Fanna Antonio, 36
Farah Diba, 133
Fauré Gabriel, 33
Fautrier Jean, 179
Fearn Raymond, ix
Fein Markus, ix, 77, 79, 105, 106
Feldman Morton, 73, 123
Fellegara Vittorio, 91, 154
Fellini Federico, 280, 281
Felsenstein Walter, 117
Feneyrou Laurent, ix, 210
Ferrari Giordano, ix, 219, 224, 228, 232
Ferrari Trecate Luigi, 66
Ferrero Mario, 157
Ferronetti Ignazio, 40
Fortner Wolfgang, 91
Franchi Franco, 280
Freud Sigmund, 65
Fromm Paul, 261, 274, 275
Fukushima Kazuo, 190
Furtwängler Wilhelm, 67
Gabrieli Giovanni, 187, 196, 202, 205, 249, 259, 264, 272
Gaipa Ettore, 116
Galuppi Bladassarre, 15
García Lorca Federico, 90, 175, 176, 218, 219, 243, 244
Gatti Guido Maria, 16
Gatto Alfonso, 65
Gawriloff Saschko, 213
Gay John, 116
Gazzelloni Severino, 96, 97, 148, 154, 159, 182, 183, 190, 191, 193, 198, 210, 214, 219, 221, 228, 230, 231, 242, 243, 244, 248, 251
Gazzolo Nando, 110

Gelmetti Umberto, 4
Geminiani Francesco, 149
Gentilucci Armando, 210
Ghedini Giorgio Federico, 36, 99, 191
Ghiringhelli Antonio, 90
Giazotto Remo, 207
Gielen Michael, 191, 196
Giovannini Marina, 12
Giulini Carlo Maria, 9
Giuranna Barbara, 89
Giuriati Domenico, 3
Glock William, 168, 172, 173
Gluck Christoph Willibald, 282
Goethe Johann Wolfgang von, 6, 178
Goeyvaerts Karel, 61, 75, 76, 82
Goldschmidt Werner, 195
Gorini Gino, 162
Gorli Sandro, 176
Gotti Tito, 241, 242, 243
Gounod Charles, 275
Gozzi Carlo, 149
Gracis Ettore, 15, 17, 18, 22, 36, 52
Gramsci Antonio, 92, 93
Grano Romolo, 31, 62
Grossato Bruno (Brunetto), 1, 2, 3, 4, 129, 188
Grossato Francesco, 1
Grossato Italia, 29
Grossato Umberto, 1, 2, 5
Guala Filiberto, 111
Guarnieri Anna Maria, 156
Guarnieri Antonio, 17, 18, 21
Guelfi Gian Giacomo, 19
Haitink Bernard, 236, 237
Hälfter Cristobal, 167

Index of Names

Händel Georg Friedrich, 196
Hangen Bruce, 275
Hartmann Karl Amadeus, 50, 51, 52, 53, 54, 60, 67, 173
Hartung Hans, 179
Haydn Franz Joseph, 19, 149, 179
Helms Hans Günter, 171, 229
Henze Hans Werner, 104, 112, 191
Hidalgo Codorniu Juan, 154
Hindemith Paul, viii, 9, 22, 24, 32, 44, 45, 60, 146, 173
Hölderlin Friedrich, 193, 198, 217, 218, 219, 220, 224, 226, 227, 228, 229, 230, 231, 239, 243, 244, 271
Holliger Heinz, 284
Honegger Arthur, 65, 93
Huisman Maurice, 238
Ingrassia Ciccio, 280
Ives Charles, 145, 178, 187, 268, 276
Izzo Leo, 41, 156
Janáček Leoš, 199
Jansen Kasper, 283, 285
Joyce James, 170, 171
Jung Annemarie, 170
Kafka Franz, 55, 56, 65, 92, 93
Karajan Herbert von, 267
Kessler Alice & Ellen, 142
Khayyâm Omar, 262, 263
Köpnik (family), 63, 102, 114, 183, 271
Köpnik Giselheid, 62
Köpnik Maderna Beate Christine, 5, 62, 63, 64, 87, 88, 99, 100, 104, 114, 123, 148, 188, 190, 211, 254, 257, 262, 265, 271
Köpnik Paul, 63
Koussewitzky Natalie, 260
Koussewitzky Serge, 260

Krenek Ernst, 73, 143, 178
Kubrick Stanley, 195
Kuhn Gustav, 253
La Guardia Fiorello, 256
Labiche Eugène, 121
Labroca Mario, 38
Landini Francesco, 202
Landré Guillaume, 234
Lattuada Alberto 40
Leibowitz René, 53, 72
Leonviola Antonio, 40, 41, 90, 109, 156
Lévi-Strauss Claude, 170
Levy Jonathan, 265, 266, 267
Lewinski Wolf-Eberhard von, 125
Leydi Roberto, 65, 94, 109, 111, 124, 142, 187
Liberatore Ugo, 156
Liebermann Rolf, 67
Lietti Alfredo, 143
Ligeti György, 187, 192, 194, 195, 199, 233, 251, 254
Liszt Franz, 189, 268, 273
Loriod Yvonne, 188
Lotti Antonio, 15
Ludwig Christa, 93
Lupi Rosita, 229
Luther Martin, 202
Lutosławski Witold, 195, 285
Maas Walter, 237
Maciunas Georges, 234
Maderna Andrea, 198, 262, 263
Maderna Carolina, 1
Maderna Caterina, 63, 104, 114, 188
Maderna Claudia, 165, 188
Magnanensi Giorgio, 13
Magnani Francesca, 177

Magri Aldo, 21
Mahler Gustav, 166, 192, 193, 200, 253, 257, 265, 267, 273, 277, 279, 285
Maldonado Tomás, 212
Malipiero Gian Francesco, vii, viii, 9, 14, 15, 16, 17, 18, 19, 21, 22, 23, 24, 25, 26, 31, 32, 35, 36, 37, 38, 40, 44, 45, 52, 54, 55, 67, 141, 145, 167, 177, 186, 202, 203, 207, 250
Malipiero Riccardo, 53
Malvezzi Piero, 91
Manfredi Ettore, 20
Manfredi Irma, 4, 5, 6, 7, 8, 9, 13, 17, 18, 20, 21, 24, 25, 28, 29, 39, 62, 63, 89, 99, 100, 104, 114, 183, 264
Mangini Giorgio, 40
Mann William, 283
Manning Peter, 252
Mantelli Alberto, 111, 170
Manzoni Giacomo, 106, 116, 118, 130, 145, 200, 228, 241
Manzù Pio, 211, 212
Marcello Benedetto, 15
Marchetti Walter, 154
Marco Tomás, 192
Marini Marino, 277
Marinković Ranko, 157
Marinuzzi Gino jr., 168
Markowski Andrzej, 168
Martignoni Massimo, 142
Martin Louis, 188
Martini Giovanni Battista, 99
Martinoja (Lieutenant-colonel), 19, 20
Martucci Giuseppe, 4
Mascagni Pietro, 13
Mastropasqua Mauro, 24
Masur Kurt, 117

Mathon Geneviève, ix, 282
Maupassant Guy (de), 234
Maurri Enzo, 113, 157
Maxwell Davies Peter, 173
Mayakowsky Vladímir, 65
Mendel Deryk, 239
Mendelssohn Bartholdy Felix, 11, 88, 158, 190, 235, 285
Mengelberg Misha, 235, 236
Mercadante Saverio, 252
Messiaen Olivier, 52, 70, 72, 73, 75, 93, 157, 173, 188, 200, 237, 285
Messinis Mario, 31, 286
Metzger Heinz-Klaus, 143, 162, 169
Meyer Leonard B., 47,
Meyer-Eppler Werner, 74, 83, 84, 85
Michaux Henry, 154
Mila Massimo, 12, 43, 49, 50, 66, 118, 120, 121, 124, 194, 201, 202, 225, 247, 286
Milhaud Darius, 91, 184, 207
Milly (pseudonym of Carolina Mignone), 116
Miotto Carlo, 23
Miotto Francesco, 3
Mitropoulos Dimitri, 31
Modugno Domenico, 41
Molinari Bernardino, 14
Molino Andrea, 26
Mondorf Hanns, 180
Montale Eugenio, 157
Montalenti Umberto, 213, 214
Montecchi Giordano, 41, 120, 121, 124, 125
Monteverdi Claudio, viii, 14, 15, 19, 36, 195, 200, 205, 206, 207, 211, 241, 249, 275

Montini Giovanni Battista (Pope Paul VI), 7
Morini Anna Maria, 96
Morley Christopher, 156
Morricone Ennio, 40
Moskowitz Imo, 64
Mozart Wolfgang Amadeus, 55, 88, 100, 104, 149, 173, 186, 187, 188, 191, 192, 193, 235, 249, 250, 252, 253, 256, 265, 272, 275, 276, 279, 285
Murray Schafer Raymond, 268
Mussorgsky Modest, 199
Mussolini Benito, 3, 16, 18, 20
Napolitano Ernesto, 208
Negri Gino, 116, 154
Neidhöfer Christoph, 106
Nicolodi Fiamma, 9, 25
Nietzsche Friedrich, 121
Nilsson Bo, 124, 145
Noller Joachim, 15, 44, 220
Nono Luigi, vii, viii, 25, 31, 32, 39, 45, 49, 52, 53, 54, 61, 62, 77, 78, 80, 81, 82, 83, 84, 85, 87, 88, 89, 90, 91, 92, 93, 99, 101, 104, 105, 115, 124, 132, 145, 146, 150, 152, 154, 157, 158, 161, 163, 164, 165, 166, 168, 169, 173, 174, 177, 180, 186, 187, 190, 191, 195, 219, 225, 241, 248, 252
Offenbach Jacques, 207, 257
Olof Theo, 192, 199, 210, 211, 253
Orff Carl, 52, 60, 83
Ormandy Eugene, 264
Orvieto Aldo, 23
Paci Enzo, 143
Pagan (family), 62
Paisiello Giovanni, 18
Palazzetti Nicolò, 25

Parrenin (Quartet), 247
Pascoli Giovanni, 10
Pasolini Pier Paolo, 280
Passannanti Benedetto, 34
Pasternak Boris, 65
Pasticci Susanna, 39, 45, 46, 280, 283
Patroni Griffi Giuseppe, 40, 109, 147
Pedrollo Arrigo, 4, 6, 7, 11, 16
Penderecki Krzysztof, 190
Peragallo Mario, 162
Pergolesi Giovanni Battista, 207
Peri Jacopo, 241
Perinello Carlo, 204
Perle George, 73
Persico Edoardo, 65
Pestalozza Luigi, 116
Petrassi Goffredo, 10, 27, 32, 83, 89, 113, 204
Petronius Arbiter, 260, 280, 281
Petrucci Ottaviano, 39, 89
Picasso Pablo, 101
Pietri Giuseppe, 149
Piovesan Alessandro, 109
Pirelli Giovanni, 91
Pizzetti Ildebrando, 6, 8, 14, 17, 32, 40
Pizzi Pier Luigi, 277
Poli Liliana, 238, 242
Ponti Gio, 35, 142
Porena Boris, 145, 154, 162
Pousseur Henri, 112, 125, 143, 144, 177
Pozzi Egidio, 107
Pozzi Raffaele, 12
Prandelli Giacinto, 41
Pressburger Giorgio, 277, 278
Prokofiev Sergej, 55, 66

Proto Gennaro, 40
Puccini Giacomo, 19, 282
Puecher Virginio, 157, 187, 210, 224, 227, 228, 229, 230, 241, 242
Purcell Henry, 184
Quantz Joachim, 236, 237
Quasimodo Salvatore, 36, 217
Questi Giulio, 41
Rameau Jean-Philippe, 199
Rass Rebecca, 200
Ravel Maurice, 187
Razzi Giulio, 111
Reinaud Madeleine, 115
Renosto Paolo, 202
Respighi Ottorino, 32
Restagno Enzo, 170, 269, 270
Riccardi Ferdinando, 206
Rifkin Joshua, 177
Righini Pietro, 143
Rizzardi Veniero, ix, 22, 26, 45, 80, 163, 218, 219, 231, 270
Rognoni Luigi, 76, 102, 103, 111, 118, 124, 142, 162, 187
Romito Maurizio, ix, 19, 38, 41, 87, 110, 156, 159, 165, 202, 209, 213, 260, 272)
Rosati Giuseppe, 9
Rudaghi, 262
Rufer Josef, 49, 142
Ruziscka Paolo, 113, 114
Ryom Peter, 37
Saadi (Abu Mohammad Moslehebn Abdollāh), 262
Salvetti Guido, 65
Salzedo Carlos, 19
Samama Leo, 249

Samama Sylvio, 248, 249, 252, 253, 255, 261, 265, 276, 285
Sanguineti Edoardo, 280
Santi Piero, 90, 111, 124, 130, 143, 153,
Sanzogno Nino, 31, 47, 48, 95, 99, 123, 284
Sapegno Natalino, 19
Satie Erik, 139
Scaldaferri Nicola, 84, 86
Scarlatti Alessandro, 97
Scarpini Pietro, 85
Schaeffer Pierre, 70, 74, 83, 84
Schat Peter, 193, 235, 236, 237
Scherchen Hermann, 38, 48, 49, 50, 51, 52, 53, 56, 60, 61, 67, 75, 78, 82, 87, 97, 115, 123, 124, 196, 250, 287
Schiffmann David, 248
Schiller Friedrich, 192
Schillinger Joseph, 73, 164
Schirk Heinz, 188
Schlüter Wilhelm, 62, 188, 195, 199, 201, 239
Schnabel Arthur, 173
Schönberg Arnold, 25, 44, 51, 53, 60, 61, 69, 72, 73, 75, 76, 77, 79, 80, 89, 93, 104, 122, 152, 166, 174, 178, 185, 186, 187, 190, 191, 226, 235, 250, 251, 253, 254, 257, 285
Schönberg Nuria, 104
Schubert Franz, 88, 190, 193, 199, 249
Schuller Gunther, 259, 260, 261, 272, 274, 276
Schumann Robert, 11, 55, 149, 196, 253, 267, 273, 275, 283, 285
Scribe Eugène, 150, 167
Sellner Gustav Rudolf, 82, 86, 89, 252
Sermonti Vittorio, 149, 150

Sessions Roger, 274
Shah of Persia, Mohammad Reza Pahlavi, 30, 95
Shakespeare William, 157, 168, 200, 277, 278, 279
Shaw George Bernard, 121
Shostakovich Dmitri, 66
Sibaldi Stefano, 167
Siciliani Francesco, 185, 186, 265
Sielter Pietro, 3
Sixt Paul, 19
Skalkottas Nikos, 166, 167
Soffer Sheldon, 248, 249, 252, 253, 255, 257, 265
Solbiati Alessandro, 209, 269, 270, 271
Solti Georg, 249, 251
Souris André, 143
Sperry Paul, 133, 265, 266, 268, 279
Spira Emile, 177
Stadlen Peter, 55
Stasi Mario, 19
Steinecke Hella, 104
Steinecke Wolfgang, 54, 58, 59, 60, 61, 62, 82, 83, 85, 88, 89, 95, 96, 97, 104, 112, 113, 114, 115, 122, 123, 124, 142, 144, 145, 147, 148, 152, 153, 154, 158, 159, 166, 168, 170, 172, 173, 174, 177, 180, 181, 204, 219, 252, 286
Steingruber Ilona, 162
Stockhausen Karlheinz, viii, 61, 75, 76, 78, 82, 83, 84, 93, 99 112, 115, 122, 123, 124, 140, 141, 143, 149, 152, 153, 158, 161, 162, 163, 177, 178, 180, 191, 195, 196, 197, 214, 237, 252, 254, 256, 286
Stone George, 203, 249
Stout Alan, 203, 249

Strasfogel Ian, 260, 275, 280
Strauss Johann jr., 19, 117, 199
Strauss Richard, 60, 90, 186
Stravinsky Igor, viii, 9, 22, 25, 27, 42, 72, 115, 186, 190, 191, 202, 249, 257, 264, 267, 273, 277, 279, 285
Strehler Giorgio, 116, 118
Strobel Heinrich, 153
Sweekhorst Angelika, 213
Taras John, 277
Tartaglia Antonio, 20
Tartaglia Raffaella, 20, 21, 30, 39, 54, 61, 62, 63, 183, 255
Taruskin Richard, 208
Tasso Torquato, 242
Tebaldi Renata, 41
Tedeschi Rubens, 286
Thiele Rolf, 64
Thomas Ernst, 180, 193, 219, 252
Thomson Virgil, 26, 31, 173, 247
Titone Antonino, 154
Togliatti Palmiro, 66
Tognazzi Ugo, 280
Togni Camillo, 35, 53, 61
Tomek Otto, 180, 181
Torchi Luigi, 38
Torelli Giuseppe, 145
Torrefranca Fausto, 38
Toscanini Arturo, 250, 267
Trezzi Giuseppe, 7
Trudu Antonio, 161, 192
Tudor David, 123, 124, 145, 151, 153, 155, 158, 159, 160, 161, 177
Turchi Guido, 8, 9, 10, 32, 35, 89
Ungaretti Giuseppe, 154
Valdambrini Francesco, 195

Valli Romolo, 156
Varèse Edgard, 63, 99, 114, 115, 145, 149
Vecchi Orazio, 82, 83, 203, 204
Vedova Emilio, 179
Veracini Francesco Maria, 97
Verdi Giuseppe, 3, 11, 13, 18, 19, 26, 27, 76, 186, 250, 267, 275
Verheul Koos, 235
Verhoeven Paul, 64
Verlaine Paul, 32, 33, 34
Verzina Nicola, 44, 92, 95, 196, 197, 218, 231, 232
Vidolin Alvise, 86
Vidussoni Aldo, 19
Vietta Egon, 86
Vildrac Charles, 90
Villani Gianni, 19
Vinay Gianfranco, 251, 272
Vincis Claudia, 205
Vis Lucas, 136, 195, 253, 260, 273, 279, 280, 281, 285
Vittorini Elio, 64
Vivaldi Antonio, viii, 14, 15, 36, 37, 97, 167, 203
Vlad Roman, 100, 124, 162
Vlijmen Jan van, 195, 235, 237
Vogel Wladimir, 53, 55, 56, 61
Wagner Richard, 4, 11, 13, 19, 41, 67, 250, 282
Weber Carl Maria von, 19
Weber Horst, 106
Webern Anton, 50, 51, 53, 69, 75, 77, 93, 104, 115, 123, 167, 191, 202, 277
Weill Kurt, 41, 60, 116, 117, 149, 199, 257
Williams Aparicio, 189
Wohlgensinger (Doctor), 85
Wolf Hugo, 149
Wolff Christian, 73, 123
Wolf-Ferrari Ermanno, 13
Wolpe Stefan, 153
Wuorinen Charles, 274
Xenakis Iannis, 52
Zafred Mario, 88
Zandonai Riccardo, 40
Zanotelli Hans, 124
Zecchi Adone, 145
Zeeman Carl, 55
Zehden Hans, 99
Zhdanov Andrei, 66
Ziani Marc'Antonio, 36
Zillig Winifried, 166
Zimmermann Bernd Alois, 283
Zoroaster, 261, 262, 263
Zuccheri Marino, 110, 118, 187, 202, 212, 278
Zuidam Rob, 236, 237

INDEX OF WORKS BY BRUNO MADERNA

ORIGINAL WORKS

Ages. 'Invenzione radiofonica' by Giorgio Pressburger and Bruno Maderna, 171, 277, 278

Alba, 11, 13, 25, 34

Amanda, Serenata, vi, 193, 194, 195, 199, 211, 224, 249

Aria, 218, 220, 222, 224, 225, 226, 227, 228, 230, 231, 232, 233, 242, 243

Aria, 1 227, 239

Aria, 2 227, 239, 241

Aulodia per Lothar, 198,

Aura, 210, 251, 269, 274, 283

Ausstrahlung, 95, 257, 258, 261, 262, 263, 269, 277

Battaglia I-IV (from Hyperion en het Geweld), 224, 239

Biogramma, 210, 269, 270, 271

Castor et Pollux (from Hyperion en het Geweld), 239, 240

Composizione in tre tempi, 39, 99, 100, 101, 102

Composizione n. 1, 44, 47, 48, 49, 50

Composizione n. 2, 44, 48, 49, 55, 56, 57, 60, 61, 79, 81, 87, 217

Concerto per due pianoforti (transcription of the Concerto per pianoforte of 1942), 22, 23

Concerto per due pianoforti e strumenti, 36, 42, 43, 44, 52, 54, 55, 60, 187

Concerto per flauto e orchestra, 96, 97, 100

Concerto per oboe e orchestra n. 1 (Konzert für Oboe und Kammerensemble, Komposition für oboe und Kammerensemble), 179, 181, 182, 183, 185, 191, 196, 261

Concerto per oboe e orchestra n. 2, 196, 197, 198, 213,

Concerto per oboe e orchestra n. 3, 283, 284, 285, 287

Concerto per pianoforte e orchestra (1942), 21 , 22, 23, 34

Concerto per pianoforte e orchestra (1959), 155, 158, 159, 160, 161, 182, 231

Concerto per violino e orchestra, 196, 199, 200, 208, 210, 211, 231, 232, 253, 268

Continuo, 119, 120, 121, 154, 163, 248

Contrasti (from Hyperion en het Geweld), 224, 239

Dark rapture crawl, 146, 159, 176

Das eiserne Zeitalter (unfinished ballet), 86

Dialodia, 258, 259

Dimensioni II. Invenzione su una voce, 170, 171, 220, 224, 228, 229, 230, 239, 248, 277

Dimensioni III, 186, 187, 195, 218, 220, 221, 222, 223, 224, 228, 229231, 232, 233

Dimensioni IV, 187, 190, 210, 222, 224, 228

Divertimento in due tempi per flauto e pianoforte, 96

Divertimento per orchestra (in collaboration with Luciano Berio), 146, 147, 159

Don Perlimplin (radio opera), 90, 109, 147, 158, 175, 176, 177, 179

Entropia I (from Dimensioni III), 224, 239,

Entropia II (from Dimensioni III), 224, 239,

Entropia III (from Suite aus der Oper Hyperion), 211, 224, 245

Fantasia e fuga per due pianoforti (B.A.C.H. Variationen), 44, 46, 55, 60

From A to Z, 200, 251

Gesti, 224

Giardino religioso, 269, 274, 275

Grande Aulodia, 208, 214, 231, 251, 257, 258

Honeyrêves, 176, 179, 182, 183, 198

Hyperion, xi, 38, 87, 148, 164, 171, 186, 187, 188, 192, 193, 194, 198, 207, 217, 218, 219, 220, 222, 223, 224, 225, 227, 228, 231, 233, 234, 235, 238, 241, 242, 243, 248, 258, 270

Hyperion en het Geweld, 199, 222, 239, 240

Hyperion-Orfeo dolente, 199, 223, 241, 242

Improvvisazione n. 1, 63, 79, 80, 81, 95

Improvvisazione n. 2, 95, 99

Intermezzi 1–4 (from Hyperion en het Geweld), 224, 239

Introduzione e Passacaglia "Lauda Sion Salvatorem," 21, 22, 23, 24, 34

Introduzione e Passacaglia "Lauda Sion Salvatorem" (version for organ), 24

Juilliard Serenade. Tempo libero II, 253, 255, 256, 257, 269

Klage (from Suite aus der Oper Hyperion), 243, 244, 245

Kranichsteiner Kammerkantate (Vier Briefe), 39, 78, 91, 92, 93, 100, 225

L'Amour maternel (from Hyperion en het Geweld), 239

L'Amour sexuel (from Hyperion en het Geweld), 239

La sera fiesolana, 10, 11

Le Rire, 187, 224, 228, 229, 230, 239

Liriche su Verlaine, 33, 42

Message (from Suite aus der Oper Hyperion), 243, 244

Musica su due dimensioni (1952), 83, 85, 86, 95

Musica su due dimensioni (1958), 148, 150, 151, 154, 159, 176, 213, 220, 248

Notturno, 118, 119, 120, 122, 144, 145, 248

Pièce pour Ivry, 257, 258

Psalm (from Suite aus der Oper Hyperion), 224, 243, 244

Quadrivium, 200, 202, 208, 209, 210, 231, 251, 257, 268

Quartetto in due tempi (1955), 103, 104, 106, 107, 108, 122, 146, 159, 160, 182, 231, 247, 252

Quartetto per archi (1940s), 21, 24, 25, 34, 44

Requiem, 21, 25, 26, 27, 29, 34, 247

Rêverie (from Hyperion en het Geweld), 239

Ritratto di città (in collaboration with Luciano Berio), 99, 109, 110, 146, 157, 174

Ritratto di Erasmo (radio opera), 200, 201, 202

Satyricon, xi, 116, 260, 277, 279, 280, 281, 282, 283, 287

Schicksalslied (from Suite aus der Oper Hyperion), 224, 243, 245

Sequenze e strutture (in collaboration with Luciano Berio), 110, 119

Serenata. Komposition Nr. 3, 124

Serenata n. 2, 96, 97, 124, 125, 150, 191, 194, 231, 248

Serenata III, 174

Serenata IV, 176, 177, 179, 182

Serenata per 11 strumenti, 35, 51

Serenata per un missile, 213

Serenata per un satellite, 200, 213, 214

Solo, 244, 257, 258,

Sottosuolo di città, 110

Stele per Diotima, 211, 218, 220, 222, 224, 231, 232, 239, 244

Studi per "Il Processo" di F. Kafka, 44, 48, 55, 56

Suite aus der Oper Hyperion, 200, 220, 223, 230, 243, 245.

Syntaxis, 119, 120, 126, 144, 145, 163

Tempo libero, 171, 212, 254, 255, 256

Tre liriche greche, 44, 45, 46, 48, 57, 87, 247

Valzer (from Hyperion en het Geweld), 224

Venetian Journal, 266, 268

Via Maestra, 110

Viola, 257, 258

Widmung, 199, 213

Y después, 244, 257, 258

Zombieschorus (from Hyperion en het Geweld), 224, 239, 240

Transcriptions, Radio Dramas, Film Music, Incidental Music

Amfiparnaso (transcription from Orazio Vecchi), 82, 83, 87, 203, 204

A Midsummer Night's Dream, (in collaboration with Luciano Berio, adaptation after Felix Mendelssohn Bartholdy), 157

Amor di violino (radio drama), 158

Aspetto Matilde (radio drama), 113, 157

Augellino belverde (adaptation for radio), 149, 150

Brigida vuole sposarsi (radio drama), 121

Cinque danze (transcription for orchestra after Franz Schubert), 190

Concerto in do maggiore per violino archi e cembalo (F 1, n. 3) (transcription after Antonio Vivaldi), 37, 167

Coriolanus (incidental music in collaboration with Mario Migliardi), 200

Diluvium universale (transcription after Giacomo Carissimi), 204

Don Giovanni e il commendatore (radio drama), 121

Historia divitis (transcription after Giacomo Carissimi), 204, 205

I misteri di Venezia (film score), 40, 90

Il cavallo di Troia (radio drama), 156

Il fabbro del convento (film score), 40

Il mio cuore è nel sud (radio drama, German version: Stadt im Süden), 40, 55, 56, 109, 110, 147

Il moschettiere fantasma (film score), 90

Il puff (incidental music for radio play), 167

Il sepolcro (transcription after Marc'Antonio Ziani), 36

In Ecclesiis (transcription after Giovanni Gabrieli), 205, 259, 264

Julius Caesar (incidental music), 157, 158

L'altro mondo, ovvero Gli stati e imperi della luna (radio drama), 162

L'incoronazione di Poppea (transcription after Claudio Monteverdi), 195, 275

La morte ha fatto l'uovo (film score), 40, 41

La scampagnata (radio drama, in collaboration with Luciano Berio), 150

Laure persécutée (radio drama), 156

Le due verità (film score), 40, 41, 90, 109, 156

Les adieux oder Die Schlacht bei Stötteritz (incidental music), 188

Macbeth (incidental music), 168

Magnificat quarti toni (transcription after Josquin Desprez), 205, 264

Mani (radio drama), 157

Massimiliano e Carlotta (in collaboration with Luciano Berio, incidental music), 157

Medea (incidental music), 126

Music of Gaity (transcription from the Fitzwilliam Virginal Book), 202, 203, 207, 257

Noi cannibali (film score), 90

Odhecaton (transcriptions for instrumental ensemble), 39, 89, 203

Opinione pubblica (film score), 90

Orfeo (transcription after Claudio Monteverdi), 200, 205, 206, 207, 211, 249

Orfeo (transcription after Giovanni Battista Pergolesi), 207

Orfeo dolente (transcription after Domenico Belli), 38, 207

Padri nemici (film score), 90

Sangue a Ca' Foscari (film score), 40

Scandalo a Sweet Spring (arrangements for the play by Gino Marinuzzi jr.), 168

Sonata pian e forte (transcription after Giovanni Gabrieli), 205